D0432066

ENCYCLOPEDIA OF
MODERN MILITARY
AIRCRAFT

ENCYCLOPEDIA OF
MODERN MILITARY
AIRCRAFT

Michael Taylor

Bison Books

Published by
Bison Books Ltd
176 Old Brompton Road
London SW5 0BA
England

Copyright © 1987 Bison Books Ltd

All rights reserved. No part of this publication may
be reproduced, stored in a retrieval system or
transmitted, in any form, by any means, electronic,
mechanical, photocopying or otherwise, without
the written permission of the publisher.

ISBN 0 86124 349 8

Printed in Hong Kong

Page 1: An MBB BO 105 CB helicopter armed with
eight TOW antitank missiles. '
Pages 2-3: F-16A Fighting Falcons of the USAF's
388th TFW, armed with Sidewinder AAMs and
bombs. The 388th was the original USAF operating
unit for this type of aircraft.
This page: A McDonnell Douglas Phantom
FGR. Mk 2 of 29 Squadron RAF.

Contents

Introduction

The genesis of air power can be said to have occurred around 200 BC when Chinese General Han Hsin made use of a kite to measure the distance between his forces and those of an enemy. From this time on the milestones in the development of military aviation were many. Twelve centuries after Han Hsin came gunpowder-fuelled rockets, less than three hundred years later bomb-laden kites took to the air, and in Germany in 1763 Melchior Bauer designed (and might have constructed) a flapping wing bomber intended to lift a 100-lb (45-kg) warload.

The age of aerial warfare in the formal sense began later, arguably when Capitano Piazza of the Italian Air Flotilla made the first use of an airplane in war on 22 October 1911, by flying a Blériot to Azizia in order to observe Turkish forces. A second reconnaissance that day, by Capitano Moizo, demonstrated the vulnerability of aircraft, when his Nieuport returned with the scars of battle. Ten days later 2nd Lt Giulio Gavotti went one stage further, dropping a Cipelli grenade onto Turkish positions at Taguira Oasis and continuing to Ain Zara where he threw out his remaining three.

The first air war proper was World War I, when aircraft were mass produced and were relatively simple. This meant that communities could, if so inclined, make gifts of a warplane, or the cost of one, when even a huge Handley Page O/100 twin-engined strategic bomber cost only £4375. However, by the next World War this sum barely paid for a small Spitfire fighter, and by the mid-1980s a single advanced long-range air-to-air missile could cost a great deal more than one hundred Spitfires, let alone the carrier aircraft whose price tag could run into many tens of millions of dollars.

For the purposes of this book 'Modern Military Aircraft' has been taken to mean aircraft that are serving with one or more air arms. 'Modern' in this sense means 'current,' and indeed some of the aircraft types detailed date from World War II. An example of an older aircraft

BAe Hawk aircraft of Britain's RAF in the various liveries of the roles they are employed in. Nearest the camera is an aircraft of No. 4 Flying Training School, accompanied by aircraft of No. 1 Tactical Weapons Unit, an aircraft in air defense colors and finally one belonging to the Red Arrows display team.

still giving good service is the Swiss FFA C-3605, built during the period 1942-44 as a fighter-bomber, but now used as a target-tug.

Every effort has been made to detail the world's most important and interesting military aircraft, covering all facets of military operations. But inevitably for a publication of this size, there are 'casualties.' Old familiar names such as the de Havilland Vampire, North American F-86 Sabre and F-100 Super Sabre, Fairchild C-123 Provider and others are among those no longer important enough to detail. Their useful lives as front-line aircraft are at an end and these aircraft are now mostly withdrawn, in store or are being used for other purposes including use as pilotless drones.

At the other end of the time scale, it was only during the course of writing that the Fairchild Republic T-46A Next Generation Trainer was deleted from the book, the USAF officially terminating the trainer's production program in March 1987. Similarly, a choice had to be made as to which aircraft currently under development should be included. This, in many respects, represented the more difficult selection. It was decided, however, to include those military prototypes flying or about to fly at the time of writing which had the greatest chance of eventually giving rise to production derivatives; not included are projects intended to mature in the far distant future or demonstrators not ever intended to spawn series production aircraft.

The Northrop Advanced Technology Bomber being developed as a follow on to the B-1B is therefore included, but the Lockheed YF-22 and Northrop YF-23 ATFs (Advanced Tactical Fighters) for future USAF service are not, as these are barely more than proposals at present. One of the greatest problems facing ATF developers may well prove to be the ability to keep within the outlined unit cost, reported in 1985 dollars to be $35 million. Higher cost could well mean the eventual production of fewer than the 750 aircraft wanted by the USAF.

Inset left: Sikorsky artist's impression of an LHX helicopter in combat form.
Main picture: British Aerospace EAP advanced technology demonstrator on its maiden flight, 8 August 1986.
Above: Lockheed-California impression of ATFs emerging from their shelters.
Overleaf: Target drone conversions of ex-USAF/ANG F-100 Super Sabres and Convair F-102As.

Notes on using this book
In the section headed 'Operators' all references are to the air forces of the countries listed unless otherwise stated. The following is a list of technical terms and abbreviations used in the book.

Technical Terms

AAM Air-to-air missile
AEW Airborne early warning
AEW&C Airborne early warning and control
AFRES Air Force Reserve, United States Air Force
ALARM Air launched antiradiation missile
AMRAAM Advanced medium-range air-to-air missile
ANG Air National Guard, United States Air Force
ARM Antiradiation missile
ASMP Air-Sol Moyenne Portée
ASRAAM Advanced short-range air-to-air missile
ASV Air-to-surface vessel or antisurface vessel
ASW Antisubmarine warfare
AUW All-up weight, or gross weight
AWACS Airborne warning and control system
Barcap Barrier combat air patrol separating friendly naval force from enemy air threat
Chaff Radar reflective material to confuse enemy radars, released from an aircraft in a cloud
COD Carrier on-board delivery

COIN Counter-insurgency
Derated Applies to an engine that is governed to restrict its power output
Drop tank Jettisonable/detachable auxiliary fuel tank
ECCM Electronic counter-countermeasures
ECM Electronic countermeasures
Elint Electronic intelligence
ESM Electronic surveillance measures, when applied to US aircraft; electronic support measures for British aircraft
Ferry range Maximum range an aircraft can fly on internal and auxiliary fuel
FLIR Forward-looking infrared
Hardpoint Strengthened section of the airframe, for attaching armaments or other stores
HARM High-speed antiradiation missile
Hovering ceiling The highest altitude at which a helicopter can hover
HUD Head-up display
IAS Indicated airspeed
IFF Identification friend or foe
IFR Instrument flight rules
IR Infrared
JATO Jet-assisted take-off (usually rocket)
JASDF Japan Air Self-Defense Force
JGSDF Japan Ground Self-Defense Force
JMSDF Japan Maritime Self-Defense Force
Km/h Kilometers per hour
Liter 0.22 (approximately) of an Imperial gallon; 0.264 of a US gallon
MAC Military Airlift Command, United States Air Force
Mach The speed of sound
MAD Magnetic anomaly detector
MATS Military Air Transport Service,

United States Air Force, now MAC
MAW Military Airlift Wing
Mph Miles per hour
Nm Nautical mile
NOS Night observation surveillance
Payload The weight of freight, passengers or weapons an aircraft can carry
Pulse-Doppler Radar emitting pulses to measure the 'returns' and evaluate them
Pylon Structure on which to attach weapons, drop-tanks and so on
Radius The distance an aircraft can fly before having to return
RAF Royal Air Force (Britain)
RPV Remotely piloted vehicle, or drone
SAC Strategic Air Command, United States Air Force
SAD Submarine anomaly detector
SAR Search and rescue
Sigint Signal intelligence
SLAR Side-looking airborne radar
STOL Short take-off and landing
TAC Tactical Air Command, United States Air Force
TANS Tactical air navigation system
TFW Tactical Fighter Wing, United States Air Force
TOW Name of an antitank missile (from Tube-launched, Optically tracked, Wire guided)
UK United Kingdom
USAF United States Air Force
USAFE United States Air Force, Europe
USMC United States Marine Corps
VFR Visual flight rules
V/STOL Vertical/short take-off and landing

U.S. AIR FORCE

The likely outcome of the ATF program is discussed in the entry on the Lockheed RF-19 highly classified reconnaissance-strike aircraft.

Another US program at present too speculative to be included is the LHX (Light Helicopter Experimental). This program aims to offer the US Army a helicopter capable of such varied missions as air-to-air combat, attack and utility, and will therefore replace several existing types. The general specifications within which the helicopter is to be designed are to some degree defined, but the eventual outcome, if the program goes ahead, could well prove to be very different.

This same argument could equally be said to apply to the European Fighter Aircraft. Progress on the EFA is gathering pace and so it is included in the text, while the forward-swept wing Grumman X-29A and British Aerospace EAP are only (but importantly) technology demonstrators, types never intended for front-line service. Conversely, the tilt-rotor machines of the V-22 Osprey series, and other combat prototypes still under construction but intended for future squadron use, are detailed. It is interesting to note that, like the EAP, the latest French, Israeli and Swedish fighter prototypes are of the close-coupled delta-wing/large foreplane configuration, a

layout pioneered by the Swedish Viggen 20 years ago and for which Saab was unable to find any export customers. And yet, with so few air forces/governments fully appreciating the operational advantages of Harrier-type V/STOL aircraft, the Viggen with its ability to operate from main roads under emergency conditions, offered European air forces one of the few aircraft that would be able to escape the crippling effects of attacks on runways that would most definitely take place at the outbreak of a major war.

Inset above: Grumman X-29A forward swept-wing demonstrator.
Main picture: Fairchild Republic T-46A NGT, no longer destined for the USAF as a T-37 replacement.
Overleaf: A Sikorsky SH-60B Sea Hawk of the US Navy.

A-Z
of Modern
Military Aircraft

Aeritalia G91
Italy

One of the greatest, and continuing difficulties facing NATO is the wide variation in aircraft types operated by the member nations. An early attempt to remedy this was to produce the Fiat (now Aeritalia) G91 strike-fighter, the thirty prototypes and pre-series examples of which were actually ordered by NATO after the NATO-inspired design competition. The first of these made its maiden flight on 9 August 1956 and two years later an Italian development squadron was formed. But the good intention came to little when only Italy and Germany took the G91 into service, the 'R' of the G91Rs representing the addition of three cameras in each aircraft to expand the possible roles. In Germany the G91R/3 was built under license by the joint effort of Bolkow, Heinkel and Messerschmitt, freeing ex-Luftwaffe (Fiat-produced) G91R/4s to be acquired by Portugal during 1965-66, followed during the 1970s and as recently as 1980 by G91R/3s for service and spares. The more recent Luftwaffe aircraft were freed by the introduction into German service of close-support and reconnaissance Alpha Jets. Similarly, Italian G91Rs and G91Ys will be displaced from 1988 by AMXs.

Specifications (G91Y data)
Weapons: Two 30-mm DEFA cannon in the air intake sides, plus up to 4000 lb (1814 kg) of attack weapons on four underwing pylons, including 1000-lb (454-kg) bombs, air-to-surface missiles or rockets, gun pods, etc.
Accommodation: The pilot.
Wingspan: 29 ft 6½ in (9.01 m).
Length: 38 ft 3½ in (11.67 m).
Maximum take-off weight: 19,180 lb (8700 kg).
Maximum speed: 690 mph (1110 km/h).
Combat radius: 466 miles (750 km).
Mission performance: Rate of climb at sea level 17,000 ft (5180 m) per min; ceiling 41,010 ft (12,500 m).
Engines: Two 4080-lb (1850-kg) thrust with afterburning General Electric J85-GE-13A turbojets.

Below: Italian Air Force Aeritalia G91Y.

Versions in service
G91R/1A and G91R/1B: Original production versions, with a single 5000-lb (2268-kg) thrust Fiat/Bristol Siddeley Orpheus 803 turbojet engine. Four 0.5-in Colt-Browning guns, 2 each side of the cockpit. 2 pylons on the 1A and 4 on the 1B, plus avionics differences. Wingspan and length of 28 ft 2½ in (8.60 m) and 34 ft 4 in (10.46 m) respectively.
G91R/3: Single Orpheus engine. 2 DEFA cannon.
G91R/4: Single Orpheus engine. 4 Colt-Browning cannon and 4 pylons.
G91T: 2-seat transonic trainer, first flown in 1960. 2 Colt-Browning guns and 2 pylons. Greater wingspan and length than the G91Rs.
G91Y: First flown in 1966 as a strike-reconnaissance aircraft using the larger airframe of the G91T trainer. 2 General Electric engines.
Operators: Italy and Portugal.

Aeritalia G222
Italy

The G222 general-purpose military transport was first flown as a prototype on 18 July 1970 and entered Italian Air Force service in this role from 1978, but only after deliveries to Dubai and Argentina. Of the 88 G222s ordered by the indigenous air force and export customers by 1986, several represent specialist variants as detailed below. Future developments could include models for an airborne early warning role, maritime patrol, use as an in-flight refuelling tanker, and RPV carrier.

Specifications (G222 data)
Radar: Meteo weather and terrain-mapping radar.
Accommodation: Flight crew of 3 plus 53 armed troops, 40 paratroops, or 19,840 lb (9000 kg) of freight or vehicles loaded via an hydraulically actuated rear ramp under the beaver tail. Alternative interiors include 36 stretchers and 4 attendants, 21 passengers in a VIP arrangement, or those for the roles given below.

Wingspan: 94 ft 2 in (28.70 m).
Length: 74 ft 5½ in (22.70 m).
Maximum take-off weight: 61,730 lb (28,000 kg).
Maximum speed: 336 mph (540 km/h).
Range: 852 miles (1371 km) with full load.
Mission performance: Rate of climb at sea level 1700 ft (520 m) per min; ceiling 25,000 ft (7620 m).
Engines: Two 3400-shp Fiat/General Electric T64-GE-P4D turboprops, with 12,000 liters of fuel standard.

Versions in service:
G222: General purpose military transport. As used by all operators mentioned below except for Libya. 5 Italian aircraft were ordered by the Ministry for Civil Defense to tackle disasters and are capable of stretcher-carrying and firefighting in addition to the transportation of emergency supplies.
G222L: Libyan Arab Air Force VIP version of the G222T. 2 built.
G222T: Transport variant with 4860-shp Rolls-Royce Tyne R.Ty.20 Mk 801 turboprops. Gross weight 63,935 lb (29,000 kg). Maximum speed 357 mph (574 km/h).
G222RM: Italian Air Force calibration model, operated by the same gruppo as the Aermacchi MB-339RMs (qv). 4 built.
G222SAA: Italian Air Force G222, quickly convertible for firefighting using palletized equipment. This includes a 6000-liter tank with two nozzles to release water or fire retardant from the opened ramp door.
G222GE: Italian Air Force electronic warfare (ECM) model. 2 built. Company designated G222VS.
Operators: Argentina (army), Dubai, Italy, Libya, Nigeria, Somali Republic, and Venezuela (air force and army).

Aeritalia/Aermacchi/EMBRAER AMX
Italy and Brazil

There were independent design programs in Italy and Brazil for a subsonic tactical fighter-bomber to supersede Aeritalia (Fiat) G91s and Lockheed F-104 Starfighters serving with the Italian Air Force and complement EMBRAER AT-26 Xavantes flying with the Brazilian Air Force. This situation led to such similar objectives that in 1980 the three participating companies from the two nations joined forces to develop a single design as the AMX. Prototypes were built by all three companies, the first from Aeritalia undertaking the maiden flight of the AMX on 15 May 1984. This was subsequently lost during a test flight in June of that year, but the flight program was able to continue with the five other prototypes that appeared over a year from November 1984 onward.

A total of 187 AMXs are now scheduled for Italian service from 1988, tasked with close support, interdiction, and counter-air (air combat); in the last role operating in partnership with Tornados and carrying Sidewinder missiles. Brazil is to receive 79 AMXs from 1989 as A-1s, mainly for attack, each carrying two 30-mm cannon and with avionics differences. Change in avionics and equipment is easily managed because of the aircraft's modular design. Indeed, the AMX is likely to greatly expand its roles as the years pass.

Construction of AMX is conventional, with aluminum alloy giving way to carbonfiber in

Above: Italian Air Force G222RM flight calibration aircraft, flying alongside a Cessna Citation II.
Right: Aeritalia/Aermacchi/EMBRAER AMX combat aircraft with wingtip AAMs.

a few areas, notably the fin and elevators. The control surfaces are hydraulically actuated. The pilot has digital data display, including a HUD.

Specifications (AMX data)
Radar: Ranging radar.
Weapons: One 20-mm M61A1 multibarrel cannon in Italian aircraft; two 30-mm DEFA 554 cannon in A-1. Up to 8377 lb (3800 kg) of weapons on 2 underfuselage and 4 underwing pylons, plus wingtip air-to-air missiles (Piranha IR homing AAMs on A-1s). Other equipment can include reconnaissance cameras and sensors.
Accommodation: The pilot.
Wingspan: 29 ft 1½ in (8.87 m).
Length: 44 ft 6½ in (13.58 m).
Maximum take-off weight: 27,558 lb (12,500 kg).
Maximum speed: Mach 0.86.
Combat radius: 230-320 miles (370-520 km) with 6000 lb (2722 kg) weapon load.
Mission performance: Ceiling 42,650 ft (13,000 m); G limits +8, −4.
Engine: One 11,030-lb (5000-kg) thrust Rolls-Royce Spey Mk 807 turbofan.
Version in service:
AMX: As detailed above. Brazilian aircraft will be designated A-1s.
Operators: Brazil and Italy from 1988-89.

Aermacchi MB.326, Atlas Impala and EMBRAER AT-26 Xavante
Italy, South Africa and Brazil

All three of these aircraft are basically the same, stemming from the original Aermacchi MB.326 two-seat basic and advanced jet trainer with light attack capability that first flew in prototype form on 10 December 1957. Production of the MB.326 in Italy ended several years ago with the introduction of the MB.339, while EMBRAER built 182 MB.326GB Xavantes between 1971 and 1983 for its indigenous air force and export to Paraguay and Togo, and Argentina received examples in 1983 (some fought during the Falklands war). South African production of Impala Mk 1s and Mk 2s lasted until about 1985, with deliveries starting in 1974. The SAAF currently operates around one hundred Impalas, the Mk 2s as single-seat attack aircraft.

Specifications (MB.326GB data)

Weapons: Can carry up to 4000 lb (1814 kg) of attack weapons on 6 underwing pylons, including 30-mm, 12.7-mm or 7.62-mm gun pods, bombs, air-to-surface missiles, 2.75-in or 80-mm rockets in launchers.
Accommodation: Student pilot and instructor in tandem.
Wingspan: 35 ft 7¼ in (10.85 m).
Length: 35 ft 0¼ in (10.67 m).
Maximum take-off weight: 11,500 lb (5216 kg).
Maximum speed: 539 mph (867 km/h).
Range: 1150 miles (1850 km).
Mission performance: Rate of climb at sea level 6050 ft (1844 m) per min; ceiling 47,000 ft (14,325 m).
Engine: One 3410-lb (1546-kg) thrust Rolls-Royce Viper 20 Mk 540 turbojet, with 1392 liters of fuel standard.

Versions in service

MB.326: Initial version with a 2500-lb (1134-kg) thrust Viper 11 engine. Delivered to the indigenous Air Force from 1962 as a basic jet trainer.

MB.326B: Similar, but with 6 pylons for attack weapons. Tunisia became a customer for this version.
MB.326E: Advanced and weapons trainer for the indigenous Air Force, with strengthened wings. Six built, plus an equal number by conversion.
MB.326F: Similar to the B but for its avionics and equipment. Ghana became a customer.
MB.326G: Trainer, suited also to COIN (counter-insurgency). Viper 20 Mk 540 engine.
MB.326GB: Similar to the G but with greater emphasis on armaments. First flown in 1967. Exports included examples to Zaire and Zambia. Similar aircraft were built under license in Brazil as AT-26 Xavantes and in South Africa as Atlas Impala Mk 1s.
MB.326H: Royal Australian Air Force and Navy version of the Viper 11-engined MB.326, built by the Commonwealth Aircraft Corporation.
MB.326K: Single-seat trainer and attack

Above: Aermacchi MB. 326H in Royal Australian Navy service.

aircraft, first flown on 22 August 1970. 4000-lb (1814-kg) thrust Viper Mk 632-43 turbojet, with 1660 liters of fuel standard. Maximum speed 553 mph (890 km/h). Two 30-mm DEFA cannon in the fuselage plus 4000 lb (1814 kg) of underwing weapons. Optional four-camera photographic reconnaissance pod. Customers included Dubai, Ghana, Tunisia and Zaire. A similar version, but with the Viper 20 Mk 540 engine, became the South African-produced Atlas Impala Mk 2.
MB.326L: Similar to the K but with a 2-seat cockpit for advanced training. Customers were Abu Dhabi and Tunisia.
Operators: Abu Dhabi, Argentina (navy), Australia (air force and navy), Brazil, Dubai, Ghana, Italy, Paraguay, South Africa, Togo, Tunisia, Zaire and Zambia.

Below: Atlas Impala 2.

Aermacchi MB-339 series
Italy

First flown as a prototype on 12 August 1976, the MB-339 is the Italian equivalent of the British BAe Hawk, French/German Alpha Jet and so on, originally satisfying the Italian Air Force's requirement for a new basic and advanced jet trainer. This service received 100 MB-339As between 1979 and 1987, including about 17 as MB-339PANs (Pattuglia Acrobatica Nazionale) for the Frecce Tricolori aerobatic display team and four MB-339RM calibration aircraft serving with the 8° Gruppo Sorveglianza Elettronica. MB-339As have also been exported and new versions have followed, as detailed below.

Aermacchi has also developed a single-seat version as the MB-339K Veltro 2, making attack the foremost role. It retains the basic straight-winged airframe of the two-seater but has a more powerful engine, a redesigned cockpit, changes to the avionics, extra fuel and fixed cannon armament. The prototype Veltro 2 first flew on 30 May 1980.

Specifications (MB-339A data)
Weapons: Up to 4000 lb (1815 kg) of weapons for training or light attack, carried on 6 underwing pylons. The very wide range of stores can include Macchi pods each containing a 30-mm DEFA 553 cannon or up to six 7.62mm Minigun pods, 2 Magic or Sidewinder air-to-air missiles, bombs of various types and purposes of up to 1000 lb (454 kg) weight each, rockets and so on.
Accommodation: Student pilot and instructor in tandem, the rear cockpit raised.
Wingspan: 35 ft 7 ½ in (10.86 m).
Length: 36 ft 0 in (10.97 m).
Maximum take-off weight: 13,000 lb (5895 kg).
Maximum speed: 558 mph (898 km/h) IAS.
Range: 1094 miles (1760 km).
Mission performance: Rate of climb at sea level 6600 ft (2010 m) per min; ceiling 48,000 ft (14,640 m); G limits +8, −4; endurance 2 h 50 min.
Engine: One 4000-lb (1814-kg) thrust Rolls-Royce Viper Mk 632-43 turbojet, with 1413 liters of fuel standard.

Versions in service
MB-339A: Standard version, for training and light attack. As detailed above.
MB-339PAN: Version of the MB-339A for the Frecce Tricolori aerobatic display team, without the otherwise integral wingtip fuel tanks.
MB-339RM: Calibration version of the MB-339A.
MB-339B: New advanced trainer model, first appearing in 1985, with improved combat capabilities. 4450-lb (2018-kg) thrust Viper Mk 680-43 turbojet and increased fuel in larger wingtip tanks. Not yet in service.
MB-339C: Under development. As for MB-339B but with a digital nav/attack system and advanced avionics. Missile armament can include AIM-9L Sidewinder, Magic, air-to-surface Maverick, and the antishipping Marte Mk II.
MB-339K Veltro 2: Single-seat attack aircraft with operational training secondary role. Engine as for MB-339B. Two 30-mm DEFA cannon in the fuselage, with 120 rounds of

Above: Aermacchi MB-339A jet trainer and attack aircraft.

ammunition per gun, plus up to 4266 lb (1935 kg) of attack weapons carried on the pylons.
Operators: All MB-339A, except Italy. Argentina (navy), Dubai, Italy (air force, 339A, 339PAN and 339RM), Malaysia, Nigeria and Peru.

Aero L-29 Delfin (NATO name Maya)
Czechoslovakia

Despite being superseded in production by the much improved L-39 Albatros during the early 1970s, the Delfin remains in widespread use; Czechoslovakia alone may have anything up to 150. In its standard form it is a tandem two-seat basic and advanced jet trainer, its only unusual feature being the adoption of a T-tail. The prototype flew for the first time on 5 April 1959 on the power of a British Viper engine, but the Motorlet M 701 produced at a factory in Jinonice, close to Prague, became standard for the production version. Subsequent development produced a camera-carrying COIN version as the L-29R and an aerobatic model as the L-29A Akrobat.

Specifications (L-29 data)
Weapons: Underwing stations for two 7.62-mm gun pods, two 220-lb (100-kg) bombs or 8 rockets.
Accommodation: Student pilot and instructor in tandem, with the rear seat raised.

Wingspan: 33 ft 9 in (10.29 m).
Length: 35 ft 5 ½ in (10.81 m).
Take-off weight: 7231 lb (3280 kg).
Maximum speed: 407 mph (655 km/h).
Range: 555 miles (894 km).
Mission performance: Rate of climb at sea
level 2755 ft (840 m) per min; ceiling
36,090 ft (11,000 m); endurance 1h 47 min on
standard fuel only.
Engine: One 1962-lb (890-kg) thrust Motorlet
M 701c 500 turbojet, with 962 liters of fuel
standard.

Versions in service
L-29: Basic and advanced trainer, as
detailed above.
L-29A Akrobat: Single-seat aerobatic version
of 1967 appearance, with a derated engine
and high maneuverability. Intended mainly
for aerobatic teams.

Operators: Afghanistan, Bulgaria,
Czechoslovakia, Egypt, East Germany,
Guinea, Hungary, Indonesia, Iraq, Mali,
Nigeria, Rumania, Soviet Union, Syria and
Uganda.

Aero L-39 Albatros
Czechoslovakia

A follow-on to the Delfin and first flown as a
prototype on 4 November 1968, the Albatros
is typical of the world's modern jet trainers
except for its massive production, which is
currently at a rate of 200 aircraft a year, which
will bring the total number built by 1990 to
around 2500. Production includes examples
of a ground attack model, designated L-39
ZA. Unlike the Delfin, the Albatros uses a
Soviet engine.

Specifications (L-39 C data)
Weapons: Two underwing stations for up to
1102 lb (500 kg) of light weapons.
Accommodation: Student pilot and instructor
in tandem, the rear seat raised.

Below: Aero L-39 ZAs in Czech Air Force service.

Wingspan: 31 ft 0 ½ in (9.46 m).
Length: 39 ft 9 ½ in (12.13 m).
Maximum take-off weight: 10,362 lb (4700 kg).
Maximum speed: 466 mph (750 km/h).
Range: 621 miles (1000 km).
Mission performance: Rate of climb at sea
level 4330 ft (1320 m) per min; ceiling
37,725 ft (11,500 m); G limits +12 ultimate at
4200-kg AUW, +5.2 operational at 5500-kg
AUW, −2.6 operational at 5500-kg AUW;
endurance 2 h 30 min.
Engine: One 3792-lb (1720-kg) thrust
Ivchenko AI-25 TL turbofan, with 1255 liters
of fuel standard.

Versions in service
L-39 C: Standard trainer version, as detailed
above.
L-39 MS: First flown in 1985, this is a much-
refined trainer with many updates that
include airframe changes and electronic
displays in the cockpit. Power is provided
by a 5291-lb (2400-kg) thrust turbofan
engine.
L-39 ZA: Development of the L-39 ZO for
attack and reconnaissance. One 23-mm
GSh-23 cannon in an underfuselage pod.
Up to 2425 lb (1100 kg) of attack weapons or
stores on four underwing pylons, including

Above: Aero L-29 Delfin trainers in Czech service.

air-to-air missiles, bombs of up to 1102-lb
(500-kg) weight, rockets and so on. Used by
Czechoslovakia and Rumania. 12,345 lb
(5600 kg) gross weight.
L-39 ZO: Combines the features of the
trainer and attack aircraft, thus best
described as an armed trainer. Reduced
maximum speed compared to the other
versions. Exported.

Operators: Afghanistan, Cuba,
Czechoslovakia, East Germany, Ethiopia,
Iraq, Libya, Nicaragua, Rumania, Soviet
Union, Syria and Vietnam.

Aerospace Airtrainer CT4 and AESL Airtourer
New Zealand

Designed in Australia by Victa, the Airtourer
two-seat all-metal light aircraft was subsequently purchased by AESL (Aero Engine
Services Ltd) of New Zealand. The RNZAF
took in a number as trainers, four of which
remain in use.

Another Victa project had produced the

Above: Aerospace Airtrainer CT4.

Specifications (AS 350L1 Ecureuil data)

Weapons: AS 350L1 can carry guns, including 7.62-mm machine-gun pods or a 20-mm GIAT M.621 gun pod with a rate of fire of 740 rounds per min, and 68-mm or 2.75-in rockets.
Accommodation: 5 or 6 persons. Optional stretchers, rescue hoist, etc.
Diameter of rotor: 35 ft 0 ¾ in (10.69 m).
Fuselage length: 35 ft 10 ½ in (10.93 m).
Maximum take-off weight: 4850 lb (2200 kg).
Cruising speed: 143 mph (230 km/h).
Range: 407 miles (655 km).
Mission performance: Rate of climb at sea level 1476 ft (450 m) per min; ceiling 14,765 ft (4500 m); hovering ceiling in ground effect 9416 ft (2870 m); hovering ceiling out of ground effect 6300 ft (1920 m).
Engine: One 641-shp Turboméca Arriel 1 turboshaft, with 530 liters of fuel standard.

Versions in service
AS 350B: Standard version with Arriel 1 turboshaft. A variant for 'hot and high' operation is the AS 350B1, with a 684-shp Arriel 1D engine. The AS 350B is also produced as the HB 350B Esquilo by Helibras in Brazil.
AS 350L1: This is a specific military version of the AS 350B1, first flown in 1985. Deliveries began in 1986.
Operators: Australia (air force and navy, AS 350B), Brazil (navy, HB 350B Esquilo), Central African Republic, Gabon, Singapore and Tunisia.

prototype of a four-seat derivative of the Airtourer, known as the Aircruiser, which AESL also subsequently took over. However, in 1973 AESL and Air Parts (NZ) Ltd merged to form New Zealand Aerospace Industries Ltd, otherwise known simply as Aerospace. Redesign and restress of the Aircruiser brought about the Airtrainer for military use, sold to three nations. A fourth, Rhodesia, had ordered examples but these were put into store because of an embargo and in 1981 were remanufactured for sale to the Royal Australian Air Force, boosting the number received by this service to 51.

Australian armed forces have received 24, undertaking training, search and rescue, and liaison duties with the RAAF and utility and survey work with the navy. Most military sales have been for the AS 350B, but in early 1985 a specialized military version based upon the AS 350B1 made its maiden flight under the designation AS 350L1. With airframe modifications that include reinforcement for carrying weapons, sliding doors, self-sealing fuel tanks and a higher undercarriage, it has the provisions for the usual armament and armored seats to protect the crew from light ground fire.

Below: Royal Australian Navy Aérospatiale AS 350B Écureuil.

Specifications (CT4 data)
Accommodation: Student pilot and instructor side by side. Optional third seat to the rear or baggage.
Wingspan: 26 ft 0 in (7.92 m).
Length: 23 ft 2 in (7.06 m).
Maximum take-off weight: 2400 lb (1088 kg).
Maximum speed: 178 mph (286 km/h).
Range: 815 miles (1311 km).
Mission performance: Rate of climb at sea level 1350 ft (411 m) per min; ceiling 17,900 ft (5455 m); G limits +6 aerobatic, −3 aerobatic.
Engine: One 210-hp Rolls-Royce/Continental IO-360-H piston, with 205 liters of fuel.
Versions in service
CT4: RAAF and Thai examples known as CT4As, and RNZAF aircraft as CT4Bs.
Operators: Australia, New Zealand and Thailand.

Aérospatiale AS 350 Ecureuil
France

The Ecureuil five/six-seat single-turboshaft light helicopter first flew on 27 June 1974. Such is its success that more than 800 production examples have passed into civil and commercial use over the ensuing years. These include *Astars* for the North American market, with 615-shp Avco Lycoming LTS 101A engines. Helibras of Brazil has also built the helicopter under the local name HB 350 Esquilo.

Though military sales have been small, the

Accommodation: 5 or 6 persons.
Diameter of rotor: 35 ft 0 ¾ in (10.69 m).
Fuselage length: 35 ft 10 ½ in (10.93 m).
Maximum take-off weight: 5732 lb (2600 kg).
Cruising speed: 139 mph (224 km/h).
Range: 436 miles (703 km).
Mission performance: Rate of climb at sea level 1280 ft (390 m) per min; ceiling 11,155 ft (3400 m); hovering ceiling in ground effect 5900 ft (1800 m); hovering ceiling out of ground effect 4430 ft (1350 m).
Engines: 2 engines, as detailed above. Fuel capacity 730 liters.

Versions in service

AS 355F: Developed for civil and commercial customers but is in military use as a general purpose helicopter.
AS 355M: French Air Force version of the AS 355F, all to be delivered by 1989.
AS 355M2: Specific military Ecureuil 2 with the antitank missile options.
Operators: Bophuthatswana, Djibouti (AS 355F), France (AS 355M) and Malawi (army)

Aérospatiale CM 170 Magister, Super Magister, CM 175 Zéphyr, AMIT Fouga and Fouga 90
France and Israel

The subject of a long and distinguished production career, the Magister outlived its three parent companies (Fouga, Potez and Sud-Aviation) to become known finally as an Aérospatiale type. Developed initially to meet the requirements of the French Air Force for a two-seat turbojet-powered trainer, the first Magister prototype took to the air on 23 July 1952. The first production example flew initially on 29 February 1956 and eventually the French Air Force received 400, including the prototypes and 130 Super

Left: Aérospatiale AS 355M2 Ecureuil 2, armed with rocket launchers.
Below: Israeli Air Force IAI AMIT Fouga, known as the Tzukit.

Aérospatiale AS 355 Ecureuil 2
France

This twin-engined derivative of the Ecureuil (first flown in 1979) offers military operators a greater variety of armament, making it particularly suitable for anti-armor and air combat missions at low altitude. This is achieved by its ability to carry GD-Hughes TOW or Euromissile Hot antitank or Matra Mistral tube-fired air-to-air missiles.

Powered by two 420-shp Allison 250-C20F turboshafts (although these are to be superseded on the production line by two 456-shp Turboméca TM 319s), the helicopter's most important military customer to date is the French Air Force (Armée de l'Air). This force ordered 50 AS 355Ms primarily for surveillance of strategic bases. These are military examples of the civil AS 355F and will eventually possess the Mistral-carrying capability. A task-designed military model is the AS 335M2, which has the antitank missile, rocket and gun options.

Specifications (AS 355 M2 Ecureuil 2 data)
Weapons: Guns and 68-mm or 2.75-in rockets in launchers, plus/or TOW or Hot antitank or Mistral AATCP air-to-air missiles (in two-round tube launchers).

Magisters. The next largest customer was West Germany, which received 62 from France and built a further 188 under license; the Luftwaffe no longer operates the type. Total production of the Magister and all variants by 1969 was 929.

From the Magister was derived the CM 175 Zéphyr for the French Navy, with deck-landing capability. A modernized Magister trainer with more powerful Astafan IIG/IVG turbofan engines flew for the first time in 1978 as the Fouga 90, featuring also an updated cockpit with the then widely accepted benefit of a raised rear seat for the instructor. Intended to be manufactured from existing airframes, it could attain 435 mph (700 km/h) at 30,000 ft (9145 m) but, despite its many improvements, little came of this program.

In addition to the German Magisters, the trainer was also built under license in Finland and Israel, and it is the latter nation that has achieved major success in the modernizing field. Israel Aircraft Industries offers its Improved Fouga update for existing airframes to provide a multimission aircraft capable of basic and advanced flight training, armament training, ground support, jet operation transition, navigation training, reconnaissance, COIN, tactical aerobatics and formation training. As well as a complete overhaul, the airframe life is extended by 5000 flight hours, offers easier maintenance, new Marboré VI engines are fitted, improvements are made to the weapon-carrying capability or the provision for other external stores, it has new wiring, anti-collision lights and improved brakes, and there are avionics options to the already improved instrumentation.

The Israeli Air Force has been receiving back examples of its Magister trainer under the local name Tzukit in AMIT form, meaning Advanced Multimission Improved Trainer. These aircraft have had all armament removed but have been modernized and rebuilt to extend their useful life with the IAF.

Specifications (Improved Fouga data)

Weapons: Two 7.62-mm Browning machine-guns with 360 rounds of ammunition, plus two 110-lb (50-kg) bombs or up to 12 air-to-ground rockets. IAI can modify aircraft to carry minigun pods, Mk 81 bombs or other stores. (Super Magister can carry 2 machine-guns plus rocket pods, bombs or an AS.11 missile.)
Accommodation: Pupil/Instructor in tandem.
Wingspan: 39 ft 10 in (12.15 m) over tiptanks.
Length: 33 ft 0 in (10.05 m).
Maximum take-off weight: 7495 lb (3400 kg).
Maximum speed: 460 mph (740 km/h).
Range: (Super Magister at 30,000 ft; 9000 m at 3100 kg AUW) 870 miles (1400 km).
Mission performance: Rate of climb at sea level 3740 ft (1140 m) per min; ceiling 25,000 ft (7620 m).
Engines: Two 1058-lb (480-kg) thrust Turboméca Marboré VI turbojets, with 980 liters of fuel, or two 881-lb (400-kg) thrust Marboré IIs.

Versions in service
CM 170 Magister: Initial version with Marboré IIA engines.
CM 170 Super Magister: First flown in 1962. As Magister but with Marboré VI engines.
CM 175 Zéphyr: Navalized Magister for the French Navy with catapult and arrester gear, 2 rearward sliding hoods instead of upward-hinged canopies, and a strengthened undercarriage. The first prototype flew initially on 31 July 1956.
Fouga 90: Modernized version.
IAI Improved Fouga: Modernized version.
IAI AMIT Fouga: Unarmed modernized trainer, used by IAF.
Operators: Algeria, Bangladesh, Belgium, Cameroon, Eire (armed for ground attack), El Salvador (IAI type), France (air force; navy Zéphyr), Gabon (armed for ground attack), Guatemala, Israel (Tzukit), Lebanon, Libya, Morocco (armed for ground attack), Senegal and Togo (armed for ground attack).

Above: Aérospatiale Epsilon primary and basic trainer.

Aérospatiale Epsilon
France

With the intention of improving its pilot training program, the French Air Force decided it needed a new propeller-driven primary/basic trainer on which to instruct pupils before they advanced to the Alpha Jet. The resulting aircraft is the Epsilon, the first prototype of which flew initially on 22 December 1979, followed eventually by the first production aircraft on 29 June 1983.

Training of student pilots using the Epsilon began at Cognac in early 1985, later at other bases. French Air Force aircraft are unarmed. One hundred and fifty production Epsilons will go into French service over several years.

Unusual for a modern trainer in being piston-engine-powered, the standard Epsilon may be joined later by a turboprop-powered version. Already the first prototype has been re-engined with a 460-shp Turboméca TP 319 turboprop, an aerobatic engine which ran for the first time in September 1985 and began flight tests on the Epsilon two months later.

A third variant of the Epsilon is an armed version, with four underwing stations for up to 661 lb (300 kg) of stores if flown as a single seater or a 440-lb (200-kg) load with both seats occupied. Three armed Epsilons were ordered by Togo.

Specifications (Epsilon data)
Weapons: The armed Epsilon can carry two 7.62-mm Matra gun pods, four Matra F2 launchers for 68-mm rockets, or two 275-lb (125-kg) bombs, or other stores.
Accommodation: Pupil and instructor in tandem. Raised rear seat.
Wingspan: 26 ft 0 in (7.92 m).
Length: 24 ft 10¾ in (7.59 m).
Maximum take-off weight: 2755 lb (1250 kg).

Maximum take-off weight (armed Epsilon): 3086 lb (1400 kg).
Maximum speed: 236 mph (380 km/h).
Mission performance: Rate of climb at sea level 1850 ft (564 m) per min; ceiling 23,000 ft (7000 m); G limits +6.7, −3.35; G limits (armed Epsilon) +6, −3; endurance 3¾ h.
Engine: Standard Epsilon has one 300-hp Avco Lycoming AEIO-540-L1B5D piston, with 210 liters of fuel.
Versions in service
Epsilon: Unarmed trainer.
Armed Epsilon: Heavier take-off weight.
Operators: France and Togo.

Aérospatiale (Nord) N 262 /Frégate and Nord N 260 Super Broussard
France

Before becoming part of Nord Aviation, Société des Avions Max Holste developed a modern-looking twin-engined light transport as the M.H.250 Super Broussard, which in production form was the M.H. 260 with 805-ehp Turboméca Bastan turboprop engines. Unlike the single-engined Broussard in every respect except for its high-mounted (unbraced) wings, it was developed further by Nord into the more rounded fuselage (cross section) and pressurized N 262, but not until the French Air Force had received a number of Super Broussards for service as liaison aircraft. Five are in service.

The prototype N 262 flew for the first time on 24 December 1962 and a number of production versions followed for commercial and military operation. Most are employed as transports, but the French Navy received 15 N 262 Series As for use also as flight-crew trainers and a further number of N 262s thereafter (mostly ex-French Air Force aircraft). About 12 N 262s remain in French Navy service, leaving the French Air Force as the largest user today with about 27 Frégates for transport, liaison and training duties.

Specifications (Frégate data)
Accommodation: 29 troops, 18 paratroops or freight up to 6780 lb (3075 kg).
Wingspan: 74 ft 1¼ in (22.60 m).
Length: 63 ft 3 in (19.28 m).

Below: Aérospatiale Frégate.

Maximum take-off weight: 23,810 lb (10,800 kg).
Maximum speed: 260 mph (418 km/h).
Maximum range: 1490 miles (2400 km).
Range with 26 troops: 900 miles (1450 km).
Mission performance: Rate of climb at sea level 1200 ft (366 m) per min; ceiling 28,510 ft (8690 m)
Engines: Two 1145-ehp Turboméca Bastan VII turboprops, with 2000 liters of fuel standard.
Versions in service
N 260 Super Broussard: Original Max Holste/Nord model with basically square-section fuselage and 805-ehp turboprop engines.
N 262 Series A: Version in service with French Navy and Angola, the latter as ex-commercially operated aircraft taken into service in 1980.
N 262 Series C: Civil version with Bastan VII engines, ordered by Gabon government for VIP role and acquired from France by Haute Volta (Burkina-Faso) as military transport.
N 262 Series D/Frégate: Military equivalent of civil Series C and operated by the French Air Force.
Operators: Angola, Burkina-Faso, France (air force and navy) and Gabon.

Aérospatiale SA 316B and SA 319B Alouette III, and ICA IAR-317 Airfox
France and Rumania

Developed as a larger seven-seat derivative of the Alouette II helicopter, the Alouette III first flew as a prototype on 28 February 1959 and production deliveries up to 1969 were of SE 3160s. With increased payload and gross weight, and strengthened rotor transmission, this helicopter became known under the revised designation SA 316B, the first flying on 27 June 1968 and deliveries starting two years later. A version of the helicopter with an Astazou XIV engine became the SA 319B. French production of these two models ended in 1985, when 1455 had been completed for civil and military use, but India, Rumania and Switzerland received licenses to build the SA 316B, production in the former two continuing today as the HAL Chetak and ICA IAR-316B respectively. In Rumania, a specialized tandem two-seat light attack and training helicopter has also been produced by modification of the IAR-316B as the

Below: One of 12 Aérospatiale SA 319B Alouette III Astazous in French Gendarmerie use.

IAR-317 Airfox. The prototype Airfox first flew in April 1984.

Specifications (IAR-316B data)
Weapons: One 7.62-mm machine-gun or 20-mm cannon, 68-mm rockets or four anti-armor missiles.
Accommodation: Pilot and 6 passengers, 2 stretchers and 2 sitting casualties/attendants, or internal/external freight. Maximum sling load is 1653 lb (750 kg).
Diameter of rotor: 36 ft 1¾ in (11.02 m).
Fuselage length: 33 ft 4½ in (10.17 m).
Maximum take-off weight: 4850 lb (2200 kg).
Cruising speed: 115mph (185 km/h).
Range: 335 miles (540 km).
Mission performance: Rate of climb at sea level 853 ft (260 m) per min; ceiling 10,500 ft (3200 m); hovering ceiling in ground effect 9350 ft (2850 m); hovering ceiling out of ground effect 4920 ft (1500 m).
Engine: One 870-shp Turboméca Artouste IIIB turboshaft (derated to 550 shp), with 575 liters of fuel.

Versions in service
SA 316B: Artouste-powered helicopter.
SA 319B: Similar helicopter but with an 870-shp Turboméca Astazou XIV turboshaft, derated to 600 shp.
Chetak: HAL-built version of the SA 316B.
IAR-316B: Rumanian license-built version of the SA 316B.
IAR-317 Airfox: Rumanian-developed attack and training helicopter, armed with two 7.62-mm guns plus up to 1653-lb (750-kg) of missiles, rockets, guns and bombs carried on outriggers.
Operators: Abu Dhabi, Angola, Argentina (army), Austria, Belgium (navy), Bophuthatswana, Burkina-Faso, Burma, Burundi, Chad, Chile (navy), China, Congo, Dominican Republic, Ecuador, El Salvador, Equatorial Guinea, Ethiopia, France (air force, navy and army), Gabon, Ghana, Greece (navy), Guinea-Bissau, India (air force and navy), Indonesia (army), Iraq (army), Ireland, Ivory Coast, Jordan, South Korea (navy), Laos, Lebanon, Malawi, Malaysia, Nepal, Netherlands (air force and army), Pakistan (air force, navy and army), Peru, Portugal, Rumania, Rwanda, Seychelles, South Africa, Spain (air force and army), Switzerland, Tunisia, Venezuela, Zaire and Zimbabwe.

Aérospatiale SA 321 Super Frelon and Changhe Zhi-8
France and China

The Super Frelon made its maiden flight on 7 December 1962 as the largest French helicopter to date, drawing from the experience of building the SE 3200 Frelon of 1959 that remained a prototype. Commercial and military versions were built and by the end of production in 1982 a total of 99 Super Frelons had been completed, the superficial Sikorsky look about the helicopter reflecting the fact that the American company assisted in its design and development. The French Navy received SA 321G antisubmarine helicopters, with duties including guarding Ile Longue nuclear submarine base and operating from a helicopter carrier. French Navy Super Frelons today carry Exocet (as do Iraqi helicopters) and also undertake commando assault roles. Of those in foreign service, the dozen Chinese examples are interesting (based on the SA 321Ja utility version and delivered during 1977-78) as some of these were the only Aviation of the People's Navy aircraft found on board ship, operating from Dajiang submarine rescue vessels with aft decks and hangars for two helicopters. The prototype of a Chinese-developed heavy helicopter based on the Super Frelon flew for the first time on 11 December 1985 as the Changhe Zhi-8. Ten are expected to be built by the end of this decade. Weight is reportedly 28,660 lb (13,000 kg), the same as for the Super Frelon.

Specifications (SA 321G data unless otherwise stated)
Radar: Doppler radar.
Weapons: 2 Exocet antiship missiles or 4 torpedoes.
Accommodation: Military versions, depending upon role. 2 or 3 crew and 27-30 troops, 15 stretchers and 2 attendants, or freight.
Diameter of rotor: 62 ft 0 in (18.90 m).
Fuselage length: 65 ft 10¾ in (20.08 m).
Maximum take-off weight: 28,660 lb (13,000 kg).
Cruising speed: 154 mph (248 km/h).
Range: 506 miles (815 km).
Mission performance: Rate of climb at sea

Below: French navy Aérospatiale SA 321G Super Frelon.

level 984 ft (300 m) per min; ceiling 10,170 ft (3100 m); hovering ceiling in ground effect 6400 ft (1950 m); endurance 4 h.
Engines: Three 1570-shp Turboméca Turmo IIIC6 turboshafts, with 3975 liters of fuel standard.

Versions in service
Super Frelon: Military versions built in several forms, the H being an air force and army model with Turmo IIIE6 engines for passengers or 11,020 lb (5000 kg) of external freight as a heavy-lift helicopter.
Changhe Zhi-8: Chinese derivative of the SA 321Ja.
Operators: China (air force and navy, Ja and Zhi-8 and used for transport and submarine support), France (navy, G), Iraq (army, H for antiship attack), Israel (K and used for transport), Libya (M/GM used mainly for SAR), Pakistan, South Africa (F/H/L types for transport) and Zaire (J for VIP transport).

Aérospatiale SA 330 Puma and AS 332 Super Puma
France

The Puma was developed for the French Army as a medium-sized all-weather helicopter for day and night operation. In some respects it looked like a scaled-down Super Frelon and the first prototype made its maiden flight on 15 April 1965. Two years later the Puma was chosen also for the RAF for tactical transport duties, and Westland Helicopters became a partner in the manufacturing program. Of the eight versions subsequently built, five were of a military nature and are detailed below. Manufacture still takes place under license in Rumania, while Indonesia also assembled Pumas but has now changed over to Super Pumas.

From the Puma was developed the Super Puma, which first flew in AS 332 form on 13 September 1978. The aim was to increase performance and payload, while also enhancing battlefield survivability and simplify maintenance. Airframe changes were evident but the most important update was the replacement of the Puma's Turmo IV engines with Makilas and uprating the transmission. To date six military versions of the Super Puma have been developed, of which the B1, F1 and M1 remain available.

Specifications (AS 332B1 Super Puma data unless stated otherwise)
Radar: Bendix RDR 1400 or RCA Primus 40/50 radar for search and rescue, or OMERA ORB 3214 radar for antisubmarine and antiship naval roles (the naval version can carry MAD, sonar and sonobuoys).
Weapons: Provision for guns and rocket pods for army and air force versions; torpedoes, Exocet and AS.15TT missiles are available for the naval model. Metal/Kevlar armor is offered to protect the crew.
Accommodation: Normally 2 crew, plus 23 troops or freight (9921-lb/4500-kg sling load). Alternatively, up to 9 stretchers and 3 attendants or a VIP cabin layout.
Diameter of rotor: 51 ft 2¼ in (15.60m).
Fuselage length: 50 ft 11½ in (15.53 m).
Maximum take-off weight: 20,615 lb (9350 kg).
Cruising speed: 163 mph (262 km/h).
Range: 384 miles (618 km).
Mission performance: Rate of climb at sea

level 1400 ft (426 m) per min; ceiling 13,450 ft (4100 m); hovering ceiling in ground effect 8850 ft (2700 m); hovering ceiling out of ground effect 5250 ft (1600 m).
Engines: Two 1877-shp Turboméca Makila IA1 turboshafts, with 1560 liters of fuel standard.

Versions in service
SA 330B Puma: Original French Army and Air Force version, entering service from 1970. Two 1328-shp Turboméca Turmo IIIC4 turboshafts. Accommodation for the crew plus 20 troops.
SA 330C Puma: Export version, with 1400-shp Turmo IVB engines.
SA 330E Puma: RAF model as the Puma HC.Mk 1, delivered from 1971. Same engines as SA 330B.
SA 330H Puma: Export version, with 1575-shp Turmo IVC engines from late 1973. Maximum cruising speed is 159 mph (257 km/h) and range 360 miles (580 km).
SA 330L Puma: Final military model of the Puma, first appearing in 1976. Composite material rotor blades, an increase in take-off weight to 16,315 lb (7400 kg) and Turmo IVC engines. Still in production in Rumania, where well over 100 have been built, mostly for the indigenous air force.
AS 332B Super Puma: Two 1780-shp Makila IA turboshaft engines. Accommodation for the crew plus 21 troops.
AS 332F Super Puma: Naval ASW, ASV and SAR version, with the same engines as for the AS 332B.
AS 332M Super Puma: Version of the AS 332B with a 2 ft 6 in (0.76 m) longer cabin for 25 troops.
AS 332B1 Super Puma: 1986 military model, with a reinforced floor. As detailed above.
AS 332F1 Super Puma: 1986 naval model. Provision for tailboom folding to assist

Below: RAF Aérospatiale Puma HC.Mk 1.

stowage. Cruise speed 149 mph (240 km/h)
SA 332M1 Super Puma: As for AS 332B1 but with 2 ft 6 in (0.76 m) longer cabin for 25 troops. 2060 liters of fuel standard.
Operators: (P=Puma, SP=Super Puma). Abu Dhabi (P and SP), Algeria (P), Argentina (army, P and SP), Brazil (P and SP), Chile (army, P and SP), Ecuador (army, P and SP), France (air force, P; navy, SP; army, P), Gabon (P), Guinea (P), Indonesia (air force, P; navy, SP), Iraq (army, P), Ivory Coast (P), Kenya (army, P), Kuwait (P and SP), Lebanon (P), Malawi (P), Mexico (P), Morocco (P), Nepal (P and SP), Nigeria (P), Oman (SP), Pakistan (army, P), Portugal (P), Qatar (SP), Rumania (P), Senegal (P), Singapore (SP), South Africa (P), Spain (P and SP), Sudan (P), Togo (P), United Kingdom (P) and Zaire (P and SP).

Aérospatiale SA 341 and SA 342 Gazelle
France and United Kingdom

It is over 20 years since the original Sud Aviation (now Aérospatiale) SA 340 Gazelle prototype was flown for the first time on 7 April 1967, highlighting the durability and popularity of this light utility helicopter. The same year saw finalization of the Anglo-French agreement under which three helicopter co-production programs were shared with Westland Helicopters in the United Kingdom; one of these was the Gazelle, and when the development phase ended Westland became responsible for some 65 percent of its structure. The initial aim of Sud had been to develop a new helicopter to eliminate the shortcomings of the Alouette III, providing one that would prove faster and more maneuverable for military operations as well as being suitable for civil use.

The first prototype had a rigid main rotor and a conventional tail rotor but the second prototype, which adopted the configuration that had been proposed for production aircraft, retained the rigid main rotor and introduced a shrouded tail rotor known as a 'fenestron' and a tall tail. Development was to prove difficult and it was not until late 1972 that the final configuration was adopted. One of the shortcomings had been the main rotor, and adoption of a semi-articulated rotor resulted in redesignation as SA 341, the early production versions being powered by a Turboméca III turboshaft; later introduction of the uprated Astazou XIV brought the change in designation to the current SA 342. By early 1987 well over 1300 Gazelles of all versions had been sold, and the type has also been built under license in Egypt and Yugoslavia.

Specifications (SA 342L data)
Weapons: Can include 2 forward-firing 7.62-mm machine-guns, or an axial GIAT 20-mm cannon, 2 rocket pods, 2 AS.12 or up to 6 Hot anti-armor missiles.
Accommodation: 5 persons.
Diameter of rotor: 34 ft 5½ in (10.50 m).
Fuselage length: 31 ft 3¼ in (9.53 m).
Maximum take-off weight: 4409 lb (2000 kg).
Cruising speed: 161 mph (260 km/h).
Range: 440 miles (710 km).
Mission performance: Rate of climb at sea level 1535 ft (468 m) per min; ceiling 13,450 ft (4100 m); hovering ceiling in ground effect 9970 ft (3040 m); hovering ceiling out of ground effect 7775 ft (2370 m).
Engine: One 858-shp Turboméca Astazou XIVM turboshaft, with 545 liters of fuel standard.

Versions in service
SA 341B: Version for British Army, which designates it Gazelle AH.Mk 1, powered by an Astazou III turboshaft.

SA 341C: Training version for the Royal Navy, which designates it Gazelle HT.Mk 2; generally similar to SA 341B.

SA 341D: Royal Air Force training version designated Gazelle HT.Mk 3; generally similar to SA 341B/C.

SA 341E: Communications version for the Royal Air Force which designates it HCC.Mk 4; generally similar to above.

SA 341F: Original version for French Army, powered by an Astazou III turboshaft.

SA 341G: Initial civil version, powered by an Astazou III turboshaft. In 1975 became the world's first helicopter to be certificated for single-pilot operation under IFR Cat I conditions; subsequently gained certification for IFR Cat II operation.

SA 341H: Company designation of the original military export version, powered by the Astazou III engine.

SA 342J: Civil version introducing the uprated Astazou XIV turboshaft and an improved 'fenestron'.

SA 342K: Military export version with the uprated Astazou XIV turboshaft, improved 'fenestron' and momentum-separation shrouds over the engine intakes.

SA 342L: Current production military version which, by comparison with earlier models, can be operated at a higher maximum take-off weight.

SA 342M: Version for France's Aviation Légère de l'Armée de Terre; differs from SA 342L by having French Army specified equipment and instrument panel.

Operators: Abu Dhabi, Angola, Burundi, Cameroon, Chad, Egypt, France (army), Guinea, Iraq (army), Ireland, Kenya, Kuwait, Lebanon, Libya, Morocco, Qatar, Rwanda, Senegal, Syria, United Kingdom (air force and army) and Yugoslavia.

Below: Aérospatiale SA 342M Gazelle, carrying Hot antiarmor missiles.

Above: US Coast Guard Aérospatiale HH-65A Dolphin.

Aérospatiale SA 365C, SA 365F/AS.15TT, SA 365N and SA 366 Dauphin 2
France

The single-engined SA 360 Dauphin and twin-engined SA 365 were developed to be modern replacements for the long-serving and highly successful Alouette III, the SA 365 making its first flight on 24 January 1975, some two-and-a-half years after the SA 360. The initial 10/14-seat SA 365C Dauphin 2 was followed by the much-changed SA 365N, the configuration remaining similar but with composite materials replacing metal over most of the airframe among the updates. The first SA 365N flew on 31 March 1979 and today production is also underway in China as the Harbin Z-9 Haitun.

Saudi Arabia ordered 24 SA 365F helicopters in 1980, based on the SA 365N. Twenty were equipped for antiship missions and four for search and rescue, some going on board new F 2000S-class frigates (*Madina, Hofouf, Abha* and *Taif*). Five SA 365Fs for SAR and fishery protection were also ordered by Ireland. Another military derivative of the SA 365N is the US Coast Guard's SA 366, known in service as the HH-65A Dolphin.

Specifications (SA 365F Dauphin 2 data)

Radar and weapons: Saudi antiship helicopters carry Thomson-CSF Agrion 15 radar, MAD, and Aérospatiale AS.15TT antiship missiles. Saudi SAR models have Omera ORB 32 radar, while Irish SAR helicopters use Bendix RDR L500 radar.
Accommodation: 2 crew, with provision for 10 passengers or freight (3527-lb/1600-kg sling load).
Diameter of rotor: 39 ft 2 in (11.93 m).
Fuselage length: 39 ft 8¾ in (12.11 m).
Maximum take-off weight: 9038 lb (4100 kg).
Cruising speed: 177 mph (285 km/h).
Range: 537 miles (865 km).
Mission performance: Rate of climb at sea level 1275 ft (390 m) per min; hovering ceiling in ground effect 7055 ft (2150 m); hovering ceiling out of ground effect 3940 ft (1200 m).
Engines: Two 700-shp Turboméca Arriel IM turboshafts.

Versions in service

SA 365C: Initial version of the Dauphin 2, powered by two 680-shp Arriel engines.
SA 365N: Two 710-shp Arriel IC engines, and smaller 13-blade fenestron ducted tail rotor than the SA 365F.
SA 365F: As detailed above. Bigger 11-blade fenestron tail rotor, of carbonfiber construction (not metal) to enhance hovering performance.
SA 366: US Coast Guard HH-65A Dolphin short-range recovery helicopter, operating from shore, cutters and icebreakers. 99 ordered, with 680-shp Avco Lycoming LTS 101-750A-1 turboshafts. Delivered between November 1984 and 1988.
Operators: Burkina-Faso (SA 365), China (air force and navy, Harbin Z-9), Dominican Republic (SA 365C), France (SA 365), Hong Kong (SA 365C), Ireland (SA 365F), Malawi (SA 365), Saudi Arabia (navy, SA 365F), Sri Lanka (SA 365C) and United States (coast guard, HH-65A).

Below: Aérospatiale SA 365M Panther.

Aérospatiale SA 365M Panther
France

The Panther is not yet in military service. Its potential is such, however, that when deliveries begin in 1988 it should greatly advance the course of combat-capable helicopters. It will be suited to carrying assault troops, providing close support or anti-armor gun, rocket or missile fire (at night using night-vision goggles), attacking low-flying aeroplanes and helicopters with cannon or missiles, performing search and rescue missions, electronic warfare, and the many other roles available to helicopters.

Based on the SA 365N airframe but with more use of composite materials, especially for the dynamic components, one of its major attractions will be its survivability under combat conditions, although, should it be disabled, it will be able to tolerate a vertical impact speed of seven meters per second at full weight. The fuel system with self-sealing tanks can tolerate twice this, greatly reducing the hazard of fire after a survivable crash. To avoid detection and homing by infrared sensors, the airframe uses a special infrared reflecting paint and the hot exhaust from the engines is mixed with cold air of the surrounding atmospheric temperature and directed upward. A radar-warning receiver allows information on enemy radars to be presented to the pilot, indicating that he has been picked up and tracked, and other survivability features include a high cruising speed, an infrared jammer and chaff dispenser to draw away enemy missiles.

Specifications (SA 365M Panther data)

Weapons: 20-mm GIAT M.621 gun pods with 180 rounds of ammunition each. 8 Matra Mistral AATCP air-to-air missiles, 68-mm or 2.75-in rockets, or up to 8 Euromissile Hot antitank missiles.
Accommodation: 2 crew plus up to 10 troops or 3527 lb (1600 kg) of slung cargo.
Diameter of rotor: 39 ft 2 in (11.93 m).
Fuselage length: 39 ft 7 in (12.07 m).

Maximum take-off weight: 9038 lb (4100 kg).
Cruising speed: 173 mph (278 km/h).
Range: 460 miles (740 km).
Mission performance: Rate of climb at sea level 1575 ft (480 m) per min; hovering ceiling in ground effect 10,500 ft (3200 m); hovering ceiling out of ground effect 8200 ft (2500 m).
Engines: Two 751-shp Turboméca TM 333-1M turboshafts.

Version in service

Not due for service until 1988.
Operators: No customers at time of writing.

Aérospatiale SE 313B and SA 318C Alouette II, and SA 315B Lama
France

The now familiar name of Alouette was introduced to a helicopter originally by the former Société Nationale de Constructions Aéronautiques de Sud-Est (SNCASE), when in 1952 its SE 3120 three-seat general-purpose helicopter took to the air. This company went on to develop the very successful SE 3130 Alouette II Artouste, using the same basic configuration but with an enlarged cabin for five persons and approximately twice the available engine power. This flew for the first time on 12 March 1955. As its name indicated, the SE 3130 was powered by a Turboméca Artouste IIC turboshaft engine. Soon after Sud-Aviation was formed in 1957 from Sud-Est and Ouest-Aviation, the Alouette II was granted its certificate of airworthiness and went on to achieve a long production run for civil and military operation, later under the designation SE 313B. Since Aérospatiale was formed in 1970, the Alouette II has been known under that title.

At the end of January 1961 a development of the SE 313B flew for the first time as the SA 318C Alouette II Astazou (originally SA 3180). This offered a substantial fuel consumption saving, higher power reserve in case of an emergency and better performance, all due to its 530-shp Turboméca Astazou IIA turboshaft engine, derated to 360 shp. Many of these were included in the total Alouette II production run of 1305 helicopters, of which more than a quarter went to the French military alone. Maximum speed of the Alouette II Astazou compared with the Artouste was 127 mph (205 km/h) against 109 mph (175 km/h).

The latest helicopter in the series is the SA 315B Lama which, though based upon a strengthened Alouette II airframe, uses the dynamics of the larger Alouette III. Developed originally to the requirements of the Indian forces, who call it the Cheetah, the prototype flew for the first time on 17 March 1969. In a demonstration of its capabilities at high altitude the same year, in the Himalayas, landings and lift-offs were made at 24,600 ft (7500 m), the greatest altitudes ever successfully attempted. A Lama also holds the absolute altitude record for helicopters, in FAI Class E.1, at 40,820 ft (12,442 m). Now operated around the world in civil and military roles, the Lama was also put into production in India by HAL and is assembled from French components as the Gavião in Brazil.

Specifications (SA 315B Lama data)

Accommodation: 5 persons, or a pilot plus 2 stretchers and an attendant, or a pilot and up to a 2502-lb (1135-kg) sling load

Above: German SA 318C Alouette IIs.

suspended beneath the helicopter (maximum take-off weight in this configuration is 5070 lb (2300 kg). Equipment can be carried for other roles, including rescue and observation.
Diameter of rotor: 36 ft 1¾ in (11.02 m).
Fuselage length: 33 ft 6¾ in (10.23 m).
Normal take-off weight: 4300 lb (1950 kg).
Maximum cruising speed: 119 mph (192 km/h).
Range: 320 miles (515 km).
Mission performance: Rate of climb at sea level 1080 ft (330 m) per min; ceiling 17,720 m (5400 m); hovering ceiling in ground effect 16,565 ft (5050 m); hovering ceiling out of ground effect 15,095 ft (4600 m).
Engine: One 870-shp Turboméca Artouste IIIB turboshaft (derated to 550 shp), with 575 liters of fuel.
Versions in service
SE 313B Alouette II: Maximum take-off weight 3527 lb (1600 kg).
SA 318C Alouette II: Developed version, with more powerful engine.
SA 315B Lama: Hybrid of Alouette II and III. 390 ordered by beginning of 1986. Indian-built Lama produced by HAL as Cheetah (140 delivered between 1973 and 1981). Helibras of Brazil assembles the helicopter as the HB 315B Gavião.
Operators: Angola (Lama), Argentina (air force and army, Lama), Belgium (Alouette), Benin (Alouette), Bolivia (Helibras Lama), Brazil (navy, Helibras Lama), Cameroon (Alouette), Central African Republic (Alouette), Chile (air force and army, Lama), Congo (Alouette), Djibouti (Alouette), Dominican Republic (Alouette), Ecuador (air force and army, Lama), France (air force, navy and army, Alouette), West Germany (army, Alouette), Guinea-Bissau (Alouette), India (Cheetah), Indonesia (navy, Alouette), Ivory Coast (Alouette),

Lebanon (Alouette), Mexico (Alouette), Peru (Alouette and Lama), Portugal (Alouette), Senegal (Alouette), Sweden (air force and navy, Alouette), Switzerland (Alouette), Togo (Lama), Tunisia (Alouette), Turkey (army, Alouette), United Kingdom (army, Alouette) and Zimbabwe (Alouette).

Aerotec A-122A Uirapuru
Brazil

Formed in 1962, Aerotec SA Industria Aeronautica developed a light aircraft for use as a primary trainer by air forces and civil flying clubs. The prototype, fitted with a 108-hp O-235 engine, flew for the first time on 2 June 1965. In production form the military variant became the A-122A and 126 were built for the home air force under the designation T-23. A further 18 went to Bolivia and eight to Paraguay.

Specifications (A-122A Uirapuru data)
Accommodation: Student pilot and instructor side by side.
Wingspan: 27 ft 10¾ in (8.50 m).
Length: 21 ft 8 in (6.60 m).

Maximum take-off weight: 1852 lb (840 kg).
Maximum speed: 141 mph (227 km/h).
Range: 497 miles (800 km).
Mission performance: Rate of climb at sea level 835 ft (255 m) per min; ceiling 14,765 ft (4500 m).
Engine: One 160-hp Avco Lycoming O-320-B2B piston, with 140 liters of fuel standard.
Version in service
A-122A: Production military version, known under the service designation T-23.
Operators: Bolivia, Brazil and Paraguay.

Agusta A 109
Italy

In basic form the A 109 is an 8-seat general-purpose helicopter of modern appearance, featuring a sleek aluminum fuselage and a retractable undercarriage. The first prototype made its maiden flight on 4 August 1971 and the initial Mk I production version was superseded in 1981 by the current Mk II. In

Below: Aerotec Uirapuru primary trainer, service-designated T-23.

Above: Coastguard version of the Agusta A 109 Mk II, with 360-degree radar scanner under the fuselage.

addition, specific military, naval and police versions have been developed, as detailed below.

Specifications (A 109A Mk II data)
Radar: Optional Bendix/FIAR RDR-1500 or Sperry Primus 300SL weather radar, or search radar for a maritime role.
Weapons: Military/naval versions can carry weapons, as detailed below.
Accommodation: The pilot and copilot/ passenger and 6 passengers. VIP configuration for 4 or 5. Alternatively, internal or external freight (2000-lb/907-kg maximum sling load), 1 or 2 stretchers and 3 attendants, etc.
Diameter of rotor: 36 ft 1 in (11.00 m).
Fuselage length: 35 ft 1½ in (10.71 m).
Maximum take-off weight: 5723 lb (2596 kg).
Cruising speed: 177 mph (285 km/h) at 4960-lb (2250-kg) gross weight.
Range: 402 miles (648 km) at 4960-lb (2250-kg) gross weight.
Mission performance: At 4960-lb (2250-kg) gross weight, rate of climb at sea level 2110 ft (634 m) per min; ceiling 15,000 ft (4575 m); hovering ceiling in ground effect 12,300 ft (3750 m); hovering ceiling out of ground effect 9450 (2880 m); endurance 3 h 12 min.
Engines: Two 420-shp Allison 250-C20B turboshafts with 560 liters of fuel standard.
Versions in service
A 109A Mk I: Initial production version. Same engines as the later Mk II but with lower-rated transmission, lower standard of avionics and other differences.
A 109 Mk II: As detailed above. Military examples include a VIP model for presidential use, flown by 31° Stormo, Italian Air Force.
Military and naval A 109A Mk II: For light attack (TOW or similar anti-armor missiles, 7.62-mm guns, rockets, etc), scouting, search and rescue, utility, surveillance and target acquisition (including use of 2 RPVs), electronic warfare, and antisubmarine/anti-surface vessel roles with optional search radar, MAD, other mission avionics, torpedoes, missiles, etc.
A 109 EOA: Italian Air Force armed

observation helicopters. 24 delivered from 1986 with 250-C20R engines, electronic warfare avionics, one 12.7-mm gun and missile launchers, and other changes from the standard Mk II.
Q 109 K: Not yet in production. Developed mainly for potential African and Middle Eastern military customers, with multirole capabilities and provision for armament on outriggers with four attachment points. Two 420-shp Turboméca Arriel IK turboshafts.
Operators: Argentina (army), Iraq, Italy (army), Libya, United Kingdom (army) and Venezuela (army).

Agusta A 129 Mangusta
Italy

The Mangusta is in production as an all-weather day and night anti-armor attack helicopter, capable also of other missions. It takes the now classic configuration of a tandem two-seater, with the pilot and copilot/ gunner in separate highly stepping cockpits within a slim fuselage. Its rotor and metal/ composite materials airframe are designed to withstand hits by 12.7-mm ammunition and other battlefield survivability features are incorporated. By keeping the Mangusta

small and light (under half the weight of an Apache, for example), Agusta has produced a low-cost specialist helicopter that might well interest many countries. Already the Dutch Army has ordered 20, which will actually be flown by the Royal Netherlands Air Force. The Italian Army is in the process of receiving 60, with at least 30 more likely to follow. The prototype Mangusta flew initially on 11 September 1983 and production deliveries to the Army started in 1987.

Specifications (A 129 Mangusta data)
Radar: Avionics include a night vision system, incorporating forward-looking infrared (FLIR), ECM and ECCM, including a radar warning receiver. Provision is made for a mast-mounted sight.
Weapons: A chin turret for a 0.50-in or 12.7-mm machine-gun can be installed, as can similar weapons or a 20-mm cannon pod under the stub wings. Other stub-wing options are 8 TOW, Hot or 6 Hellfire anti-armor missiles, rockets, 2 Stinger missiles for air-to-air use, etc, up to a maximum weight of 2205 lb (1000 kg).
Accommodation: Pilot and copilot gunner in stepped tandem cockpits.
Diameter of rotor: 39 ft 0½ in (11.90 m).
Fuselage length: 40 ft 3 in (12.28 m).
Maximum take-off weight: 9040 lb (4100 kg).
Maximum speed: 196 mph (315 km/h).
Mission performance: Rate of climb at sea level 2090 ft (637 m) per min; hovering ceiling in ground effect 10,795 ft (3290 m); hovering ceiling out of ground effect 7840 ft (2390 m); endurance 3 h.
Engines: Two 825-shp Piaggio-built Rolls-Royce Gem 2 Mk 1004D turboshafts.
Version in service
A 129 Mangusta: As detailed above. Two future developments have been proposed, comprising a naval antishipping version carrying radar, and an advanced multimission army version known as the Tonal, which reportedly could interest the indigenous army and those of the Netherlands, Spain and the United Kingdom.
Operators: Italy (army) and the Netherlands (army/air force).

Below: Agusta A 129 Mangustas armed with rocket launchers.

Above: AIDC AT-3 jet trainer.

AIDC AT-3
Taiwan

Although there is an abundance of modern basic and advanced jet trainers on the world market, few nations with the ability to design, develop and produce their own type can resist the opportunity and thereby advance their national aircraft industry. With export markets difficult to break into, the indigenous forces have to be capable of accepting a sufficient number to make the high costs of development worthwhile, and in the case of the CAF (Chinese Nationalist Air Force) it requires more than 50 home-produced AT-3s. As far as it is known, no export orders for the trainer had been received by the end of 1986.

The AIDC AT-3 is typical of the modern generation of jet trainers, having tandem cockpits for the two crew, the rear one raised for good forward vision. It is powered by two non-afterburning engines, fitted in nacelles on the fuselage sides at the wingroots. What makes this aircraft different is its armament arrangement, with a total load only slightly less than that for the BAe Hawk but greater than the equally popular Alpha Jet. For armament training and, presumably, light strike missions, weapons can be carried in a bay under the rear cockpit, on a centerline pylon, four underwing pylons and two wingtip rails, the latter for air-to-air missiles.

The first prototype AT-3, referred to by the name Tse Tchan, achieved its maiden flight on 16 September 1980 and delivery of production aircraft began in March 1984.

Specifications (AT-3 data)
Weapons: Up to 6000 lb (2721 kg) of weapons. The bay can house various armaments, including semi-recessed gun packs. Usually bombs, rocket launchers and so on can be carried on the pylons, those inboard capable of using triple ejector packs, while the centerline pylon can carry a 2000-lb (907-kg) store or an aerial target system. Air-to-air missiles are mounted on wingtips.
Accommodation: Student pilot and instructor in tandem cockpits.
Wingspan: 34 ft 3¾ in (10.46 m).
Length: 42 ft 4 in (12.90 m).
Maximum take-off weight: 17,500 lb (7938 kg).
Maximum speed: 562 mph (904 km/h).
Range: 1416 miles (2279 km).
Mission performance: Rate of climb at sea level 10,100 ft (3078 m) per min; ceiling 48,000 ft (14,625 m); endurance 3 h 12 min.
Engines: Two 3500-lb (1588-kg) thrust Garrett TFE731-2-2L turbofans, with 1630 liters of fuel standard.
Version in service
AT-3: Conventional jet trainer, although with a weapons bay. All-metal construction, except for the limited use of graphite/epoxy in areas of the fuselage. Supercritical section 'straight' wings.
Operator: Taiwan.

AIDC T-CH-1 Chung Hsieng
Taiwan

In 1981 the production program ended of this turboprop-powered basic trainer for the Chinese Nationalist Air Force. Fifty aircraft had been constructed, with T53 engines license-built at Kang-Shan. The performance and range of the T-CH-1 clearly makes other military roles possible.

Specifications (T-CH-1)
Accommodation: Tandem cockpits for the student pilot and instructor that are not stepped.
Wingspan: 40 ft 0 in (12.19 m).
Length: 33 ft 8 in (10.26 m).
Maximum take-off weight: 11,150 lb (5057 kg).
Maximum speed: 368 mph (592 km/h).
Range: 1250 miles (2010 km).
Mission performance: Rate of climb at sea level 3400 ft (1035 m) per min; ceiling 32,000 ft (9755 m).
Engine: One license-built 1451-shp Avco Lycoming T53-L-701 turboprop, with 963 liters of fuel.
Version in service
T-CH-1: The first prototype made its maiden flight on 23 November 1973. The second prototype was configured to carry armament, suited to weapons training and counter-insurgency.
Operator: Taiwan.

Airtech CN-235
Spain and Indonesia

Airtech (Aircraft Technology Industries) is a company founded by CASA of Spain and IPTN of Indonesia to develop a twin-turbo-prop short-haul commuter transport aircraft known as the CN-235. The first prototype to fly was that assembled by CASA, on 11 November 1983. Full production aircraft appeared in 1986. Military examples have been ordered by Indonesia and Saudi Arabia, the former order represented by 32 for the air force and 18 for the navy, with four CN-235s destined to join the Royal Saudi Air Force. Military CN-235 versions include one for antisubmarine warfare and maritime patrol with a search radar and weapon stations (see below), and others for ECM, photography, etc. Those aircraft ordered to date are believed to have been assigned transport roles.

Below: AIDC T-CH-1 Chung Hsieng trainers.

Above: Camouflaged Airtech CN-235.

Specifications (CN-235 data)
Radar: Collins Pro Line WXR-300 weather radar.
Weapons: Two fuselage and four underwing stations for up to 7716 lb (3500 kg) of weapons, including Exocet antiship missiles and torpedoes on ASW/patrol version.
Accommodation: Crew of 2 plus 48 troops, 41 paratroops, 24 stretchers and 4 attendants, or up to 11,025 lb (5000 kg) of cargo.
Wingspan: 84 ft 8 in (25.81 m).
Length: 70 ft 1 in (21.35 m).
Maximum take-off weight: 31,745 lb (14,400 kg).
Maximum speed: 276 mph (445 km/h).
Range with reserves: 373 miles (600 km) with a full payload; 2933 miles (4720 km) with a 3968-lb (1800-kg) load and full fuel.
Mission performance: Rate of climb at sea level 1525 ft (465 m) per min; ceiling 26,600 ft (8110 m).
Engines: Two 1700-shp General Electric CT7-&A turboprops, with 5268 liters of fuel.
Version in service
CN-235: Developed for commercial and military use.
Operators: Indonesia (air force and navy) and Saudi Arabia.

Below: Antonov An-2 biplanes at Kabul.

Antonov/PZL Mielec An-2 Antek and Huabei Y-5 (NATO name Colt)
Soviet Union, Poland and China

This ancient-looking Jack-of-all-trades general-purpose biplane has proved so successful in its chosen roles that production continues 40 years after the prototype flew on 21 August 1947. Designed originally for the Soviet Ministry of Agriculture and Forestry, it subsequently entered civil and military service for an incredible variety of tasks including agricultural ones. The secret of its success lay in its ability to fly almost anywhere, needing only 560 ft (170 m) and 610 ft (185 m) respectively to take off from and land on grass; while undercarriage options include compressed-air shock absorbers for rough field use, twin floats or skis. Production in the Soviet Union was undertaken between 1948 and 1960, by which time around 5000 An-2s had been completed. Thereafter WSK-PZL Mielec in Poland took over and has produced some 12,000 more, of which more than two-thirds have been exported back to the Soviet Union. In addition, China builds its own version as the Huabei Y-5. It is believed some 1000 Y-5s have been completed.

Specifications (An-2P data)
Accommodation: 2 crew plus 12 passengers, 14 paratroops or 2734 lb (1240 kg) of freight.

Wingspan: 59 ft 7¾ in (18.18 m) upper, 46 ft 8½ in (14.24 m) lower.
Length: 40 ft 8¼ in (12.40 m).
Maximum take-off weight: 12,125 lb (5500 kg).
Maximum speed: 160 mph (258 km/h).
Range: 559 miles (900 km) with 1102-lb (500-kg) load.
Mission performance: Rate of climb at sea level 690 ft (210 m) per min; ceiling 14,435 ft (4400 m).
Engine: One 1000-hp Shvetsov ASz-621R radial piston (PZL Kalisz built for Polish examples), with 1200 liters of fuel.
Versions in service
An-2LW: Polish general-purpose transport with float undercarriage.
An-2P: Soviet and Polish passenger/troop/paratroop/freight transport.
An-2PK: Polish 5-passenger VIP version.
An-2P-Photo: Polish special model for photogrammetry.
An-2S: Polish 6-stretcher ambulance version.
An-2T: Polish utility transport.
An-2TD: Polish paratroop training model, for 12 paratroops.
An-2TP: Polish passenger derivative of the TD, with similar tip-up seats along the cabin sides.
An-2V: Soviet twin-float version of its An-2P.
Y-5: Chinese model with a similar engine built as the Huabei 5 at Zhuzhou.
Y-5 turboprop: China is believed to be developing a variant of the Y-5 with an 1850-shp turboprop engine.
An-3: Antonov turboprop conversion of existing An-2s, each with 1450-shp Glushenkov TVD-20 engine and lengthened fuselage. A Polish version with this engine is the An-3M, mainly for agricultural work. No turboprop An-3s are believed in military service.
Operators: Afghanistan, Albania, Angola, Benin, Bulgaria, China, Cuba, Czechoslovakia, Egypt, East Germany, Hungary, Iraq, North Korea, Laos, Mali, Mongolia, Nicaragua, Poland, Rumania, Somali Republic, Soviet Union, Tanzania and Vietnam.

Antonov An-12 and Shaanxi Y-8 (NATO name Cub)
Soviet Union and China

The An-12 is the Soviet equivalent of the West's C-130 Hercules, also dating from the 1950s but, unlike the C-130, its importance as a military transport is diminishing with the arrival of newer and better aircraft such as the Il-76. It also differs from the C-130 in having tail armament for self protection, something Western transports have not been given. The cargo cabin of the An-12 is 44 ft 3 in (13.50 m) in length and 11 ft 6 in (3.50 m) wide, with straight-in loading via hinged doors under the upswept rear fuselage. More than 200 An-12BPs still operate with the Soviet VTA, the same version as that in production in China as the Y-8. In addition to the transport roles, the An-12 has been adopted for various electronic warfare missions.

Specifications (An-12BP data)
Weapons: Two 23-mm Nudelman-Rikter NR-23 cannon in a tail turret.
Accommodation: 44,092 lb (20,000 kg) of

Above: Shaanxi Y-8, the Chinese version of the Antonov An-12 Cub.

freight, 60 paratroops, or 90 armed troops.
Wingspan: 124 ft 8 in (38.00 m).
Length: 108 ft 7 in (33.10 m).
Maximum speed: 483 mph (777 km/h).
(61,000 kg).
Maximum speed: 483 mph (777 km/h).
Range: 3542 miles (5700 km).
Mission performance: Rate of climb at sea level 1970 ft (600 m) per min; ceiling 33,460 ft (10,200 m).
Engines: Four 4000-ehp Ivchenko AI-20K turboprops, with 18,100 liters of fuel.
Versions in service
An-12BP: Standard transport model with the Soviet forces since 1959. A version of this is also built at the Shaanxi factory in Hanzhong, China as the Y-8, powered by Wojiang-6 engines of 4250-ehp. The NATO name is Cub.
Cub-A: NATO name for a special elint (electronic intelligence) derivative.
Cub-B: NATO name for Soviet Navy elint aircraft, modified from transports.
Cub-C: NATO name for an electronic countermeasures version of the An-12. A tailcone carrying some of the aircraft's electronics replaces the tail armament and turret.
Cub-D: NATO name for a second ECM version to complement Cub-C.
Operators: Algeria (Cub), China (Y-8), Czechoslovakia (Cub), Egypt (Cub*), Ethiopia (Cub), Guinea (Cub), India (Cub) Iraq (Cub), Jordan (Cub), Malagasy Republic (Cub), Poland (Cub), Soviet Union (air force Cub, Cub-A, Cub-C and Cub-D; navy, Cub-B, Cub-C and Cub-D) and Syria (Cub).
* The Cub-C has been photographed in Egyptian markings, though then on short-term deployment.

Antonov An-22 Antheus
(NATO name Cock)
Soviet Union

Until the advent of the new Antonov An-124, this was the largest heavy-transport aircraft in operational service with the Soviet Air Forces and the civil airline Aeroflot, second in size only to the US Galaxy. First flown as a prototype on 27 February 1965, it was designed to accommodate the largest Soviet main battle tanks and, indeed, was until recently the only aircraft available to the Soviet forces

capable of airlifting the T-62 MBT with a combat weight of 88,185 lb (40,000 kg). Since then heavier tanks have entered the Soviet forces, including the T-72 of 90,390 lb (41,000 kg). To lift a payload of 176,370 lb (80,000 kg), the aircraft uses four of the largest turboprop engines developed, driving pairs of contra-rotating propellers.

Each of the approximately 55 An-22s remaining active has a main cabin normally intended for freight carrying. It is 108 ft 3 in (33 m) long and 14 ft 5 in (4.4 m) wide (and high), with a reinforced titanium floor. Unlike the Galaxy and An-124 it only loads via an aft ramp under the huge beaver tail, with the assistance of powerful winches. However, as the majority of An-22s are stationed within close access of the Soviet airborne divisions, the troop/paratroop transport role is clearly an important function of the aircraft.

Specifications (An-22 data)
Accommodation: 6 crew and 29 persons in a cabin aft of the flight deck. Main cabin for 176,370 lb (80,000 kg) of vehicles, freight or missiles, or a large number of troops/paratroops.
Wingspan: 211 ft 4 in (64.40 m).
Length: 190 ft 0 in (57.92 m).
Maximum take-off weight: 551,155 lb (250,000 kg).
Maximum speed: 460 mph (740 km/h).
Range: 6805 miles (10,950 km).
Engines: Four 15,000-shp Kuznetsov NK-12MA turboprops.
Version in service
An-22: As detailed above. Civil-registered examples can be made available to the Soviet forces.
Operator: Soviet Union.

Antonov An-24, An-26, An-30, An-32 and Xian Y-7 (NATO names Coke, Curl, Clank, Cline and Coke)
Soviet Union and China

With the requirement for a turboprop-powered aircraft to replace the large number of piston-engined transports in service with Aeroflot, Antonov initiated the design of a new transport that had some similarity to the Fokker F 27. Designated An-24, this was first flown in prototype form on 20 December 1959, and was subsequently allocated the NATO name Coke. Deliveries began in 1962.

A substantial number of An-24s passed also to military operators, able to accommodate 38 armed troops, 30 paratroops, 24 stretchers and an attendant, or up to 12,565 lb (5700 kg) of freight. The door under the rear fuselage facilitates handling of bulky items. When production ended in the Soviet Union during 1978, a total of more than 1100 had been built, but in 1987 production was continuing in China, where a developed model is designated Xian Y-7.

Below: Antonov An-22 Antheus in Aeroflot markings.

Above: Hungarian Air Force Antonov An-26.

When first seen at Paris in 1969, the An-26 was at first thought to be an An-24 variant. However the new designation was seen to be justified when it was realized that this was a specialized cargo version of the An-24 with a completely new rear fuselage section incorporating a full-width door/ramp in the undersurface of the tail to facilitate loading of bulky items and vehicles. It also has mechanized cargo-handling equipment, tip-up seats at the sides of the cargo compartment for a maximum 40 paratroops, or in the same area can accommodate 24 stretchers and a medical attendant. The ensuing An-30, first flown in 1974 and known to NATO as Clank, is a mapping/survey aircraft based on the An-24/An-26 design. Easy external identification is provided by a raised flight deck, a glazed nose, and fewer cabin windows as part of the interior is used as a darkroom. Up to five cameras can be carried, as well as special survey equipment. The final member of this An-24/An-26 family is the An-32 (NATO Cline), a short-range transport optimized for use in 'hot and high' areas. Improved performance results from new high-lift devices, as well as more powerful Ivchenko AI-20M turboprop engines. The first major order came from the Indian Air Force, to whom deliveries began in July 1984; the IAF at present plans to procure a total of 95 and has named the type Sutlej.

Specifications (An-26 data)
Radar: Weather and navigation radar.
Accommodation: 5 crew plus up to 12,125 lb (5500 kg) of freight, vehicles, paratroops/troops or up to 24 stretchers loaded via the rear ramp door.
Wingspan: 95 ft 9½ in (29.20 m).
Length: 78 ft 1 in (23.80 m).
Maximum take-off weight: 52,910 lb (24,000 kg).
Cruising speed: 273 mph (440 km/h).
Range: 684 miles (1100 km) with full load.
Mission performance: Rate of climb at sea level 1575 ft (480 m) per min; ceiling 24,600 ft (7500 m).
Engines: Two 2820-ehp Ivchenko AI-24VT turboprops and one auxiliary turbojet in an engine nacelle for performance enhancement or self-start of main engines, with 7050 liters of fuel standard.

Versions in service
An-24: The An-24V was the initial production model with seating for 28 to 40. The An-24V Series II was an improved version of 1967 appearance, seating 50. This has two 2550-ehp AI-24A turboprops. Wingspan is 95 ft 9½ in (29.20 m), length 77 ft 2½ in (23.53 m) and cruising speed 280 mph (450 km/h). The generally similar An-24RV introduced an auxiliary turbojet, while the An-24T and An-24RT were built as specialized freighters with a freight door in the underside of the rear fuselage, the latter aircraft having an auxiliary turbojet. These are the most important military versions.
Xian Y-7: Developed version of the An-24, built in China.
An-26: The initial version and the An-26B (introduced in 1981 with a revised freight-handling system) are specialized freighters.
An-30: Aerial mapping/survey aircraft derived from the An-24 and An-26. Two 2820-ehp AI-24VT engines. Wingspan as for the An-26. Length 79 ft 7 in (24.26 m). Maximum speed 336 mph (540 km/h).
An-32: Short/medium-range version of the An-24/26 family. Initial production for the Indian Air Force. Wingspan as for the An-26. Length 77 ft 8 in. (23.68 m). Cruising speed 329 mph (530 km/h), accommodation for 39 troops, 30 paratroops, 24 stretchers with an attendant, or 14,771 lb (6700 kg) of freight.
Operators: Afghanistan (An-26), Algeria (An-26), Angola (An-26), Bangladesh (An-24/An-26), Benin (An-26), Bulgaria (An-24/An-26/An-30), Cape Verde (An-32), China (Xian Y-7/An-26), Congo (An-24/An-26), Cuba (An-24/An-26/An-32), Czechoslovakia (An-24/An-26), Egypt (An-24), East Germany (An-24/An-26), Ethiopia (An-26), Guinea-Bissau (An-26), Hungary (An-24/An-26), India (An-32), Iraq (An-24/An-26), North Korea (An-24), Laos (An-24/An-26), Malagasy (An-26), Mali (An-24), Mongolia (An-24), Mozambique (An-26), Nicaragua (An-26), Peru (An-26), Poland (An-24/An-26), Rumania (An-24/An-26/An-30), Somali Republic (An-24), Soviet Union (An-24/An-26/An-30), Syria (An-24/An-26), Tanzania (An-26/An-32), Vietnam (An-24), North Yemen (An-24/An-26), South Yemen (An-24), Yugoslavia (An-26) and Zambia (An-26).

Antonov An-124
(NATO name Condor)
Soviet Union

The An-124 and the Condor bird have something in common – both are the largest of their species to fly in our modern skies. The Antonov can be viewed as a C-5 Galaxy look-alike, though it has a larger wingspan and heavier gross weight and, more importantly, a greater payload capacity. But it also first flew as recently as 26 December 1982, a full 14 years after the United States transport. The tremendous weight of the An-124 would have been higher still had it not been for the substantial use of composite materials such as glassfiber and carbonfiber. Other noteworthy features include a quadruple redundant fly-by-wire control system.

Below: Antonov An-124, the world's largest operational aircraft.

Now in Soviet Air Force service as well as with Aeroflot, to supersede the turboprop-powered giant, the An-22, it has an upward lifting nose-visor door and rear ramp for straight-through loading/unloading from both ends. Its huge cabin volume allows the largest and heaviest main battle tanks or other vehicles (including an SS-20 mobile ballistic missile system) to be carried over long ranges.

Specifications (An-124 data)
Radar: Weather radar and terrain-mapping/ navigation radar.
Accommodation: Crew of 6 and provision for 88 passengers/troops on the upper deck. Lower deck cargo cabin of 118 ft 1 in (36.00 m) length, 21 ft (6.40 m) width and 14 ft 5 in (4.4 m) height for up to 330,690 lb (150,000 kg) of freight or vehicles.
Wingspan: 240 ft 5¾ in (73.30 m).
Length: 226 ft 8½ in (69.10 m).
Maximum take-off weight: 892,872 lb (405,000 kg).
Cruising speed: 537 mph (865 km/h).
Range: 10,252 miles (16,500 km) with maximum fuel; 2796 miles (4500 km) with maximum load.
Engines: Four 51,588-lb (23,400-kg) thrust Lotarev D-18T turbofans.
Version in service
An-124: Operations began in 1986.
Operator: Soviet Union.

Atlas Alpha XH1
South Africa

First flown on 3 February 1985, more than a year before its existence was made public, the Alpha XH1 is a light attack helicopter derived in only small part from the French Alouette III. Though experimental at present, clearly it is intended for production. The main features are a slim fuselage of part-composites construction, tandem stepped cockpits for the two crew members, and armament that includes a GAI 20-mm cannon in a trainable underfuselage turret linked to the weapon operator's helmet-mounted sight.

Specifications (XH1 data)
Weapons: One 20-mm cannon as detailed above, or four 7.62-mm machine-guns. Stub wings will undoubtedly be fitted later for anti-armor missiles and rockets.
Accommodation: Weapons operator/copilot and pilot in separate stepped tandem cockpits.
Diameter of rotor: 36 ft 1¾ in (11.02 m).
Length, including rotors: 42 ft 1½ in (12.84 m).
Maximum take-off weight: 4850 lb (2200 kg).
Maximum speed: About 130 mph (210 km/h).
Combat radius: About 171 miles (275 km/h).
Mission performance: Rate of climb at sea level about 800 ft (244 m) per min.
Engine: One 870-shp Turboméca Artouste IIIB turboshaft, derated to 570 shp.
Version in service
XH1: Experimental only at the present time.
Operator: None at present.

Atlas C4M Kudu
South Africa

Designed as a six to eight-seat or cargo-carrying light plane, able to operate from rough airstrips, it was not until the third prototype appeared that a military version flew (18 June 1975). However, all 40 production C4Ms were of the military type for the indigenous air force. It is believed that one of the two operational liaison squadrons to receive Kudus still flies the type (No 41 Squadron), while others are still with No 84 Advanced Flying School at Potchefstroom.

Specifications (C4M Kudu data)
Accommodation: 2 crew plus 4 or 6 passengers. Alternatively 1235 lb (560 kg) of freight. Can be used for supply or paratroop dropping. Some Kudus are fitted out for casualty evacuation.
Wingspan: 42 ft 10¾ in (13.08 m).
Length: 30 ft 6½ in (9.31 m).
Maximum take-off weight: 4497 lb (2040 kg).
Maximum speed: 161 mph (259 km/h).
Mission performance: Rate of climb at sea level 800 ft (244 m) per min; ceiling 14,000 ft (4270 m); endurance 8 h.
Engine: One 340-hp Piaggio/Avco Lycoming GSO-480-B1B3 piston, with 432 liters of fuel.
Version in service
C4M Kudu: Strut-braced high-wing monoplane, with a fixed undercarriage. Mostly metal construction, but with glassfiber wingtips and tailcone.
Operator: South Africa.

Above: Atlas C4M Kudu.

Below: Atlas Alpha XH1 light attack helicopter.

Above: Atlas Cheetah, developed in South Africa from the Mirage III.

Atlas Cheetah
South Africa

Because of the United Nations arms sales embargo on South Africa, that nation has considered it increasingly important to equip its own forces with indigenous products. Where this is not possible, modification or refurbishing of existing equipment is sometimes undertaken to extend capabilities and/or service life. Such is happening to the Air Force's Mirage IIIs, becoming in modified form Atlas Cheetahs.

According to reports, much of the Mirage airframe is reconstructed to produce the Cheetah, additions including swept fore-planes carried on the air intakes, dog-tooth wing leading-edges, and strakes fitted to the longer nose and lower forward fuselage. The modified nose could house multimode radar, under which could be an infrared seeker. Modern navigation and weapon systems are carried. Both air-to-air and attack weapons are options, as for the SAAF Mirages, but now with the indigenous Armscor V3B highly maneuverable IR-homing dogfight missile as the principal air-to-air weapon. In overall configuration the Cheetah looks remarkably like the Israeli Kfir, which was also based on the Mirage airframe. The first publicly revealed Cheetah was modified from a Mirage III-D2Z trainer.

BAC Jet Provost and BAe Strikemaster
United Kingdom

The Jet Provost was developed from the earlier Hunting Percival Provost as a primary and basic jet trainer, with a Viper turbojet replacing the Alvis Leonides radial piston engine of the earlier aircraft. First flown on 26 June 1954, the Jet Provost became the standard side-by-side two-seat jet trainer of the RAF and was exported. S312 Tucanos now being built by Shorts are replacing these.

From the Jet Provost, BAC (now BAe) developed an inexpensive armed counter-insurgency (COIN) aircraft for export as the Strikemaster, retaining the same layout but with a higher-powered engine, greater weapon-carrying capability and fixed wing-tip tanks. The first flight of a Strikemaster was recorded on 26 October 1967.

Specifications (Strikemaster data)
Weapons: Two 7.62-mm FN machine-guns, each with 550 rounds of ammunition, plus up to 3000 lb (1360 kg) of weapons on 4 underwing pylons including up to 1102-lb (500-kg) bombs, rocket launchers, gun packs, etc. Alternatively, 5-camera photographic reconnaissance pods or stores.
Accommodation: 2 crew, side by side.
Wingspan: 36 ft 10 in (11.23 m).
Length: 33 ft 8½ in (10.27 m).
Maximum take-off weight: 11,500 lb (5216 kg).
Maximum speed: 481 mph (774 km/h).
Range: 1382 miles (2224 km).
Mission performance: Rate of climb at sea level 5250 ft (1600 m) per min; ceiling 40,000 ft (12,190 m).
Engine: One 3410-lb (1547-kg) thrust Rolls-Royce Viper Mk 535 turbojet, with 1664 liters of fuel.

Left: Sultan of Oman's Air Force BAC Strikemaster Mk 82, carrying rockets and bombs.

Versions in service

Jet Provost: RAF T.Mk 5 has one 2500-lb (1134-kg) thrust Viper Mk 202 turbojet. Maximum speed 440 mph (708 km/h). Provision for two 7.62-mm guns and underwing weapons/practice weapons.
Strikemaster: COIN derivative, as detailed above, also used for training. 146 ordered. Production ended in 1978.
Operators: Ecuador (Strikemaster Mk 89), Kenya (Strikemaster Mk 87), Kuwait (Strikemaster Mk 83), New Zealand (Strikemaster Mk 88), Oman (Strikemaster Mk 82/A), Saudi Arabia (Strikemaster Mk 80/A), Singapore (Strikemaster Mk 84), Sudan (Jet Provost and Strikemaster Mk 55), United Kingdom (Jet Provost) and Venezuela (Jet Provost).

BAC Lightning
United Kingdom

The only totally British production supersonic aircraft, the Lightning all-weather interceptor was derived from the P.1 research aircraft of August 1954 which proved the unusual superimposed engine arrangement, 60-degree swept wing with ailerons across the tips, low slab tailplane and main undercarriage units that folded outward near the wingtips. The Lightning F.Mk 1, which made its maiden flight on 4 April 1957, entered service with the RAF in 1960, but was extremely limited in weapons and endurance though fast in climb and dash. The F.Mk 3 brought more fuel and the F.Mk 6 more powerful engines, double the fuel capacity and a revised wing with greater chord outboard for better maneuverability at high altitudes. Most F.Mk 3s were converted to this model. Thanks to sparkling performance as an air defense interceptor and a complete absence of vices, the Lightning has always been popular with pilots who would otherwise have criticized its extremely light armament and short endurance, although a fixed inflight refuelling probe and overwing ferry tanks can be added. RAF No 5 and 11 Squadrons and the Lightning Training Flight at Binbrook are in their final weeks of life, LTF using a few dual side-by-side T.Mk 5 trainers which retain full weapon capability.

Saudi Arabia became an operator of the Lightning in F.Mk 52 and 53 interceptor/attack, and T.Mk 54 and 55 training forms, and Kuwait in F.Mk 53 and T.Mk 55 forms. The latter put its aircraft in store in 1977 and purchased French Dassault-Breguet Mirage F1s, while Saudi Arabia purchased F-15 Eagles as replacements.

Specifications (Lightning F.Mk 6 data)
Radar: Ferranti Airpass fire-control radar in the air intake centerbody.
Weapons: Two 30-mm Aden cannon, with 120 rounds of ammunition each.
2 Red Top or Firestreak air-to-air missiles.
Accommodation: The pilot.
Wingspan: 34 ft 10 in (10.61 m).
Length: 55 ft 3 in (16.84 m).
Maximum take-off weight: 50,000 lb (22,680 kg).
Maximum speed: Mach 2.3.
Range: 800 miles (1290 km).
Mission performance: Rate of climb at sea level 50,000 ft (15,240 m) per min; ceiling above 60,000 ft (18,290 m).

Engines: Two 16,360-lb (7420-kg) thrust with afterburning Rolls-Royce Avon 301 turbojets.
Versions in service
F.Mk 3: No cannon armament, and introduced Red Top as alternative missiles to Firestreak. First production example made its maiden flight on 16 June 1962.
F.Mk 6: Final production version for the RAF, entering service at the end of 1965. More than twice the fuel capacity, combined with extended and cambered outer wing leading-edges to reduce subsonic drag.
T.Mk 5: Side by side two-seat operational trainer based on the F.Mk 3, with Avon 301 turbojets. First flown on 29 March 1962 and entered service in 1965.
Operator: United Kingdom.

BAe 125 and Dominie T.Mk 1
United Kingdom

Design of what became the highly successful 125 business jet was begun by de Havilland, with the first flight of a prototype taking place on 13 August 1962. Becoming a Hawker Siddeley and later a British Aerospace product, several versions have been built over the

Above: No 5 Squadron, RAF, has some of the few remaining Lightning F.Mk 6s.

years which culminate today in the 125 Series 800. Of those 125s in military use, all are communication transports except for Dominie T.Mk 1 navigation trainers serving with the RAF. The most recent model in military use is the Series 700B.

Specifications (BAe 125 Series 700B data)
Accommodation: 2 or 3 crew and 8 to 14 passengers.
Wingspan: 47 ft 0 in (14.33 m).
Length: 50 ft 8½ in (15.46 m).
Maximum take-off weight: 25,500 lb (11,566 kg).
Cruising speed: 502 mph (808 km/h).
Range: 2785 miles (4482 km) with reserves.
Mission performance: Ceiling 41,000 ft (12,500 m).
Engines: Two 3700-lb (1678-kg) thrust Garrett TFE731-3-1RH turbofans, with 5369 liters of fuel.
Versions in service
Series 2: Version from which the RAF's Dominie T.Mk 1 navigation trainer was developed. The first Dominie flew on 30

Below: BAe Dominie T.Mk 1.

December 1964. 3000-lb (1361-kg) thrust Rolls-Royce Viper 520 turbojet engines.
Series 400B: Brazilian VC/VU-93 VIP transports (scheduled for replacement), Argentine and South African Mercurius transports, and RAF's CC.Mk 1. Two 3360-lb (1524-kg) thrust Viper 522 turbojets. CC.Mk 1s being converted to CC.Mk 3.
Series 600B: RAF's CC.Mk 2. Two 3750-lb (1701-kg) thrust Viper 601-22 turbojets. Being converted to CC.Mk 3 standard.
Series 700B: RAF's CC.Mk 3, Irish and Malawi transports.
Operators: Argentina (navy), Brazil, Ireland, Malawi, South Africa and United Kingdom.

BAe 146
United Kingdom

The BAe (British Aerospace) 146 short-haul airliner, that first flew as a prototype on 20 May 1981, is now used by the RAF's The Queen's Flight. Replacing Andover CC.Mk 2s, the two Series 100 aircraft are available to the Queen, the Royal Family, the Prime Minister and senior ministers, the Chief of Staff and visiting foreign VIPs. The first 146 CC.Mk 2 was accepted by the RAF on 23 April 1986.

Specifications (BAe 146 data)
Radar: Weather radar.
Accommodation: Pilot, copilot, navigator, crew chief and engineer, plus a police officer and steward. Variable VIP accommodation, including a 4-person settee/bed and 2 single chairs.
Wingspan: 86 ft 5 in (26.34 m).
Length: 85 ft 11 in (26.19 m).
Maximum take-off weight: 84,000 lb (38,100 kg).

Below: BAe 146 CC.Mk 2 transport of The Queen's Flight, RAF.

Cruising speed: 440 mph (709 km/h).
Range: 1077-1924 miles (1733-3096 km) with reserves and allowance for 150-nm diversion.
Engines: Four 6970-lb (3161-kg) thrust Avco Lycoming ALF 502R-5 turbofans, with 11,728 liters of fuel standard.
Version in service
146 CC.Mk 2: Serving with The Queen's Flight, RAF.
Operator: United Kingdom.

BAe 748 and Andover
United Kingdom

The short/medium-range 748 twin-turboprop commercial transport made its maiden flight as a prototype on 24 June 1960. Military examples entered RAF service as the Andover, including the CC.Mk 2 for The Queen's Flight and E.Mk 3 for calibration (modified from retired C.Mk 1s), while New Zealand took over 10 ex-RAF CC.Mk 1 transports with rear loading. The Andover CC.Mk 2's being superseded by the BAe 146 CC.Mk 2. The 748 remains available for purchase, and HAL in India has license-assembled examples that include 72 for its indigenous air force.

Specifications (current military 748 data)
Radar: Bendix RDR 1300 weather radar.
Accommodation: 2 crew plus 58 troops, 48 paratroops, 24 stretchers and 9 attendants, VIP layout, or 12,861-17,302 lb (5833-7848 kg) of freight.
Wingspan: 102 ft 6 in (31.24 m).
Length: 67 ft 0 in (20.42 m).
Maximum take-off weight: 51,000-lb (23,133-kg) overload weight, 46,500-lb (21,092-kg) normal.
Cruising speed: 282 mph (454 km/h).
Range: 1159 miles (1865 km) with full payload and reserves.
Mission performance: Rate of climb at sea

level 1420 ft (433 m) per min; ceiling 25,000 ft (7620 m).
Engines: Two 2280-ehp Rolls-Royce Dart RDa.7 Mk 552 turboprops. 6546 liters of fuel.
Versions in service
748: Series 1 was built with 1740-ehp RDa.6 Mk 514 engines, the first version received by India; Series 2 built with 2105-ehp RDa.7 Mk 531 engines; Series 2A with 2280-ehp RDa.7 Mk 532, 534 or 535 engines, as used by Belgium, Brazil, Ecuador, Nepal and others; and Series 2B with increased wingspan and 536-2 engines, as used by Colombia. The current version is based on the Super 748, as detailed above.
Andover: RAF name. The CC.Mk 1 has two 3245-ehp RDa.12 Mk 301 turboprops, giving a 265-mph (426-km/h) cruising speed and 15,350-lb (6963-kg) payload. Other Andover versions as detailed above.
Operators: Australia, Belgium, Brazil, Burkina-Faso, Colombia, Ecuador, India, South Korea, Malagasy, Nepal, New Zealand, Sri Lanka, Tanzania, Thailand, United Kingdom, Venezuela and Zambia.

BAe EAP
United Kingdom

This technology demonstrator is not intended for production, though it encompasses technologies to be used in the EFA Eurofighter. See Introduction.

BAe Harrier
United Kingdom

The Harrier is the production version of the Hawker Siddeley Kestrel development aircraft, itself stemming from the P.1127 prototype that flew for the first time in tethered form on 21 October 1960 and which made its first free-hovering test on 19 November that year. Six years of development, trials and evaluation followed before the first Harrier proper flew on 31 August 1966.

This light tactical attack and reconnaissance machine, which unexpectedly also proved to have great potential as an air-combat fighter, pioneered the use of jet lift in order to operate without the need of an airfield. Thus, it was the first of what must one day become the usual kind of combat aircraft, able to survive in actual warfare.

It was made possible because of the development of the unique Pegasus engine, a turbofan with four jet nozzles which can be rotated in unison through an angular range of 98.5 degrees in order to provide vertical upthrust (lift), forward thrust or a rearward braking force. Thereby, the wing can be very small, matching the Harrier to high speed at low level even with heavy weapon loads. The aircraft's small size, odd shape, lack of smoke and ability to make 'impossible' maneuvers (because of the vectored-thrust engine) makes it a tricky customer in a dogfight. All weapons and the multi-sensor reconnaissance pod are carried externally. The RAF has three front-line squadrons and a conversion unit, the US Marine Corps has the same (con-

Above right: Royal Air Force BAe Andover.
Right: BAe Harrier GR.Mk 3, equipping three front-line RAF squadrons and an OCU.

verting to the Harrier II, described separately) and the Spanish Navy one squadron. The last two services often operate from carriers or amphibious-warfare ships, for example in support of landings on hostile shores. All three users also operate a lengthened tandem two-seat trainer version. This has only one gun, but otherwise retains full weapons capability and in an emergency would be flown by instructors as part of a front-line unit.

Total deliveries to the RAF amounted to 120 single-seaters, all upgraded to GR.3 standard with a radar-warning receiver (with aerials facing to front and rear at the tail) and a laser ranger and marked-target seeker in the 'thimble' nose. The RAF also received 23 two-seaters, upgraded to T.4 or (without laser nose) T.4A standard. The US Marines received 102 AV-8A single-seaters, many being upgraded to AV-8C standard, and eight two-seat TAV-8As. The Spanish Navy received 11 AV-8S Matadors and two TAV-8Ss, while the Royal Navy uses four T.4RN trainers and the Indian Navy three T.60s.

Specifications (Harrier GR.Mk 3 data)
Equipment: Avionics include the Ferranti FE 541 inertial navigation and attack system, Marconi radar warning receiver, and Ferranti laser ranger and marked target seeker.
Weapons: Normally up to 5000 lb (2270 kg) of weapons on one underfuselage and 4 underwing attachments, and two 30-mm Aden cannon can replace the underfuselage strakes. All single-seaters now have Sidewinder air-to-air missile capability.
Accommodation: The pilot.
Wingspan: 25 ft 3 in (7.70 m).
Length: 45 ft 7 in (13.89 m).
Maximum take-off weight: 25,200 lb (11,430 kg).
Maximum speed: 730 mph (1176 km/h).

Below: BAe Hawk 200 armed with four Sidewinder AAMs.

Range: 414 miles (666 km) with a 4400-lb load.
Mission performance: Ceiling 51,200 ft (15,605 m).
Engine: One 21,500-lb (9752-kg) vectored thrust Rolls-Royce Pegasus Mk 103 turbofan, with 4 rotatable nozzles, and 2864 liters of fuel standard.

Versions in service
Harrier GR.Mk 3: Current RAF version, as detailed above. Fought during the 1982 Falklands conflict, operating from HMS *Hermes.* Four made a 4000-mile (6437-km) nonstop flight from the United Kingdom to Ascension Island using inflight refuelling, in a little over 9 hours, then flew a similar distance to land on the carrier in an elapsed time of 18 hours. 3 Harriers were lost during the fighting, but all pilots survived.
Harrier T.Mk 4, 4A and 4RN: RAF and Royal Navy two-seat combat-capable training versions.
Harrier T.Mk 60: 2-seat trainer for the Indian Navy to instruct Sea Harrier pilots. Fitted with Sea Harrier avionics, with the exception of the radar.
AV-8A: US Marine Corps version, for close support and reconnaissance. Fitted with an F402-RR-402/-402A (Pegasus 803) turbofan. AV-8As are not equipped with the laser designator and marked target seeker of RAF aircraft. Known to BAe as the Harrier Mk 50.
TAV-8A: 2-seat trainer version of the AV-8A, known to BAe as the Mk 54.
AV-8C: 47 AV-8As upgraded to incorporate lift improvement devices, radar warning and other avionics.
AV-8S Matador: Spanish Navy version of the AV-8A, operated by the 8a Escuadrilla and flown from the aircraft carrier *Dedalo.* BAe Mks 50 and 55.
TAV-8S: Spanish Navy 2-seat training version, known to BAe as Mk 54.
Operators: India (navy), Spain (navy), United Kingdom and United States (marine corps).

BAe Hawk, Goshawk and Hawk 200
United Kingdom

To provide the Royal Air Force with a two-seat aircraft suitable for basic and advanced jet training, competing submissions for the requirement were made by the British Aircraft Corporation and Hawker Siddeley. In October 1971 the latter company's P1182 design was declared the winner and some five months later the Rolls-Royce/Turboméca Adour in a nonafterburning version was selected to power it. One pre-production and 175 production aircraft were ordered for the RAF, the single pre-production example making the type's maiden flight on 21 August 1974.

Subsequently named the Hawk, as a result of changing fortunes in Britain's aircraft industry this aircraft has become the responsibility of British Aerospace (BAe), which continues to build the type for export customers. It has proved particularly successful in a keenly-contested export market, not only in the training role for which the RAF required it but also as a very capable all-round tactical combat aircraft. It can be deployed effectively for long-range strike and air-combat missions at a cost far lower than that of more powerful (and much more expensive) aircraft, and has demonstrated extremely low maintenance costs. Such capability has engendered the demand for a single-seat equivalent dedicated to the tactical role, and in 1985 BAe began the design and construction of such a prototype under the designation Hawk 200. First flown on 19 May 1986, this aircraft was soon lost in a tragic accident, but an investigation cleared the aircraft's structure from being responsible. Construction of a new prototype was initiated, and first flew on 24 April 1987.

To meet a US Navy requirement for a comprehensive VTXTS training system BAe, in partnership with McDonnell Douglas and Sperry in the United States, submitted an overall aircraft and training system that was

Above: BAe Hawk Mk 51 in Finnish Air Force markings.

the clear winner of the contest. In May 1986 an initial contract was finalized for 60 aircraft which the US Navy has designated T-45A Goshawk. It will differ from the BAe Hawk primarily by having new landing gear, an arrester hook and associated structural strengthening, plus cockpit avionics and displays to render it suitable for carrier operation. The US Navy intends to procure a total of 300 T-45A aircraft.

Specifications (Hawk 60 series data)

Weapons: 4 underwing pylons for a total weapon load of up to 6800 lb (3084 kg), which can include a wide range of tactical bombs, missiles, rockets and auxiliary tanks. Provision for a 30-mm cannon in self-contained centerline pod or, alternatively, one Sea Eagle antiship missile.
Accommodation: Student pilot and instructor in tandem.
Wingspan: 30 ft 9¾ in (9.39 m).
Length: 36 ft 7¾ in (11.17 m) without the probe.
Maximum take-off weight: 18,890 lb (8568 kg).
Maximum speed: 644 mph (1036 km/h).
Combat radius: 620 miles (998 km) with 5000-lb weapon load.
Mission performance: Rate of climb at sea level 11,800 ft (3597 m) per min; ceiling 50,000 ft (15,240 m); G limits +8, −4.
Engine: One 5700-lb (2585-kg) thrust Rolls-Royce/Turboméca Adour 861 turbofan, with 1705 liters of fuel standard.

Versions in service

Hawk T.Mk 1: Basic 2-seat trainer for the RAF, powered by a 5200-lb (2360-kg) thrust Adour 151 turbofan. It has an underfuselage 30-mm gun pack and 2 underwing hardpoints.
Hawk T.Mk 1A: Designation of 85 RAF Hawks which have been equipped to carry two AIM-9L Sidewinder air-to-air missiles as air defense aircraft, presumably guided in groups to their targets by a radar-equipped fighter.
Hawk 50 Series: Initial export version with 5335-lb (2420-kg) thrust Adour 851 engine and 4 underwing pylons, the inboard pair carrying auxiliary fuel tanks.
Hawk 60 Series: Developed and current export production version with 5700-lb

(2585-kg) thrust Adour 861. Introduces a number of improvements and has provisions for Sidewinder or Matra Magic air-to-air missile.
Hawk 200: Single-seat combat version, able to be fitted with a wide range of avionics, equipment and weapons to suit particular roles. All-weather operation could be provided by Ferranti Blue Fox or similar multimode radar.
T-45A Goshawk: US Navy version, that is carrier capable. As detailed above. One 5450-lb (2475-kg) thrust Rolls-Royce F405-RR-400 turbofan.
Operators: Abu Dhabi (Mk 63), Dubai (Mk 61), Finland (Mk 51), Indonesia (Mk 53), Kenya (Mk 52), Kuwait (Mk 64), Saudi Arabia (Mk 65), United Kingdom (T.Mk 1 and Mk 1A), United States (navy, T-45A Goshawk) and Zimbabwe (Mk 60).

BAe Jetstream
United Kingdom

What is now a highly successful light commuter and executive transport had a rather turbulent beginning. The Jetstream started life as the Handley Page HP.137 and was first flown as a prototype on 18 August 1967.

Thereafter it was taken over by Jetstream Aircraft and Scottish Aviation, before finally becoming one of the British Aerospace range.

The only military operators to date are the RAF and Royal Navy, who use Jetstreams for training (as detailed below). Also available, however, is the Jetstream 31 Special Role, suited to transport, training, communications, calibration and other duties, with a more specialized model for offshore patrol as the radar-carrying Jetstream 31EZ (indicating operation in exclusive economic zones).

Specifications (Jetstream T.Mk 1 data unless otherwise stated)

Radar: Jetstream T.Mk 3 has Racal ASR 360 search radar carried under the fuselage.
Accommodation: Pilot and trainee, plus 4 passengers.
Wingspan: 52 ft 0 in (15.85 m).
Length: 47 ft 1½ in (14.37 m).
Maximum take-off weight: 12,566 lb (5700 kg).
Maximum speed: 282 mph (454 km/h).
Range: 1380 miles (2224 km).
Mission performance: Rate of climb at sea level 2500 ft (762 m) per min; ceiling 25,000 ft (7620 m).
Engines: Two 996-ehp Turboméca Astazou XVID turboprops, with 1746 liters of fuel.

Versions in service

Jetstream T.Mk 1: RAF multi-engine pilot trainer, with 'eyebrow' windows and avionics/instrumentation differences compared to the civil Jetstream Series 200 from which it derives. Superseded the Vickers Varsity.
Jetstream T.Mk 2: Royal Navy variant of the T.Mk 1 type, superseding Hunting Sea Princes in the observer training role. MEL E 190 weather and ground mapping radar.
Jetstream T.Mk 3: The latest Royal Navy version, based on the Jetstream 31. 'Eyebrow' windows, TANS computer and Doppler, and radar as detailed above. 4 delivered to No 750 Naval Air Squadron at Culdrose in 1986 for helicopter observer training. Cabin is installed with two training consoles. Powered by two 940-shp Garrett TPE331-10 turboprops.
Operator: United Kingdom (air force and navy).

Below: Royal Navy BAe Jetstream T.Mk 3.

Above: BAe Nimrod MR.Mk 2P, carrying Sidewinder AAMs for self-protection.

BAe Nimrod
United Kingdom

In the past there have been many successful civil airliners that were derived from the basic airframe of an aircraft intended for use as a bomber. Conversely, many civil airliners have been adapted by armed services for deployment in a variety of military roles and the BAe Nimrod is an excellent example of this. For the RAF from 1951 the task of long-range maritime reconnaissance had been placed firmly on the shoulders of the Avro Shackleton, a derivative of the Lincoln bomber. With a decade of valuable service behind it, it was clear by the early 1960s that the piston-engined 'Shack' would very soon need a replacement. The chosen vehicle for this task was the de Havilland Comet 4C airliner, its adaptation for the role being carried out by Hawker Siddeley at Woodford under the project designation HS.801, soon to be named Nimrod.

By comparison with the Comet, the major changes resulted in a modified pressurized fuselage, reduced in length by 6 ft 6 in (1.98m), with a new unpressurized lower lobe added to house equipment and weapons that would enable the new aircraft to be deployed not only for maritime patrol but also for ASW and antishipping strike. Other changes saw revised inlets to give the Rolls-Royce Spey turbofans (chosen to replace the Comet's Avons) the required amount of air, larger windows on the flight deck, and the provision of ESM and MAD equipment. The first of two prototypes (conversions of Comet 4C airframes) was flown initially on 23 May 1967, with the first production version flying on 28 June 1968. Service introduction, initially with the RAF's Maritime Operational Training Unit (later No 236 OCU) began on 2 October 1969. Since that time the Nimrod, a potent warplane that looks deceptively innocent, has provided and will continue to provide RAF Strike Command with an important maritime asset. There is an ironic twist to this success story, for there can be few readers who will be unaware of the failure of the Nimrod AEW.Mk 3 to meet the RAF's

requirement for an airborne early-warning aircraft. Inadequacy of its high-technology radar equipment has resulted in selection of the Boeing E-3 AWACS for the RAF, and until the first of the six or eight E-3s enter service some three years hence Britain's AEW task will in the main rely upon the old Avro Shackleton AEW.Mk 2.

Specifications (Nimrod MR.Mk 2 data)
Radar: Thorn EMI ARI.5980 Searchwater radar with long-range detection able to resolve such small targets as submarine snorts and periscopes at extreme ranges.
Weapons: The 48 ft 6 in (14.78 m) long weapons bay can accommodate a maximum disposable load of 13,500 lb (6123 kg), including bombs, torpedoes and auxiliary fuel tanks. Sonobuoys are carried in a bay in the pressurized fuselage and a hardpoint below each wing can carry gun or rocket pods, sea mines, an antiship Harpoon or two self-defense Sidewinder missiles.
Accommodation: 12 crew.
Wingspan: 114 ft 10 in (35.00 m).
Length: 129 ft 1 in (39.35 m).
Maximum take-off weight: 192,000 lb (87,089 kg).
Maximum speed: 547 mph (880 km/h).
Ferry range: 5755 miles (9262 km) without flight refuelling.
Mission performance: Ceiling 42,000 ft (12,800m); patrol speed 230 mph (370 km/h); endurance 12 h.
Engines: Four 12,140-lb (5506-kg) thrust Rolls-Royce RB168-20 Spey Mk 250 turbofans, with 48,778 liters of fuel standard.
Versions in service
Nimrod MR.Mk 1: Designation of three aircraft converted for the electronic intelligence role, with radomes forward of the wing tanks and replacing the MAD 'stinger'.
Nimrod MR.Mk 1P: Redesignation of one R.Mk 1 following the installation of inflight refuelling equipment for Falklands operations.
Nimrod MR.Mk 2: Redesignation of original MR.Mk 1s following the incorporation of advanced avionics and self-defense Sidewinders.
Nimrod MR.Mk 2P: Redesignation of those MR.Mk 2s which were given inflight refuelling equipment for the Falklands

operations. It is anticipated that all MR.2s will eventually be modified to this standard.
Operator: United Kingdom.

BAe (BAC) One-Eleven, BAe (Hawker Siddeley) Trident and Vickers Viscount
United Kingdom

These three very different British-built airliners serve with the air forces of seven nations but in such small numbers as not to warrant separate entries. Tridents form the largest single block by far, when in 1982 CAAC (Civil Aviation Administration of China) passed 18 Trident 2Es of its total Trident fleet of 37 to the Air Force. It is this aircraft type that is detailed below.

Specifications (Trident 2E data)
Accommodation: 3 crew plus up to 132 passengers.
Wingspan: 98 ft 0 in (29.87 m).
Length: 114 ft 9 in (34.97 m).
Maximum take-off weight: 144,000 lb (65,315 kg).
Cruising speed: 605 mph (972 km/h).
Range: 2464 miles (3965 km) with 21,378-lb (9696-kg) load.
Engines: Three 11,960-lb (5425-kg) thrust Rolls-Royce Spey RB.163.25 Mk 512-5W turbofans, with 29,094 liters of fuel standard.
Versions in service
Trident 2E: Originally a de Havilland design (DH.121), the Trident first flew on 9 January 1962 in its initial version. 33 Trident 2Es were acquired by CAAC during the 1970s for commercial operation, 18 of which were passed to the Air Force of the People's Liberation Army.
One-Eleven: First flown on 20 August 1963, this short-range airliner remains in production today under license in Rumania. Apart from 4 in RAF service for nonoperational tasks, the Royal Australian Air Force uses 2 as operational transports and 3 are with the Sultan of Oman's Air Force. The latter are based on the Series 475, with quick-change interiors for passenger/freight layouts and each has a large forward freight door. Wingspan and

Above: Royal Aircraft Establishment BAC One-Eleven.

length are both 93 ft 6 in (28.50 m). Maximum take-off weight 98,500 lb (44,678 kg). Maximum speed 541 mph (871 km/h). Range 1865 miles (3000 km). Accommodation is for a crew of 2 and 89 passengers or 21,527 lb (9764 kg) of freight. Engines are two 12,500-lb (5693-kg) thrust Rolls-Royce Spey Mk 512 DW turbofans.

Viscount: The world's first turboprop-engined commercial transport in airline service, first flown as a prototype on 16 July 1948. Ones and twos are in military service today, all used as transports except for those with the RAF which has the only Series 800s in military use. The Viscount with the SAAF is a Type 781, based on the 700D series and delivered as new to the government with a VIP interior. Power for this example is provided by four 1600-shp Rolls-Royce Dart 510 turboprops. Normal Viscount 700 series accommodation is for up to 59 passengers. Wingspan 93 ft 8½ in (28.56 m). Length 81 ft 9 in (24.92 m). Maximum take-off weight 64,500 lb (29,256 kg). Cruising speed with 40 passengers 334 mph (538 km/h).

Operators: Australia (One-Eleven), China (Trident), Laos (Viscount), Oman (One-Eleven), South Africa (Viscount), Turkey (Viscount) and United Kingdom (One-Eleven and Viscount).

BAe Sea Harrier
United Kingdom

After years of indecision the go-ahead for a version of the Harrier for the Royal Navy was received in May 1975, and the first was flown on 20 August 1978. The designation Sea Harrier FRS.Mk 1 indicates its roles are fighter reconnaissance and strike, operating from three Invincible-class light aircraft carriers with ski jumps for STO operations. The airframe is based on that of the RAF Harrier, but with marinized (noncorroding) materials and with a completely new nose. The latter provides room for a Ferranti Blue Fox multimode radar (which folds to reduce length aboard small carriers), as well as many other new avionic boxes and additional cockpit

equipment. The need to raise the Martin-Baker Mk 10H automatic ejection seat (usable at zero speed and altitude) automatically gave the pilot a better all-round view.

Sea Harriers proved decisive during fighting near the Falklands in spring 1982 when 28 (out of 32) Sea Harriers were virtually the only British air-combat-capable aircraft. Armed with the new AIM-9L version of the Sidewinder they downed 24 aircraft, plus seven more hit by cannon fire. No Sea Harrier was lost in combat, though one slid off an icy deck and two are thought to have collided in cloud.

Today further batches have brought total Royal Navy orders to 57, and the Indian Navy has 16 (plus three trainer aircraft), which differ in having gaseous (instead of liquid) oxygen systems and in using the Matra Magic dogfight missile. During 1987-90 all Royal

Below: Royal Navy BAe Sea Harrier FRS.Mk 1s, some carrying Sidewinder AAMs.

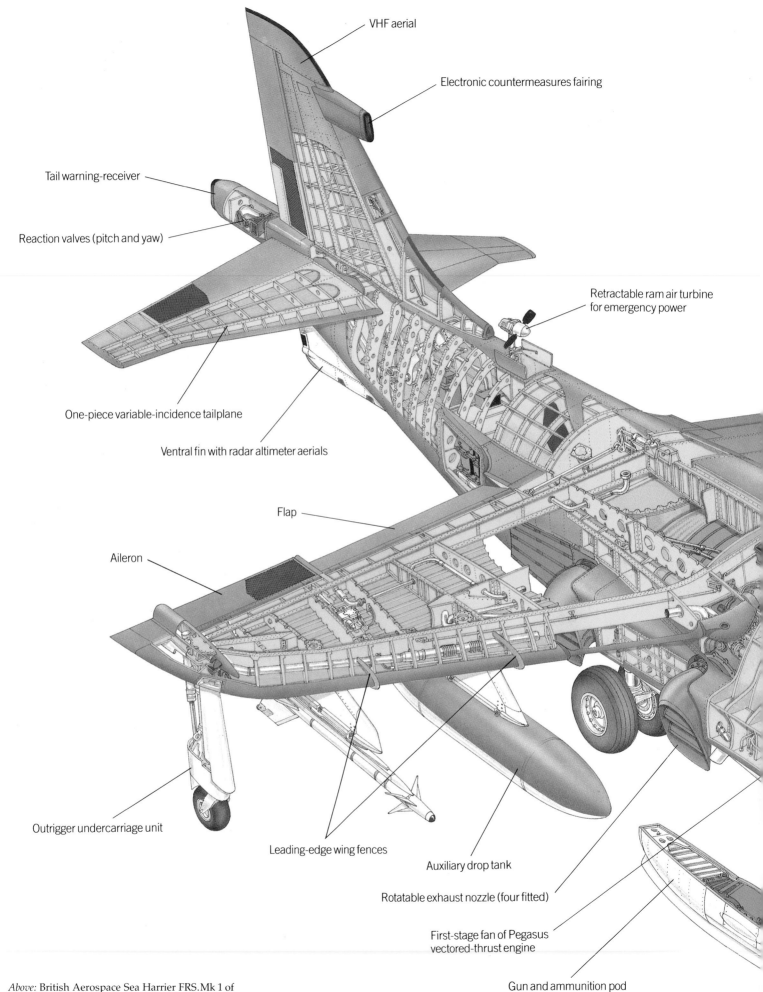

VHF aerial

Electronic countermeasures fairing

Tail warning-receiver

Reaction valves (pitch and yaw)

Retractable ram air turbine
for emergency power

One-piece variable-incidence tailplane

Ventral fin with radar altimeter aerials

Flap

Aileron

Outrigger undercarriage unit

Leading-edge wing fences

Auxiliary drop tank

Rotatable exhaust nozzle (four fitted)

First-stage fan of Pegasus
vectored-thrust engine

Gun and ammunition pod

Above: British Aerospace Sea Harrier FRS.Mk 1 of
No 700A Intensive Flying Trials Unit of the Royal
Navy.

Navy Sea Harriers will be upgraded to FRS.Mk.2 standard, with the advanced Blue Vixen radar to give lookdown/shootdown capability using the new AMRAAM air-to-air missiles, and with long target-detection range matching the Sea Eagle cruise missile. The cockpit will be modernized, and other new avionics will include the Guardian radar warning, Zeus active countermeasures, a secure voice data-link and the JTIDS (joint tactical information distribution system).

Specifications (Sea Harrier FRS.Mk 1 data)
Radar: Ferranti Blue Fox multimode radar with interception, air-to-surface search and strike, and ground mapping functions.
Weapons: Provision for two 30-mm Aden cannon pods, plus 4 Sidewinder air-to-air missiles, 2 Sea Eagle or similar antiship missiles, bombs etc, up to a total weight of 8000 lb (3630 kg) for short take-offs and 5000 lb (2270 kg) for vertical take-offs.
Accommodation: The pilot.

Wingspan: 25 ft 3 in (7.70 m).
Length: 47 ft 7 in (14.50 m).
Maximum take-off weight: 26,200 lb (11,880 kg).
Maximum speed: Mach 1.25.
Combat radius (strike): 288 miles (463 km).
Mission performance: G limits +7.8, −4.2.
Engine: One 21,500-lb (9752-kg) vectored-thrust Rolls-Royce Pegasus Mk 104 turbofan, with 2864 liters of fuel standard.
Versions in service
FRS.Mk 1: Initial production version, delivered to the Royal Navy from June 1979. Ship trials performed on HMS *Hermes,* the last large Royal Navy aircraft carrier that has now been sold to India to join INS *Vikrant.* First-line Sea Harrier Squadrons are Nos 800 and 801, with No 899 HQ Squadron on shore.
FRS.Mk 2: Upgraded FRS.Mk.1, with Blue Vixen pulse-Doppler radar, bestowing all-weather lookdown/shootdown capability, track-while-scan, multiple target engagement, and improvements to the range, ECCM and acquisition of surface targets. Other upgrades include wingtip extensions, a 46 ft 3 in (14.10 m) length, redesigned cockpit, HOTAS (hands on throttle and stick) control for the aircraft/radar/weapon systems, and weapon pylons including underwing, centerline, and 2 others under the fuselage for 2 Aden cannon, two 25-mm gun packs or AMRAAM AAMs. The wide range of weapons include 2 ALARM antiradiation missiles. FRS.Mk 2s by conversion will be redelivered to the Royal Navy from 1989, with newly built aircraft following in 1990.
FRS.Mk 51: Indian Navy version of the FRS.Mk.1, with Magic missiles. First used by No 300 'White Tiger' Squadron on board INS *Vikrant.*
T.Mk 4N: Royal Navy 2-seat trainer of standard 2-seat Harrier type.
T.Mk 60: Indian Navy 2-seat trainer.
Operators: India (navy) and United Kingdom (navy).

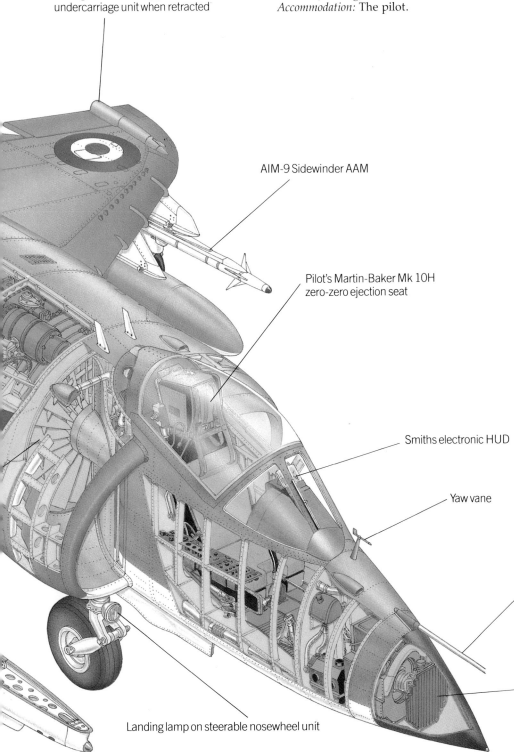

Fairing to house outrigger undercarriage unit when retracted

AIM-9 Sidewinder AAM

Pilot's Martin-Baker Mk 10H zero-zero ejection seat

Smiths electronic HUD

Yaw vane

Pitot head

Ferranti Blue Fox radar

Landing lamp on steerable nosewheel unit

Above: Beechcraft T-44A pilot trainer operated by the United States Navy.

Beagle Basset and Husky, and BAe (Scottish Aviation) Bulldog
United Kingdom

The Beagle Basset CC.Mk 1 is a five to eight-seat twin-engined light transport, of which just three are in RAF service as utility aircraft. The first CC.Mk 1 flew initially on 24 December 1964. The Husky, of which only one remains with the RAF, was used as a primary trainer.

By far the most important of the trio of aircraft is the Bulldog, a two/three-seat primary trainer of conventional all-metal construction with a fixed undercarriage. Although normally unarmed, four underwing stations have been provided. The first prototype, by Beagle, made its maiden flight on 19 May 1969, followed by the second by Scottish Aviation in 1971.

Specifications (Bulldog Series 120 data)
Weapons: Up to 640 lb (290 kg) of weapons if required, including bombs weighing up to 110 lb (50 kg) each, missiles, 7.62-mm gun pods, grenade launchers, etc.
Accommodation: Student pilot and instructor side by side, with an observer's seat to the rear.
Wingspan: 33 ft 0 in (10.06 m).
Length: 23 ft 3 in (7.09 m).
Maximum take-off weight: 2350 lb (1066 kg).
Maximum speed: 150 mph (241 km/h).
Range: 621 miles (1000 km).
Mission performance: Rate of climb at sea level 1035 ft (315 m) per min; ceiling 16,000 ft (4875 m); G limits +6 fully aerobatic, −3 fully aerobatic; endurance 5 h.
Engine: One 200-hp Avco Lycoming IO-360-A1B6 piston, with 145 liters of fuel.
Versions in service
Basset CC.Mk 1: Utility aircraft, powered by two 310-hp Rolls-Royce/Continental GIO-470A piston engines.
Husky: Powered by one 160-hp Avco Lycoming O-320 piston engine.
Bulldog: As detailed above.
Operators: All Bulldog, unless otherwise stated. Botswana, Ghana, Hong Kong, Jordan, Kenya, Lebanon, Malaysia, Nigeria, Sweden and United Kingdom (Basset, Bulldog and Husky).

Beechcraft Baron/T-42A Cochise, King Air/VC-6/U-21 Ute/T-44A, Queen Air/U-8 Seminole, Twin-Bonanza/U-8 Seminole, and 99 Airliner
United States

This series of Beech twin-engined light transports is used by many nations for tasks including transport itself, liaison, navigation and instrument training, and reconnaissance/electronic intelligence. The individual types are listed below.

Specifications (King Air C90 data)
Accommodation: 2 crew plus 4 to 8 passengers.
Wingspan: 50 ft 3 in (15.32 m).
Length: 35 ft 6 in (10.82 m).
Maximum take-off weight: 9650 lb (4377 kg).
Cruising speed: 256 mph (412 km/h).
Range: Up to 1474 miles (2374 km).
Mission performance: Rate of climb at sea level 1950 ft (595 m) per min; ceiling 28,100 ft (8560 m).
Engines: Two 550-ehp Pratt & Whitney Canada PT6A-21 turboprops, with 1454 liters of fuel.
Versions in service and Operators
King Air series: In 1963 Beech modified a Queen Air to use PT6A-6 turboprops and this served as the prototype of the U-21A Ute transport (10 troops, 6 or 8 personnel, or 3 stretchers) for the US Army. Deliveries began on 16 May 1967 and later U-21 models

Below: BAe Bulldog primary trainer in RAF markings.

followed, including some for the USAF. Army RU-21 reconnaissance and elint derivatives, some with 680-shp PT6A-29 engines, are also still used. VC-6B is a USAF VIP transport version of the King Air C90, while the T-44A is a US Navy advanced pilot trainer. Though the US Army's U-21F 9-seat VIP transport and those for Spain were based on the King Air A100 (a stretched version of the 90 series), most military King Airs have been of the 90 series, of which 226 military examples had been delivered by 1986. Operators of the King Air series are Chile, Ecuador (air force and army), Indonesia, Jamaica, Japan (navy), Mexico, Morocco, Spain, Thailand (army), United States (air force, navy and army) and Venezuela (navy and army).

Queen Air series: The Queen Air appeared in 1958 in Model 65 form. It was developed through the series to the B80, which came out of production in the late 1970s. Military examples include the US Army's U-8F 6-seat light transport, powered by two 340-hp Avco Lycoming IGSO-480-A1B6 piston engines. Wingspan of this model is 45 ft 10½ in (13.98 m), length 35 ft 6 in (10.82 m) and maximum speed 239 mph (384 km/h). Operators of this series are Argentina (navy and army), Dominican Republic, Israel, Japan (air force and navy, transport and navigation trainer), Peru, Pakistan (army), Thailand, United States (army), Uruguay, and Venezuela (air force and army).

Twin Bonanza series: The Twin Bonanza first appeared in 1949 as a twin-engined version of the Bonanza. Seating 6 or 7, progressive versions used more powerful engines until the final model, the J50, had two 340-hp Avco Lycoming IGSO-480-A1B6s. Wingspan 45 ft 11½ in (13.99 m), length 31 ft 6½ in (9.61 m); cruise speed 223 mph (358 km/h). The US Army's U-8D Seminole transport was based on the E50 with 340-hp O-480 engines and the U-8E Seminole on the D50 with 295-hp GO-480-G2F6 engines, giving a maximum speed of 214 mph (344 km/h). The U-8G designation applies to early U-8s modified to have better accommodation and GO-480 engines. Operators are Chile, Pakistan, Switzerland and US Army.

Baron series: The 4- to 6-seat Baron appeared in 1960. The US Army selected the B55B model as an instrument trainer under the designation T-42A Cochise, which also went to Turkey. Two 260-hp Continental IO-470-L engines, bestowing a maximum speed of 236 mph (380 km/h). Wingspan 37 ft 10 in (11.53 m) and length 27 ft (8.23 m). Used by Brazil, Haiti, Honduras, Spain, and Turkish and US armies.

99 Airliner: The 99 Airliner appeared in 1966. Chile purchased 15-seat 99As with 680-shp Pratt & Whitney PT6A-27 turboshaft engines, a wingspan of 45 ft 10½ in (13.98 m), length 44 ft 6¾ in (13.58 m) and cruising speed 284 mph (457 km/h). Other operators of the 99-type are Peru and Thailand (army).

Beechcraft F33A/C Bonanza, Musketeer, Sierra 200 and Sundowner 180
United States

These Beechcraft lightplanes are in military service as trainers, although both the Mexican Navy and Ivory Coast Air Force also employ Bonanzas for liaison. F33Cs sold to the Netherlands are with the Government Flying School.

Specifications (F33A/C data)
Accommodation: 4 persons, with optionally 5 for the F33A.
Wingspan: 33 ft 6 in (10.21 m).
Length: 26 ft 8 in (8.13 m).
Maximum take-off weight: 3400 lb (1542 kg).
Maximum speed: 209 mph (338 km/h).
Range: Up to 1025 miles.
Mission performance: Rate of climb at sea level 1165 ft (356 m) per min; ceiling 17,860 ft (5440 m).
Engine: One 285-hp Continental IO-520-BB piston, with 280 liters of fuel.
Versions in service
F33A/C Bonanza: Cabin lightplane, first flown on 14 September 1959. As detailed above. The aerobatic version is the F33C, and is flown at a gross weight of 2800 lb (1270 kg) for aerobatics.
Musketeer: Normally used as a 2-seat flying

Below: Canadian Armed Forces Beechcraft CT-134 Musketeer.

Above: US Army Beechcraft RC-12D Improved Guardrail V special-missions electronic aircraft.

and instrument trainer. First flown in 1961. The Canadian Armed Forces operates the type under the designation CT-134. One 150-hp Avco Lycoming IO-320-E2C piston engine, bestowing a maximum speed of 140 mph (225 km/h) and range of 883 miles (1420 km). Wingspan 32 ft 9 in (9.98 m) and length 25 ft (7.62 m).

Sierra 200: 4- or 6-seat cabin lightplane, based on the Musketeer. One 200-hp Avco Lycoming IO-360-A1B6 piston engine, bestowing a maximum speed of 167 mph (269 km/h) and range of 790 miles (1271 km). Wingspan 32 ft 9 in (9.98 m) and length 25 ft 9 in (7.85 m).

Sundowner 180: Similar to the Sierra but with an 180-hp O-360-A4K piston engine. Maximum speed 147 mph (237 km/h) and range 737 miles (1187 km). Known in Canadian Armed Forces service as the CT-134 Musketeer II.

Operators: Algeria (Sierra), Canada (CT-134 Musketeer), Haiti (Bonanza), Iran (Bonanza), Ivory Coast (Bonanza), Mexico (air force, Bonanza and Musketeer; navy Bonanza), Netherlands (see introduction) and Spain (Bonanza).

Beechcraft Super King Air 200 series/C-12, Maritime Patrol 200T/ B200T and 1900C/C-12J
United States

First flown on 27 October 1972 as a heavier and more powerful development of the King Air light transport, with a greater wingspan and fuel capacity, and a T-tail, the civil Super King Air too has found acceptance with military forces for various duties as detailed below. It is worth noting that the first few aircraft off the production line were acquired by the US Army for its Cefly Lancer program as RU-21J electronic warfare testbeds, but these have since been converted into VIP transports. A maritime patrol derivative appeared in 1979.

The Beechcraft 1900C is a considerably larger aircraft than the Super King Air, developed as a commuter airliner for commercial operations. It flew for the first time in prototype form on 3 September 1982. Six were ordered by the US Army's Aviation Systems Command as C-12Js, entering service from 1987 as mission support aircraft with the Air National Guard and superseding the ageing Convair C-131s which had first entered US service in 1954.

Specifications (Maritime Patrol B200T data)

Radar and equipment: Search radar is carried in an underfuselage radome, affording 360-degree scanning. Equipment can include electronic surveillance measures, forward-looking infrared (FLIR), low light-level television, sonobuoys and the associated processing equipment, on-top position indicator, multispectral scanner, photographic gear, and survival equipment that can be released through a fuselage hatch (useful for search and rescue missions).

Wingspan: 56 ft 7 in (17.25 m) over the removable 201-liter wingtip tanks.

Length: 43 ft 9 in (13.34 m).

Maximum take-off weight: 14,000 lb (6350 kg).

Cruising speed: 305 mph (491 km/h).

Range: 2061 miles (3317 km).

Mission performance: Rate of climb at sea level approximately 2450 ft (746 m) per min; ceiling approximately 35,000 ft (10,670 m); patrol speed 161 mph (259 km/h); endurance on station with wingtip tanks fitted 9 h.

Engines: Two 850-shp Pratt & Whitney Canada PT6A-42 turboprops, with 2461 liters of fuel (including wingtip tanks).

Versions in service

Maritime Patrol 200T and B200T: The B200T

is the current maritime model, as detailed above. Including the original 200T model, the largest operator to date is the Japan Maritime Safety Agency, which acquired 15. 3 have been delivered each to Australia and Chile and 2 to the government defense ministry of Algeria. The only specified navy to use this aircraft is the Uruguayan, while the Irish Air Corps has two 200Ts.

C-12A: US Army (60 aircraft) and USAF (30 aircraft) designation for the original service model of the Super King Air light transport, accommodating 8 passengers (in addition to the crew) or freight. Powered by two 750-shp PT6A-38 turboprops. US Army C-12As are now powered by 850-shp PT6A-41s. [*See C-12E.*]

C-12C: US Army designation for 14 transports delivered with PT6A-41 turboprop engines.

C-12D: Similar to the C-12C for the US Army but with optional wingtip tanks, a large cargo door and a high-flotation undercarriage. 27 received, with 5 more ordered.

C-12E: Designation of USAF C-12As refitted with PT6A-42 turboprops.

C-12F: Operational support aircraft for MAC (Military Airlift Command), USAF. Total of 40 delivered from 1984.

C-12J: Not a Super King Air but a Beechcraft 1900C Airliner, of which 6 have gone into Air National Guard service to replace C-131s. Accommodating 19 passengers plus crew, it has a wingspan of 54 ft 5¾ in (16.61 m), length of 57 ft 10 in (17.63 m), take-off weight of 16,600 lb (7530 kg) and a cruising speed of 295 mph (474 km/h).

RC-12D Improved Guardrail V: 19 aircraft (with 6 more ordered) operated by the US Army as special mission battlefield communications intercept and direction finding aircraft.

RC-12K Improved Guardrail V: Special missions electronic aircraft for the US Army. 9 delivered.

UC-12B: US Navy/Marine Corps utility transport aircraft with PT6A-41 engines. 89 delivered.

Super King Air: As for the civil version for liaison, communications, light transport, survey and training duties.

Operators*: Super King Airs, unless stated to be a specific model. Algeria, Argentina (navy), Bolivia, Chile, Ecuador (navy and army), Greece (army), Guatemala, Guyana, Ireland (air corps, Maritime Patrol and Super King Air), Ivory Coast, Pakistan,

Above: Beechcraft T-34C-1 trainers in the markings of Morocco (nearest), Ecuador and Peru.

Peru, Thailand, United States (air force, navy/marine corps and army, as detailed under 'versions in service'), Uruguay (navy, Maritime Patrol) and Venezuela (air force, navy and army).

* Maritime Patrol 200T/B200Ts are not included where specific military use by *air forces* is not undertaken or is uncertain.

Beechcraft T-34 Mentor and T-34C; Fuji LM-1 Nikko, KM-2 and KM-2B
United States and Japan

In 1948 the Beech Aircraft Corporation flew the prototype of a new tandem two-seat primary trainer derived from its Bonanza light aircraft, as the T-34. Powered by a 225-hp Continental O-470-13A piston engine, it was eventually ordered in hundreds for the USAF and US Navy, exported (partly under military assistance programs) and built under license in Argentina, Canada and Japan.

Under US Navy contract, a modernized turboprop-powered version was developed as the T-34C. It first flew on 21 September

1973. A total of 334 were eventually delivered to the US Naval Air Training Command, and examples of the T-34C-1 armaments trainer have been exported. The latter has four underwing pylons for up to 1200 lb (544 kg) of weapons or target-towing equipment, which also makes it suitable for light attack missions and forward air-control duties if required.

Apart from its local production of T-34s, Fuji of Japan developed a liaison derivative for the JGSDF as the LM-1 Nikko, featuring a wider fuselage accommodating four seats. A more powerful conversion with a fifth seat became the LM-2. Very few LM-1s remain in use. Basically similar to the LM-2 was the KM-2, which entered service with the JMSDF as a primary trainer (about 38 currently operated), while the strictly two-seat KM-2B entered JASDF service as the T-3 trainer, of which about 50 remain on strength.

Specifications (T-34C-1 data)
Weapons: For armaments training and light attack missions, up to 1200 lb (544 kg) of weapons can be carried on four underwing pylons. These can include containers for flares or practice bombs, incendiary bombs, antitank missiles, rocket or gun pods.
Accommodation: Student pilot and instructor in tandem cockpits.
Wingspan: 33 ft 4 in (10.16 m).
Length: 28 ft 8½ in (8.75 m).
Maximum take-off weight: 5500 lb (2494 kg).
Maximum speed: 241 mph (387 km/h).
Combat radius with auxiliary fuel and weapons: 345 miles (555 km).

Below: Italian Army Agusta-Bell 47G-3B-1.

Mission performance: Rate of climb at sea level 1430 ft (436 m) per min; ceiling above 30,000 ft (9145 m); G limits +6, −3.
Engine: One 715-shp Pratt & Whitney Canada PT6A-25 turboprop, with 492 liters of fuel.

Versions in service
LM-1 Nikko: Fuji 4-seat liaison aircraft, developed from the Mentor.
KM-2: 2- or 4-seat trainer built by Fuji for the JMSDF. Power is provided by a 340-hp Avco Lycoming IGSO-480-A1C6 piston engine.
KM-2B: Tandem 2-seat trainer built by Fuji for the JASDF, with whom it is designated T-3. IGSO-480-A1A6 engine of 340-hp is fitted.
KM-2D: Proposed Allison 250-B17D turboprop conversion of the JMSDF's remaining 32 KM-2s.
T-34 Mentor: Original piston-engined primary trainer, from which all the other aircraft described here were derived.
T-34B: Originally for US Navy, with extra equipment. Production ended in 1957.
T-34C: Turboprop development of the Mentor, featuring slightly larger dimensions, updated avionics, and a marginally redesigned tail unit with a long dorsal fin added.
T-34C-1: Armaments trainer, also suited to light attack and FAC duties.

Operators: Algeria (T-34C), Argentina (air force, T-34A; navy T-34C-1), Chile (T-34A), Colombia (T-34A and B), Dominican Republic (T-34B), Ecuador (air force and navy, T-34C-1), El Salvador (T-34A), Gabon (T-34C-1), Indonesia (T-34C-1), Japan (air force, T-34A and KM-2B; navy T-34A and KM-2; army LM-1), Mexico (navy, T-34A), Morocco (T-34C-1), Peru (navy, T-34C-1), Spain (T-34A), Turkey (T-34A), United States (navy, T-34B and T-34C), Uruguay air force, T-34A and B; navy T-34B and T-34C-1) and Venezuela (T-34A).

Bell Model 47 and Kawasaki KH-4
United States and Japan

The Bell Model 47 is remembered historically as the first helicopter to gain a Type Approval Certificate for commercial operation, on 8 March 1946. Having first flown as a prototype light general-purpose helicopter on 8 December 1945, it was among the first major production helicopters in the world and indeed was built by the parent company until 1974. Many Model 47s of various versions found their way into military service, most with the familiar 'goldfish bowl' enclosure that was introduced on the Model 47D. Today the G and J models remain in military service, known by the name Sioux. License production also took place in Italy and the United Kingdom, by Agusta and Westland respectively, and in Japan where the four-seat Kawasaki KH-4 derivative was also developed and manufactured. KH-4 production ended in 1975 and Agusta-Bell production in 1976. Among Agusta versions was the four/five-seat Model 47J-3 for ASW, though most Sioux types were three-seaters used for observation, training and rescue.

Specifications (Model 47G-3B-1 Sioux data)
Accommodation: Pilot plus 2 passengers.
Diameter of rotor: 37 ft 1½ in (11.32 m).

Length: 31 ft 7 in (9.63 m).
Maximum take-off weight: 2950 lb (1338 kg).
Maximum speed: 105 mph (169 km/h).
Range: 315 miles (507 km).
Engine: One 270-hp Avco Lycoming TVO-435-25 piston.

Versions in service

Bell Model 47: Many sub-types of the Model 47G and J remain, with engines from 240 to 280 hp. US military designation was H-13, under which some military Model 47s operate abroad.

Agusta-Bell 47: Italian license-built models and the final examples to be manufactured.

Kawasaki KH-4: 4-seater with a new cabin enclosure, modified control system and instrument layout, and increased fuel capacity.

Operators: Argentina, Brazil, Chile, Colombia, Greece (air force and army), Indonesia (army?), Italy (air force and army), Japan (navy), Lesotho, Libya, Malta, Mexico, New Zealand, Pakistan (air force and army), Paraguay (air force, navy and army), Spain (air force and navy), Taiwan (army), Thailand (army), Turkey (army), Uruguay (navy), Venezuela (national guard) and Zambia.

Bell Model 206 JetRanger/OH-58 Kiowa/TH-57 SeaRanger, Model 206L LongRanger, Model 400 Combat Twin, and Model 406/OH-58D
United States and Canada

On 8 December 1962 the initial flight took place of Bell's new Model 206, designed to a 1960 US Army request for a light turboshaft-powered observation helicopter to supersede OH-13s and OH-23s. This competition was cancelled but out of its Model 206 Bell developed the improved Model 206A JetRanger five-seat general-purpose civil helicopter. The first 206A was flown on 10 January 1966 and it proved a huge success. As a result of the reopened LOH competition, in 1968 Bell was selected to provide the US Army with similar OH-58A Kiowas, later also being exported. Similar helicopters went to the US Navy as TH-57A SeaRanger trainers. Improved models of the JetRanger produced the Model 206B JetRanger II and III, and new Kiowa/SeaRanger versions appeared by conversion and new manufacture. A longer, seven-seat derivative of the JetRanger first flew in September 1974 as the LongRanger, while on 30 June 1984 a new helicopter retaining the basic shape of the Model 206 types flew as the Model 400 TwinRanger. This is being manufactured in Canada and includes the Combat Twin among its versions. A program to upgrade US Army Kiowas has brought about the Model 406, US Army designated OH-58D.

Including those helicopters built under license by Agusta in Italy and as Kalkadoons (Kiowas) by the Commonwealth Aircraft Corporation in Australia for the indigenous army, by 1986 more than 7000 helicopters of the series had been built for civil or military use.

Specifications (OH-58C Kiowa data)
Weapons: 7.62-mm Minigun.
Accommodation: 2 crew plus 2 passengers or freight.

Diameter of rotor: 35 ft 4 in (10.77 m).
Fuselage length: 32 ft 7 in (9.93 m).
Maximum take-off weight: 3200 lb (1451 kg).
Cruising speed: 117 mph (188 km/h).
Range: 305 miles (490 km).
Mission performance: Rate of climb at sea level 1800 ft (550 m) per min; ceiling 18,500 ft (5640 m); hovering ceiling in ground effect 13,200 ft (4023 m); hovering ceiling out of ground effect 9700 ft (2960 m).
Engine: One 420-shp Allison T63-A-720 turboshaft, with 276 liters of fuel.

Versions in service

Model 206A/B JetRanger I/II/III: Basically a civil five-seater, originally with a 317-shp Allison 250-C18A engine and now the latest model with a 420-shp Allison 250-C20J engine. Used for utility, search and rescue, ECM, training, etc.

OH-58A Kiowa: Initial US Army light observation model, corresponding with the Model 206A JetRanger and powered by a 317-shp Allison T63-A-700 engine but with a larger rotor. 2200 delivered to the US Army between 1969 and 1973. Canadian Armed Forces received similar CH-136s, those used for training having been superseded by JetRanger IIIs. CAC in Australia assembled Kiowas for the indigenous army.

OH-58B Kiowa: The Austrian Air Force took 12.

OH-58C Kiowa: 435 US Army OH-58As upgraded to this standard by 1985, the T63-A-720 engine fitted with 'Black Hole' infrared suppression.

Model 406/OH-58D Kiowa: Under AHIP (Army Helicopter Improvement Program), Bell is upgrading possibly 578 OH-58As to OH-58D standard by 1991. Powered by a 735-shp Allison 250-C34R engine and with new avionics that include a mast-mounted sight, the OH-58D is intended to carry out observation, surveillance, intelligence-gathering and armed support missions.

Above: Agusta-Bell AB 206A JetRanger, operated by the Swedish Navy as the HKP 6.

Armament can be four TOW anti-armor missiles, Stinger air-to-air missiles, 70-mm rockets or guns.

TH-57A SeaRanger: 40 Model 206As for primary helicopter training with the US Navy.

TH-57B SeaRanger: New version, based on the JetRanger III. 51 received.

TH-57C SeaRanger. 89 instrument trainers, based on the JetRanger III.

Model 206L LongRanger: Lengthened JetRanger for seven persons, 2 stretchers and attendants or freight. Latest 206L-3 LongRanger III is powered by a 650-shp Allison 250-C30P engine.

Model 400A TwinRanger: Produced by Bell Helicopter Canada. Seven-seater, powered by a 937-shp Pratt & Whitney Canada PW209T coupled twin-turboshaft engine. An armored derivative is the Combat Twin, with an optional mast-mounted sight, survivability features, and armed with TOW or Stinger missiles, 7-round 2.75-in rocket launchers or guns/cannon. The TwinRanger first flew on 30 June 1984.

Operators: All JetRanger types, and air forces, unless stated otherwise. Argentina (army), Australia (army, Kiowa), Austria (Kiowa), Bangladesh (LongRanger), Brazil (navy and army), Brunei, Canada (CH-136), Chile (navy and army), Colombia, Dubai (police), Greece (air force and army), Guatemala (LongRanger), Guyana, Indonesia, Iran, Israel, Italy (army), Jamaica, Libya, Mexico, Morocco, Oman, Pakistan (army), Peru (air force and navy), Saudi Arabia, Spain (air force and army), Sri Lanka, Sweden (navy), Thailand (army, Kiowa), Turkey (army), Uganda, United States (navy and army), Venezuela (army) and North Yemen.

Above: Italian Navy Agusta-Bell 212ASW all-weather antisubmarine helicopter.

Bell Model 212 Twin Two-Twelve/ UH-1N and 412
United States

The Model 212 was developed to a Canadian requirement for a twin-engined Iroquois-type general-purpose helicopter. Power plant was specified as the PT6T-3, comprising two PT6 engines couple to a single gearbox. Like the Iroquois itself, the Model 212 has been selling widely. The first examples went to the USAF in 1970 as UH-1Ns to serve with the Special Operations Force for 'unconventional' missions. Canadian CUH-1Ns were delivered from the following year, now redesignated CH-135s. Other users are many, including the US Navy and Marine Corps and encompass those customers choosing the Italian license-produced Agusta-Bells. Specialist mission versions have also been developed by Bell and Agusta, but notably the latter.

The Model 412 is basically an improved version of the 212, with a four-blade rotor to improve performance and lower noise and vibration levels.

Specifications (UH-1N data)
Radar: Optional weather radar.
Accommodation: The pilot and 14 passengers/troops, internal or up to 5000 lb (2268 kg) of externally slung cargo, stretchers, rescue equipment, or other layouts.
Diameter of rotor: 48 ft 2¼ in (14.69 m).
Fuselage length: 42 ft 4¾ in (12.92 m).
Maximum take-off weight: 11,200 lb (5080 kg).
Cruising speed: 115 mph (185 km/h).
Range: 261 miles (420 km).
Mission performance: Rate of climb at sea level 1320 ft (402 m) per min; ceiling 13,000 ft (3960 m); hovering ceiling in ground effect 11,000 ft (3350 m).
Engines: One 1800-shp Pratt & Whitney PT6T-3B Turbo Twin Pac, flat-rated at 1290 shp, with 814 liters of fuel standard.

Versions in service
Bell Model 212/UH-1N: As described above.
Bell Model 412: Version of the 212 with an advanced 4-blade rotor and a transmission rating of 1400 shp. Cruising speed 143 mph (230 km/h).
Bell Model 412AH: Attack version of the 412, with a detachable Lucas turret under the nose housing a 0.50-in machine-gun with 875 rounds of ammunition, linked to a helmet sight. Provision for 38 air-to-surface rockets.
Agusta-Bell 212: Italian version, with a 48-ft (14.63-m) rotor.
Agusta-Bell 212ASW: Much modified all-weather antisubmarine derivative of the A-B 212 for day and night operations, with an 1875-shp PT6T-6 power plant, crew of 3 or 4, Doppler radar, ASW navigation computer, sonar and 2 torpedoes or depth charges. Antisurface vessel model has Ferranti Seaspray search radar, Sea Skua or Marte Mk 2 antishipping missiles. Can also perform a midcourse guidance role for ship-fired Otomat 2 missiles, or passenger/freight transport and other missions.
Agusta-Bell 412: Italian license-built version of the Bell Model 412.
Agusta-Bell Griffon: Special Italian-developed multipurpose version of the 412, for roles including reconnaissance, troop transport, battlefield/fire support, etc, with many features to enhance survivability.
Operators: Argentina, Austria, Bangladesh, Bahrain, Brunei, Canada, Colombia, Ecuador, Finland (border guard), Ghana, Greece (air force and navy), Guatemala, Guyana, Iraq (navy), Iran (air force and navy), Israel, Italy (air force, navy and army), Jamaica, South Korea, Lebanon, Lesotho, Mexico, Morocco, Nigeria (police), Panama, Peru (air force and navy), Philippines, Saudi Arabia, Singapore, Somali Republic, Spain (army), Sri Lanka, Sudan, Thailand (air force, navy and army), Tunisia, Turkey (navy and army), Uganda (army), United States (air force, navy and marine corps), Venezuela, North Yemen, Zambia and Zimbabwe.

Bell Model 214
United States

The Model 214 series of military and commercial helicopters was founded upon an order for 287 examples from the US Army, destined through United States government funding to serve with the pre-revolution Iranian Army as Model 214A Isfahans. The first of these flew on 13 March 1974 and deliveries started just over a year later. At that time a production line was also to be established in Iran for the construction of hundreds more. Though the Isfahans and further numbers of Bell-manufactured 214s were delivered, including SAR 214Cs, Iranian production never happened. The current version of the Model 214 is the ST SuperTransport. Though basically a commercial version, it has also gone into military service in Peru, Thailand and Venezuela.

Specifications (Model 214ST data)
Radar: Optional radar.
Accommodation: 2 crew plus 18 passengers/troops or cargo. Optional rescue equipment.
Diameter of rotor: 52 ft 0 in (15.85 m).
Fuselage length: 49 ft 3½ in (15.02 m).
Maximum take-off weight: 17,500 lb (7938 kg).
Cruising speed: 161 mph (259 km/h).
Range: 533 miles (858 km).
Mission performance: Rate of climb at sea level 1780 ft (543 m) per min; hovering ceiling in ground effect 4800 ft (1460 m).
Engines: Two 1625-shp General Electric CT7-2A turboshafts, with 1647 liters of fuel standard.

Versions in service
214A: Initial Iranian model with one 2930-shp Avco Lycoming LTC4B-8D turboshaft, used mainly as a 16-seat utility helicopter.
214B BigLifter: Developed as a commercial passenger or freight-carrying version of the 214A, with a T5508D turboshaft of the same power. Main and tail rotors have raked tips, and the main rotor has elastometric bearings on the flapping axis.
214C: SAR version of the 214A for Iran.
214ST Super Transport: As described above.
Operators: Dubai, Ecuador (army), Iran (air force and army), Peru, Philippines, Thailand, Uganda and Venezuela.

Bell AH-1 HueyCobra, SeaCobra and SuperCobra
United States

From the beginning of United States' involvement in Vietnam, in 1961, it became clear that helicopters used to transport troops and supplies were vulnerable to ground fire. Armed versions of the UH-1 attempted to act as escorts, but on many occasions they proved too slow, with too little firepower. Not surprisingly Bell had been among the first to recognize the shortcomings and in 1962 completed a mock-up of a specialist armed attack helicopter based on the Iroquois, known as the Iroquois Warrior. While the Army saw the importance of an armed escort, especially with its new large Chinook about to enter service, it considered the armed modification of a large helicopter an adequate solution. However, when eventually the specifications were widened to include a speed of 200

Above: Bell Model 214 eighteen-passenger (plus crew) transport helicopter.

knots, Bell became convinced that only a new design would fulfill the requirement.

As any efforts in this direction had to be company-funded, in July 1963 Bell flew its Model 207 Sioux Scout, a demonstrator specialist attack helicopter based on the low-powered H-13. Features included tandem stepped cockpits for the crew of two in a slimmer than normal fuselage, stub wings, and a 'chin' gun turret. This convinced the Army of the need for a new design and the AAFSS (Advanced Aerial Fire Support System) program was initiated. However the required AAFSS design was so advanced that Bell considered an interim attack helicopter would almost certainly be needed, and set to work on its own company-funded Model 209. The judgment proved correct. In August 1965 the Army began looking for an interim attack helicopter and, because of its foresight, Bell was able to fly its prototype Model 209 Huey-Cobra on 7 September, featuring a fuselage only 3 ft 2 in (0.97 m) wide to make it a difficult target. In November it was evaluated against modified S-61s and UH-2s and in April 1966 the first 110 AH-1G HueyCobras were ordered. Deliveries started in June 1967 and deployment began that August.

Subsequent armament changes brought TOW missiles onto the HueyCobra, AH-1Gs being modified into AH-1Qs, while an advanced version became the AH-1S by conversion of Gs and new production. A twin-turboshaft version of the HueyCobra, initially for US Marine Corps service but also exported to Iran, became the AH-1J SeaCobra. The latest advanced version is the AH-1W SuperCobra, examples of which are going to the US Marine Corps by new production and modification of AH-1S SeaCobras. It is also interesting to note that two ex-Army AH-1Gs are used by the United States Customs Service for night missions, while, of the HueyCobra/SeaCobras exported, the Spanish Navy flies its Z.14s (AH-1Gs) on antishipping missions from its aircraft carriers.

Specifications (AH-1S data)
Equipment: Avionics include Doppler navigation, radar warning receiver and infrared jammer.
Weapons: Either an M28 chin turret with 7.62-mm guns or 40-mm grenade launchers (or one of each), or more recently a General Electric turret with 20-mm/30-mm cannon. 8 TOW anti-armor missiles and launchers for 2.75-in rockets carried on the stub-wings.
Accommodation: Pilot to the rear and higher than the forward copilot/gunner.
Diameter of rotor: 44 ft 0 in (13.41 m).
Length with rotors: 53 ft 1 in (16.18 m).
Maximum take-off weight: 10,000 lb (4536 kg).
Maximum speed: 141 mph (227 km/h) while carrying TOW missiles.
Range: 315 miles (506 km).
Mission performance: Rate of climb at sea level 1620 ft (495 m) per min; ceiling 12,200 ft (3718 m).
Engine: One 1800-shp Avco Lycoming T53-L-703 turboshaft, with 980 liters of fuel.

Versions in service
AH-1G HueyCobra: Initial production version, with a 1400-shp T53-L-13 engine (derated to 1100 shp). The US Army received 1075, the US Marine Corps 38, Israel six and Spain eight. Of those in US Army service, 92 were modified into AH-1Qs (themselves converted into AH-1Ss) and 344 directly into AH-1Ss. Others became TH-1G dual-control trainers. Over 300 AH-1Gs remained as such in 1986. Gun, grenade launcher and rocket armament. Maximum speed is 172 mph (277 km/h).
AH-1J SeaCobra: First 'twin-engined' version, with an 1800-shp Pratt & Whitney Canada T400-CP-400 coupled turboshaft. 69 built and delivered between 1970-75, of which the majority are believed to remain in use. Iran received 202 but the number remaining serviceable is unknown, while it was reported that South Korea received 8 in 1978. Armament comprises a 20-mm cannon in the turret, and rockets and guns under the stub-wings. USMC helicopters might now carry Hellfire anti-armor missiles and a night vision system. Maximum speed is 207 mph (333 km/h).
AH-1S HueyCobra: Improved version of the AH-1G/Q, with a more powerful engine, upgraded gearbox and transmission, TOW missiles, an antiglint flat-plate cockpit canopy and other features. 'Production' is by the conversion of AH-1Gs and Qs and by new manufacture. Also serves with the United States Army National Guard. Some US Army AH-1Ss have automatic airborne laser trackers to acquire targets. 10 US Army AH-1Ss by conversion have been further modified into dual-control trainers under the designation TH-1S, to train Apache

Below: JGSDF Bell AH-1S HueyCobra attack helicopters.

crews in the use of FLIR and helmet sighting systems. Foreign AH-1S users are Japan, Jordan and Pakistan, which ordered 30, 24 and 20 respectively.

AH-1T Improved SeaCobra: 57 helicopters for the USMC, most with TOW missile capability and all powered by a 1970-shp T400-WV-402 engine arrangement. About 40 remain in use.

AH-1W SuperCobra: An advanced attack helicopter for the US Marine Corps, with 2 General Electric T700-GE-700 turboshafts, giving a combined rating of about 3200 shp. 44 were delivered between 1986 and 1988, and are being followed by AH-1Ts modified to this standard. Weapon choices include the 20-mm cannon with 750 rounds of ammunition plus 2 Sidewinder air-to-air missiles, the cannon plus eight TOW or Hellfire anti-armor missiles, or the cannon and rockets (perhaps 76 2.75-in). Maximum speed is 218 mph (350 km/h).

Operators: Greece (army, AH-1S), Iran (army, AH-1J), Israel (AH-1G and AH-1S), Japan (army, AH-1S), Jordan (AH-1S), South Korea (army, AH-1J?), Pakistan (army, AH-1S), Spain (navy, AH-1G), Turkey (army, AH-1S) and United States (marine corps, AH-1J, T and W; army AH-1G, S, TH-1G and TH-1S).

Bell UH-1 Iroquois
United States

The UH-1 Iroquois, which is often referred to as the 'Huey' because of its original service designation HU-1, was the result of a 1955 US Army competition for a front-line helicopter capable of utility, casualty evacuation and instrument training roles. The first prototype Model 204, Army designated XH-40, flew initially on 22 October 1956. Delivery to the US Army of six-seat UH-1As started on 30 June 1959, followed by the UH-1B with capacity for two crew and seven troops or three stretchers and attendant. As early as 1962 UH-1As were flying in Vietnam as experimental armed escort helicopters and

Below: Bell Iroquois of the Indonesian Army (Model 205).

similar missions were also undertaken by UH-1Bs (with provision of SS.11 missiles in addition to guns and rockets). With the full commitment of the United States to Vietnam in 1965 came the extensive deployment of Iroquois helicopters for all manner of duties, later including psychological warfare, though troop and freight/armaments transport was always its primary task.

After the UH-1C, Bell switched to the Model 205 for continued Iroquois production, the UH-1D introducing a longer fuselage for up to 14 troops but retaining the engine of the 'C'. The final version of the Model 205 was the UH-1H, of which 3573 went to the US Army alone and a further 1317 to export customers by 1987 (earlier models had also been exported). Agusta in Italy and Fuji in Japan built Model 204 and 205 series Iroquois helicopters under license, while Dornier-built UH-1Ds for the West German forces and AIDC in Taiwan produced UH-1Hs Agusta also developed its own anti-submarine version as the Agusta-Bell 204AS with a 1290-shp T58-GE-3 engine and carrying AN/APN-195 search radar, sonar and torpe-does (delivered originally to the Italian and Spanish navies), and an antisurface vessel version with Bendix radar and missiles. Agusta production of the Model 205 had not ended in 1986. Although the Sikorsky Black Hawk is being manufactured in the US to supersede the Iroquois as the US Army's main assault transport, that service plans to retain a force of about 2700 UH-1Hs into the next century to perform troop transport, evacuation, mine emplacement, command and control, electronic warfare and other tasks. To help survivability in the ever more dangerous battlefield environment, improvements are being made to these UH-1Hs, including the installation of infrared jammers to deter heat-seeking missiles, chaff/flare dispensers and a radar-warning receiver.

Specifications (Bell UH-1H data)
Accommodation: Pilot plus up to 14 troops or 3880 lb (1759 kg) of freight.
Diameter of rotor: 48 ft 0 in (14.63 m).
Fuselage length: 41 ft 10¾ in (12.77 m).
Maximum take-off weight: 9500 lb (4310 kg).

Maximum speed: 127 mph (204 km/h).
Range: 318 miles (511 km).
Engine: One 1400-shp Avco Lycoming T53-L-13 turboshaft, with 844 liters of fuel standard.

Versions in service
UH-1B: Second production version of the Model 204, with a 960-shp T53-L-5 or 1100-shp T53-L-11 turboshaft. The export version was designated Model 204B, with the latter engine. Also the first Agusta- and Fuji-built models.
UH-1C: Similar to the more powerful UH-1B but with wider-chord rotor blades.
UH-1D: First Model 205 version. T53-L-11 engine with a larger rotor. More cabin space for up to 14 troops. Also built by Agusta and Dornier.
UH-1E: Version of the B with a rescue hoist and carrying two 7.62-mm machine-guns, used by the US Marine Corps.
UH-1F: USAF missile site support helicopter. T58-GE-3 engine and based on the Model 204.
TH-1F: USAF instrument trainer.
UH-1H: Final Model 205 version, as detailed above. Also built by Agusta, Fuji and AIDC.
UH-1L/TH-1L: US Navy utility and training helicopters, with 1400-shp T53-L-13 engines, derated to 1100 shp.
UH-1M: Hunter-killer version with Hughes INFANT night fighter and night tracker system. First operated in Vietnam in 1970 to detect and strike at targets in darkness.
UH-1P: USAF phychological warfare helicopter, converted from UH-1Fs.
EH-1H: Electronic countermeasures version, with communications interception, emitter locating and jamming equipment. Modified from UH-1Hs.
HH-1H: USAF base rescue helicopter.
UH-1V: Medical evacuation helicopter, modified from UH-1Hs.
204B and AS: Export and license-built versions of the Model 204, the latter as a specialized ASW and ASV helicopter developed by Agusta in Italy.
Operators: License-built versions are given the appropriate suffix letter when known. Argentina (air force and army, H), Australia (air force, B and H; navy B), Austria (204B), Brazil (H), Burma (H), Canada (CH-118 = H), Chile (air force and army, H), Colombia (B and H), Dominican Republic (205), Dubai (205), Ecuador (H), West Germany (air force and army, D), Greece (air force, H; army, D and H), Guatemala (D), Honduras (B and H), Indonesia (204B and 205), Iran (navy, 205; army, 205), Israel (D), Italy (air force, 204B; navy AS 204AS; army, 204B and 205), Japan (army, B and H), South Korea (air force and army, B and H), Mexico (205), Morocco (205), New Zealand (D and H), Norway (B), Oman (205), Pakistan (army, H), Panama (B,D and H), Philippines (air force and army, H), Saudi Arabia (205), Singapore (B and H), Spain (air force, 205; army, B and H), Sweden (air force and army, 204B), Taiwan (army, H), Tanzania (205), Thailand (air force, H; navy, H; army, B and H), Tunisia (H), Turkey (air force, H; navy, 204AS; army, D and H), Uganda (205), United States (air force, TH-1F, UH-1F, HH-1H and UH-1P; navy/marine corps, E and L; army, B, C, D, H, M, EH-1H and UH-1V), Uruguay (B and H), Venezuela (air force, D and H; army, H), Vietnam (?) and Zimbabwe (205).

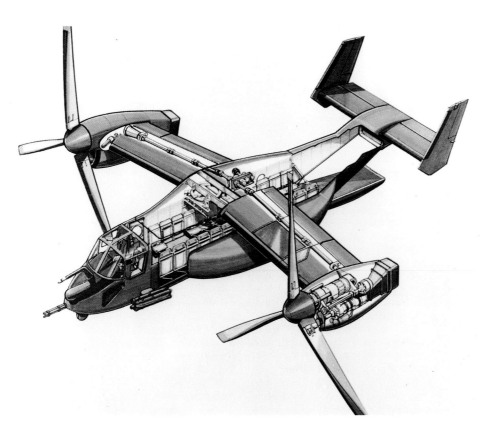

Above: Artist's impression of the Bell/Boeing V-22 Osprey tilt-rotor multimission aircraft.

Bell/Boeing Vertol V-22 Osprey
United States

In a unique program Bell and Boeing Vertol have joined forces to develop a tilt-rotor multimission aircraft for future service with the US Air Force, Navy/Marine Corps and Army. Following earlier demonstrations of tilt-rotor technology with the Bell XV-15, the V-22 is being funded by the United States government under the USAF/USN Joint Services Advanced Vertical Lift Aircraft program, previously known as JVX. The missions intended for the V-22 are given below with their required performances, while other capabilities are to include a ferry range of 2100 nautical miles, flight refuelling capability, all-weather navigation at low levels, and the ability to lift a 10,000-lb (4536-kg) sling load. Six flying prototypes are being built, together with three for ground testing. The first is due to fly initially in June 1988, with delivery of production MV-22As beginning in late 1991.

Incorporating fly-by-wire control, the V-22 is designed to fly as a helicopter and aeroplane. Each engine is fitted with a large rotor/propeller. For vertical take-off and landing the engines/rotors face upward. To achieve high-speed forward flight, the engines are rotated down once the V-22 is flying at the optimum speed, thereafter the wings providing 'lift.' STOL, with its inherent benefits to payload, can be achieved by tilting the engines forward by just 20 degrees.

Specifications (Provisional data)
Radar: Texas Instruments AN/APQ-168 multimode radar, incorporating also beacon and weather modes.
Diameter of each rotor/propeller: 38 ft (11.58 m).
Length: 57 ft 4 in (17.47 m).
Maximum take-off weight: 59,000 lb (26,760 kg) STOL.
Cruising speed: 391 mph (630 km/h).
Engines: Two 6000-shp Allison 501-M80C turboshafts.
Versions for service
CV-22A: Designation of 80 aircraft required for special missions by the USAF, carrying 12 troops or 2880 lb (1306 kg) of equipment at 250 knots over a radius of 700 nm.
HV-22A: Designation of 50 SAR aircraft to supersede HH-3 helicopters with the US Navy, accommodating 4 survivors. Radius of action will be 460 nm.
MV-22A: Designation of US Marine Corps assault transports, accommodating 24 equipped troops and able to fly at 250 knots over a mission radius of 200 nm. These will supersede Sea Knights and Stallions. 552 required, with ship-borne capability.
V-22: Other so-far undesignated versions will include US Navy ship-borne antisubmarine aircraft (300 required) and US Army transports (231 required).
Operators: None at present.

Beriev Be-6 and Be-12 Tchaika
(NATO names Madge and Mail)
Soviet Union

Large amphibious flying-boats were widely operated by the Allied powers during World War II but, with peace and the development of specialized long-range landplanes for maritime duties they passed out of British use in the postwar period and US Navy operation of new very large and jet-powered types (such as the Martin Marlin) ended in 1966. The Soviet Union, on the other hand, having established an important role for flying-boats during the war to patrol and protect sea approaches, has never given up their operation and today maintains the world's largest force, which complements maritime patrol landplanes of Ilyushin Il-38 type. The only nation to rival the Soviet Union is Japan, though the number of Shin Meiwas operated is tiny in comparison.

The old Beriev Be-6 can still be found flying with the Air Force of the Chinese People's Liberation Army and People's Navy, which have small numbers in service. First flown in 1949 the Be-6 resembles the Be-12 which superseded it in Soviet use but is powered by two 2400-hp Shvetsov ASh-73TK radial piston engines mounted on the leading edges of the high wings. With five 23-mm NR-23 cannon for defensive armament (each with 200-275 rounds of ammunition) and the normal offensive ASW weapons it can fly at 257 mph (415 km/h).

The Soviet Navy force of approximately 80 or more Beriev Be-12s is mainly distributed around bases of the Black Sea and Northern Fleets and are tasked with surveillance and antisubmarine duties. Using nose radar and MAD equipment carried out in a tail 'sting' the Be-12 can patrol hundreds of miles out to sea for long periods and mount attacks on submarines or surface craft with internally or externally carried weapons. It has been reported that the People's Army Air Force of Vietnam also has a dozen Be-12s in its inventory. This, however, may not be the case but may merely represent Soviet aircraft operated out of that country, as were once a number of Be-12s from Egypt. Be-12s entered Soviet service in the mid-1960s.

Below: Beriev Be-12 Tchaika (NATO Mail) ASW and patrol amphibian.

Specifications (Be-12 data)

Weapons: Torpedoes, mines, depth charges and sonobuoys in the hull bay, plus rockets, bombs or antiship missiles under the wings.
Accommodation: 5 crew.
Wingspan: 97 ft 5½ in (29.71 m).
Length: 98 ft 11¾ in (30.17 m).
Maximum take-off weight: 68,343 lb (31,000 kg).
Maximum speed: 378 mph (608 km/h).
Range: 4660 miles (7500 km).
Mission performance: Rate of climb at sea level 2995 ft (912 m) per min; ceiling 37,075 ft (11,300 m).
Engines: Two 4190-ehp Ivchenko AI-20D turboprops, with 11,000 liters of fuel.

Versions in service

Be-6: Predecessor to the Be-12, with piston engines. Withdrawn from the ASW/patrol role with the Soviet Navy during the 1970s, although some continued for a short time thereafter in fishery protection and utility capacities. Only currently operated by China.
Be-12: Turboprop development of Be-6, currently the second largest military flying-boat in service.
Operators: China (air force and navy, Be-6) and Soviet Union (navy, Be-12).

Boeing Model 707/C-135 Stratotanker/Stratolifter and Model 720, E-8A and EC-18A
United States

The Boeing Model 367-80 was first flown on 15 July 1954 as a tanker-transport demonstrator, developed at company expense and the first United States turbojet-powered transport to fly. Massive orders for KC-135 tanker-transports for the USAF followed quickly, while in July 1955 Boeing was given permission to manufacture commercial airliner variants as Model 707s. No fewer than

Below: Boeing KC-135R Stratotanker, with CFM turbofan engines and its 'flying boom' lowered.

732 KC-135A Stratotankers were built, followed by C-135 Stratolifters with the refuelling equipment deleted. The tankers were ideal for refuelling the fast combat jets then in service or planned, able to match their speeds and altitudes, something the previous Boeing KC-97 was struggling to do. The French air force also received a dozen C-135Fs to refuel Mirage IV supersonic strategic bombers, and since then other nations have had 707s converted into tankers, including those for the Canadian armed forces, Royal Moroccan Air Force and the Royal Saudi Air Force (latter as KE-3As). A feature of tanker versions is that they possess a dual role, able to perform as troop/freight transports when required.

Saudi KE-3As differ from standard 707s in having CFM International CFM56 turbofan engines fitted, and this same engine is currently being retrofitted into existing USAF KC-135As to extend their useful lives well into the next century and make them far more economical to operate. The first of an expected total of 630 KC-135As to be modified into KC-135Rs were redelivered to the 384th Air Refuelling Wing in July 1985. The French tankers are also being modified, the first C-135FR going back into service in August 1985. In a similar program KC-135s in Air Force Reserve and Air National Guard squadrons are being updated to use JT3D turbofans and other components from ex-airliners. These follow on from a small number of C-135E/KC-135E/NKC-135E/EC-135H/EC-135K/EC-135N/EC-135P/RC-135T USAF special mission aircraft similarly re-engined and returned in 1981. Foreign modifications include a single Argentine Air Force 707 that has been converted by IAI in Israel for electronic countermeasures and signal intelligence roles and two as flight refuelling tankers.

The USAF has many special-purpose versions of the C-135, the better known of which are detailed below. In addition, two ex-American Airlines 707s are being modified as demonstrator USAF/US Army E-8A J/STARS (Joint Surveillance Target Attack Radar

System) aircraft, to fly from 1988, with perhaps up to ten production aircraft to follow in the 1990s. Six other ex-AA 707s are becoming EC-18B ARIAs (Advanced Range Instrumentation Aircraft) for use by the 4950th Test Wing and have the largest-ever steerable radar antenna to be fitted in an aircraft. These will support US Army/Navy ballistic and cruise missile testing, the Shuttle program and satellite launches.

Specifications (KC-135A Stratotanker data)

Accommodation: 6 crew plus 80 passengers, 56,000 lb (25,400 kg) of freight or a total of 118,105 liters of fuel as a flight refuelling tanker. Uses the flying-boom and probe-and-drogue fuel transfer systems.
Wingspan: 130 ft 10 in (39.88 m).
Length: 136 ft 3 in (41.52 m).
Maximum take-off weight: 297,000 lb (134,717 kg).
Cruising speed: 585 mph (941 km/h).
Range: Carrying 120,000 lb of fuel to transfer, 1150 miles (1850 km).
Mission performance: Ceiling 50,000 ft (15,240 m).
Engines: Four 13,750-lb (6237-kg) thrust Pratt & Whitney J57-PW-59W turbojets.

Versions in service

C-135A/B Stratolifters, RC-135E/M and WC-135B: 13 of the 45 C-135s built for MAC (then MAT), USAF, remain in service in one form or another: as 126-troop/87,100 lb (39,510 kg) freight/44-stretcher and 54 seated casualty C-135A or B transports (J57-PW-59W turbojet and TF33-P-5 turbofan engines respectively), some C-135Bs being modified to have VIP interiors; RC-135C and M electronic reconnaissance aircraft; and WC-135B long-range weather reconnaissance aircraft.
C-135F and FR: French Air Force tankers, the latter designation after CFM56-2B-1 turbofans have been fitted in an update program.
C-137B and C: Five VIP 707s flown by the 89th Military Airlift Wing, USAF, including two 707-320Cs (one as 'Air Force One,' the Presidential transport). The latter two are to

Above: Boeing T-43A navigation trainer.

be superseded by C-25As.

EC-135A/C/G/K/L/H/P/Y: Airborne command post and communications relay aircraft, assigned to Strategic Air Command, Tactical Air Command, Pacific and European commands of the USAF. SAC EC-135Cs can direct bomber- and land-based ballistic missile forces if the normal ground command stations are made inoperable by enemy action, one remaining airborne at all times. EC-135Hs, Ks and Ps were among the 18 special mission aircraft originally converted to use JT3D turbofans.

EC-135N: JT3D turbofans. ARIA aircraft, each with a bulbous nose carrying an antenna. To be superseded by EC-18Bs.

KC-135A and R Stratotanker: Tanker-transports, as detailed above. These are being upgraded to KC-135R standard with CFM56-2B-1 turbofans. Reserve Stratotankers have been brought up to KC-135E standard.

KC-135E: AFRES and ANG KC-135A Stratotankers after modification, including the use of Pratt & Whitney JT3D-3B turbofans and modifications to the braking system. 128 KC-135s have been modified to this standard.

NKC-135: Testbed aircraft. Airborne laser laboratory models are used in the High Energy Laser (HEL) research program. Two NKC-135Es have been re-engined with JT3D turbofans.

RC-135S/T/U/V/W: Electronic reconnaissance models.

WC-135B: Ten C-135Bs were modified for long-range weather reconnaissance duties, but not all remain.

E-8A J/STARS: Initially 2 Joint Surveillance Target Attack Radar System aircraft, based on 707-323C airliners. The first to fly in 1988.

EC-18B ARIA: Four to supersede EC-135Ns in Advanced Range Instrumentation Aircraft configuration, with bulbous noses (each containing steerable antenna) and wingtip probe antenna.

Model 707: Several Model 707 airliners serve with air forces, some converted into flight refuelling tankers and others into electronic warfare aircraft (*see* Introduction). Saudi tankers are designated KE-3As and are powered by CFM-56 engines.

Model 720: Improved performance version of the Model 707, with modified wings (greater sweepback and reduced thickness/chord ratio). The 720's turbojet engines were superseded by JT3D turbofans on the 720B. Ecuador and Taiwan operate 720Bs.

Operators: Argentina (707), Australia (707), Canada (707 designated CC-137), Colombia (707?), Ecuador (707 and 720B), Egypt (707), France (C-135F/FR), West Germany (707), Indonesia (707), Iran (707), Israel (707), Morocco (707), Saudi Arabia (KE-3A), Taiwan (720B) and United States (air force, navy/marine corps; versions as above).

Boeing Model 737, T-43A and Surveiller
United States

This short-range airliner was Boeing's first twin jet, making its maiden flight on 9 April 1967. Five air forces use Model 737s in transport roles but with two others the missions are more specialized. The USAF's T-43A is a navigation trainer based on the Model 737-200, with equipment as given below. The Indonesian Air Force received three Surveillers, the specialized maritime surveillance model but in this case fitted with 14 first-class and 88 tourist-class seats for use also as government transports.

Specifications (T-43A data)
Equipment: Radar, inertial and celestial navigation systems, long-range navigation (LORAN), and other radio systems.
Accommodation: 3 instructors, 4 navigator proficiency pupils and 12 trainees.
Wingspan: 93 ft 0 in (28.35 m).
Length: 100 ft 0 in (30.48 m).
Maximum take-off weight: 115,500 lb (52,390 kg).

Maximum speed: 586 mph (943 km/h).
Range: 2995 miles (4820 km).
Mission performance: Rate of climb at sea level 3760 ft (1145 m) per min; endurance 6 h.
Engines: Two 14,500-lb (6577-kg) thrust Pratt & Whitney JT8D-9 turbofans.

Versions in service
Model 737: Transport aircraft in military service are based upon the Model 737-200/C, with seating for 115-130 passengers or freight.

Surveiller: Specialized maritime surveillance version of the Model 737-200, with Motorola APS-94D side-looking airborne modular multimission radar (SLAMMR) that can detect small vessels in heavy seas to a distance of 100 nm to port and starboard when the aircraft is flying at 30,000 ft (9150 m). Indonesian aircraft have passenger seats as detailed above.

T-43A: USAF navigation trainer, based upon the Model 737-200. T-43As form the air element of the Undergraduate Navigator Training System, complemented by land-based Honeywell T-45 electronic simulators.

Operators: Brazil (737), India (737), Indonesia (Surveiller), Mexico (737), Thailand (737), United States (T-43A) and Venezuela (737).

Boeing Model 747, C-19A and C-25A
United States

The Islamic Republic of Iran Air Force operates between seven and nine Model 747Fs as tanker-transports.

In addition to the E-4 Command Post aircraft the USAF will operate two Model 747-200Bs from 1988/89 as C-25A 'Air Force Ones,' superseding Model 707-320Cs as the airlift aircraft for the President of the United States. Each will have the very latest communications equipment installed.

Under the Civil Reserve Air Fleet (CRAF) program 19 Pan American Model 747s have been modified so that they can provide bulk freight transportation for the military in an

Above: Impression of the C-25A 'Air Force One' US Presidential transport, for delivery in November 1988.

emergency. Designated C-19As, they remain flying in a commercial capacity until needed. Each has a strengthened floor, a new freight door and a freight handling system, raising the aircraft's empty weight.

Specifications (C-25A data)
Accommodation: 23 crew and 80 passengers.
Wingspan: 195 ft 8 in (59.64 m).
Length: 231 ft 10 in (70.66 m).
Maximum take-off weight: 803,700 lb (364,550 kg).
Range: More than 6910 miles (11,120 km).
Engines: Four 56,750-lb (25,740-kg) thrust General Electric CF6-80C2B1 turbofans 202,940 liters of fuel.
Versions in service
As above.
Operators: Iran (747F) and United States (C-25A and C-19A in an emergency).

Boeing B-52 Stratofortress
United States

In the late 1940s the global strategic bombing missions of the USAAF Strategic Air Command could not be flown by a jet. Then in 1949-50 the advent of the powerful and economical J57 engine made this possible, but the B-52 had to be so big it needed eight of these engines. Other unusual features included giant spoilers along the top of the wings, and four main undercarriage trucks which could be steered in unison to line them up with the runway in crabwise cross-wind landings. The first prototype flew on 15 April 1952, and the initial production model entered service in 1955. A total of 744 were delivered in eight major versions. Today the only models in service are the last two, the B-52G (193 built) and B-52H (102 built). The G introduced a 'wet wing,' with the structure itself forming vast integral fuel tanks. It also moved the tail gunner forward into the main pressurized crew compartment where he could fire the four 0.5-in tail guns by remote control, and the vertical tail was made 8 ft

(2.44 m) shorter. Large pylons were added under the inner wings, and today these are used for either 12 SRAMs or 12 ALCMs (*see* data). A further eight of either type of missile can be attached to a rotary launcher in the internal weapons bay, though many of the aircraft have not yet been converted to fire the cruise missile. The engines are advanced versions of the original J57, driving the accessories directly through shafts inside the engine pods, whereas the earliest models bled hot air from the engines and used this to drive small accessory-power turbines in the fuselage.

The chief advance in the B-52H was the switch to the TF33 turbofan engine, which greatly extended the mission radius. This model also has a single tail gun of the 20-mm 'Gatling' type as used in fighters. Both the G and H have been progressively updated with many new avionics systems for better navigation, self-defense electronic warfare capability, global communications and safe flight at low levels. Altogether 99 Gs are being converted to carry cruise missiles, the other 69 of an active force of 168 being equipped to

Above: Boeing B-52G Stratofortress eight-engined strategic bomber.
Below: AGM-86B air-launched cruise missiles under the wings of a B-52G.

carry nuclear or conventional bombs or, in the maritime role, the Harpoon antiship missile (superseding B-52Ds). The whole active force of 96 B-52H bombers will be converted to carry cruise missiles.

Specifications (B-52H data unless otherwise stated)

Radar: New OAS (Offensive Avionics System) is currently being fitted to the B-52G and H, comprising a Teledyne Ryan Doppler radar, Honeywell AN/ASN-131 gimballed electrostatic airborne inertial navigation system, IBM/Raytheon ASQ-38 analog bombing/navigation system with digital processing, Norden improved strategic radar with upgraded terrain avoidance and ground mapping, and other systems. Westinghouse AN/ALQ-153 pulse-Doppler tail warning radar for detection of threats from the rear, and Emerson AN/ASG-21 fire-control radar for the tail cannon of the B-52H; B-52G uses AN/ASG-15 fire-control radar for its tail guns.

Weapons: One 20-mm M61 Vulcan multibarrel cannon in the tail plus 12 air-launched cruise missiles underwing and 8 SRAM short-range nuclear attack missiles together with free-fall bombs in the bay. Eventually ALCMs will be a bay option also on all B-52Hs, making 20 ALCMs.

Accommodation: 6 crew.

Wingspan: 185 ft 0 in (56.39 m).

Length: 160 ft 11 in (49.05 m).

Maximum take-off weight: 488,000 lb (221,350 kg).

Maximum speed: 595 mph (957 km/h).

Range: Over 10,000 miles (16,090 km) unrefuelled.

Mission performance: Ceiling 55,000 ft (16,765 m).

Engines: Eight 17,000-lb (7711-kg) thrust Pratt & Whitney TF33-P-3 turbofans, with 174,129 liters of fuel standard.

Versions in service

B-52G: Four 0.50-in machine guns. 12 ALCMs, 8 SRAMs and nuclear free-fall bombs. Those B-52Gs assigned a maritime role carry 8-10 Harpoon antishipping missiles. Eight 13,750-lb (6237-kg) thrust J57-P-43WB turbojets.

B-52H: As detailed above.

Operator: United States.

Boeing E-3 Sentry
United States

By deploying the E-3 Sentry, the USAF introduced by far the most capable airborne early warning and control aircraft ever put into service anywhere. Based on the airframe of a Boeing 707-320B airliner, the E-3 has as its principal sensor system a Westinghouse AN/APY-2 surveillance and early warning radar, the scanner of which is carried with other equipment in an above-fuselage rotodome that rotates at a rate of six revolutions every minute during actual operations. When flying at its operating altitude, the E-3 can scan to a range of hundreds of miles, detecting, tracking and identifying targets flying at high and low levels in all weather conditions and over all terrain, combining also a maritime surveillance capability. Among the most difficult targets to detect are low-flying aircraft and missiles, but even these can be picked up at a range of about 200 nautical miles. This detection/tracking ability is coupled with another to guide friendly air defense forces on to the incoming targets, thereby making the best use of what could be outnumbered resources (including operations within NORAD – North American Air Defense Command), while E-3s can also be used to assist friendly strike aircraft evade enemy defenses as part of tactical missions. Because AWACS (airborne warning and control system) aircraft would be prime targets at the outbreak of war, their best work could be undertaken in the days or even hours before hostilities started, though they are designed to be capable of surviving and resist jamming.

E-3s are not confined just to the USAF, as detailed below, and the RAF looks set to be a future user now that Nimrod AEW.3 has been cancelled. NATO E-3s have operating bases in West Germany, Greece, Italy, Norway and Turkey. Several civilian support roles are also offered by the E-3, included among which are those assisting the United States drug-enforcement agencies.

Specifications (Standard E-3A data)

Radar: Westinghouse surveillance radar, as detailed above. Much other equipment and avionics.

Weapons: A number of the E-3s have underwing pylons that could carry self-defense weapons if required.

Below: NATO/OTAN Boeing E-3A Sentry.

Accommodation: Flight crew of 4 plus 16 avionics operators.
Wingspan: 145 ft 9 in (44.42 m).
Length: 152 ft 11 in (46.61 m).
Maximum take-off weight: 325,000 lb (147,415 kg).
Maximum speed: 530 mph (853 km/h).
Mission performance: Ceiling more than 29,000 ft (8840 m); endurance over 11 h without flight refuelling.
Engines: Four 21,000-lb (9525-kg) thrust Pratt & Whitney TF33-PW-100 or 100A turbofans.

Versions in service

E-3A: Initial version, sometimes referred to as the Core E-3A, first going to Tactical Air Command's 552nd Airborne Warning and Control Wing in Oklahoma (the home of the first EC-121C Constellation AWACS aircraft in 1953). 24 delivered to the USAF. The first prototype had flown as an EC-137D trial aircraft on 9 February 1972.
Standard E-3A: USAF and NATO (OTAN) version, covering 10 aircraft delivered from 1981. Changes to the radar give maritime surveillance capability. Underwing pylons for weapons and extra electronic countermeasures equipment if required.
E-3B: 22 E-3As and 2 prototypes are being updated to this standard, with many improvements to the avionics.The first became operational again in 1984.
E-3C: This designation covers 10 USAF Standard E-3As after the addition of extra avionics to improve command and control.
E-3A and KE-3A Peace Sentinel: Of the 13 E-3 type aircraft delivered to the Royal Saudi Air Force between 1986 and 1987 (CFM56-2 engines), 8 are KE-3A tanker versions.
Operators: NATO, Saudi Arabia (E-3A and KE-3A), eventually United Kingdom and United States.

Boeing E-4B
United States

Just four aircraft make up the USAF's E-4B fleet, assigned the task of advanced airborne command post and providing a communica-

Below: Boeing E-4B NEACP (National Emergency Airborne Command Post).

tions link between the US strategic forces and the US National Command Authority in the event of an attack upon the United States.

First flown on 13 June 1973, the initial aircraft and the following two began as E-4As but were subsequently brought up to the same standard as the fourth aircraft which was built to full E-4B form. Operated by Strategic Air Command from a base in Nebraska, each E-4B has nuclear thermal shielding to improve survivability, a high-power very low frequency communications system that is difficult for an enemy to jam and can function in a nuclear atmospheric environment, and can use satellites which further reduces the possible effects of enemy electronic warfare. The aircraft's very low frequency communications system uses two trailing wire antennae, the longer approximately 26,000 feet (7925 m) long. The super high frequency satellite link employs dish antennae carried inside the large blister above the forward fuselage.

Specifications

Radar: E-4B carries research radar in nosecone.
Accommodation: 94 crew members can be

Above: Boeing E-6 Tacamo US Navy communications relay aircraft.

carried, including flight crew, battle staff and rest crews.
Wingspan: 195 ft 8 in (59.64 m).
Length: 231 ft 4 in (70.51 m).
Maximum take-off weight: 800,000 lb (362,873 kg).
Mission performance: Unrefuelled endurance about 12 h; refuelled endurance 72 h.
Engines: Four 52,500-lb (23,814-kg) thrust General Electric CF6-50E turbofans.

Version in service

E-4B: 4 aircraft, as advanced airborne command posts for SAC.
Operator: United States.

Boeing E-6A Tacamo
United States

Tacamo (TAke Charge And Move Out) is the name given to US Navy aircraft assigned the difficult and specialist role of relaying emergency mission communications between the US National Command Authority and the Navy's ballistic missile submarine fleet. At least one Tacamo assigned each to the Pacific and to the Atlantic and Mediterranean is airborne at all times, with others ready on the ground as backups in case they are needed. This ensures a link between ground or airborne command authorities and the retaliatory submarines even in the event of a major attack upon the United States. At present this mission is undertaken by the EC-130Q version of the Lockheed Hercules, but as the Trident submarine becomes increasingly important so the major share of Tacamo support is being handled by the new E-6A.

Based upon the same Model 707/C-135 airframe as the E-3 Sentry, it is intended that by 1993 the US Navy will have a Tacamo complement of 15 E-6As, alongside just 10 EC-130Qs. The first Boeing E-6A flew in early 1987 and initial operational capability is scheduled for November 1988.

The E-6A carries a great deal of specialized avionics and equipment, hardened to remain operational in an electromagnetic interference environment. Using a very low frequency antenna, comprising a 26,000 ft (7925 m) wire aerial with a drogue at its end (which is winched out) and another 4000 ft (1219 m) dipole aerial, a link is established with the ground authorities and the submarines. Further links are established with airborne command post aircraft and the Presidential Boeing E-4, to satellites (satcom) and the emergency rocket communications system (ERCS).

Specifications
Radar: Bendix AN/APS-133 digital color radar in the nosecone, a high-performance weather, tanker-beacon homing, short-range terrain mapping and waypoint display system. In the air-to-air mode, it detects and tracks tanker aircraft for flight refuelling. A fuel-receiving boom is carried over the flight deck to prolong missions up to 72 hours.
Accommodation: Flight crew of four, plus specialist mission operators.
Wingspan: 145 ft 9 in (44.42 m).
Length: 152 ft 11 in (46.61 m).
Maximum take-off weight: 342,000 lb (155,130 kg).
Maximum speed: 604 mph (972 km/h).
Unrefuelled range: 7715 miles (12,415 km).
Mission performance: Ceiling 42,000 ft (12,800 m); patrol altitude 25,000-30,000 ft (7620-9145 m); unrefuelled endurance on station 16 h.
Engines: Four 22,000-lb (9979-kg) thrust CFM International F108-CF-100 turbofans.
Version in service
E-6A Tacamo: For service with the US Navy from 1988.
Operator: United States (navy).

Below: RAF Boeing Vertol Chinook HC.Mk 1.

Boeing Vertol CH-47 Chinook
United States

First flown as a prototype on 21 September 1961, the Chinook is the standard medium transport helicopter of the US Army, has been exported, and has also been built in Italy by Elicotteri Meridionali as well as in Japan. A typical Boeing Vertol design, the twin tandem rotors (both pylon-mounted and with the rear higher than the forward and overlapping) turn in opposite directions to compensate for torque. Entry into the main cabin is via a rear ramp which permits easy loading, fast deployment of troops, or air dispatch of free-falling or parachute-assisted cargo.

Specifications (CH-47D Chinook data)
Accommodation: 2 or 3 crew plus up to 44 troops, 24 stretchers and 2 attendants, vehicles or freight. A sling load of 28,000 lb (12,700 kg) is possible as a flying crane.
Diameter of each rotor: 60 ft 0 in (18.29 m).
Fuselage length: 51 ft 0 in (15.54 m).
Maximum take-off weight: 50,000 lb (22,680 kg).
Maximum speed: 181 mph (291 km/h) at 33,000-lb (14,968-kg) AUW.
Mission radius: 115 miles (185 km) at 44,000-lb (19,958-kg) AUW.
Mission performance: Rate of climb at sea level 1980 ft (605 m) per min at 44,000-lb (19,958-kg) AUW; ceiling 12,800 ft (3,900 m) at 33,000-lb (14,968-kg) AUW; hovering ceiling out of ground effect 10,000 ft (3050 m) at 44,000-lb (19,958-kg) AUW.
Engines: Two 3750-shp Avco Lycoming T55-L-712 turboshafts, with 3899 liters of fuel.
Versions in service
CH-47A: First production version, with

2200-shp Avco Lycoming T55-L-5 or 2650-shp T55-L-7 turboshafts. Existing US Army CH-47As have had their transmissions uprated to a combined total of 7500 shp. 4 were delivered to Thailand.
CH-47B: US Army version of 1967 initial delivery, with 2850-shp T55-L-7Cs and new rotors incorporating blades with cambered leading edges. Transmissions uprated.
CH-47C: Two 3750-shp T55-L-11A turboshafts, strengthened transmissions, and increased fuel capacity. Delivered to the US Army from 1968. Currently being fitted with glassfiber rotor blades. Nine acquired by Canada as CH-147s and many Spanish Chinooks are of this type. Some RAF Chinook HC.Mk 1s are similar, with T55-L-11E engines (to be retrofitted with T55-L-712s) and allowance for composites material rotor blades; they carry Doppler radar and other avionics including radar-warning receivers, and accommodate 44 troops, freight, or 24 stretchers and attendants. EM-built Chinooks from Italy are of this type.
CH-47D: Current program to modernize to this standard existing US Army CH-47As, Bs and Cs. The total could reach 436 helicopters. Redelivery to the US Army began in 1982. The RAF has received 8 similar new helicopters.
CH-47D International Chinook: Export version, originally known as the Model 414. Also assembled/built in Japan by Kawasaki as the CH-47J for its indigenous air force and army. Spanish Internationals carry Bendix RDR-1400 weather radar in the nose.
Operators: Argentina (air force and army), Australia, Canada, Egypt, Greece (air force and army), Iran (army), Italy (army), Japan (air force and army), South Korea (?), Libya, Morocco, Spain (army), Thailand, United Kingdom and United States (army).

Boeing Vertol H-46 Sea Knight/ Kawasaki KV107
United States and Japan

When in 1960 Boeing took over the former Vertol company, it inherited the Model 107 which had first flown as a prototype on 22 April 1958 and had a touch of the Piasecki 'flying banana' look about it (Vertol having been formed out of the Piasecki Helicopter Corporation in 1956). Boeing Vertol delivered 624 Sea Knights to the US Navy and Marine Corps between 1964 and 1971 for assault, transport and vertrep (vertical replenishment), for ship and shore operation under CH-46 and UH-46 designations. From 1977, 273 of these were upgraded to CH-46E standard, with 1870-shp General Electric T58-GE-16 turboshafts and other changes including automatic navigation systems. Canada received CH-113 Labradors for its air force and CH-113A Voyageurs for its army, and the Swedish Air Force and Navy received HKp 4s with British Bristol Siddeley Gnome H.1200 turboshafts for search and rescue and antisubmarine warfare.

Some of the Swedish helicopters came from Japan, where in 1962 Kawasaki had flown its first Model 107 built under license, and in 1965 gained full worldwide sales rights for the helicopter from Boeing Vertol. The KV107IIA from Kawasaki is the currently available model.

Above: US Marine Corps Boeing Vertol CH-46E Sea Knight with safety, reliability and maintainability (SR&M) improvements.

Specifications (KV107IIA data)
Radar: Provision for radar.
Weapons and equipment: Antisubmarine weapons, mine countermeasures/minesweeping/retrieving equipment, SAR equipment, etc for appropriate helicopters.
Accommodation: 2 or 3 crew plus 26 troops, freight including vehicles, 15 stretchers and attendants, etc.
Diameter of rotor: 50 ft 0 in (15.24 m).
Fuselage length: 44 ft 7 in (13.59 m).
Maximum take-off weight: 21,400 lb (9706 kg).
Maximum speed: 158 mph (254 km/h).
Range: 222-682 miles (357-1097 km) depending on fuel carried.
Mission performance: Rate of climb at sea level 2050 ft (625 m) per min; ceiling 17,000 ft (5180 m); hovering ceiling in ground effect 11,700 ft (3565 m); hovering ceiling out of ground effect 8800 ft (2680 m).
Engines: Two 1400-shp General Electric CT58-140-1 turboshafts (or Ishikawajima-Harima-built examples). 1324 to 3785 liters of fuel.
Versions in service
C/UH-46 Sea Knight: Boeing Vertol versions, delivered to the US Navy and Marine Corps in CH-46A (1250-shp T58-GE-8B engines), CH-46D (1400 shp T58-GE-10 engines), CH-46F (similar to the D but with increased avionics and changes to the instrument panel), and UH-46A/D (US Navy vertrep) forms. CH-46E applies to updated early Sea Knights, as detailed above.
CH-113 and CH-113A: Canadian helicopters for transport and search and rescue.
HKp 4: Swedish helicopter with British engines for antisubmarine and search and rescue. As detailed above.
KV107: Kawasaki series, built in KV107IIA form since 1968. Models include the KV107IIA-3 mine countermeasures helicopter for the JMSDF, A-4 transport for the JGSDF, A-5 SAR helicopter for the

JASDF, and A-SM-1/2/3/4 versions for Saudi Arabia and used respectively for firefighting, aeromedical, VIP transport and ambulance roles.
Operators: Canada, Japan (air force, navy and army), Saudi Arabia, Sweden (air force and navy) and United States (navy and marine corps).

Breguet 1050 Alizé
France

Alizés have been the standard carrier-borne antisubmarine warfare aircraft of the French Navy since entering service in 1959. In configuration they are conventional turboprop-powered aircraft with hydraulically folding outer wing panels and a retractable 'dustbin' radome in the rear of the fuselage housing the search radar.

The French Navy received 75 production Alizés, of which 34 remain in service. Of these 28 have recently been modified to extend their useful life into the next decade, being equipped with new Thomson-CSF Iguane radar, a new navigation system and ESM equipment. The Alizés operate with 6F Flottile at Nîmes-Garons.

In addition to French Navy aircraft, the Indian Navy received 17 Alizés from 1961, of which five or six remain operational.

Specifications (1050 Alizé data)
Radar: Thomson-CSF Iguane sea surveillance and maritime warfare radar, replaced earlier DRAA2A radar.
Weapons: Weapons bay for a torpedo or three depth charges, and underwing stations for two more depth charges and six 5-in rockets or two AS.12 air-to-surface missiles. Sonobuoys are carried in the forward section of the undercarriage nacelles.
Accommodation: 3 crew.
Wingspan: 51 ft 2 in (15.60 m).
Length: 45 ft 5¾ in (13.86 m).
Maximum take-off weight: 18,078 lb (8200 kg).
Maximum speed: 292 mph (470 km/h).
Range: 1553 miles (2500 km).
Mission performance: Rate of climb at sea level 1378 ft (420 m) per min; ceiling 20,000 ft (6100 m); patrol speed 149-230 mph (240-370 km/h); endurance 5 h 10 min with standard fuel, 7 h 40 min with auxiliary fuel.
Engine: One 2100-ehp Rolls-Royce Dart RDa 7 Mk 21 turboprop, with 2101 liters of fuel standard.
Versions in service
Alizé: As above. All French Navy aircraft had been returned after modifications by 1986. Both French Navy carriers, *Clemenceau* and *Foch*, can carry one flight of Alizés. Indian Navy Alizés operate from the aircraft carrier *Vikrant*. (The ex-Royal Navy carrier HMS *Hermes* was purchased by India in 1986.)
Operators: France (navy) and India (navy).

Below: Breguet Alizé in its latest French Navy form.

Above: Canadair Challenger 600 used by the Canadian Department of National Defense for the electronic support/training role.

Canadair Challenger 600 and 601
Canada

Developed as a 12/19-passenger business and commuter transport from a William Lear Sr design known as the LearStar 600, the twin-turbofan Challenger flew for the first time on 8 November 1978. Specialized military versions have been offered and the Canadian Armed Forces has received seven Challenger 601s as special air mission transports and and four each of Challenger 600s and 601s as VIP transports. In addition, the West German Luftwaffe received seven Challenger 601s as special air mission transports and China ordered three Challenger 601s. Two Challenger 600s delivered to Malaysia for air force use are believed to have been handed back.

Specifications (Challenger 601 data)
Accommodation: Crew plus up to 19 passengers, according to requirements.
Wingspan: 64 ft 4 in (19.61 m) over winglets.
Length: 68 ft 5 in (20.85 m).
Maximum take-off weight: 43,100 lb (19,550 kg).
Cruising speed: 529 mph (851 km/h).
Range: 3960 miles (6371 km).
Mission performance: Maximum operating altitude 41,000 ft (12,500 m); G limit +2.6.
Engines: Two 9140-lb (4145-kg) thrust General Electric CF34-1A turbofans, with 9278 liters of fuel including auxiliary tank.
Versions in service
Challenger 600: Variant with two 7500-lb (3400-kg) thrust Avco Lycoming ALF 502L-2/L-3 turbofans and no winglets as standard. However winglets have been retrofitted/fitted to many aircraft of this version.
Challenger 601: Higher-powered version, with winglets as standard. Luftwaffe aircraft include 12/16-passenger, mixed passenger/cargo and air ambulance layouts.
Operators: Canada, China and West Germany.

Canadair CL-41 Tutor and Tebuan
Canada

Looking superficially like the earlier Cessna T-37 jet trainer but with many differences including the use of a single engine carried in the rear fuselage to exhaust from the tail, the CL-41 Tutor basic jet trainer first flew on 13 January 1960 and 190 CL-41As entered RCAF service between 1963 and 1966. More than 120 of these remain in use.

In addition, Canadair developed the CL-41G dual trainer/light attack version with a more powerful engine, additional armor protection and six stations for up to 4000 lb (1814 kg) of weapons. Malaysia became the only customer, taking 20 as Tebuans. However, with the delivery of Aermacchi MB-339As during the 1980s, the 10 remaining Tebuans were sent for maintenance before being passed to reserve forces.

Specifications (CL-41A data unless otherwise stated)
Weapons: 2 underwing pylons for 500-lb bombs, gun pods, rocket launchers, etc.
Accommodation: Student pilot and instructor side by side.
Wingspan: 36 ft 6 in (11.13 m).
Length: 32 ft 0 in (9.75 m).
Maximum take-off weight: 7397 lb (3355 kg).
Maximum speed: 498 mph (801 km/h).
Range: Tebuan 1340 miles (2157 km).
Mission performance: Ceiling 43,000 ft (13,100 m).
Engine: One 2633-lb (1195-kg) thrust Orenda/General Electric J85-CAN-40 turbojet.
Versions in service
CL-41A Tutor: Ab initio and basic jet trainer.
CL-41G Tebuan: Current status uncertain.
Operators: Canada (Tutor) and Malaysia (reserve, Tebuan?)

Canadair CL-215
Canada

First flown on 23 October 1967, the CL-215 is a highly successful general-purpose amphibian that is best known as a water-bomber for combating forest fires but has also been adopted for military use. It is an all-metal aircraft with a single-step hull, with wells in the hull sides into which the main undercarriage units retract. Military CL-215s are used mainly for search and rescue, Spain's eight being typical of this, though other uses can include patrol and transport. In addition to the air forces and navy listed below as operators, the governments of France, Italy and Venezuela received examples. Weapons are not carried by CL-215s, which can operate from bays, inland waterways, lakes or land.

Specifications (Canadair CL-215 data)
Radar: Search radar is available for SAR.

Below: Royal Malaysian Air Force Canadair CL-41G Tebuan.

Above: Spanish Air Force Canadair CL-215 amphibian.

Accommodation: Crew of 6 in a SAR role, including the 2 pilots, a navigator, flight engineer and observers. In a transport role, up to 26 passengers can be carried or 8518 lb (3864 kg) of cargo. (As a water-bomber, 5346 liters of water can be carried in fuselage tanks; chemicals can also be dropped when fire-fighting.)
Wingspan: 93 ft 10 in (28.60 m).
Length: 65 ft 0½ in (19.82 m).
Maximum take-off weight: 43,500 lb (19,731 kg).
Cruising speed: 181 mph (291 km/h).
Range: 1300 miles (2094 km).
Mission performance: Rate of climb at sea level 1000 ft (305 m) per min.
Engines: Two 2100-hp Pratt & Whitney R-2800-CA3 radials, with 5910 liters of fuel.

Below: Spanish Air Force CASA C-101EB Aviojets, military designated E.25 Mirlos.

Versions in service
CL-215: General-purpose amphibian, as detailed above. Spanish Air Force designation UD.13.
CL-215T: Proposed turboprop variant with 2000-shp PW100 engines. The first flight is expected to take place in 1988.
Operators: Spain, Thailand (navy) and Yugoslavia.

CASA C-101 Aviojet
Spain

Spain, like many other countries with thriving aircraft industries, decided to fulfill its own requirement for a modern basic and advanced jet trainer with light attack capability by developing an indigenous product, the resulting Aviojet making its maiden flight as a prototype on 27 June 1977. Assistance in its design was given by MBB of West Germany and Northrop of the United States. Chile, the most important export customer in terms of

units ordered, has set up its own assembly line at Santiago, ENAER-completed T-36 Halcóns joining the 1st Air Group's flying school in 1983. CASA and ENAER collaborated on a program to develop a higher-powered version with enhanced attack capability (C-101CC), as detailed below. One of the principal design features of the Aviojet is the fuselage bay into which interchangeable gun, camera, laser designator and electronic countermeasures packs can be fitted.

Specifications (C-101CC data)
Weapons: Fuselage bay accommodates a detachable pack carrying either a 30-mm DEFA cannon, two 12.7-mm guns, or the equipment mentioned above. 6 underwing pylons for up to 4960 lb (2250 kg) of weapons, including guns, rocket launchers, bombs, two Maverick air-to-surface missiles, etc.
Accommodation: Student pilot and instructor in tandem, the rear seat raised.
Wingspan: 34 ft 9½ in (10.60 m).
Length: 41 ft 0 in (12.50 m).
Maximum take-off weight: 13,890 lb (6300 kg).
Maximum speed: 518 mph (834 km/h).
Combat radius: 374 miles (602 km) with 2 Mavericks and a DEFA cannon pack, and reserves.
Mission performance: Rate of climb at sea level 4900 ft (1494 m) per min; ceiling 42,000 ft (12,800 m); G limits +7.5 at 10,582-lb (4800-kg) AUW, −3.9 at 10,582-lb (4800-kg) AUW; endurance 7 h.
Engine: One 4300-lb (1950-kg) thrust Garrett TFE731-5-1J turbofan, with 2414 liters of fuel.

Versions in service
C-101EB: Spanish trainer, known as the E.25 Mirlo. Powered by one 3500-lb (1588-kg) thrust TFE731-2-2J engine. Same weapon positions and total load as for C-101CC, but fewer options (no Maverick, for example).
C-101BB: Export version, with a 3700-lb (1678-kg) thrust TFE731-3-1J engine. License-assembled by ENAER as the T-36 Halcón.
C-101CC: Most powerful version, enhanced for attack missions. As detailed above. License-assembled by ENAER as A-36 Halcón.

C-101DD: Latest version, principally for training but with the TFE731-5-1J engine. Equipment includes a HUD, weapon-aiming computer and inertial attitude/heading reference system, and more.
Operators: Chile (T-36 and A-36), Honduras (C-101BB), Jordan (C-101CC) and Spain (E.25 Mirlo).

CASA C-212 Aviocar
Spain

A light STOL utility transport capable also of fulfilling other specialized roles such as photographic, navigation trainer, antisubmarine (ASW), maritime patrol, SAR and electronic missions (ECM and elint) with the appropriate equipment fitted. The Series 100 prototype first flew on 26 March 1971 and by 1986 Aviocar orders had peaked 390, about half for military use.

Specifications (C-212 Series 200 data)
Radar: Bendix or Sperry weather radar. Eaton AN/APS-128 surveillance radar in a nose radome for the maritime patrol and SAR version, which has optional FLIR. Underfuselage radar with 360-degree scanning for the ASW model, which also features electronic support measures, sonobuoys, etc.
Weapons: All military Aviocars have the option of gun pods or rocket launchers on the fuselage sides. Weapons for ASW maritime patrol include torpedoes (including Sting Ray) and air-to-surface missiles of AS.15TT or Sea Skua types.
Accommodation: 2 crew plus 24 troops/paratroops, 12 stretchers and 4 sitting casualties/attendants, or up to 6107 lb (2770 kg) of freight loaded via the rear ramp/door.
Wingspan: 62 ft 4 in (19.00 m).
Length: 49 ft 8½ in (15.15 m).
Maximum take-off weight: 16,424 lb (7450 kg).
Cruising speed: 227 mph (365 km/h).
Range: 253-1094 miles (408-1760 km).

Below: The Royal Jordanian Air Force has CASA C-212A and C-212AV Aviocars in operation.

depending on payload.
Mission performance: Rate of climb at sea level 1555 ft (474 m); ceiling 28,000 ft (8535 m); G limits +3, −1.2.
Engines: Two 900-shp Garrett TPE331-10R-511C turboprops, with 2040 liters of fuel standard.
Versions in service
C-212A: Series 100 version for military transport work. Acquired by Indonesia (as IPTN NC-212S), Jordan, Nicaragua, Portugal and Spain. 776-ehp TPE331-5-251C engines.
C-212AV: Series 100 VIP transport for Jordan and Spain.
C-212B: Series 100 photographic survey version for Portugal and Spain.
C-212E: Series 100 navigation trainer for Spain.
C-212 Series 200: Superseded the Series 100 in 1979. Used for many roles, as detailed above. The ASW/maritime patrol/SAR models are used by Spain, Sweden (as the TP89), Sudan, Uruguay and Venezuela. The elint/ECM model is in use with Portugal and others.
C-212 Series 300: 1987 model, with 925-shp TPE331-10R-513C turboprops, a payload of 6217 lb (2820 kg), and a cruising speed of 228 mph (367 km/h).
Operators: Abu Dhabi, Angola (army), Chad, Chile (air force, navy and army),

Above: Cessna T-37B jet trainer.

Colombia, Equatorial Guinea, Indonesia (air force, navy and army), Jordan, Malaysia, Mexico (navy), Nicaragua, Panama, Portugal, Somali Republic, Spain, Sudan, Sweden (navy and coast guard), Uruguay, Venezuela (navy) and Zimbabwe.

Cessna A-37 Dragonfly, OA-37B and T-37
United States

First flown on 12 October 1954, the T-37 was the first jet trainer designed as such to join the USAF, which it did as a basic trainer in 1957. A staggering 1268 T-37s of all versions had been built by the end of production in 1977, including those exported to other air forces. Today the USAF retains over 600 T-37s, which may continue for some years yet if the proposed re-engining and modification program is funded following the cancellation of the Fairchild Republic T-46As.

A COIN (counter insurgency) derivative had flown as a prototype on 22 October 1963, and production of this version began by converting T-37s. New production began after the 39 A-37As with the A-37B, and 538 were eventually built. Flown in Vietnam, a substantial number remained with the South

Vietnamese Air Force when the war ended, allowing Vietnam to remain a major user until recently. Other A-37Bs were exported or transferred. The A-37B as such is no longer in USAF or reserve service, although a number have been modified into OA-37Bs for Air National Guard use as forward air control (FAC) aircraft, superseding O-2As.

Specifications (T-37B data)
Accommodation: Student pilot and instructor side by side.
Wingspan: 33 ft 9¼ in (10.30 m).
Length: 29 ft 3 in (8.92 m).
Maximum take-off weight: 6600 lb (2993 kg).
Maximum speed: 426 mph (685 km/h).
Range: 870 miles (1400 km).
Mission performance: Rate of climb at sea level 3020 ft (920 m) per min; ceiling 35,100 ft (10,700 m).
Engines: Two 1025-lb (465-kg) thrust Continental J69-T-25 turbojets, with 1170 liters of fuel standard.

Versions in service
A-37B: Production attack version, first flown in 1967. One 7.62-mm GAU-2B/A minigun in the fuselage, plus bombs, rocket launchers, gun pods, etc, carried on 8 underwing pylons.
OA-37B: FAC modification of the A-37B for ANG service. Armament capabilities retained. Powered by two 2850-lb (1293-kg) thrust General Electric J85-GE-17A turbojets, as for A-37B. Maximum speed 507 mph (816 km/h).
T-37B: Second production of the A-37 trainer, as detailed above.
T-37C: Export model. Similar to T-37B but with provision for 250-lb (113-kg) bombs or Sidewinder air-to-air missiles, or reconnaissance cameras.
Operators: Burma (T-37C), Chile (A-37B and T-37B/C), Colombia (A-37B and T-37C), Ecuador (A-37B), El Salvador (A-37B), West Germany (T-37B), Greece (T-37C), Guatemala (A-37B and T-37C), Honduras (A-37B), Jordan (T-37C), South Korea (T-37C), Pakistan (T-37C), Peru (A-37B and T-37B/C), Portugal (T-37C) Thailand (A-37B and T-37B), Turkey (T-37C), United States (T-37B and OA-37B) and Uruguay (A-37B).

Cessna Models 310/320 Skyknight, 340, 401, 402, 404 Titan, 411, 414, 421 Golden Eagle, Citation I and Citation II
United States

This grouping covers a wide range of Cessna twin-engined light transports and light twin-jets that undertake various utility, survey, liaison, transport and training roles with the air forces given below. Arguably the most important of these are the 15 Model 552 Citation IIs taken into US Navy service as T-47As, superseding T-39Ds in the role of training flight crews in the use of airborne radar equipment.

Specifications (Model 552/T-47A data)
Radar: Emerson AN/APQ-159 radar in nose.
Accommodation: Pilot, instructor and three trainees.
Wingspan: 46 ft 6 in (14.18 m).
Length: 47 ft 10¾ in (14.60 m).
Maximum take-off weight: 15,000 lb (6804 kg).

Cruising speed: 463 mph (746 km/h).
Range: 2300 miles (3700 km).
Engines: Two 2900-lb (1315-kg) thrust Pratt & Whitney Canada JT15D-5 turbofans, with 3263 liters of fuel.
Versions in service and Operators
Model 310/320 Skyknight: Appeared in 1954. 6-seat light transport, powered by 2 Continental O-470 series engines of 240-260 hp. 160 Model 310As and 35 all-weather Model 310Es became U-3A and U-3B utility aircraft with the USAF, but today only the Navy and Army fly US examples. Operators are Bolivia (310), Dominican Republic (310), Ecuador (navy, 320), France (310), Guatemala (310), Indonesia (310), Iran (army, 310), Malagasy, Mexico (310), Peru (air force, 320; navy, 310), Philippines (310), Tanzania (310), United States (navy and army), Uruguay (310), Venezuela (navy, 310) and Zaire (310).
Model 340: Developed from the Model 310 as a pressurized 6-seater. Introduced in 1971. Two 310-hp Continental TSIO-520-NB piston engines initially. Operated by Thailand.
Model 401: 6/8-seat and larger development of the Model 310 type, first flown in 1965. Two 300-hp TSIO-520-E piston engines. Operators are Indonesia and Trinidad and Tobago.
Model 402: 6/10-seat transport, similar to the Model 410 but available with a convertible passenger/freight cabin. Same engines initially but with 325-hp TSIO-520-VBs. Operators are Bolivia, Comores Islands, Haiti, Indonesia, Malaysia, Mexico (navy), Panama, Paraguay and Venezuela (navy).
Model (404) Titan: 10-passenger, utility or freight transport, delivered to customers from 1976. Two 375-hp Continental GTSIO-520-M piston engines. Operators are Hong Kong, Sweden and Tanzania.
Model 411: 6/8-seat transport, of similar appearance to the Model 402. Two 340-hp Continental GTSIO-520-C piston engines. Operated by the French Air Force for liaison duties.
Model 414: First flown in 1968 as a 6/7-seat transport with pressurization. Two 310-hp Continental TSIO-520 piston engines. Operated by the Bolivian Air Force for utility.

Above: US Navy Cessna T-47A.

Model 421 Golden Eagle: Pressurized 6/8-seat transport of 1965 first flight, powered by two 375-hp Continental GTSIO-520N piston engines. Operators are Bolivia, Ivory Coast, New Zealand, Pakistan, Sri Lanka, Turkey (army) and Zimbabwe.
Citation I and II: First flown on 15 September 1969, the Citation was developed as an eight-passenger executive jet, powered by two 2200-lb (998-kg) thrust Pratt & Whitney Canada JT15D-1B turbofans. In 1977 the larger Citation II (Model 550) appeared with room for the pilot and 10 passengers, powered by two 2500-lb (1134-kg) thrust JT15D-4 turbofans. An updated model with many airframe refinements and JT15D-4B engines first flew in 1984 as the S550 Citation S/II, and this is the basic model for the US Navy's T-47As (although with a change of engine and other modifications as the Model 552). An 8/11-seat long-range Citation is the Model 650 Citation III. Citation I and II operators are Argentina (army, for survey), Burma, Chile (army), China, Spain (navy), Turkey, United States (navy, T-47A) and Venezuela.

Cessna O-1 Bird Dog, 150, 152, 172/T-41 Mescalero, 180/185 Skywagon, 182/Skylane, Stationair, 208 Caravan I/U-27A, and 210 Centurion
United States

This series of Cessna single-engined light aircraft fulfills varies roles, including observation, reconnaissance, liaison, utility, transport and training.

Specifications (O-1E Bird Dog data)
Accommodation: The pilot and observer seated in tandem.
Wingspan: 36 ft 0 in (10.97 m).
Length: 25 ft 10 in (7.89 m).
Maximum take-off weight: 2430 lb (1102 kg).
Maximum speed: 115 mph (185 km/h).
Range: 530 miles (853 km).
Mission performance: Rate of climb at sea level 1150 ft (350 m) per min; ceiling 18,500 ft (5640 m).

Engine: One 213-hp Continental O-470-11 piston, with 155 liters of fuel.

Versions in service and Operators

O-1 Bird Dog: Actually the Cessna Model 305, the prototype of this strut-braced high-wing cabin monoplane flew in January 1950. Production, beginning with the O-1A, included examples for observation, reconnaissance, liaison and training. Current users are Austria, Indonesia, Italy (army), Japan (army), South Korea, Laos, Libya, Norway (army), Pakistan (army), Philippines, Thailand (air force and army), Turkey and Vietnam.

Models 150 and 152: First flown in September 1957, the 150 was built as another two-seat strut-braced high-wing monoplane. This (100-hp Continental O-200-A), and the more powerful and refined 152, were also produced in France by Reims Aviation. The 152 has a 110-hp Avco Lycoming O-235-L2C engine. Wingspan is 32 ft 8½ in (9.97 m), length 24 ft 1 in (7.34 m), and cruising speed 123 mph (198 km/h). Operating air forces (unless stated otherwise) are Botswana (152), Burundi (150), Haiti (152), Iran (150), Ivory Coast (150), Mexico (navy, 150), Paraguay (navy, 150), Somali Republic (150), Sri Lanka (150 and 152) and Zaire (150).

Model 172/T-41 Mescalero: The 172 is a 2/4-seat strut-braced high-wing monoplane that first appeared in 1955. Continental O-300 piston engines were fitted to early models, thereafter changing to Avco Lycoming O-320s or Continental IO-360s. Reims Aviation also produced the aircraft. As the T-41A and C Mescalero, it became a basic trainer with the USAF, the T-41B being a US Army trainer and liaison aircraft and the T-41D an export version of the T-41B (provided under military assistance programs). The T-41A is powered by a 145-hp Continental O-300-C piston engine, has a wingspan and length of 36 ft 2 in (11.02 m) and 26 ft 6 in (8.07 m) respectively, and a maximum speed of 138 mph (222 km/h). Operating air forces (unless stated otherwise) are Angola, Argentina (army), Bolivia, Chile (air force and army), Colombia, Dominican Republic, Ecuador, El Salvador, Greece, Guatemala,

Below: Argentine Cessna T-41D Mescaleros.

Haiti, Honduras, Indonesia, Ireland, Israel, South Korea, Laos, Liberia, Malagasy, Paraguay, Peru, Philippines, Saudi Arabia, Thailand (army), Turkey, United States (air force and army) and Uruguay.

180/185 Skywagon/U-17 and Stationair: The Skywagon 180 appeared in 1953 as a strut-braced high-wing 4-seater, powered by a 225-hp Continental O-470 piston engine. The 1981 and last model progressed to a 6-seater with a 230-hp engine. The 185 was developed as a more powerful and strengthened version, seating up to 6 or the pilot and cargo. An underfuselage Cargo-Pack was also made available, with a 300-lb (136-kg) capacity. The 185 has a 300-hp Continental IO-520-D piston engine, a wingspan and length of 35 ft 10 in (10.92 m) and 25 ft 7½ in (7.81 m) respectively, and a cruising speed of 169 mph (272 km/h). The USAF designation for 185s supplied to other air forces under military assistance programmes is U-17. The Stationair (originally the U206) is similar to the 185 but for minor variations in the engine, a tricycle undercarriage and double cargo doors. A seven-seater is the Stationair 7 (or 207 Turbo Stationair T207). The USAF designation of the Turbo Stationair is U-26A. Operating air forces (unless stated otherwise) are Argentina (army, U-17 and 207), Bolivia (185 and 206), Burma (180), Chile (180), Djibouti (206), El Salvador (180 and 185), Greece (army, U-17), Guatemala (180 and 206), Guyana (206), Honduras (180 and 185), Indonesia (185 and 207), Iran (air force, 180; army 185), Israel (180 and 206), Jamaica (185), Liberia (185 and 207), Mexico (air force, 206; navy, 180), Nicaragua (185), Panama (air force, 180, 185 and 207), Paraguay (navy, 206), Philippines (U-17), South Africa (185), Surinam (206), Thailand (navy, U-17), Turkey (army, U-17 and 206), Uruguay (U-17) and Vietnam (U-17).

Model 182 and Skylane: First flying in 1956, the 182 is a higher-performing strut-braced high-wing monoplane, accommodating 4 persons. Several models were produced, including the deluxe Skylane; it was also built in France by Reims Aviation and by DINFIA in Argentina. A typical version has a 230-hp Continental O-470-R piston engine, a wingspan and length of 35 ft 10 in (10.92 m) and 28 ft 0½ in (8.54 m)

respectively, and a maximum speed of 165 mph (266 km/h). Operating air forces (unless stated otherwise) are Argentina (army), Dubai, Ecuador (army), El Salvador, Uruguay and Venezuela (air force and army).

Model 208 Caravan I/U-27A: This is thought only to be operated currently by the Liberian Army, although Cessna is demonstrating it to the US Army for ambulance, RPV control and other possible uses. Like all the others in this batch of Cessna lightplanes, the U-27A is a strut-braced high-wing monoplane. It can accommodate 10-14 persons or the pilot and 3000 lb (1360 kg) of freight, has a 600-shp Pratt & Whitney Canada PT6A-114 turboprop engine, a wingspan of 52 ft 1 in (15.88 m), length 37 ft 7 in (11.46 m) and cruising speed of 212 mph (341 km/h).

Model 210 Centurion: Built in standard and pressurized models, the 210 differs from the others by having a cantilever high-wing and a retractable undercarriage. Typically powered by a 300-hp Continental IO-520-L piston engine (though Bolivia for one uses the Turbo-Centurion with a turbocharged engine), it has a wingspan of 36 ft 9 in (11.20 m), a length of 28 ft 2 in (8.59 m), and a cruising speed of 193 mph (310 km/h). First flown in 1957, current operators are the air forces of Bolivia, Jamaica and Philippines.

Cessna Skymaster, O-2, Reims/Cessna FTB 337 and Summit Sentry
United States and France

The Cessna Model 337 Skymaster first flew as a prototype four/six-seat light aircraft on 28 February 1961, featuring an unusual tandem layout for its two engines (one in the nose and the other in the rear of the fuselage pod). In 1966, during the Vietnam war, the USAF ordered Skymasters as O-2A forward air control aircraft, equipped for target identification and marking, reconnaissance, coordination of air and land forces, and other missions. A psychological warfare version with special communications and broadcasting equipment was also ordered as the O-2B.

In France, Reims Aviation also put the Skymaster into production, its versions including the FTB 337 with STOL characteristics (high-lift trailing-edge flaps) suited to many military roles from COIN and overland/coastal patrol to stretcher carrying (two), navigation/IFR training and rescue.

In addition to the former newly-built versions from Cessna and Reims Aviation, an all-military modification of the Cessna T337 has also been made available by another American company, Summit Aviation. Taken into service by Haiti, Honduras, Nicaragua, Senegal and Thailand, the Sentry O2-337 can perform the missions detailed above and is said also to be capable of helicopter escort, aerial photography and other specialized missions. It has four NATO pylons under the wings (as for O-2s and some Reims models), each pylon capable of carrying 350 lb (159 kg) of weapons ranging from 7.62-mm and 12.75-mm gun pods to rocket launchers, bombs, markers and flares.

Specifications (O-2A data)

Weapons: 4 pylons for light ordnance,

Above: Summit Sentry O2-337s before delivery to the Royal Thai Navy.

including a 7.62-mm Minigun pack, bombs and rockets.
Accommodation: 2 crew plus 4 passengers or light freight.
Wingspan: 38 ft 2 in (11.63 m).
Length: 29 ft 9 in (9.07 m).
Maximum take-off weight: 4630 lb (2100 kg).
Maximum speed: 206 mph (332 km/h).
Range: 1290 miles (2076 km).
Mission performance: Rate of climb at sea level 1100 ft (335 m) per min; ceiling 18,000 ft (5485 m); ceiling (Sentry) 28,500 ft (8690 m).
Engines: Two 210-hp Continental IO-360-C pistons, with 348 liters of fuel standard. Auxiliary tanks in wings.

Versions in service
Cessna and Reims Skymaster: Similar to civil Skymaster for liaison, transport.
Cessna O-2: Specific military models, originally for USAF for FAC and psychological warfare. O-2As active.
Reims FTB 337: STOL model with Rolls-Royce/Continental TSIO-360-Ds of 225 hp each. Can be equipped for many varied duties and armed for COIN.

Below: Calspan-modified Convair 580, with an extended nose and vertical control surfaces on the wings. Initially used by the Flight Dynamics Laboratory at Wright Patterson Air Force Base as the unique Total In-flight Simulator for research purposes, it has been further improved.

Summit Sentry O2-337: Only model of Skymaster still being offered, though produced for military use by rebuilding existing airframes. If a sufficiently large order was received, new airframes for the Sentry would be manufactured by Cessna. Operator with the largest number to date is the Royal Thai Navy.

Operators: Chad (Reims), Chile (army, Cessna), Ecuador (air force and navy, Cessna), El Salvador (Cessna), Gabon (Cessna), Guinea-Bissau (Reims), Haiti (Summit), Honduras (Summit), Iran (Cessna), Jamaica (Cessna), South Korea (Cessna), Malagasy (Reims), Mauritania (Reims), Mexico (navy, Cessna), Nicaragua (Summit), Niger (Reims and Cessna), Paraguay (Cessna), Portugal (Reims), Senegal (Summit), Sri Lanka (Cessna), Thailand (navy, Summit), Togo (Reims and Cessna), United States (Cessna) and Zimbabwe (Reims).

Convair C-131 Samaritan and Canadair CC-109 Cosmopolitan
United States and Canada

The C-131 Samaritan, the United States military transport version of the piston-engined Convair-Liner 240 airliner, entered USAF service in 1954 as its first pressurized twin-engined casualty evacuation aircraft. Subsequent versions of the C-131 were based on the

CV-340 and CV-440, and their transport duties took in also passengers and VIPs. Canadair produced the similar Cosmopolitan for its home forces, based on the CV-440. These were service-designated CC-109s, of which perhaps seven are still in use. Only 27 C-131s remain with the USAF, assigned to the Air National Guard for airlift support duties.

Specifications (C-131H data)
Accommodation: 4 crew plus 44 passengers.
Wingspan: 105 ft 4 in (32.10 m).
Length: 79 ft 2 in (24.13 m).
Maximum take-off weight: 54,600 lb (24,766 kg).
Cruising speed: 342 mph (550 km/h).
Range: 1605 miles (2583 km).
Mission performance: Rate of climb at sea level 2050 ft (625 m) per min.
Engines: Two 3750-shp Allison T56-A-9 turboprops.

Versions in service
C-131 Samaritan: CV-340 and CV-440 versions remain. Bolivian aircraft are based upon the CV-440 and CV-580.
CC-109 Cosmopolitan: Canadian military version of the CV-440.
Operators: Bolivia, Canada (CC-109s) and United States (air force and navy).

Convair F-106 Delta Dart
United States

The last surviving member of the 'Century Series' of fighters in USAF first-line service, the all-weather Delta Dart was developed as a more powerful derivative of the F-102 Delta Dagger, flying for the first time on 26 December 1956. Total production accounted for 277 single-seat F-106As and 63 tandem two-seat F-106B trainers. The Hughes MA-1 system was subsequently fitted to allow the interceptor to work within SAGE (Semi-Automatic Ground Environment), the computer-controlled radar and communications air defense network for interceptors and surface-to-air missiles. A further update, begun in 1973, introduced a cannon to the armament, the Vietnam War having shown this type of weapon to be useful in dogfights but which had been left off many missile fighters built during the earlier period.

Since the 48th Fighter Interceptor Squadron at Langley received the F-15 Eagle, this new fighter has largely taken over the US air defense role from the F-106. However in 1986 105 Delta Darts were still counted as active

Above: The last 'Century Series' fighter fulfilling a major role within the USAF and reserve forces is the Convair F-106 Delta Dart.

with five regular and Air National Guard squadrons, but even these will be finally off the scene by 1988, when they will become QF-106 target drones. Interestingly, NASA uses one F-106B for storm-hazard tests, flying into storm-cloud areas to measure the number of lightning strikes on the aircraft.

Specifications (F-106A data)
Weapons: One 20-mm M-61A1 cannon on most aircraft. Four AIM-4F or G Super Falcon air-to-air missiles carried in the fuselage bay.
Wingspan: 38 ft 3½ in (11.67 m).
Length: 70 ft 8¾ in (21.56 m).
Maximum take-off weight: About 42,400 lb (19,230 kg).

Maximum speed: Mach 2.
Mission performance: Ceiling 65,000 ft (19,800 m).
Range: 1200 miles (1930 km).
Engine: One 24,500-lb (11,113-kg) thrust Pratt & Whitney J75-P-17 turbojet.
Versions in service
F-106A: Single-seat interceptor.
F-106B: Tandem 2-seat combat trainer.
Operator: United States.

Dassault Mirage IV-A and IV-P
France

France, like Britain, entered the age of the nuclear deterrent by deploying atomic bombs on strategic bombers, though in the case of the Mirage IV-A the bomber was supersonic. Configured as an enlarged two-seat Mirage III, and powered by two Atar 09 afterburning

turbojets, the prototype made its maiden flight on 17 June 1959 and a total of 62 production IV-As were received by the Force de Frappe between 1964 and 1968. Headquarters for their operation was in an underground station near Paris; it was as hardened against an enemy strike as the aircraft in their protective shelters from which they could emerge with their engines running.

With the subsequent deployment of ballistic submarines and land-based missiles, Air Force IV-As became displaced in the strategic role, thereafter undertaking low-level tactical strike with tactical nuclear or conventional high-explosive bombs. Today the remaining force of about 43 aircraft is assigned various roles. Eighteen operated by CFAS (Commandement des Forces Aériennes Stratégiques) have the new IV-P designation, indicating their recent modification to carry the Mach 3 ASMP medium-range nuclear missile. Other updates in the IV-P are given below. IOC (initial operational capability) with the IV-P was attained by the Gascogne squadron of 91e Escadre de Bombardement, based at Mont-de-Marsan, in May 1986. Of the remaining IV-As, most are still operating as strike aircraft, although some were assigned to a strategic reconnaissance role and are held in reserve.

Specifications (Mirage IV-A and IV-P data)
Radar: The IV-P has Thomson-CSF Arcana pulse-Doppler radar to update the navigation system and dual inertial systems.
Weapons: ASMP is carried by the IV-P, with a 150-kT warhead. An AN-22 nuclear bomb

Below: Dassault Mirage IV-P strategic bomber carrying ASMP.

can be carried semi-recessed under the fuselage of the IV-A or alternative armament can be sixteen 1000-lb (454-kg) bombs or Martel air-to-surface missiles.
Accommodation: 2 crew.
Wingspan: 38 ft 10½ in (11.85 m).
Length: 77 ft 1¼ in (23.50 m).
Maximum take-off weight: 73,800 lb (33,475 kg).
Maximum speed: Mach 2.2.
Tactical combat radius: IV-A. 771 miles (1240 km).
Engines: Two 15,432-lb (7000-kg) thrust with afterburning SNECMA Atar 09K turbojets. Two 2000-liter auxiliary fuel tanks are available to increase range.

Versions in service
IV-A: Original model, used in both low-level tactical strike and strategic reconnaissance roles.
IV-P: 18 modified aircraft, with ASMP, Arcana radar, Thomson-CSF jamming pod, Matra Phimat chaff dispenser and radar warning receivers.
Operator: France.

Dassault-Breguet Atlantic and Atlantique 2
France

On 16 April 1957 a panel set up by the NATO Armaments Committee met to begin the preparation of a specification for a NATO maritime patrol aircraft, this representing one of many attempts to standardize NATO equipment among member nations. This was required to supersede the Lockheed P-2 Neptune that was then tasked with most of the long-range overwater reconnaissance. Some two years later the French government initiated development through Breguet (now Dassault-Breguet) of this new maritime reconnaissance aircraft which by then had been named Atlantic. Breguet set up a joint company which it named SECBAT (Société Européenne pour la Construction du Breguet

Below: Dassault-Breguet Atlantique 2.

Atlantic) which combined several manufacturers to build the Br.1150 Atlantic, with Breguet responsible not only for construction of sections of fuselage, but also for final assembly and flight testing. The resulting midwing monoplane incorporated a 'double-bubble' fuselage to simplify pressurization and the provision of a large weapons bay. The first prototype was flown on 21 October 1961, followed subsequently by the first production aircraft on 19 July 1965.

By the time the Atlantic entered service, initially with the Aéronavale on 10 December 1965, most of the NATO nations had followed their own procurement policies. The result was that production of the Atlantic totalled only 87, for France (40 – three later acquired by Pakistan), Italy (18), Netherlands (9) and West Germany (20). In 1977 the French government made moves for the procurement of an improved version which was known initially as the ANG (Atlantique Nouvelle Génération). Now identified as the Dassault-Brequet Atlantique 2, the first of two prototypes was flown initially on 8 May 1981. Current procurement plans envisage that 42 will be built for the Aéronavale, with work being shared as before. The Atlantique 2 will differ primarily by incorporating improved construction techniques, and by the installation of state-of-the art avionics and operational equipment. An order for the first two aircraft was finalized in mid-1985 with the first scheduled to fly in July 1988.

Specifications (Atlantique 2 data)
Radar: Thomson-CSF Iguane sea surveillance and attack radar.
Weapons: Maximum weapons load of 7716 lb (3500 kg), which can comprise a wide range of NATO weapons including Mk 46 homing torpedoes in the weapons bay and AM39 Exocet missiles on underwing pylons.
Accommodation: 12 crew plus relief crew or 12 passengers.
Wingspan: 122 ft 9¼ in (37.42 m).
Length: 107 ft 0¾ in (32.63 m).
Maximum take-off weight: 101,854 lb (46,200 kg).

Maximum speed: 403 mph (648 km/h).
Combat radius: 2072 miles (3335 km) plus 2-hour loiter for search in target area.
Mission performance: Rate of climb at sea level 2900 ft (884 m) per min at 66,139 lb (30,000 kg) gross weight; ceiling 30,000 ft (9145 m).
Engines: Two 5665-shp Rolls-Royce Tyne RTy.20 Mk 21 turboprops, with 23,120 liters of fuel standard.

Versions in service
Atlantic: Original version, with the same engines as given above. Wingspan 119 ft 1 in (36.30 m) and length 104 ft 2 in (31.75 m). Maximum speed 409 mph (658 km/h). Range 5592 miles (9000 km).
Atlantique 2: As detailed above.
Operators: France (navy, Atlantic and Atlantique 2), West Germany (navy), Italy (navy), Netherlands (navy) and Pakistan.

Dassault-Breguet Etendard and Super Etendard
France

Few aircraft of such limited capability have had such a successful impact on the world scene as the Super Etendard, which in the 1982 war in the South Atlantic destroyed a British destroyer and a large merchant ship and in 1986 wrought havoc among tankers in the Persian Gulf. This happened because of its ability to launch the AM.39 Exocet missile, though any alert warship ought to be able to offer an effective defense.

The original Etendards were a series of light fighters of 1955-57, which failed to be accepted as a NATO type. Fortunately for Dassault a customer appeared in the form of the Aéronavale (French naval aviation), which bought the Etendard IVM as a light carrier-based attack machine and the IVP for reconnaissance. Both were given an inflight-refuelling probe and could refuel each other by the 'buddy' method. The IVM has been withdrawn, but the IVP remains in service and will do so until superseded by the navalized Rafale B.

The Aéronavale planned to replace both versions with the supersonic Jaguar M, but despite successful tests this part-British aircraft was cancelled and replaced by the Super Etendard, thought to be much cheaper and to meet most of the Aéronavale's needs. A key factor was the big AM.39 missile, normally carried under the right wing only, with a drop tank balancing it under the left wing. The Super closely resembles the IVM but has an improved airframe, better engine, Agave multimode radar and upgraded EW (electronic warfare) equipment. Navigation is assisted by fitting an inertial system made under license from Kearfott of the United States. The planned force of 100 was cut back to 71 by inflation. The first Super (a converted IVM) flew on 28 October 1974, and deliveries began nearly four years later. The Super equips squadrons (Flotilles) 11F, 12F, 14F and 17F. A further 14 were supplied to Argentina, where five had arrived with a few Exocets, but with no manuals or trained personnel, by the time of the Falklands war. Iraq requested Super Etendards and Exocets, and despite international pressure the Aéronavale loaned that country five aircraft and also supplied missiles, which were soon put to use. In 1990

Above: French Navy Dassault-Breguet Super Etendards on deck.

flight development is expected to begin of a Super fitted with the improved Anémone radar, better inertial system and new cockpit displays.

Specifications (Super Etendard data)
Radar: Thomson-CSF/ESD Agave lightweight multimode radar, with search, designation, automatic tracking, ranging and mapping functions.
Weapons: Two 30-mm DEFA cannon, with 125 rounds of ammunition each, plus up to 4630 lb (2100 kg) of attack/air-to-air weapons including the ASMP nuclear missile, AN-52 nuclear bomb, one AM.39 Exocet antishipping missile, conventional bombs of up to 882-lb (400-kg) weight each, four 18-round 68-mm rocket pods, 2 Matra Magic air-to-air missiles, etc, carried on 4 underwing and 1 underfuselage pylon. 'Buddy' refuelling pack or reconnaissance pack optional.
Accommodation: The pilot.
Wingspan: 31 ft 6 in (9.60 m).
Length: 46 ft 11½ in (14.31 m).
Maximum take-off weight: 26,455 lb (12,000 kg).
Maximum speed: About Mach 1.
Combat radius: 528 miles (850 km) with an Exocet and 2 auxiliary fuel tanks.
Mission performance: Ceiling 44,950 ft (13,700 m).
Engine: One 11,023-lb (5000-kg) thrust SNECMA Atar 8K-50 turbojet, with 3270 liters of fuel standard.
Versions in service
Etendard IVP: Unarmed reconnaissance aircraft, with 5 Omera cameras. One 9700-lb (4400-kg) thrust Atar 8B turbojet.
Super Etendard: As detailed above. Delivered to the Aéronavale from June 1978. Argentine aircraft ordered in 1979.
Operators: Argentina (navy), France (navy) and Iraq.

Dassault-Breguet Mirage III, 3NG and 5
France

In 1953 the Armée de l'Air issued a specification covering a lightweight high-altitude all-weather interceptor, the most demanding parameter being an ability to carry its weapons to a height of 60,000 ft (18,290 m) in not more than six minutes. Dassault's contender for this requirement, the MD.550 Mystère Delta, later renamed Mirage I, was first flown on 25 June 1955 and subsequent testing was to show that it was not only too small but also unable to achieve the required performance despite having two turbojets and a rocket motor. A larger Mirage II with more powerful turbojets and two rocket motors failed to win a prototype construction order, resulting in the Mirage III which introduced an area-ruled fuselage, a modified delta wing that benefitted from British research with the Fairey Delta 2, and with a 9921-lb (4500-kg) thrust SNECMA afterburning turbojet replacing the twin turbine/rocket motor power plant proposed for the Mirage II. When first flown, on 17 November 1956, it was clear that Dassault had produced the right formula for success.

Of conventional all-metal construction, the elevons of the Mirage III's delta wing and the rudder of its swept vertical surfaces are hydraulically powered. Although intended purely as an interceptor, the Mirage III was soon found to be equally effective if deployed for ground attack or reconnaissance missions, and this tractability combined with an aircraft that was found to be easy to maintain and operate has ensured its continued success and production. The type was also manufactured under license in Australia and Switzerland. A dedicated VFR ground attack version was developed as the Mirage 5, flown for the first time on 19 May 1967; this retains the airframe and power plant of the Mirage III-E, has increased fuel capacity, can deploy a wider range of weapons and is easier to maintain. It can be used as an interceptor carrying two AAMs and external fuel, and at the customer's option can trade-off fuel/weapon load to provide greater IFR/all-weather capability.

Dassault-Breguet developed more recently a Nouvelle Génération version of the Mirage III, designated Mirage 3NG, and based upon the same airframe. It introduces the 15,783-lb (7200-kg) thrust SNECMA Atar 9K-50 afterburning turbojet that powers the Mirage 50, new aerodynamic features which include fixed sweptback foreplanes and highly swept-wing leading-edge root extensions, and a fly-by-wire system adapted from that of the Mirage 2000. The improved capability of the Mirage 3NG stems from a state-of-the art nav/attack system that can be complemented to customer option with advanced forward-looking sensors. So far only the prototype has been built, first flown on 21 December 1982.

Specifications (Mirage III-E data)
Radar: Thomson-CSF Cyrano II fire-control radar in nose; optional is the Thomson-CSF/ESD Agave radar if the primary role is naval attack.
Weapons: For ground attack standard armament includes two DEFA 552A 30-mm cannon, each with 125 rounds. Maximum external weapon load 8818 lb (4000 kg) on five hardpoints, and can include an AN 52 tactical nuclear weapon, conventional bombs, combined tank/bomb carriers, an HSD/Matra AS 37 Martel ARM or Matra R.530E AAM, Matra R.550 Magic AAMs, Philips-Matra Phimat chaff dispensers and a variety of drop tanks.
Wingspan: 26 ft 11½ in (8.22 m).
Length: 49 ft 3½ in (15.03 m).
Maximum take-off weight: 30,203 lb (13,700 kg).
Maximum speed: 1460 mph (2350 km/h) at 39,370 ft (12,000 m).
Combat radius: Ground attack 745 miles (1200 km).

Below: The Dassault-Breguet Mirage 50. This aircraft is derived from the Mirage III/5 but it is far less successful commercially.

Mission performance: Climb to 49,210 ft (15,000 m) 6 min 50 sec; service ceiling 55,775 ft (17,000 m); service ceiling 75,460 ft (23,000 m) with optional rocket motor.
Engine: One 13,670-lb (6200-kg) thrust Atar 9C afterburning turbojet, with one SEPR 844 3307-lb (1500-kg) thrust rocket motor optional.

Versions in service
III-B: 2-seat trainer generally similar to pre-production III-A with SNECMA Atar 9B turbojet, but with tandem seating in a fuselage lengthened by 1 ft 11½ in (0.60 m). Retains strike capability carrying a Matra AS.30 air-to-surface missile or bombs beneath the center fuselage and other conventional weapons beneath the wings.
III-C: All-weather interceptor and day ground attack fighter with SNECMA Atar 9B turbojet, with SEPR 841 rocket motor available optionally. For ground attack carries weapons as noted above for III-B, and as interceptor one Matra R.530 air-to-air missile or, optionally, two 30-mm cannon and two AIM-9 Sidewinders.
III-D: Export 2-seat trainer/ground attack version of Mirage III-E, basically similar to Mirage III-DO of the Royal Australian Air Force.

III-DO: Australian 2-seat version of the license-built Mirage III-O.
III-E: Long-range fighter-bomber/intruder version; standard power plant one SNECMA Atar 9C with one SEPR 844 rocket motor optional. The Armée de l'Air has 2 squadrons of III-Es which are equipped to carry the AN 52 tactical nuclear weapon.
III-O: Australian license-built variant of the III-E, sometimes designated III-O(A), which differs primarily in some items of installed equipment.
III-R: Reconnaissance version of III-E with self-contained navigation system, nose radar replaced by an installation of 5 Omera 31 cameras suitable for low/medium/high and/or night missions, and with provisions to carry air-to-surface weapons.
III-R2Z: Variant of III-R for service with the South African Air Force; differs by having 15,873-lb (7200-kg) thrust SNECMA Atar 9K-50 turbojet installed.
III-RD: Variant of III-R with Omera 33 and 40 cameras and an improved Doppler navigation system.
III-S: Swiss license-built variant of the III-E for service with the Swiss Air Force; differs primarily by having the Cyrano II radar replaced by Hughes TARAN nav/attack radar system.
Operators: Abu Dhabi (III-E, 5), Argentina (III-E, III-B, III-C, III-D, 5), Australia (III-DO, III-O), Belgium (5), Brazil (III-D,

III-E), Chile (III-B), Colombia (5), Egypt (5), France (III-B, III-C, III-E, III-R/RD, 5), Gabon (5), Lebanon (III-B; III-E), Libya (5), Pakistan (III-D, III-E, III-R, 5), Peru (5), South Africa (III-B, III-C, III-D, III-E, III-R, III-R2Z), Spain (III-D, III-E), Switzerland (III-B, III-D, III-R, III-S), Venezuela (III-E, 5) and Zaire (5).

Dassault-Breguet Mirage 50
France

Derived from the Mirage III and 5 but with a more powerful engine to increase acceleration and rate of climb, the prototype of this multirole fighter took to the air for the first time on 15 April 1979. Yet, despite other advantages, such as improved maneuverability, it was only taken into service by Chile (16).

Specifications (Mirage 50 data)
Radar: Was made available with Cyrano IV-M multifunction radar for interception, ground attack and antishipping missions, or the lightweight Agave multifunction radar.
Weapons: As for the Mirage III and 5, but the Matra 530 air-to-air missile suiting the Cyrano radar and Magic the Agave.
Accommodation: The pilot.
Wingspan: 26 ft 11½ in (8.22 m).

Length: 51 ft 0¾ in (15.56 m).
Maximum take-off weight: 30,203 lb (13,700 kg).
Maximum speed: Mach 2.2.
Combat radius: 776 miles (1250 km) carrying 1764 lb (800 kg) of bombs and a total of 6810 liters of standard and auxiliary fuel.
Mission performance: Rate of climb at sea level 36,615 ft (11,160 m) per min; service ceiling 59,050 ft (18,000 m).
Engine: One 15,873-lb (7200-kg) thrust with afterburning SNECMA Atar 9K-50 turbojet, with 3410 liters of internal fuel.
Version in service
Mirage 50: More powerful derivative of the Mirage III and 5.
Operator: Chile.

Dassault-Breguet Mirage 2000
France

Retaining the familiar delta wing and vertical tail only configuration synonymous with most Mirages, the 2000 was chosen by the French Air Force as its standard multipurpose combat aircraft for the remainder of this century and beyond, to be joined later by the even more advanced Rafale B. First flown on 10 March 1978, it has a fly-by-wire system to actuate the control surfaces and some use is made of composite materials in its construction. The basic Mirage 2000 is principally an interceptor and air superiority fighter, but can just as easily be used for attack and reconnaissance. A two-seater for low-level penetration missions carrying the new ASMP nuclear missile is the Mirage 2000N, able to fly at 690 mph (1110 km/h) at very low level. Naturally this requires terrain-following radar, and this is provided by the Electronique Serge Dassault Antilope V which also has air-to-air, air to ground, maritime and navigation (ground-mapping) functions. Mirage 2000C production single-seaters first became operational with the French Air Force (Escadron de Chasse [EC] 1/2 *Cigognes*) in 1984 and the Mirage 2000N in 1988. Export customers for the Mirage 2000 include India, with whom it is known as the Vajra and entered service in 1985.

Specifications (Mirage 2000C data)
Radar: Thomson-CSF RDI pulse-Doppler radar now being fitted, with about a 56-mile (90-km) range.
Weapons: Two 30-mm DEFA 554 cannon, each with 125 rounds of ammunition. Up to 13,890 lb (6300 kg) of air-to-air and/or attack, antishipping weapons, or other stores on 4 underwing and 5 fuselage pylons. Interception armament is 4 air-to-air missiles of Matra 530D, Super 530, Magic or Magic 2 types.
Accommodation: The pilot.
Wingspan: 29 ft 11½ in (9.13 m).
Length: 47 ft 1 in (14.36 m).
Maximum take-off weight: 37,479 lb (17,000 kg).
Maximum speed: Above Mach 2.2.
Range: 920 miles (1480 km) with 2205 lb (1000 kg) of bombs.
Mission performance: Rate of climb at sea level 56,000 ft (17,060 m) per min; ceiling 59,050 ft (18,000 m); G limit +9 normal.
Engine: One 21,385-lb (9700-kg) thrust with afterburning SNECMA M53-P2 turbofan, with 3980 liters of fuel standard.
Versions in service
Mirage 2000C: French Air Force single-seat multirole fighter, of which 66 have been ordered of a much larger planned total for eventual service.
Mirage 2000B: 2-seat trainer version of the C, first flown in 1980. No fixed cannon armament. Twenty-one ordered for the French Air Force out of a larger planned total for eventual service.
Mirage 2000N: 2-seat penetration model, carrying ASMP as one weapon option. No fixed cannon armament. First flown on 2 February 1983. 47 ordered for the French Air Force out of a larger planned total for eventual service.
Mirage 2000EAD, RAD and DAD: 36 export aircraft for Abu Dhabi, including 8 Mirage 2000RAD reconnaissance aircraft.
Mirage 2000EGM and BGM: 40 export aircraft for the Hellenic Air Force.
Mirage 2000EM and BM: Export Egyptian models, with C engines. 20 aircraft initially.
Mirage 2000H and TH: Export Indian models, of which 30 of the 40 ordered were delivered with temporary M53-5 engines of 19,842-lb (9000-kg) thrust with afterburning.
Mirage 2000P and DP: Export Peruvian models, totalling 14.
Operators: Abu Dhabi, Egypt, France, Greece, India and Peru.

Above: Spanish Dassault-Breguet Mirage III-E.

Left: Dassault-Breguet Mirage 2000Cs and a 2000B, single- and two-seat versions of the latest French multirole fighter.
Below: Cutaway drawing of a French Air Force Mirage 2000.

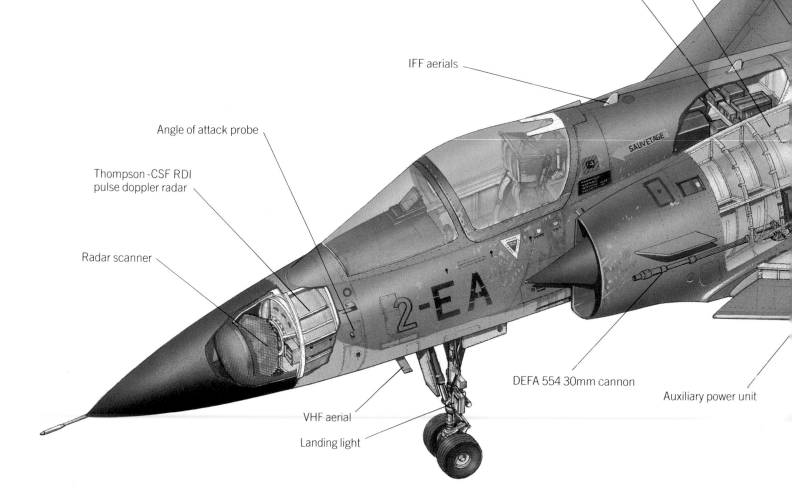

Hydraulic accumulator

Foreward fuselage integral fuel tank

Radio & electronic equipment

IFF aerials

Angle of attack probe

Thompson-CSF RDI pulse doppler radar

Radar scanner

DEFA 554 30mm cannon

Auxiliary power unit

VHF aerial

Landing light

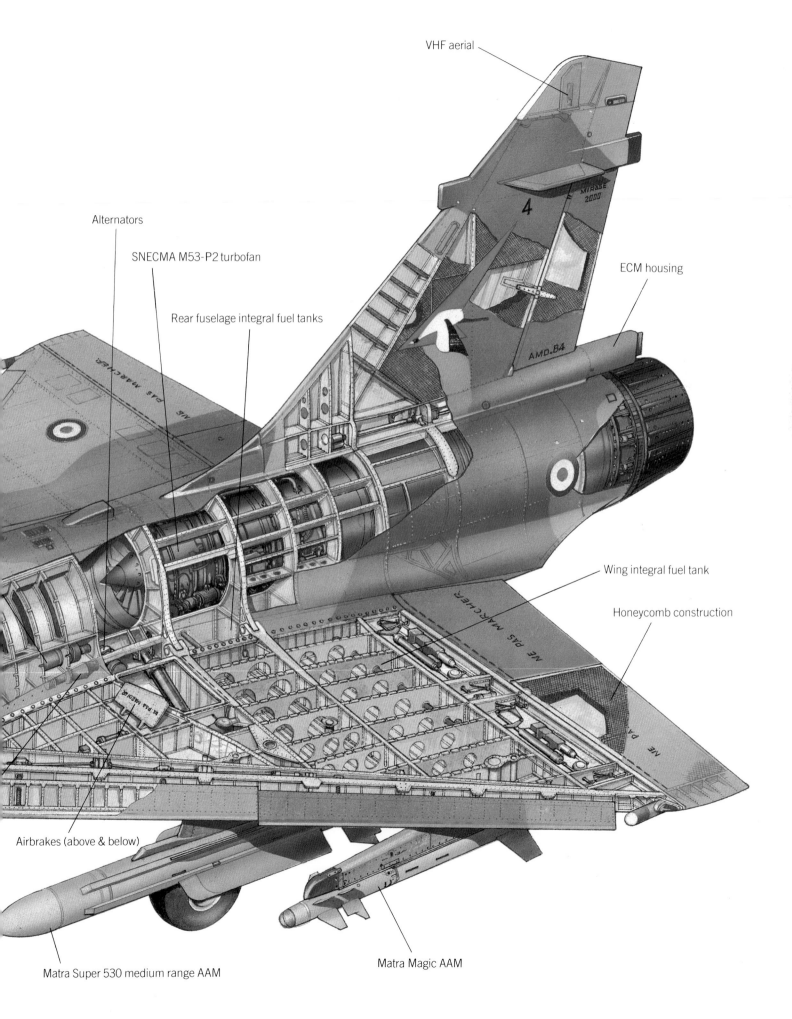

VHF aerial

Alternators

SNECMA M53-P2 turbofan

Rear fuselage integral fuel tanks

ECM housing

Wing integral fuel tank

Honeycomb construction

Airbrakes (above & below)

Matra Super 530 medium range AAM

Matra Magic AAM

Dassault-Breguet Mirage F1
France

The F1 was developed by Dassault as a private-venture replacement for the Mirage III, concurrently with the larger French-government-sponsored Mirage F2 which only got to prototype stage. Unlike all other Mirage combat aircraft that have entered production since the Mirage III, the F1 does not use the familiar delta wings but has swept wings and an all-moving tailplane. The prototype F1 first flew on 23 December 1966 and the initial production version was the F1-C all-weather interceptor, deliveries to the French Air Force beginning in 1973 and first going to 30e Escadre based in Reims. Several versions have followed for French use and export, as detailed below, with sales exceeding 670 aircraft worldwide by 1986.

Specifications (F1-C data)
Radar: Thomson-CSF Cyrano IVM multifunction radar, for air-to-air, air-to-ground and maritime missions. The F1-C-200 uses Cyrano IVMR, with additional ground mapping (optional Doppler-beam sharpening), contour mapping and terrain avoidance for low-level missions in all weathers.
Weapons: Two 30-mm DEFA 553 cannon in the fuselage, with 135 rounds of ammunition per gun, plus 5 underwing/underfuselage pylons and 2 wingtip AAM launchers for up to 13,890 lb (6300 kg) of air-to-air and/or attack weapons. Primary armament for interception is 2 Matra Super 530 and two Matra Magic or Sidewinder missiles. Attack weapons can include various types of bombs, an AM 39 Exocet antishipping or ARMAT antiradar missile, AS.30L missiles and associated laser designator, etc.
Accommodation: Pilot only.
Wingspan: 27 ft 6¾ in (8.40 m).
Length: 50 ft 2½ in (15.30 m).

Below: Dassault-Breguet Mirage F1-CR-200 fighter-reconnaissance aircraft.

Maximum take-off weight: 35,715 lb (16,200 kg).
Maximum speed: Mach 2.2.
Combat radius: 265 miles (425 km) with a 7716-lb (3500-kg) attack load.
Mission performance: Rate of climb at sea level 41,925 ft (12,780 m) per min; ceiling 65,615 ft (20,000 m); endurance 2 h 15 min with 2 Super 530 missiles and an auxiliary fuel tank.
Engine: One 15,875-lb (7200-kg) thrust with afterburning SNECMA Atar 9K-50 turbojet, with 4300 liters of fuel standard.

Versions in service
F1-A: Out of production day attack-fighter, with fewer avionics than the other versions.
F1-B: 2-seat training version of the F1-C.
F1-C: First production version, principally for interception.
F1-C-200: F1-C built with provision for, or modified retrospectively to have, a removable flight refuelling probe to enhance range for emergency reinforcement. French Air Force version.
F1-OCU: Designation of 20 F1-Bs serving with the French 5e Escadre at Orange, with F1-C armament and avionics but minus the 30-mm guns and with less fuel. Used for conversion training.
F1-CR-200: French Air Force version of the F1-R, serving with 3 squadrons of the 33e Escadre de Reconnaissance in Strasbourg. Equipment can include an Omera 33 camera, an Omera 40 or SAT Super Cyclope SCM 2400 infrared sensor, side-looking airborne radar and an Omera 400 sight recorder. Flight refuelling capability. Operational since 1983.
F1-D: 2-seat training version of the F1-E.
F1-E: Export multimission aircraft, suitable for fighter, attack and reconnaissance roles.
F1-R: Day and night single-seat reconnaissance aircraft.

Operators: Ecuador (B and E), France (B, C-200, OCU and CR), Greece (C), Iraq (B and E), Jordan (B, C and E), Kuwait (B and C), Libya (A, B and E), Morocco (C and E), Qatar (B and E), South Africa (A and C) and Spain (B, C and E).

Dassault-Breguet Mystère-Falcon and Guardian/Gardian series
France

The Mystère-Falcon series of executive jets began with the Mystère-Falcon 20, an 8- to 14-passenger pressurized transport of low-wing configuration that flew for the first time in prototype form on 4 May 1963. Several versions have been built over the years, some of which found their way into military service as light transports, for training duties (such as the Falcon ST used for radar and navigation training of Mirage III pilots), target towing and calibration. The French Air Force, for example, uses Mystère-Falcon 20s for all these roles. More specialized military variants have also been produced, such as the HU-25A Guardian surveillance aircraft ordered by the US Coast Guard and based upon the Mystère-Falcon 20 Series G, and ECM/training models which have found several purchasers including Canada, Morocco and Norway. The Mystère-Falcon 200 took over from the 20 during the early 1980s, introducing systems changes and other updates but most importantly Garrett engines and increased fuel capacity. The 200 formed the basis of the French Navy's Gardian maritime surveillance aircraft, inspired by the USCG HU-25As, entering service in 1983 to supersede Lockheed P-2H Neptunes on Pacific duty. A simplified development is the Gardian 2.

Well before the 200 appeared, back in 1970, a smaller development of the Mystère-Falcon 20 made its maiden flight as the four- to seven-passenger Mystère-Falcon 10. The French Navy purchased seven as 10MERs. These are suited to night flying and instrument training, communications, evacuation transport, and calibration of ship radars, but their most interesting task is to act as intruders as part of the interception training program for Super Etendard pilots. One Mystère-Falcon 10MER can carry weapons or ECM pods on four underwing pylons. The current version of the 10 is known as the Mystère-Falcon 100, though none is in military service.

On 7 November 1976 the prototype Mystère-Falcon 50 flew as a three-turbofan

Below: Dassault-Breguet Gardians.

executive jet with seats for 8 to 12 passengers. The French Air Force operates five as VIP transports for the President and ministers, and a similar VIP role is associated with those 50s delivered to eight other countries. Italian Air Force aircraft combine as air ambulances, with three stretchers and two attendants each.

Specifications (Mystère-Falcon 20 data)
Accommodation: 2 crew and up to 14 passengers in a transport role.
Wingspan: 53 ft 6 in (16.30 m).
Length: 56 ft 3 in (17.15 m).
Maximum take-off weight: 28,660 lb (13,000 kg).
Cruising speed: 536 mph (862 km/h).
Range: 2051 miles (3300 km) with 8 passengers.
Mission performance: Ceiling 42,000 ft (12,800 m).
Engines: Two 4500-lb (2041-kg) thrust General Electric CF700-2D-2 turbofans, with 5180 liters of fuel.

Versions in service
Mystère-Falcon 10MER: French Navy aircraft, as detailed above.
Mystère-Falcon 20: Original executive jet version, forming also the basis of the HU-25A Guardian. Canadian Armed Forces aircraft are designated EC-117 for the ECM variant and CC-117 for the transports, while Spanish transports are known as TM.11s.
Mystère-Falcon 200: Current version of the 20, with 5200-lb (2358-kg) thrust Garrett ATF 3-6A-4C turbofans and a fuel capacity of 6000 liters.
Guardian and Gardian 2s: Maritime surveillance derivatives of the 200, the former used by the French Navy. Both have Thomson-CSF Varan search radar, the latter though representing a simplified aircraft. The Gardian 2 has 4 underwing weapons and equipment pylons, and can perform target designation (including over-the-horizon), antiship (with 2 Exocet missiles), light attack, elint and ECM, and target-towing missions.
Mystère-Falcon 50: Powered by three 3700-lb (1678-kg) Garrett TFE 731-3 turbofans, with 8765 liters of fuel in fuselage and wing tanks. Used as a VIP transport.
Operators*: Australia (20), Belgium (20), Canada (20), France (air force, 20 and 50; navy, 10MER and Gardian), West Germany (50), Guinea-Bissau (20), Iran (air force and navy, 20), Iraq (50), Italy (50), Jordan (50), Libya (50), Morocco (20 and 50), Norway (20), Pakistan (20), Peru (20), South Africa (50), Spain (20 and 50), United States (coast guard, HU-25A) and Yugoslavia (50).
* Includes Mystère-Falcon 50s used as state VIP transports.

Dassault-Breguet Rafale
France

Although in many respects the Rafale A, which first flew on 4 July 1986, is like the BAe EAP in so much as it is an experimental combat aircraft, Rafale is worthy of a full entry by virtue of being intended for production in Rafale B form.

Rafale B, which should first fly in prototype form in 1990, is intended to supersede Mirage III-Es and SEPECAT Jaguars with the French Air Force in ACT tactical form and Vought Crusaders and Etendard IVPs in carrier-based ACM form. It will look similar to the Rafale A but be of marginally smaller size and will not have an air intake at the root of the tail fin.

Rafale has been designed to cope with a wide spectrum of enemy aircraft, ranging in the air-to-air role from helicopters to super-

Above: Dassault-Breguet Rafale A.

sonic jets. Basic missile armament will be four to eight Mica medium-range missiles and two Magic dogfight missiles. The look-down/shootdown radar will be capable of tracking eight targets at once, an essential quality if the Air Force's demands are to be met for the ability to launch at least six missiles in rapid succession. Rafale also has good ground attack capabilities, designed to carry a 7716-lb (3500-kg) warload to a target 350 nautical miles from its station.

In configuration Rafale is typical of the next generation of combat aircraft currently under development in various countries. The wings are of compound delta form and constructed mainly of carbonfiber and aluminum-lithium alloy, with some titanium and aramid fiber. Control surfaces, actuated by a fly-by-wire system, comprise three-section trailing-edge elevons and three-section leading-edge slats, which can operate together automatically to change the wing camber and thereby the degree of 'lift' achieved. The composite materials foreplanes are 'active' (movable) and the fuselage is built of the same alloy and composites as the wings.

Rafale A went supersonic on its first-ever flight (Mach 1.3) and achieved Mach 1.8 on its sixth. The Rafale B production model will be powered by two 16,860-lb (7650-kg) thrust SNECMA M88 turbofan engines. It will carry

ECM for self protection and its Mica missiles have been designed to function in a heavy ECM combat environment. AMRAAM missiles will be an air-to-air option.

Specifications (Rafale A data unless otherwise stated)
Radar: Thomson-CSF RDX multifunction radar, currently under development for Rafale.
Weapons: One 30-mm DEFA 554 cannon and 12 stations for air-to-air missiles or attack weapons.
Accommodation: The pilot on a seat reclined at 30-40 degrees.
Wingspan: 36 ft 9 in (11.2 m).
Wingspan, Rafale B: Approximately 35 ft 3in (10.75 m).
Length: 51 ft 10 in (15.8 m).
Length, Rafale B: Approximately 46 ft 7 in (14.20 m).
Combat configured weight: 30,864 lb (14,000 kg).
Maximum speed: Mach 2.
Mission performance: G limit +9.
Engines: Two 16,000-lb (7257-kg) thrust General Electric F404-GE-400 turbofans, with 4250 kg of fuel standard. Capable of flight refuelling.
Versions for service
Rafale A: Experimental combat aircraft, known originally as ACX.
Rafale B ACT: Projected French Air Force version.
Rafale B ACM: Projected French Navy version, with a modified and strengthened undercarriage for catapult launching and maybe use of a 'ski jump' on board ship, plus an arrester hook.
Operator: Rafale B is not yet in French service.

Dassault-Breguet/Dornier Alpha Jet
France and West Germany

One of the most curious aspects of modern aviation is that the combat capability of some jet trainers is so good that not only can they undertake secondary attack missions in an emergency but have spawned purpose-built combat variants that, in some cases, have replaced aircraft genuinely designed as warplanes. A good example of this is the Alpha Jet basic and advanced jet trainer, close support examples of which superseded Aeritalia G91s with the Luftwaffe.

Alpha Jet is a joint program of Dassault-Breguet of France and Dornier of West Germany, and is also being built in Egypt by the AOI (Arab Organization for Industrialization) in Helwan. The first prototype flew on 26 October 1973 and by 1986 480 had been delivered in several versions. Most of its construction is of metal and the comprehensive avionics include a head-up display on German aircraft, NGEA and Lancier, the latter which also has radar. All Alpha Jets have two choices of power plant, the standard (as detailed below) and the 3175-lb (1440-kg) thrust Larzac 04-C20, though this is, itself, standard on the NGEA and Lancier.

Specifications (Alpha Jet with Larzac 04-C6 engines data)
Weapons: Many different weapon combinations are possible. Provision for one 30-mm DEFA or 27-mm Mauser cannon, with 150 rounds of ammunition, in

an underfuselage pod. 4 underwing pylons for more than 5510 lb (2500 kg) of weapons, including air-to-air and air-to-surface missiles, bombs of up to 882-lb (400-kg) size, rockets, guns and much else. Other stores include a 4-camera photographic reconnaissance pod and decoy launcher.
Accommodation: Student pilot/copilot and instructor/pilot in tandem, the rear cockpit raised.
Wingspan: 29 ft 10¾ in (9.11 m).
Length: 40 ft 3¾ in (12.29 m).
Maximum take-off weight: 17,637 lb (8000 kg).
Maximum speed: Mach 0.86.
Mission radius: 335-764 miles (540-1230 km).
Mission performance: Rate of climb at sea level 11,225 ft (3420 m) per min; ceiling 48,000 ft (14,630 m); G limits +12 ultimate, −6.4 ultimate; endurance up to 3 h 30 min.
Engines: Two 2976-lb (1350-kg) thrust SNECMA/Turboméca Larzac 04-C6 turbofans, with 1900 or 2040 liters of fuel.

Above: Dassault-Breguet/Dornier Alpha Jet NGEA.

Versions in service
Trainer: Originally called the Alpha Jet E. Delivered from 1978, originally to the French Air Force which has received 176. Many export customers. Known in Egypt as the MS1.
Close support: Originally called the Alpha Jet A. Delivered from 1979 to the Luftwaffe, which ordered 175 as fighter-bombers and reconnaissance aircraft.
Close support, updated: Flown in 1982, this model features a new nav/attack system which includes a laser rangefinder, HUD and inertial platform. Known in Egypt as the MS2.
NGEA: More powerful attack model, with

Below: Three of Ivory Coast's seven Alpha Jet trainers.

the nav/attack system of the MS2 type and provision for Magic 2 air-to-air missiles and larger drop tanks.

Lancier: Top of the range day or night combat version, with Thomson-CSF/ESD Agave radar, improved computer, FLIR, HUD, passive and active ECM, and more added to NGEA features. Wider range of weapon options to take in such missions as air-to-air combat, including antihelicopter and antishipping.

Operators: Belgium (Trainer), Cameroon (Close support updated), Egypt (MS1, MS2/NGEA), France (Trainer), West Germany (Close support), Ivory Coast (Trainer), Morocco (Trainer), Nigeria (Trainer), Qatar (Trainer) and Togo (Trainer).

De Havilland Dove, Devon/Sea Devon and Heron/Sea Heron
United Kingdom

This series of closely related light transports originated with the Dove, an eight-passenger airliner that has the historic distinction of being the first new British commercial transport aircraft to take to the air after the end of World War II, first flying on 25 September 1945. Though Doves went into military service, the actual military derivative was called the Devon, or Sea Devon in Royal Navy operation. A 'stretched' four-engined derivative became the 14- to 17-passenger Heron, or Sea Heron with the Royal Navy. A conversion of the Heron with supercharged Avco Lycoming engines, by Riley in the United States, became known as the Riley Turbo Skyliner.

Specifications (Devon CC.Mk 2 data)
Accommodation: 2 crew and 9 passengers.
Wingspan: 57 ft 0 in (17.37 m).
Length: 39 ft 3 in (11.96 m).
Maximum take-off weight: 8950 lb (4060 kg).
Maximum speed: 230 mph (370 km/h).
Range: 880 miles (1416 km) with reserves.
Mission performance: Ceiling 21,700 ft (6615 m).

Engines: Two 400-hp de Havilland Gipsy Queen 175 pistons.
Versions in service
Dove: Basically a commercial transport, with different Gipsy Queen engines according to the version. Typically, Dove 8s have 400-hp Gipsy Queen 70 Mk 3s.
Devon: Military version of the Dove. Some fitted with larger canopies.
Sea Devon: Royal Navy liaison aircraft, similar to the Devon.
Heron: Larger derivative of the Dove, with four 250-hp de Havilland Gipsy Queen 30-2 engines.
Sea Heron: Royal Navy liaison aircraft, similar to the Heron.
Riley Turbo Skyliner: Basically a commercial conversion of the Heron, with four 290-hp Avco Lycoming IO-540-K1C5 supercharged engines. Maximum speed increased to 285 mph (458 km/h).
Operators: India (Dove and Devon?), Iraq (Heron), Jordan (Dove?), Lebanon (Dove), Sri Lanka (Heron and Riley Turbo Skyliner) and United Kingdom (air force, Devon CC.Mk 2; navy, Sea Devon and Sea Heron).

Above: Royal Navy de Havilland Canada Chipmunk.

De Havilland Canada DHC-1 Chipmunk
Canada

In 1928 de Havilland Aircraft in the United Kingdom established a Canadian subsidiary. This only added aircraft manufacturing to its activities during World War II, and after designed and produced its first indigenous design as the DHC-1 Chipmunk trainer. The prototype Chipmunk made its maiden flight on 22 May 1946, the type then viewed as a Tiger Moth biplane replacement. However, by far the largest proportion of the 1232 Chipmunks produced came from the British parent company. Today most of the Chipmunks flying are T.Mk 10s with the British forces, used as general-purpose aircraft. A flying selection squadron of the RAF has a number,

Below: Royal Aircraft Establishment de Havilland Devon.

and a few are based in Germany and fly around the Berlin area.

Specifications (DHC-1 Chipmunk data)
Accommodation: 2 crew in tandem under a bubble or framed canopy.
Wingspan: 34 ft 4 in (10.46 m).
Length: 25 ft 5 in (7.75 m).
Maximum take-off weight: 2014 lb (914 kg).
Maximum speed: 138 mph (222 km/h).
Range: 280 miles (450 km).
Mission performance: Rate of climb at sea level 900 ft (274 m) per min; ceiling 15,800 ft (4820 m).
Engine: One 145-hp de Havilland Gipsy Major 8 piston, with 114 liters of fuel.
Versions in service
T.Mk 10: RAF version, generally superseded by the Bulldog. More than 100 still remain with the 3 British services.
T.Mk 21: British-produced model currently in service in Sri Lanka.
OGMA Chipmunk: Oficinas Gerais de Material Aeronáutico of Portugal built a number of Chipmunks for home use.
Operators: Portugal, Sri Lanka and United Kingdom (air force, navy and army).

De Havilland Canada DHC-2 Beaver
Canada

De Havilland Canada's second design, following the Chipmunk trainer, the Beaver began a family of STOL utility transports that today includes the DHC-8. The Beaver was designed as an extremely rugged utility transport, able to operate on wheels, floats or skis. The prototype made its maiden flight in August 1947 and very large numbers of production aircraft were built for military and civil operation. Today the number of Beavers remaining in military service is fairly small, and no Turbo-Beavers (first flown in 1963) are military-flown.

Specifications (Beaver landplane data)
Accommodation: Pilot plus 2 passengers on lightweight collapsible seats or freight in 120 cu ft of the cabin space.
Wingspan: 48 ft 0 in (14.64 m).
Length: 30 ft 4 in (9.24 m).
Maximum take-off weight: 5100 lb (2313 kg).
Maximum speed: 140 mph (225 km/h).
Range: 483-778 miles (777-1252 km).
Mission performance: Rate of climb at sea

Below: De Havilland Canada DHC-2 Beaver.

level 1020 ft (311 m) per min; ceiling 18,000 ft (5485 m).
Engine: One 450-hp Pratt & Whitney R-985-AN-1/AN-3 radial piston, with 359 liters of fuel.
Versions in service
DHC-2 Beaver: As described above. US Army designation U-6A. British Army designation Beaver AL.1. Most of the latter's Beavers are in store.
Operators: Argentina, Colombia, Haiti, Indonesia (army), Laos, Turkey (army), United Kingdom (army), United States (army) and Zambia.

De Havilland Canada DHC-3 Otter
Canada

A larger development of the Beaver, the Otter first flew as a prototype on 12 December 1951 and a great many eventually went into military and commercial use. Like the Beaver, it can operate on wheels, floats or skis and, indeed, at least seven nations used the aircraft on Antarctic expeditions and operations; the Royal Canadian Air Force/ Canadian Armed Forces used Otters for Arctic search and rescue as well as for other more commonplace duties. Today Otters are flown in small numbers as utility transports and for liaison.

Above: De Havilland Canada DHC-3 Otter, flown by the US Army as the U-1A.

Specifications (Otter landplane data)
Accommodation: 2 crew plus up to 10 passengers, 6 stretchers and 4 seated attendants or casualties, 7 passengers plus 3 stretchers, or freight in main cabin space of 272 cu ft.
Wingspan: 58 ft 0 in (17.69 m).
Length: 41 ft 10 in (12.80 m).
Maximum take-off weight: 8000 lb (3629 kg).
Maximum speed: 153 mph (246 km/h).
Range: 945 miles (1520 km).
Mission performance: Rate of climb at sea level 850 ft (260 m) per min; ceiling 18,800 ft (5730 m).
Engine: One 600-hp Pratt & Whitney R-1340-S1H1-G/S3H1-G radial piston, with 809 liters of fuel.
Version in service
DHC-3 Otter. As described above. US Army designation U-1A. The designation U-1B applied to Otters flown by the US Navy for Antarctic operation. India is currently the largest military user with approximately 20 in service.
Operators: Argentina, Canada, India, Nicaragua, Panama, Paraguay and United States (army).

De Havilland Canada DHC-4A Caribou
Canada

The Caribou was de Havilland Canada's first tactical STOL transport, very different in style to its earlier Beaver and Otter utility transports. An early boost in the program was the support of the US Army. The first prototype undertook its initial flight on 30 July 1958. The US Army placed orders for AC-1s (later redesignated CV-2As) and higher gross weight CV-2Bs, the latter relating to the company designation DHC-4A. In total the US Army received 159 Caribous, most of which were passed to the USAF in 1967, becoming C-7As. Of the other users, the RCAF received only a few as CC.108s, four of which worked with United Nations units in the Congo.

Above: Spanish Air Force de Havilland Canada DHC-4A Caribou, service-designated T.9.

Specifications (DHC-4A data)
Accommodation: Pilot and copilot plus up to 8740 lb (3964 kg) of freight, vehicles, 32 troops, 26 paratroops, or 22 stretchers and 8 medical attendants/sitting casualties.
Wingspan: 95 ft 7½ in (29.15 m).
Length: 72 ft 7 in (22.13 m).
Maximum take-off weight: 28,500 lb (12,927 kg).
Maximum speed: 216 mph (348 km/h).
Range: 242 miles (389 km) with full payload.
Mission performance: Rate of climb at sea level 1350 ft (411 m) per min; ceiling 24,800 ft (7560 m).
Engines: Two 1450-hp Pratt & Whitney R-2000-7M2 radial pistons, with 3137 liters of fuel.
Versions in service
DHC-4: Initial production version, with 26,000-lb (11,793-kg) AUW.
DHC-4A: Higher gross weight version, as detailed. Spanish military designation T.9.
Operators: Australia, Cameroon, India, Kenya, Malaysia, Spain, United States (air force and army), Vietnam and Zambia.

De Havilland Canada DHC-5 Buffalo
Canada

The Buffalo STOL transport was developed as a more modern and turboprop replacement for the Caribou, offering a much enhanced payload. A rear-loading door is provided as before, but under a less upswept 'beaver' rear fuselage, while the cargo cabin is longer, wider and higher, the volume increasing from 1150 cu ft for the Caribou to 1580 cu ft. The first Buffalo flew initially on 9 April 1964 and today the DHC-5A and D versions are in service, the former with the Canadian Armed Forces as CC-115 SAR/ transports and Brazil as C-115s.

Specifications (DHC-5D data)
Radar: Weather radar.
Accommodation: 3 crew plus 41 troops, 35 paratroops, 24 stretchers and 6 sitting casualties/attendants, or 18,000 lb (8164 kg) of freight. Can use a low-altitude parachute extraction system (LAPES), whereupon a 5000-lb (2268-kg) load can be parachute-dropped with precision from an altitude of about 200 ft (61 m) on to a drop zone.
Wingspan: 96 ft 0 in (29.26 m).

Length: 79 ft 0 in (24.08 m).
Maximum take-off weight: 49,200 lb (22,316 kg).
Cruising speed: 261 mph (420 km/h).
Range: 3800 miles (6115 km).
Engines: Two 3133-shp General Electric CT64-820-4 turboprops, with 7978 liters of fuel.
Versions in service
DHC-5A: Early version, with two 3055-eshp General Electric CT64-820-1 turboprops.
DHC-5D: Current and major model.
Operators: Abu Dhabi, Brazil, Cameroon, Canada, Ecuador, Egypt, Mauritania, Oman, Peru, Sudan, Tanzania, Togo, Zaire and Zambia.

De Havilland Canada DHC-6 Twin Otter
Canada

Bearing no configurational relationship to the DHC-3 Otter, the Twin Otter first flew on 20 May 1965 as a twin-turboprop STOL

Below: Canadian Armed Forces de Havilland Canada CC-115 Buffalo.

Above: Canadian Armed Forces Twin Otters.

transport for civil and military use. Over 800 have been delivered to more than 70 countries, those currently using military examples being listed below. Apart from transport, the aircraft can undertake more specialized roles, such as geophysical/photographic survey and SAR, but as yet no DHC-6-300M weapon-carrying military transport/counter-insurgency aircraft have been sold. A single 300MR maritime reconnaissance variant was delivered to the Senegal Department of Fisheries in 1982. The Twin Otter can operate on a wheel undercarriage, floats or wheel/skis, taking off in just 700 ft (213 m) with wheels fitted.

Specifications (Series 300 data)
Radar: Optional weather radar.
Accommodation: 2 crew plus 20 passengers, stretchers, or up to 4280 lb (1941 kg) of freight.
Wingspan: 65 ft 0 in (19.81 m).
Length: 51 ft 9 in (15.77 m).
Maximum take-off weight: 12,500 lb (5670 kg).
Cruising speed: 210 mph (338 km/h).
Range: 806 miles (1297 km) with a 2500-lb (1134-kg) load.
Mission performance: Rate of climb at sea level 1600 ft (488 m) per min; ceiling 26,700 ft (8135 m).
Engines: Two 620-shp Pratt & Whitney Canada PT6A-27 turboprops, with 1446 liters of fuel standard.
Versions in service
Series 100: Initial production version, with 579-ehp PT6A-20 turboprops.
Series 200: Similar to the Series 100 but with greater baggage volume in the rear of the fuselage and in a longer nose.
Series 300: Current production version, as detailed above. Three USAF aircraft are designated UV-18B and are Academy parachute-jump trainers. US Army UV-18As are transports.
Series 300MR: Litton AN/APS-504(V)2 search radar under the nose, plus a

searchlight and four underwing pylons.
Operators: Argentina (air force and army), Botswana, Canada (designated CC.138s), Chile, Ecuador, Ethiopia (army?), France, Haiti, Norway, Panama, Paraguay, Peru, Senegal and United States (air force and army).

De Havilland Canada DHC-7 Dash 7
Canada

Designed as a short/medium-range STOL airliner for 50 to 54 passengers, to be quiet in operation, the DHC-7 flew for the first time on 27 March 1975. Only a tiny number have found their way into military service as transports. A Dash 7IR variant of the latest heavier Series 150, for ice reconnaissance and equipped with SLAR 100 side-looking radar and a unique observation cabin above and to the rear of the flight deck, is used by the

Canadian Department of the Environment (but is civil-registered).

Specifications (DHC-7 Dash 7)
Accommodation: 50-54 passengers or 11,310 lb (5130 kg) of freight.
Wingspan: 93 ft 0 in (28.35 m).
Length: 80 ft 6 in (24.54 m).
Maximum take-off weight: 44,000 lb (19,958 kg).
Cruising speed: 266 mph (428 km/h).
Range: 795 miles (1279 km) with 50 passengers.
Mission performance: Rate of climb at sea level 1220 ft (372 m) per min; ceiling 21,000 ft (6400 m).
Engines: Four 1120-shp Pratt & Whitney Canada PT6A-50 turboprops, with 5600 liters of fuel standard.
Versions in service
Dash 7 Series 100 and 101: The Series 100 is the standard passenger version. All-cargo version is the Series 101. Known in Canadian Armed Forces service as the CC-132.
Dash 7 Series 150: Higher-weight version. Used as the basis for the Dash 7IR civil-registered ice reconnaissance model.
Operators: Canada and Venezuela (navy).

De Havilland Canada DHC-8 Dash 8
Canada

The Dash 8 is a short-range commercial transport aircraft, designed to be quiet and economical. Eight, however, are in military service. The Canadian Department of National Defence ordered six, four as navigation trainers and two as passenger and cargo transports for European operations, all under the designation Dash 8M. Apart from the necessary changes to the avionics, the Dash 8Ms have increased fuel capacity, reinforced cabin floors and strengthened undercarriages for rough field take-offs and landings. Two Dash 8s are also flown by the USAF, as airborne data link/relay aircraft. Fitted with AN/APS-128D sea-search radar,

Below: De Havilland Canada DHC-7 Dash 7, designated CC-132 in CAF service.

Above: USAF de Havilland Canada DHC-8 Dash 8 before delivery as an airborne telemetry relay aircraft.

Dornier Do 27, Do 28, Do 28 D Skyservant, and Do 128
West Germany

This series of STOL aircraft from Dornier covers single- and twin-engined models produced over a period of more than 30 years. The Do 27 first flew as a prototype on 27 June 1955 and the Federal German Luftwaffe and Army alone received 428, while other military users included Spain where fifty were built under license as CASA C.127s.

From the single-engined Do 27 (used for utility, transport and ambulance duties and currently mainly occupied in a liaison role), the Do 28 was developed. The Do 28 prototype flew on 29 April 1959. This was basically no more than a twin-engined derivative, but with the Do 28 D Skyservant a completely new design was chosen although still of Do 28 general layout. The prototype Do 28 D made its maiden flight on 23 February 1966.

In 1980 an improved ten-seat Skyservant appeared as the 128-2. This was followed by a turboprop version as the 128-6, of which deliveries to civil and military customers began in 1981.

Below: Dornier Do 28 D-2s.

Above: USAF de Havilland Canada DHC-8 Dash 8 before delivery as an airborne telemetry relay aircraft.

phased-array antenna and other specialized avionics, their function is to relay voice, telemetry and tracking information with aircraft undertaking training and test missions. Both aircraft fly off the Florida coast.

DHC-8 Dash 8 200M is the designation given to a proposed armed antisubmarine warfare version of the Dash 8.

Specifications (Standard Dash 8 Series 100 data unless otherwise stated)
Radar: 2 USAF aircraft have surveillance radar, as noted above. Standard for the Dash 8 is Primus 800 weather radar.
Weapons: The Dash 8 200M is proposed with fuselage and underwing armament.
Accommodation: Normal seating is for a flight crew of 2 and up to 40 passengers. Alternatively, up to 9410 lb (4268 kg) of cargo.
Wingspan: 85 ft 0 in (25.91 m).
Length: 73 ft 0 in (22.25 m).
Maximum take-off weight: 33,000 lb (14,968 kg).
Cruising speed: 309 mph (497 km/h).
Range with 40 passengers: 1025 miles (1650 km).
Mission performance: Rate of climb at sea level 2070 ft (631 m) per min.
Engines: Two 1800-shp Pratt & Whitney Canada PW120A turboprops, with 3160 to 5655 liters of fuel.
Versions in service
Dash 8M: Canadian DND version, as detailed above.
USAF Dash 8: Military service designation not given at the time of writing. 2 aircraft for data link missions, for service in 1987.
Dash 8 200M: Proposed antisubmarine warfare version, with search radar, MAD, ESM, FLIR, sonobuoy information processing, weapons, etc.
Operators: Canada and United States.

Specifications (Do 28 D-2 data)

Accommodation: Up to 15 persons (including the pilot/s), or the pilot and 5 stretchers and 5 sitting casualties/attendants, or cargo.
Wingspan: 51 ft 0¼ in (15.55 m).
Length: 37 ft 5¼ in (11.41 m).
Maximum take-off weight: 8470 lb (3842 kg).
Maximum speed: 202 mph (325 km/h).
Range: 652 miles (1050 km).
Mission performance: Rate of climb at sea level 1160 ft (354 m) per min; ceiling 25,200 ft (7680 m).
Engines: Two 380-hp Avco Lycoming IGSO-540-A1E pistons, with 893 liters of fuel standard.

Versions in service

Do 27: Cantilever high-wing monoplane, with a fixed undercarriage and a 270-hp Avco Lycoming GO-480-B1A6 or 340-hp GSO-480-B1B6 engine mounted in the nose. Several versions were produced, the Do 27 A-4, Q-5 and Q-6 possessing a maximum speed of 130 mph (210 km/h). Accommodation for 6 to 8 persons (including the crew).
Do 28: Initial twin-engined version, retaining the Do 27's wing layout (though of increased span and area) and round-section fuselage. Engines carried on stub wings each side of the lower fuselage. A and B series variants were completed, the B-1 with two 290-hp IO-540 engines and possessing a maximum speed of 184 mph (290 km/h).
Do 28 D Skyservant: This redesigned variant of the Do 28 was built in D, D-1 and D-2 models. Square-section fuselage.
128-2 Skyservant: Developed from the Do 28 D-2 and powered by two 380-hp Avco Lycoming IGSO-540-A1E piston engines. Maximum speed is 202 mph (325 km/h).
128-6: Turboprop development of the 128-2, first flown on 4 March 1980. Strengthened undercarriage. Powered by two 400-shp Pratt & Whitney Canada PT6A-110s, giving a maximum speed of 211 mph (339 km/h)

Below: Dornier 228-201 in Luftwaffe markings.

and a range of 1134 miles (1825 km). A maritime patrol version with a MEL Marec maritime surveillance radar is also available as the 128-6MPA.
Operators: Burundi (army, Do 27), Cameroon (Do 28 B and 128-6MPA), West Germany (air force and navy, Do 28 D-2; 2 navy Skyservants now carry surveillance equipment to detect oil pollution), Greece (Do 28 D-2), Guinea-Bissau (Do 27), Israel (Do 28B), Kenya (Do 28 D-2), Malawi (army, Do 27 and Do 28 D), Morocco (Do 28 D-2), Niger (Do 28 D-2), Nigeria (Do 28 D-2, 128-2, 128-6), Rwanda (Do 27), Spain (CASA C.127 and Do 28A), Sweden (army, Do 27), Switzerland (Do 27), Turkey (army, Do 27, Do 28B and Do 28 D-1) and Zambia (Do 28 D-1).

Dornier 228 and Maritime Patrol
West Germany

The Dornier 228 is a larger stablemate of the 128-6, and of substantially different design. The larger wing has tapered outer panels with raked tips, the engines are carried below the wing, and the undercarriage retracts. Accommodation is for 21 troops in the Series 100 model and 25 in the lengthened Series 200. The maximum payload in a cargo configuration is 4689 lb (2127 kg) and 4394 lb (1993 kg) respectively. Each model also has a derivative with a strengthened fuselage and new tires for higher operating weights. Two maritime patrol derivatives are also available, as detailed below.

The Kanpur division of HAL in India is producing the 228 under license. These operate with the Indian Air Force for transport and other duties as replacements for older types such as the de Havilland Devon, de Havilland Canada Otter and Douglas C-47, and with the Navy and Coast Guard in maritime form. The Air Force requirement has been reported at 80 and 116 aircraft, though which is correct is not as yet clear. The Navy order has been reported as 24.

Specifications (228-200 data)

Accommodation: As detailed above.
Wingspan: 55 ft 8 in (16.97 m).
Length: 54 ft 4 in (16.56 m).
Maximum take-off weight: 12,566 lb (5700 kg).
Cruising speed: 266 mph (428 km/h).
Range: 372-1680 miles (600-2704 km).
Mission performance: Rate of climb at sea level 2030 ft (618 m) per min; ceiling 29,600 ft (9020 m).
Engines: Two 715-shp Garrett TPE331-5-252D turboprops, with 2386 liters of fuel.

Versions in service

228-100: Initial version, delivered from early 1982. Same engines as for 228-200.
228-101: Higher-weight version of the 228-100, with a maximum take-off weight of 13,183 lb (5980 kg). Possible load increased to 4667 lb (2117 kg).
228-200: As detailed above.
228-201: Higher-weight version of the 228-200, with the same take-off weight as the 228-101 and a possible load of 4482 lb (2033 kg).
228 Maritime Patrol A: Crew of five, comprising two pilots, two observers and an operator for the MEL Marec II maritime reconnaissance radar. Roles include coastal patrol, fishery protection, pollution detection, antismuggling missions, and search and rescue (two 20-person liferafts are available). Indian Coast Guard examples (three based on the 228-101) may be capable of carrying air-to-surface missiles and Indian Navy examples may carry antishipping missiles.
228 Maritime Patrol B: Fitted with side-looking airborne radar (SLAR) and other equipment. No known orders at the time of writing.
Operators: India (air force, 228-200, navy and coast guard Maritime Patrol A) and Nigeria (228-100 and -200). The German Luftwaffe and Navy evaluated the 228-201 in 1986.

Douglas A-4 Skyhawk
United States

Designed to provide the US Navy with a single-engined carrier-based daylight attack aircraft of high performance, and one that would be suitable also for such roles as dive-bombing, close support and interdiction, the key to the success of what became the Douglas A-4 was undoubtedly its small size and simple lightweight construction.

Features of the design included a wing of modified delta planform which was small enough to eliminate the need for wing folding, and one which incorporated continuous wingtip-to-wingtip spars, one-piece wing skins, automatic leading-edge slats, split trailing-edge flaps and powered ailerons. The fuselage comprised forward and rear assemblies, the forward section with a detachable nosecone containing communications and IFF avionics, and an easily removable rear section to facilitate an engine change. The tail unit also had powered control surfaces, with a rudder of unique design that comprised a central skin and external stiffeners. A stalky retractable tricycle undercarriage provided adequate clearance beneath the wing for a comprehensive weapon load, and power plant was originally a Wright J65 turbojet, which was a

Above: Douglas Skyhawk of the Israeli Air Force carrying two Gabriel III A/S standoff missiles.

license-built version of the Armstrong Siddeley Sapphire.

First flown in XA4D-1 prototype form on 22 June 1954, the capability of this new aircraft was confirmed at an early date when on 15 October 1955 the second pre-production aircraft established a 500-km closed-circuit world speed record of 695.163 mph (1118.756 km/h). Initial deliveries to US Navy Squadron VA-52 began on 26 October 1956 and now, more than 30 years later, the type still remains in use with both the US Navy and Marine Corps in some numbers, in the latter case primarily for training. When A-4 Skyhawk production ended on 27 February 1979 a total of 2960 had been built for the USN/USMC, comprising 2405 attack aircraft and 555 trainers. Early versions displaced from USN/USMC service were soon acquired by other air forces and included some comprehensive conversions by Lockheed Aircraft Service Company for the Republic of Singapore Air Force. Israel Aircraft Industries has upgraded the A-4s in service with the Israeli Air Force and is offering a similar package to other operators of the A-4; items covered by the update include a life-extension overhaul, the replacement of all wiring and the introduction of several items including a steerable nosewheel, brake-chute, 30-mm (instead of 20-mm) cannon and a new fully inertial weapon delivery/navigation system. Also, currently Grumman is remanufacturing 40 Royal Malaysian Air Force Skyhawks for longer service, comprising single-seat A-4PTMs and six TA-4PTM two-seat trainers. Apart from refurbished engines, new avionics, etc, these have seven weapon stations.

Specifications (A-4M Skyhawk data)
Radar: APN-153(V) radar nav with ASN-41 nav computer.
Weapons: Weapon stations on the fuselage centerline and four under the wings, with maximum external load limited to 8200 lb (3719 kg). In addition to the two standard 20-mm Colt Mk 12 cannon, each with 100 rounds, a very wide range of weapons can include conventional or nuclear bombs;

free-fall, retarded and guided bombs; and missiles that can include the AIM-9 Sidewinder AAM and Hughes AGM-12 Bullpup or AGM-65 Maverick ASMs.
Accommodation: The pilot.
Wingspan: 27 ft 6 in (8.38 m).
Length: 40 ft 3½ in (12.28 m).
Normal take-off weight: 24,500 lb (11,113 kg).
Maximum speed: 685 mph (1102 km/h) 'clean' at sea level.
Combat radius: 340 miles (547 km) with 4000-lb (1814-kg) weapon load.
Mission performance: Rate of climb at sea level 10,300 ft (3140 m) per min.
Engine: One 11,200-lb (5080-kg) thrust Pratt & Whitney J52-P-408A turbojet, with 3028 liters fuel standard.

Versions in service
A-4E: Originally A4D-5. Similar to earlier A-4C all-weather attack version, but with 5 weapon stations and J52-P-6A engine.
A-4F: Last USN attack version, differed from above by introducing a zero-zero ejector seat, nosewheel steering, wing spoilers, an upper fuselage hump aft of the cockpit for additional avionics and uprated J52-P-8A engine.
TA-4F: 2-seat advanced trainer of A-4F with a fuselage lengthened by 2 ft 6 in (0.76 m) to accommodate second cockpit; both cockpits with zero-zero ejector seats.
A-4H: Version basically similar to A-4E for operation from land bases by Israeli Air Force, but with J52-P-8A engine, square-tipped fin and rudder and provided with ribbon-type drag-chute and two 30-mm DEFA cannon in lieu of 20-mm cannon.
TA-4H: 2-seat trainer version of A-4H.
TA-4J: Similar to TA-4F but with some weapons systems deleted and J52-P-6A engine installed.
A-4K: Version of A-4H for Royal New Zealand Air Force.
TA-4K: two-seat version of A-4K for RNZAF.
A4-KU: Version for the Kuwait Air Force, generally similar to the A-4M (see below).
TA-4KU: 2-seat version of the A-4KU for the Kuwait Air Force.
A-4M: Improved version for US Marine Corps introducing uprated J52-P-408A engine with self-start capability, more electric power generating capacity,

modified refuelling probe, doubled ammunition capacity, enlarged cockpit canopy, and with the modified tail surfaces and brake-chute of the A-4H.
OA-4M: 2-seat forward air control version of TA-4F for use by the US Marine Corps.
A-4N: Version of A-4M for Israeli Air Force, but introducing new navigation/weapons delivery system and, as with earlier IAF aircraft, two 30-mm DEFA cannon.
A-4P: Designation of refurbished A-4B and A-4C aircraft for service with the Argentine Air Force.
A-4PTM: Conversions by Grumman of A-4C/L aircraft for Malaysian Air Force.
TA-4 PTM: Malaysian Air Force 2-seat trainers.
A-4Q: Designation of refurbished A-4B aircraft for service with Argentina's Comando de Aviación Naval.
A-4S: Designation of refurbished A-4Bs for the Singapore Air Force. Following extensive repair of the airframe these A-4S aircraft were modernized by the installation of solid-state electronics, had a redesigned cockpit for new instrumentation, introduced the A-4M type of refuelling probe and A-4H drag-chute, and had Aden 30-mm cannon installed; the J65 engines were overhauled and upgraded.
TA-4S: Modification of A-4Bs to provide tandem 2-seat trainers for Singapore Air Force; differ from all other two-seaters by having individual cockpit canopies.
A-4S-1: Designation of refurbished A-4Cs for the Singapore Air Force, introducing new avionics and upgraded weapon pylons.
TA-4S-1: Designation of TA-4B trainers following modification for the Singapore Air Force.
Operators: Argentina (air force A-4P; navy A-4Q), Indonesia (A-4E, TA-4H), Israel (A-4E, A-4H, A-4N, TA-4H, TA-4J), Kuwait (A-4KU, TA-4KU), Malaysia (A-4PTM, TA-4PTM), New Zealand (A-4K, TA-4K); Singapore (A-4S, A-4S-1, TA-4S, TA-4S-1) and United States (navy/marine corps A-4E, A-4F, A-4M, OA-4M, TA-4F, TA-4J).

Douglas C-47 and Lisunov Li-2
(Li-2 NATO name Cab)
United States and Soviet Union

C-47 was the designation given to the original military derivative of the DC-3 fourteen-passenger airliner, the latter of which first flew on 17 December 1935. Immediately successful as a prewar commercial transport, it became the subject of intense production during World War II to provide the backbone for Allied military transport operations. It remained in production for a short time after peace returned, finally ending after nearly 11,000 had been constructed. Most of these were for use as transports.

Despite its obsolescence among modern transports, typified by its slanting cargo floor which makes loading difficult, C-47s remain in service around the world. Also in very limited use is the 'Spooky' gunship version, which demonstrated its effectiveness at suppressing ground fire during the Vietnam War. The Soviet equivalent of the DC-3, the Lisunov Li-2, also remains in military operation, the greatest number serving with the Chinese forces.

Above: Hellenic Air Force Douglas C-47.

Specifications (C-47 data)

Weapons: The AC-47 'Spooky' gunship conversion of the C-47 can carry three 7.62-mm Miniguns.
Accommodation: Up to 28 armed troops, or 6000 lb (2722 kg) of cargo, or 18 stretchers and medical attendants.
Wingspan: 95 ft 0 in (28.95 m).
Length: 64 ft 5½ in (19.64 m).
Maximum take-off weight: 26,000 lb (11,793 kg).
Maximum speed: 229 mph (369 km/h).
Range: 1500 miles (2414 km).
Mission performance: Ceiling 24,100 ft (7350 m).
Engines: Two 1200-hp Pratt & Whitney R-1820-92 radial pistons.

Versions in service
C-47: Military derivative of the commercial DC-3, named Skytrain and Dakota. Various sub-variants were produced.
AC-47: So-called 'Spooky' gunship conversion.
TC-47: Trainer.
Lisunov Li-2: Soviet-built DC-3 with 1000-hp ASh-62IR radials. China is the largest operator today, with about 75.
Operators: All C-47s, unless stated otherwise. Albania (Li-2), Argentina, Australia, Benin, Cameroon, Canada, Central African Republic, Chad, Chile, China (Li-2), Colombia, Congo Republic,

Below: Colombian Air Force Douglas C-54 Skymaster.

Dominican Republic, Ecuador, El Salvador (AC-47), Greece, Guatemala, Guinea-Bissau, Haiti, Honduras, Hungary, India, Indonesia (air force, navy and army), Israel, North Korea (Li-2), Laos (C-47, TC-47 and AC-47), Libya, Malagasy, Mali, Mexico, Mozambique, Panama, Paraguay (air force and navy), Peru (air force and navy), Philippines, Rwanda, Somalia, South Africa, Sri Lanka, Taiwan, Thailand (C-47 and AC-47), Turkey, Venezuela, Vietnam (C-47 and Li-2), North Yemen, Zaire and Zimbabwe.

Douglas C-54 Skymaster
United States

Designed as a big brother to the DC-3, the DC-4's commercial program was also interrupted by World War II and became the C-54 military transport, first flying in this guise in 1942. Apart from its greater accommodation and four engines, it was important from the point of view of having a tricycle undercarriage which provided level cabins and thereby made loading and unloading much easier.

Specifications (C-54 Skymaster data)
Accommodation: 50 armed troops or 32,000 lb (14,515 kg) of cargo.
Wingspan: 117 ft 6 in (35.81 m).
Length: 93 ft 11 in (28.63 m).
Maximum take-off weight: 73,000 lb (33,110 kg).
Maximum speed: 274 mph (441 km/h).

Normal range: 1500 miles (2414 km).
Mission performance: Rate of climb at sea level 1070 ft (326 m) per min; ceiling 22,500 ft (6855 m).
Engines: Four 1450-hp Pratt & Whitney R-2000 radial pistons.

Version in service
C-54 Skymaster: Became the standard transport of the USAF and US Navy, but neither service retains any today. Small numbers are operated as transports by 8 air forces worldwide.
Operators: Central African Republic, Chad, Colombia, South Korea, Mexico, Niger, South Africa and Taiwan.

Douglas C-118 Liftmaster, DC-6 and DC-7
United States

First flown on 15 February 1946, the Liftmaster (originally designated C-112) was the military version of the DC-6 airliner and represented a larger and more powerful successor to the earlier DC-4/Skymaster. Of similar overall configuration to the Skymaster, the Liftmaster was given thermal de-icing and pressurization for the cabins among other features. Although most Liftmasters in service today carry the C-118 military designation in one form or another (such as the US Navy's C-118Bs), ex-DC-6B airliners are among those transports in military use.

It is believed that a single DC-7B is the only remaining example of this transport in military service today, operated by Mexico. The DC-7 was evolved as a slight scale-up of the DC-6, with accommodation for 95 persons in a longer fuselage and more powerful engines fitted.

Specifications (C-118 Liftmaster data)
Accommodation: 76 troops or up to 27,000 lb (12,247 kg) of cargo.
Wingspan: 117 ft 6 in (35.81 m).
Length: 105 ft 7 in (32.18 m).
Maximum take-off weight: 107,000 lb (48,534 kg).
Maximum speed: 360 mph (579 km/h).
Range: 3860 miles (6212 km).
Mission performance: Rate of climb at sea level 1070 ft (326 m) per min.
Engines: Four 2500-hp Pratt & Whitney R-2800-52W radial pistons.

Versions in service
C-118 Liftmaster: Military counterpart of the DC-6 airliner.
DC-7B: Development of the DC-6, with four 3400-hp Wright R-3350-18 engines.

A-3B, had an all-up weight of 82,000 lb (37,195 kg). Yet, despite the enormous weight, it could attain 610 mph (982 km/h) on the power of just two Pratt & Whitney J57 turbojet engines, with the optional assistance at take off of twelve jettisonable rockets on the rear fuselage sides.

Apart from attack bomber versions, photographic-reconnaissance, electronic countermeasures and training models were produced. Flight Refuelling Inc also developed a pack that could fit into the bomb-bay to enable the Skywarrior to perform as a tanker, and in 1959 one such aircraft flew from USS *Independence* at a weight of 84,000 lb (38,100 kg). Other Skywarrior versions were developed by modification. Today the only Skywarriors in service are 21 EA-3Bs with the US Navy for elint (electronic intelligence)and two reserve squadrons of KA-3B tankers. The latter can each carry 19,025 liters of fuel.

Specifications (EA-3B Skywarrior data)
Equipment: Includes electronic countermeasures equipment, and forward- and side-looking radars.
Accommodation: Flight crew of 3 plus 4 equipment operators in the bomb-bay compartment.
Wingspan: 72 ft 6 in (22.10 m).
Length: 76 ft 4 in (23.27 m).
Maximum take-off weight: 73,000 lb (33,110 kg).
Maximum speed: 610 mph (982 km/h).
Mission performance: Ceiling 45,000 ft (13,715 m).
Engines: Two 10,500-lb (4763-kg) thrust

Above: French government agency Securité Civile Douglas DC-6B water-bomber.

Operators: El Salvador (C-118), France (government, Sécurité Civile), Guatemala (DC-6), Honduras (C-118), Mexico (DC-6B and DC-7B), Paraguay (DC-6B), United States (navy, C-118) and Yugoslavia (DC-6B).

Below: Douglas KA-3B Skywarriors.

Douglas EA-3 and KA-3B Skywarrior
United States

The Skywarrior was nothing short of revolutionary when it entered US Navy service as a carrier-borne high-speed attack bomber in March 1956. The heaviest aircraft ever produced to operate from aircraft carriers, it had first flown as a prototype on 28 October 1952 (under the original A3D designation) and the most important production version, the

Pratt & Whitney J57-P-10 turbojets.

Versions in service

EA-3B: ECM versions, of which 21 remain active.

KA-3B: Tanker version, of which 2 squadrons remain with the US Navy Reserve.

Operator: United States (navy and reserve, EA-3B and KA-3B).

EH Industries EH 101
Italy and United Kingdom

With both the Royal Navy and the Italian Navy requiring a new antisubmarine warfare helicopter for future deployment (mainly from ship and shore respectively), Agusta and Westland joined forces to develop such an aircraft under the management of a newly founded company, EH Industries. Three versions are now planned, the naval with ASW as one role, a utility model for 24 to 35 troops, cargo or vehicles driven into the main cabin via a rear loading ramp, and a commercial type. The first EH 101 was exhibited in early 1987 and deliveries of production helicopters are scheduled for the 1990s.

Specifications (Naval EH 101 data unless otherwise stated, with estimated performance)

Radar: Ferranti Blue Kestrel search radar in the British service version, with a flat aperture antenna. ASW model will carry dipping sonar, sonobuoys and GEC AQS-903 processing equipment, and ESM.

Weapons: Will include four homing torpedoes. The antishipping version will be armed with air-to-surface missiles as one option, and the antiship surveillance and tracking model will be capable of over-the-horizon targeting and midcourse guidance for frigate-launched missiles, and surveillance.

Accommodation: Troops, vehicles in utility model, or cargo to a maximum of 10,000 lb (4535 kg) as a slung load.

Diameter of rotor: 61 ft 0 in (18.59 m).

Length with rotors: 75 ft 3 in (22.94 m).

Maximum take-off weight: 28,660 lb (13,000 kg).

Cruising speed: 173 mph (278 km/h).

Time on station with full naval load: 5 h.

Versions in service

None as yet.

Operators: None as yet.

Below: EH Industries EH 101 multirole helicopter mock-up, in antiship configuration.

EMBRAER EMB-110 Bandeirante and EMB-111
Brazil

One of the great success stories of modern aviation, the Bandeirante twin-turboprop transport has found world markets in commercial form and has been included in the inventories of several air forces. The first prototype achieved its maiden flight on 26 October 1968 and by 1986 454 production aircraft had been delivered to customers in 32 countries. Details of the various models in military use can be found below.

From the EMB-110, EMBRAER developed the EMB-111 as a land-based maritime surveillance aircraft. The initial customer was the home air force's Coastal Command, which took 12 for service with the 7° Grupo de Aviação. The six Chilean Navy aircraft have several equipment changes, and the Gabonese Air Force operates a single aircraft.

Specifications (EMB-110 Bandeirante data unless otherwise stated)

Radar (EMB-111): Eaton AN/APS-128 surveillance radar in the nose radome, which also doubles as a weather radar with a range of 200 nautical miles. Standard equipment includes passive ECM.

Weapons: Four underwing pylons for weapons and/or equipment, the latter optionally comprising a searchlight,

Above: Gabonese Air Force EMBRAER EMB-111.

loudhailer, etc. Armament can be up to eight 5-in HVAR or four launchers for 2.75-in FFAR air-to-surface rockets. Chute in the lower fuselage for marker buoys, flares or chaff.

Accommodation: See 'Versions in service' below.

Wingspan: 50 ft 3½ in (15.33 m).

Length: 49 ft 6½ in (15.10 m).

Maximum take-off weight: 12,500 lb (5670 kg).

Maximum speed: 286 mph (460 km/h).

Range: 1244 miles (2000 km).

Mission performance: Rate of climb at sea level 1788 ft (545 m) per min; ceiling 22,500 ft (6860 m).

Engines: Two 750-shp Pratt & Whitney Canada PT6A-34 turboprops, with 1720 liters of fuel. EMB-111 has a fuel capacity of 1914 liters, plus a further 636 liters in permanent tiptanks.

Versions in service

EMB-110: Initial version, flown as a 12-seat transport by the Brazilian Air Force under the military designation C-95.

EMB-110A: Navigation aid calibration aircraft, flown by the Brazilian Air Force as the EC-95.

EMB-110B: Photogrammetric aircraft with Zeiss and Wild cameras. Decca Doppler navigation equipment. Flight crew plus 3 systems operators. Brazilian Air Force designation R-95. Convertible 14 passenger/photogrammetric version became the EMB-110B1, ordered by the Uruguayan Air Force.

EMB-110C: 15-passenger transport, purchased by the Chilean Navy and Uruguayan Air Force.

EMB-110K1: Cargo version with a large upward-hinging door. Fuselage lengthened from 45 ft 1 in to 47 ft 10½ in, allowing for an overall length of 49 ft 6½ in. Brazilian Air Force designation C-95A.

EMB-110P1K: Utility version of the commercial P1 quick-change model, for military use including paratroop dropping. Brazilian Air Force designation C-95B. Used also by Gabon.

EMB-110P1K SAR: Search and rescue aircraft. Accommodation includes 6

stretchers. Can also be used for paratroop dropping. Brazilian Air Force designation SC-95B.

EMB-111: Maritime surveillance derivative, with search radar.

Operators: Brazil (EMB-110 and EMB-111), Chile (navy, EMB-110 and EMB-111), Gabon (EMB-110 and EMB-111) and Uruguay (EMB-110).

EMBRAER EMB-120 Brasilia
Brazil

First flown as a prototype on 27 July 1983, the Brasilia was designed and developed as a twin-turboprop civil transport aircraft, accommodating up to 30 passengers or 7650 lb (3470 kg) of freight. Mixed passenger/freight, corporate and military versions are now also available, and in the latter form two were ordered for the Chilean Air Force and a much larger number for the Brazilian Air Force.

Specifications (EMB-120 Brasilia data)
Radar: Collins WXR-270 or, optionally, WXR-300 weather radar.
Accommodation: Perhaps up to 30 persons or freight as given above.
Wingspan: 64 ft 10¾ in (19.78 m).
Length: 65 ft 7½ in (20.00 m).
Maximum take-off weight: 25,353 lb (11,500 kg).
Maximum speed: 378 mph (608 km/h).
Range with 30 passengers and reserve fuel: 1088 miles (1750 km).
Mission performance: Rate of climb at sea level 2120 ft (646 m) per min; ceiling 29,805 ft (9085 m).
Engines: Two 1800-shp Pratt & Whitney Canada PW118 turboprops, with 3340 liters of fuel.

Version in service
EMB-120 Brasilia: No Brazilian Air Force military designation given at the time of writing. Ordered by Brazil (12 or 24) and Chile as transports.
Operators: Brazil and Chile.

Below: EMBRAER EMB-120 Brasilia.

EMBRAER EMB-121A Xingu
Brazil

Under the designation VU-9, the Brazilian Air Force received Xingu Is as VIP transports, operating with the Grupo de Transporte Especial. The only other country to operate the Xingu as a military aircraft is France, the French Air Force and Navy using it as a light transport/liaison aircraft and aircrew trainer. Deliveries to France began in 1982.

Specifications (EMB-121A Xingu I data)
Accommodation: Flight crew of one or 2 and up to 9 passengers in a transport role.
Wingspan: 46 ft 1 in (14.05 m).
Length: 40 ft 2 in (12.25 m).
Maximum take-off weight: 12,500 lb (5670 kg).
Cruising speed: 280 mph (450 km/h).
Range: 1460 miles (2352 km).
Mission performance: Rate of climb at sea level 1400 ft (426 m) per min; ceiling 26,000 ft (7925 m).
Engines: Two 680-shp Pratt & Whitney Canada PT6A-28 turboprops, with 1666 liters of fuel.

Above: French Navy EMBRAER Xingu.

Version in service
Xingu I: Flown as a prototype for the first time on 10 October 1976. Most production aircraft have gone into civil use. Brazilian Air Force designation VU-9.
Xingu II: EMB-121A1, used by France.
Operators: Brazil and France (air force and navy).

EMBRAER EMB-312 and Shorts S312 Tucano
Brazil and United Kingdom

EMBRAER, a company formed to promote the national aircraft industry of Brazil, was founded in 1969 and yet in this relatively short period it has made major inroads into world commercial and military markets in the face of established competition. There can surely be no better illustration of this point than the EMB-312 Tucano basic trainer, which has been ordered by several air forces and beat all-comers to satisfy Air Staff Target 412 to provide the RAF with a trainer to replace the long-serving Jet Provost.

First flown as a prototype on 16 August 1980, the EMB-312 Tucano had been conceived originally for the Brazilian Air Force which required a replacement for the Cessna T-37C and T-25 Universal. Under the military designation T-27, all 118 examples ordered were delivered between 1983 and 1986. Of these, two were assigned to the Air Force Academy and six to the Esquadrilha da Fumaca aerobatic team. Options were placed on a further 50 T-27s. Others have been exported, as detailed below.

The Tucanos of two export customers are worthy of particular attention. Egypt ordered 120 aircraft, two-thirds on behalf of Iraq, of which all but the initial 10 were to be assembled or built in Egypt by the Arab Organization for Industrialization based at Heliopolis. Delivery of Egyptian-assembled Tucanos began in 1985. In its bid to win a British Ministry of Defence order for 130 aircraft to replace Jet Provosts, EMBRAER was joined by Shorts to present a modified version of the Brazilian aircraft featuring much British equipment including a new cockpit arrangement, an 1100-shp Garrett TPE331-12B turboprop

Above: EMBRAER-built prototype of the Shorts S312 Tucano.

engine to increase speed, a strengthened structure, and the adoption of a hydraulic ventral airbrake among other changes. In this form it was selected in 1985. The RAF's Tucano T.Mk 1 weighs 5842 lb (2650 kg) at take-off and can achieve 315 mph (507 km/h) at 10,000 ft or higher and 308 mph (496 km/h) at sea level. High speed at low level enhances the aircraft's strike capabilities. The latest Tucano customer, Argentina, is to have 30.

Specifications (EMB-312 Tucano data)

Weapons: Up to 2205 lb (1000 kg) of weapons on 4 underwing pylons, including machine-gun pods, rocket launchers and bombs.
Accommodation: Student pilot and instructor in tandem cockpits under a single canopy, the rear cockpit raised.
Wingspan: 36 ft 6½ in (11.14 m).
Length: 32 ft 4¼ in (9.86 m).
Maximum take-off weight: 7000 lb (3175 kg) with weapons.
Maximum speed: 278 mph (448 km/h).
Range: 1145 miles (1844 km).
Mission performance: Rate of climb at sea level 2230 ft (680 m) per min; ceiling 30,000 ft (9145 m); endurance approximately 5 h; G limits, aerobatic +6, −3; G limits 7000-lb (3175-kg) AUW and armed +4.4, −2.2.
Engine: One 750-shp Pratt & Whitney Canada PT6A-25C turboprop, with 694 liters of fuel standard.
Versions in service
EMB-312: Standard version, designated T-27 by the Brazilian Air Force.
Shorts S312: RAF version with the modifications as detailed above. Rate of climb is 3510 ft (1070 m) per min, and ceiling is 34,000 ft (10,365 m). Deliveries began in 1987.
Operators: Argentina, Brazil, Egypt, Honduras, Iraq, United Kingdom and Venezuela.

ENAER T-35 Pillán and T-35TX Aucán
Chile

Design of the Pillán basic, intermediate and instrument trainer was, in fact, based upon the Piper Cherokee series of light aircraft to reduce the cost of development. Indeed, the prototypes, the first of which made its maiden flight on 6 March 1981, were developed by Piper. Pilláns ordered for the Spanish Air Force are delivered as kits for assembly by CASA. A turboprop-powered variant is the Aucán, which flew initially on 14 February 1986. Production is scheduled to begin in 1988.

Specifications (T-35 Pillán data)

Weapons: 2 underwing stations for weapons.
Accommodation: Student pilot and instructor in tandem, with the rear seat raised for improved forward view.
Wingspan: 28 ft 11 in (8.81 m).
Length: 26 ft 3¾ in (8.02 m).
Maximum take-off weight: 2950 lb (1338 kg).
Maximum speed: 193 mph (311 km/h).
Range: 829 miles (1334 km).
Mission performance: Rate of climb at sea level 1525 ft (465 m) per min; ceiling 19,100 ft (5820 m); G limits +6, −3; endurance up to 5 h 39 min.
Engine: One 300-hp Avco Lycoming IO-540-K1K5 piston, with 291 liters of fuel.
Versions in service
T-35A: Primary trainer for the Chilean Air Force.
T-35B: Instrument trainer for the Chilean Air Force with upgraded avionics.
T-35C: Primary trainer for the Spanish Air Force, with whom it is known as E.26 Tamiz.
T-35TX Aucán: Prototype turboprop derivative, with a 420-shp Allison 250-B17D.
Operators: Chile and Spain.

English Electric Canberra
United Kingdom

First flown on 13 May 1949 and remembered as the first jet bomber to fly with the RAF, the Canberra seemed at first a very ordinary machine compared with the exciting jet bombers then flying elsewhere. But this quality proved to be its strength and large numbers are still used in many roles, including bombing, reconnaissance and ground attack. It was notable for its generous wing area which despite the low power of its engines (installed in long nacelles centered on the wings), conferred exceptional high-altitude capability and outstanding maneuverability at low speeds and altitudes. Features include a circular-section fuselage, with a pressurized nose crew compartment, a bomb-bay amidships with tankage above, manual flight controls, multifinger airbrakes extended above and below the outer wings, and, in

Below: ENAER T-35 Pillán trainers, mostly in Chilean Air Force colors.

most versions, cartridge starters and tip-mounted tanks.

Most versions resemble the original B.2 (Australian B.20), a visual light bomber with a navigator and bombardier seated side-by-side behind the pilot, the bombardier going forward to his sight in the nose when necessary. Trainer versions have side-by-side dual controls. Some, such as the Indian B(I).58 and South African B(I).12, have a fighter-type canopy offset to the left and the navigator in the nose. The PR.9 is an upgraded model with numerous changes for high-altitude reconnaissance. Five are being completely rebuilt by Shorts for special radar/elint reconnaissance with the RAF.

Specifications (B(I).8 data and similar types)
Weapons: Up to 6000 lb (2722 kg) of bombs in the bay; 2000 lb (907 kg) of bombs, rocket pods or missiles on underwing pylons.
Accommodation: 3 crew.
Wingspan: 63 ft 11½ in (19.51 m).
Length: 65 ft 6 in (19.96 m).
Maximum take-off weight: 56,250 lb (25,515 kg).
Maximum speed: 541 mph (871 km/h).
Range: 3630 miles (5842 km).
Mission performance: Rate of climb at sea level 3400 ft (1036 m) per min; ceiling 48,000 ft (14,630 m).
Engines: Two 7400-lb (3356-kg) thrust Rolls-Royce Avon 109 turbojets, with 12,570 liters of fuel standard.
Versions in service
B.2: Light bomber. Two 6500-lb (2948-kg) thrust Avon 101s.
T.4: 3-crew trainer version of the B.2.
B.6: Light bomber. Similar to the B.8 but with 55,000-lb (24,948-kg) gross take-off weight, maximum speed of 580 mph (933 km/h) and range of 3790 miles (6100 km).
PR-7: 7-camera photographic reconnaissance aircraft, with Avon 109 engines.
B(I).8: Long-range night interdictor and high-altitude bomber. Greater fuel capacity.
PR.9: High-altitude strategic reconnaissance model, with increased wingspan and 11,000-lb (4,990-kg) thrust engines.
B (I).12: Modified B (I) 8.
E.15: RAF radar and radio calibration model.

T.17: RAF ECM trainer with blisters around the nose.
TT-18: RAF target tug.
T.22: Royal Navy radar target version.
B.56, 58, 62, 72, 82, 88 and PR.57, 83 and T.4, 13 84: Similar to earlier mentioned versions, taking the final digit as the mark reference.
Operators: Argentina (B.62 and T.64), Chile (PR.9), Ecuador (B.6), India (B (I).12, B (I).58, PR.57, T.4 and T.13), Peru (B (I).8, B (I).58, B.72 and T.4), South Africa (B (I).12 and T.4), United Kingdom (air force, B.2, B.6, B (I).8, E.15, PR7, PR.9, T.4 and TT-18*; navy T.22), Venezuela (B.82, B (I).82, PR.83, B (I).88 and T.84) and Zimbabwe (B.2 and T.4).
* RAF aircraft do not undertake any armed offensive roles. Those bomber variants still in the inventory have miscellaneous uses.

Eurocopter HAP, PAH-2 and HAC-3G
West Germany and France

Eurocopter GmbH was set up in 1985 to manage cooperation between the West German company MBB and Aérospatiale of France in

Above: Refurbished Venezuelan English Electric B (I).82 Canberra.

the design, development and production of a new and battlefield-survivable combat helicopter. Though basically a single design, three separate versions are planned: the French Army is expected to receive 75 HAPs (Hélicoptère d'Appui et de Protection) for helicopter escort and support missions and 140 HAC-3Gs (Hélicoptère Anti-Char) for anti-armor missions; the German Army requires 212 PAH-2s altogether for anti-armor warfare.

All versions use the now established layout of a crew of two in tandem in stepped cockpits, though French aircraft will seat the pilot in the forward cockpit. A prototype is expected to fly in 1988, but delivery of production aircraft will not begin until 1993, when the first HAPs will enter service. This model will carry FLIR, TV, a laser rangefinder and direct-optics sensors in above-fuselage positions, and will have a chin turret containing a 30-mm GIAT AM-30781 cannon. Stub-

Below: Model of the Eurocopter PAH-2 Federal German Army antiarmor helicopter.

wing weapons will comprise two launchers for a total of 44 68-mm rockets and four Mistral air-to-air missiles. Both antitank versions, for delivery from 1995 (PAH-2) and 1996 (HAC-3G), will eventually each carry eight PARS 3LR 'fire and forget' antitank missiles with a range of 2.8 miles. The missile also has an antihelicopter capability, and is currently under development by Euromissile Dynamics. However, the PAH-2 may at first be armed with a similar number of Hot 2s. Accompanying Stinger 2s will provide an air-to-air capability for the German version, which has no cannon. The PAH-2 and HAC-3G have nose-mounted night-vision sights, the latter also with mast-mounted sensor systems.

Specifications (HAP and HAC-3G data)

Weapons: As detailed above.
Accommodation: 2 crew in stepped tandem cockpits.
Rotor diameter: 42 ft 7¾ in (13.00 m).
Maximum take-off weight: 11,900 lb (5400 kg).
Cruising speed: 174 mph (280 km/h).
Mission performance: Rate of climb at sea level 1968 ft (600 m) per min; hovering ceiling out of ground effect (PAH-2) 6560 ft (2000 m); endurance, with reserve fuel, 2h 50 min.
Engines: Two 120-shp MTU-Turboméca MTM 385R turboshafts, currently under development by this Franco-German company.

Versions in service

None as yet.

Operators: Eventually France (army) and West Germany (army).

Eurofighter EFA/JF-90
West Germany, Italy, Spain and United Kingdom

Intended for delivery to the air forces of West Germany (250), Italy (200), Spain (100) and the United Kingdom (250) from 1995 at the earliest, the airframe design for the European

Below: British Aerospace impression of the future Eurofighter.

Above: Argentine Fairchild Merlin IVA.

Fighter Aircraft has yet to be completed and no prototype will fly until 1990. There is, therefore, little point in expanding this entry to take in speculative data, other than to say that it will have large delta wings with rear elevons and canard control surfaces, and be primarily for air defense, with secondary attack capability. It will be built with stealth technologies incorporated in new metal alloys and carbonfiber reinforced plastics. Missile armament will comprise AMRAAMs and ASRAAMs, Skyflash 90s or other air-to-air missiles in the fighter role, or a wide range of attack weapons including perhaps 12 1000-lb (454-kg) bombs when carrying two auxiliary fuel tanks to extend range. EFA will have a maximum speed of at least Mach 1.8 on the power of two 20,250-lb (9185-kg) thrust Eurojet EJ200 turbofans. It will be capable of full combat while carrying the maximum internal fuel load; wingspan will be 35 ft 11½ in (10.96 m). The stated empty weight will be 21,495 lb (9750 kg); maximum weight 37,480 lb (17,000 kg).

Fairchild Metro III, Merlin IIIA/B and IVA
United States

Although the US forces have reserved the designation C-26A for the Metro III commuter airliner, so far there have been no known orders. This leaves just a single example in Swedish Air Force service as a VIP transport, known as the TP88. A Special Missions version of the Metro III is also available for roles ranging from ASW and maritime patrol (with Litton AN/APS-504[V], [V]5, or Eaton AN/APS-128D surveillance radar and optionally FLIR and much more besides) to calibration, airborne early warning and ECM. At least 34 Special Missions aircraft have been sold but it is not clear who are the users.

The Merlin IIIA is an 8- to 11-seat transport, while the Merlin IIIB has more powerful engines and other changes which include airframe refinements. The Merlin IVA was developed as the corporate version of the Merlin range, with the long fuselage of the Metro II airliner and so with a higher seating capacity.

Specifications (Metro III data)

Accommodation: 2 crew plus up to 20 passengers.
Wingspan: 57 ft 0 in (17.37 m).
Length: 59 ft 4¼ in (18.09 m).
Maximum take-off weight: 14,500 lb (6577 kg).
Cruising speed: 320 mph (515 km/h).
Range: 1001 miles (1610 km) with reserve fuel.
Mission performance: Rate of climb at sea level 2370 ft (723 m) per min; ceiling 27,500 ft (8385 m).
Engines: Two 1100-shp Garrett TPE331-11U-611G turboprops, with 2453 liters of fuel.

Versions in service

Metro III and Special Mission: As detailed above. Swedish military designation TP88; US military designation C-26A.
Merlin IIIA: Designed as a pressurized executive transport. Two 840-shp Garrett

TPE331-3U-303G turboprops. Wingspan
46 ft 3 in (14.10 m), length 42 ft 2 in (12.85 m)
and cruising speed 325 mph (523 km/h).
Merlin IIIB: Follow-up version to the Merlin
IIIB, with 900-shp Garrett TPE331-10U-501G
engines.
Merlin IVA: Two 940-shp Garrett TPE331-
3UW-304G engines. Wingspan as for Merlin
IIIA. Length 59 ft 4¾ in (18.10 m). Cruising
speed 310 mph (499 km/h).
Operators: Argentina (air force, Merlin IVA;
army Merlin IIIA), Belgium (Merlin IIIA),
Ivory Coast (Metro), Seychelles (Merlin
IIIB), Sweden (Metro III) and Thailand
(Merlin IVA).

Fairchild Republic A-10A Thunderbolt II
United States

The A-10A is unique among the West's aircraft, being an extremely hard-hitting, fairly
low-speed close-support aircraft, with the
ability to destroy armor with its 30-mm
seven-barrel Avenger cannon and deliver up
to an amazing 16,000 lb (7258 kg) of other
weapons. It is of interest to note that the
Soviet Union deployed an aircraft for a similar role in the 1980s as the Sukhoi S-25, initially for service in Afghanistan. This is
noteworthy as it reflects development for a
particular form of warfare, much as the
A-10A can be viewed as the culmination of
USAF experience in Vietnam when subsonic
aircraft with very heavy payloads proved an
operational necessity.

The initial prototype YA-10A made its
maiden flight on 10 May 1972, and the first
combat-ready Wing with production A-10As
was the 354th Tactical Fighter Wing, in 1977.
Altogether, a total of 713 A-10As were produced up to 1983, of which today some are
based also in West Germany, South Korea,
Alaska and the United Kingdom. A-10As

Below: The USAF's principal close support aircraft
is the Fairchild Republic A-10A Thunderbolt II.

have also passed to units of the Air National
Guard and Air Force Reserve, historically the
first currently frontline combat aircraft ever
to be handed over to the ANG.

The A-10A is of unusual appearance, with
its two podded turbofans exhausting between the twin tailfins. Survivability in the
battle area is enhanced by the aircraft's excellent maneuverability and ability to fly very
low to make the best use of the terrain and to
surprise. The pilot is protected by a bulletproof windshield and a titanium armor 'bath-
tub' that can withstand a 23-mm impact. The
aircraft's controls have redundant features
and are armor-protected. The fuel tanks are
filled with reticulated foam and supply pipes
have self-sealing covers. Electronics also play
their part in enhancing survivability, and
include a head-up display so that the pilot
can keep his eyes ahead, target-penetration
aids, a radar homing and warning system,

Above: Indonesian Air Force FFA AS 202/18A3
Bravo.

and active and passive ECM. A recent modification to some A-10As has provided self-
defense capability with Sidewinder air-to-air
missiles.

Specifications (A-10A Thunderbolt II data)
Weapons: One 30-mm General Electric
GAU-8/A Avenger 7-barrel cannon, carried
at a depressed angle in the nose, with 1174
rounds of ammunition, plus up to 16,000 lb
(7258 kg) of attack weapons on 8 underwing
and 3 underfuselage pylons. The wide
range of options include various types of
general-purpose, retarded, incendiary,
cluster, laser-guided and electro-optically
guided bombs (typically twenty-eight 500-lb
bombs or six 2000-lb bombs), 6 Maverick
air-to-surface missiles, gun pods, etc.
Sidewinder air-to-air missiles are available
to some aircraft. The Pave Penny target
designation pod is standard equipment.
Accommodation: The pilot.
Wingspan: 57 ft 6 in (17.53 m).
Length: 53 ft 4 in (16.26 m).
Maximum take-off weight: 50,000 lb
(22,680 kg).
Maximum speed: 439 mph (706 km/h).
Combat radius: 288-620 miles (463-1000 km)
according to mission.
Mission performance: Rate of climb at sea
level 6000 ft (1830 m) per min.
Engines: Two 9065-lb (4112-kg) thrust
General Electric TF34-GE-100 turbofans,
with 10,700 lb of fuel standard. Three
2271-liter drop-tanks can be carried.
Version in service
A-10A: As detailed above.
Operator: United States (air force, including
AFRES and ANG).

FFA AS 202/18A Bravo
Switzerland

FFA is responsible for the manufacture and
development of the Bravo aerobatic trainer,
under the terms of an agreement with the
Italian company SIAI-Marchetti. To date

three main versions have flown, though only one of these, the AS 202/18A, has found its way into military service.

First flown on 7 March 1969, the Bravo is a conventional light aircraft of aluminum construction, with a fixed undercarriage for simplicity and a rearward-sliding canopy that affords the crew an excellent all-round view. The largest military customer to date has been the Iraqi Air Force.

Specifications (AS 202/18A Bravo data)
Accommodation: Instructor and student pilot side by side. In non-aerobatic utility form, a third person can be carried or 100 kg of goods.
Wingspan: 31 ft 11¾ in (9.75 m).
Length: 24 ft 7¼ in (7.50 m).
Maximum take-off weight: 2315 lb (1050 kg).
Maximum speed: 150 mph (241 km/h).
Range: 600 miles (965 km).
Mission performance: Rate of climb at sea level 905 ft (276 m) per min; ceiling 18,010 ft (5490 m); endurance 5 h 30 min.
Engine: One 180-hp Avco Lycoming AEIO-360-B1F piston, with 170 liters of fuel.
Version in service
AS 202/18A: This version took to the air for the first time on 22 August 1974. It is also in civil operation.
Operators: Indonesia (AS 202/18A3), Iraq (AS 202/18A2), Jordan (AS 202/18A2), Morocco (AS 202/18A1), Oman (AS 202/18A) and Uganda (AS 202/18A1).

FFA C-3605
Switzerland

The C-3605 is a target-tug conversion of the EKW C-3603 fighter-bomber, the latter of which 144 were constructed between 1942 and 1944. Twenty-three C-3603s were modified as C-3605s and these remain in service today. The conversion entailed lengthening the forward fuselage to maintain the CG position, the addition of a third tailfin, and installation of an Avco Lycoming turboprop in place of the original 1020-hp Hispano-Suiza 12Y-51 piston engine. The first modified C-3605 made its maiden flight on 19 August 1968. C-3605s operated by the Zeilfliegerkorps operate out of Sion, alongside a small number of Vampire FB.6s.

Below: FFA C-3605 target tug.

Above: FMA IA 58C Pucará Charlie.

Specifications (C-3605 data)
Equipment: The SZW 52 target-towing winch with 2000 m of cable is carried in the rear cockpit.
Accommodation: Two crew in tandem cockpits.
Wingspan: 45 ft 1 in (13.74 m).
Length: 39 ft 5¾ in (12.03 m).
Maximum take-off weight: 8192 lb (3716 kg).
Maximum speed: 268 mph (432 km/h).
Range: 610 miles (970 km).
Mission performance: Rate of climb at sea level 2470 ft (753 m) per min; ceiling 32,810 ft (10,000 m).
Engine: One 1100-shp Avco Lycoming T53-L-7 turboprop, with 510 liters of fuel standard.
Version in service
C-3605: Target-tug.
Operator: Switzerland.

FMA IA 58 Pucará
Argentina

Fábrica Militar de Aviones (FMA) is closely connected to the Argentine Air Force, being responsible for the design and manufacture of aircraft among other activities. One of its most successful products has been the Pucará counter-insurgency and close-support aircraft, which first flew as a prototype on 20 August 1969 and joined squadrons from 1976.

In appearance the Pucará is a sleek aircraft of duralumin construction, using a light airframe and two powerful French turboprops to achieve good all-round performance. In many respects it is an uncomplicated aircraft, with such items as electronic countermeasures, weather radar and IFF (identification friend or foe) falling among the manufacturer's options rather than standard fitted equipment. The crew seated in tandem under a common canopy (the rear cockpit raised) are protected from ground fire by armor plating in the floor, this being designed to withstand rounds of 7.62-mm ammunition fired from a distance of 150 meters.

Combat experience during the Falklands war of 1982, during which twenty-four IA 58As were lost, advanced the idea of extending the aircraft's capabilities to pack a harder punch, undertake a wider range of missions, and carry air-to-air missiles for self-protection against attack and for emergency low-altitude air defense missions. The latter could, perhaps, best be achieved if a number of Pucarás were directed onto targets by an accompanying radar-equipped aircraft. In particular, it was thought that the Pucará could achieve good results attacking helicopters and warships, both of which had played decisive roles in the British operations of 1982. One step towards achieving this was the conversion of some early IA 58As into single-seaters, with the rear cockpit given over to an additional fuel tank to increase range.

To take the single-seat concept further and demonstrate the mission benefits, a new version of the Pucará has been undergoing flight testing as a fully converted single-seater with more equipment and improved armament. Known as the IA 58C Pucará Charlie, a prototype flew for the first time at the end of 1985. This version has a new fighter-style canopy over what was the rear seat position, the forward cockpit being deleted entirely. The pilot is protected by more armor. The longer nose enables two 30-mm DEFA 553 cannon to be added to the standard guns, and weapons that can be carried underwing now include two R.550 Magic air-to-air missiles or a similar number of CITEFA Martin Pescador Mach 2.3 tactical missiles with 40-kg warheads. The additional avionics allow Nap-of-the-earth missions, give warning of enemy radars and improve communications. The

Above: Argentine FMA IA 58A Pucará close support aircraft.

FAA (Fuerza Aérea Argentina) has about 72 IA 58As, some of which have been converted into the interim single-seaters. If the IA 58C becomes a fully operational model, it is unclear whether existing IA 58As will be so converted or whether this model will be newly constructed.

Specifications (IA 58A data)

Weapons: Built-in armament of four 7.62-mm FN-Browning M2-30 machine-guns and two 20-mm Hispano DCA-804 cannon, with 900 and 270 rounds of ammunition per gun each respectively, plus 3307 lb (1500 kg) of externally carried weapons or stores including air-to-surface missiles, rocket launchers, gun pods, bombs and cluster bombs, napalm, torpedoes, cameras, etc.
Accommodation: 2 crew in tandem, the rear copilot's seat raised.
Wingspan: 47 ft 7 in (14.50 m).
Length: 46 ft 9 in (14.253 m).
Maximum take-off weight: 14,990 lb (6800 kg).
Maximum speed: 310 mph (500 km/h).
Combat radius: 217 miles (350 km) with full weapon load in hi-lo-hi mission.
Mission performance: Rate of climb at sea level 3545 ft (1080 m) per min; ceiling 32,810 ft (10,000 m); G limits +6, −3.
Engines: Two 978-shp Turboméca Astazou XVIG turboprops, with 1280 liters of fuel standard.

Versions in service

IA 58A: Standard 2-seat production version, detailed above. Some now converted into single-seaters but not to IA 58C level.
IA 58B: Designation of improved model with a deeper forward fuselage, and avionics and armament upgrading. First flown in 1979 but later abandoned.
IA 58C Pucará Charlie: Fully developed single-seat Pucará, expected to enter FAA service at a future date. More powerful built-in armament, upgraded avionics and options that include a head-up display, jamming equipment, flares and chaff.
IA 66: Prototype only of a version of the Pucará with more powerful 1000-shp Garrett TPE331-11-601W turboprops.
Operators: Argentina and Uruguay.

FMA IA 63 Pampa
Argentina

To supersede its Morane-Saulnier MS.760 Paris trainers, the FAA (Argentine Air Force) decided to request a new trainer of indigenous design and manufacture, using FMA (*see* IA 58 Pucará entry) as the contractor. The program began in 1979 and the West German company, Dornier, was brought in to offer technical assistance as well as subsequently

Below: FMA IA 63 Pampa jet trainer.

to assemble the wings and tailplanes for the static and flying prototypes. Not altogether surprisingly, therefore, the resulting Pampa has a hint of the Alpha Jet about it, though it uses a single engine and the wings are straight.

The first Pampa prototype took to the air on 6 October 1984 and by the end of 1986 it had been joined by two further prototypes and a number of pre-production aircraft. The FAA intends to receive 64 Pampa trainers for basic and advanced flying training, entering service from 1988. More may be ordered later as combat proficiency trainers. The development of a specialized close-support variant is a future option.

Specifications

Weapons: Up to 2557 lb (1160 kg) of stores on 4 underwing and one underfuselage pylon, including a 30-mm DEFA cannon pod with 145 rounds of ammunition, 7.62-mm gun pod, bombs, rockets, etc.
Accommodation: Student pilot and instructor in tandem, the rear seat raised.
Wingspan: 31 ft 9¼ in (9.68 m).
Length: 35 ft 9¼ in (10.90 m).
Maximum take-off weight: 11,023 lb (5000 kg).
Maximum speed: 509 mph (819 km/h) estimated.
Range with internal fuel: 621 miles (1000 km).
Mission performance (estimated): Rate of climb at sea level 5950 ft (1913 m) per min; ceiling 42,320 ft (12,900 m); G limit +4.5 sustained.
Engine: One 3500-lb (1588-kg) thrust Garrett TFE731-2-2N turbofan, with standard fuel capacity of 980 liters.

Version in service

IA 63: Basic and advanced jet trainer for the FAA and available for export from 1990.
Operator: Ordered for Argentina.

Below: Senegal Fokker F27 Mk 400Ms.

Fokker F27 Friendship, 50, and Fairchild F-27/Fairchild Hiller FH-227
Netherlands and United States

On 24 November 1955 Fokker flew the first prototype of a twin-turboprop short-range airliner that subsequently proved so successful that production lasted until 1986 and was also manufactured under license in the United States by Fairchild (later Fairchild Hiller) between 1957 and 1974. The very last of 786 F27s were examples of a maritime version for the Royal Thai Navy, just two of many military F27s in service that include specialized versions as detailed below.

The basic F27 configuration and concept is, however, being retained by the new Fokker 50, which is also offered in maritime and surveillance versions as Mk 2 models of the Maritime/Maritime Enforcer/Sentinel/Kingbird series, in addition to the more usual transport. The 50 makes use of new technology engines, avionics and constructural materials, also raising comfort levels for the 46 to 58 passengers; Fokker 50 engines are two 2160-shp Pratt & Whitney Canada PW124 turboprops driving six-blade propellers.

Specifications (F27 Mk 400M data)

Radar: Bendix weather radar.
Accommodation: Crew plus 46 paratroops, 24 stretchers and 9 sitting casualties/attendants, or 14,193 lb (6438 kg) of freight.
Wingspan: 95 ft 1¾ in (29.00 m).
Length: 77 ft 3½ in (23.56 m).
Maximum take-off weight: 45,900 lb (20,820 kg).
Cruising speed: 298 mph (480 km/h).
Range: 1375 miles (2213 km).
Mission performance: Rate of climb at sea level 1620 ft (494 m) per min; ceiling 30,000 ft (9145 m); endurance 7 h 25 min.
Engines: Two 2210-shp Rolls-Royce Dart

Mk 552 turboprops, with 5136 liters of fuel standard.

Versions in service

F27: Military transport versions of the F27 carry the suffix 'M' and include the Mk 300M, 400M and lengthened 50-paratroop/30-stretcher 500M. The Mk 400M is detailed above.
Maritime: Coastal patrol, fishery and environmental protection, and SAR (search and rescue) aircraft, normally without weapons. Litton AN/APS-504(V)2 radar in an underfuselage radome. Based on the Mk 200 airframe, with Dart Mk 552 engines.
Maritime Enforcer: Same airframe and engines as Maritime, for surveillance, ASW and ASV, and with provision for weapons which can include two or four torpedoes or antiship missiles such as Exocet, Sea Eagle, and Harpoon, carried on fuselage and underwing pylons. Litton AN/APS-504(V)5 radar, plus other mission avionics including sonar, sonobuoys and processing system, radar receiver equipment, infrared detector, MAD.
Sentinel: Version for patrolling borders and for stand-off reconnaissance, using mainly Motorola AN/APS-135(V) SLAR (side-looking airborne radar) and long-range oblique cameras or infrared linescan. Based on the Mk 200 airframe and Dart Mk 552 engines.
Kingbird: Envisaged airborne early warning version, which is currently offered in Fokker 50 Mk 2 form with a Thorn EMI Skymaster radar in a retractable underfuselage radome.
Fokker 50: All the above roles are currently offered by Fokker 50 equivalents, known in the case of the Maritime, Maritime Enforcer, Sentinel and Kingbird as Mk 2s.
Fairchild F-27 and Fairchild Hiller FH-227: License-built F27s, retaining Rolls-Royce engines. See introduction above.
Operators: All air forces unless otherwise stated; those used for maritime reconnaissance and/or SAR are denoted by the letters MR. Algeria (navy, MR), Angola (MR), Argentina, Bolivia, Burma, Finland, Ghana, Guatemala, Indonesia, Iran (army), Mexico, Netherlands (transport and MR), New Zealand, Nigeria (MR), Pakistan, Peru (navy, MR), Philippines (transport and MR), Senegal, Spain (MR), Thailand (navy, MR) and Uruguay.

Fokker F28 Fellowship
Netherlands

Production of the Fellowship short/medium-range airliner ended in 1986 after more than 240 had been built for operation in 39 different countries. Its place has been taken over by the new Fokker 100. Of the F28s, not many are in military service but include the Presidential transport of Peru. The prototype F28 had made its maiden flight on 9 May 1967.

Specifications (F28 Mk 3000 data)

Radar: RCA weather radar.
Accommodation: Flight crew of 2 or 3, plus 55-65 passengers. Alternative 15-passenger VIP layout.
Wingspan: 82 ft 3 in (25.07 m).
Length: 89 ft 10¾ in (27.40 m).
Maximum take-off weight: 73,000 lb (33,110 kg).

Above: Ghana Air Force Fokker F28 Fellowship.

Cruising speed: 523 mph (843 km/h).
Range: 1704 miles (2743 km).
Mission performance: Maximum cruising
height 35,000 ft (10,675 m).
Engines: Two 9900-lb (4490-kg) thrust
Rolls-Royce RB183-2 Mk 555-15P turbofans,
with 9740 liters of fuel standard.
Versions in service
Mk 1000: First production model and most
common variant in military use. Mk 1000C
option with a freight door, for all-freight or
mixed passenger/freight layout. 9850-lb
(4468-kg) thrust RB183-2 Mk 555-15 engines.
Mk 3000: As detailed above.
Mk 4000: Up to 85 passengers in a
lengthened fuselage. Overall length
97 ft 1¾ in (29.61 m). Same engines as for
Mk 3000.
Operators: Argentina (air force and navy),
Colombia, Ghana, Indonesia, Ivory Coast,
Peru and Togo.

Below: Fuji T1 jet trainer.

Fuji T1
Japan

Under the Fuji designation T1F, the company
developed a very fine-looking intermediate
jet trainer to supersede North American T-6G
Texans then operating with the JASDF. Two
versions were built, one with a British engine
as the T1F2 and the other with a Japanese
2645-lb (1200-kg) thrust Ishikawajima-
Harima J3-IHI-3 turbojet as the T1F1. It was
the T1F2 that first flew as a prototype, on 19
January 1958, and two batches of 20 production aircraft entered service, deliveries taking
place up to 1962. Meanwhile, by converting a
T1F2, the prototype T1F1 flew on 17 May 1960,
thereby becoming the first postwar jet aircraft
of completely Japanese design and manufacture. Twenty full production aircraft entered
service as T1Bs.

Specifications (T1A data)
Weapons: One 0.50-in machine-gun in the
nose, with 220 rounds of ammunition, and
up to 1500 lb (680 kg) of weapons

underwing including Sidewinder air-to-air
missiles, guns, rockets, bombs, etc.
Accommodation: Student and instructor in
tandem.
Wingspan: 34 ft 5 in (10.50 m).
Length: 39 ft 9 in (12.12 m).
Maximum take-off weight: 11,023 lb (5000 kg).
Maximum speed: 575 mph (925 km/h).
Range: 1212 miles (1950 km) with two
455-liter drop-tanks.
Mission performance: Rate of climb at sea
level 6500 ft (1980 m) per min.
Engine: One 4000-lb (1815-kg) thrust Bristol
Siddeley Orpheus 805 turbojet, with 1400
liters of fuel standard.
Versions in service
T1A: Initial version, with British engine.
T1B: Fully Japanese version. Deliveries
completed by 1963. A large number of T1As
and Bs remain in use.
Operator: Japan.

GAF Missionmaster and Searchmaster
Australia

The Missionmaster and Searchmaster are
military derivatives of the Nomad STOL utility transport aircraft, the prototype of which
made its maiden flight on 23 July 1971. In configuration it is a no-nonsense strut-braced
high-wing monoplane, with a rectangular
section fuselage offering maximum accommodation for passengers, freight or equipment. So as not to take up cabin space, the
main undercarriage units retract into small
nacelles at the tips of short stub wings. The
Missionmaster is based upon the short-fuse-
lage version of the Nomad and is suitable for
surveillance and armed support in addition
to its basic transport role. The Searchmaster
is a specialized coastal patrol aircraft, itself
available in two versions with different levels
of equipment, as detailed below.

**Specifications (Missionmaster and
Searchmaster data)**
Radar: The Searchmasters carry search
radar, as detailed under 'Versions in
service'.
Weapons: The Missionmaster and
Searchmaster can carry up to 500 lb (227 kg)
of weapons on four underwing pylons,
including rocket and gun pods. Night
vision and surveillance equipment can be
carried optionally in the nose.
Accommodation: 14 (including crew) or crew
plus freight.
Wingspan: 54 ft 2 in (16.51 m).
Length: 41 ft 3 in (12.57 m).
Maximum take-off weight: Missionmaster
8500 lb (3855 kg); Searchmaster L 9100 lb
(4127 kg).
Cruising speed: 193 mph (311 km/h).
Range: 840 miles (1352 km).
Mission performance: Rate of climb at sea
level 1460 ft (445 m) per min; ceiling
21,000 ft (6400 m).
Engines: Two 420-shp Allison 250-B17C
turboprops, with 1018 liters of fuel
standard.
Versions in service
Missionmaster: Military light transport
version.
Searchmaster B: Coastal patrol derivative of
the Missionmaster, with a nose radome
carrying Bendix RDR 1400 radar which has a

Above: Australian Army Air Corps GAF Missionmaster.

weather mode and search modes to detect boats and other small sea objects, oil slicks, and can be used for precision ground mapping.

Searchmaster L: Sophisticated version of the Searchmaster with Litton APS-504(V)2 search radar in a chin radome.

Operators: Australia (army, Missionmaster, plus Searchmaster used by customs), Indonesia (navy, Searchmaster B and L), Papua New Guinea (Missionmaster), Philippines (Missionmaster) and Thailand (air force, Missionmaster; navy, Searchmaster B).

Gates Learjet series
United States

The Learjet series of executive jets began in the early 1960s with the Learjet 23 and today includes the Learjet 55. Although basically a civil aircraft, a substantial number have found their way into military service. The most important of these is the Learjet 35A, which is offered by the company in 'special mission' forms. In addition, the USAF selected the 35A for its Operational Support Aircraft program, receiving eighty during 1984-5 as C-21As to supersede Sabreliners in the roles of priority and passenger transport, medevac and pilot-proficiency training.

Specifications (Learjet 35A data)
Radar: Sperry Primus 300SL weather radar.
Accommodation: 2 crew plus 8 passengers. Maximum payload is 3000 lb (1361 kg).
Wingspan: 39 ft 6 in (12.04 m).
Length: 48 ft 8 in (14.83 m).
Maximum take-off weight: 17,000 lb (7711 kg) standard.
Maximum speed: 542 mph (872 km/h).
Range: 2634 miles (4240 km).
Mission performance: Rate of climb at sea level 4760 ft (1450 m) per min; ceiling 45,000 ft (13,715 m).
Engines: Two 3500-lb (1588-kg) thrust

Garrett TFE731-2-2B turbofans, with 3524 liters of fuel.

Versions in service
Learjet 24D: First flown in 1963, this has accommodation for the crew plus 6 passengers. Two 2950-lb (1338-kg) thrust General Electric CJ610-6 turbojets. One user is Mexico.

Learjet 25 series: First flown in 1966. Current model is the 25D, accommodating the crew plus 8 passengers. Powered by two 2950-lb (1338-kg) thrust CJ610-8A turbojets. Users of the 25 series include Peru (which also has a 36A) for reconnaissance.

Learjet 35A and 36A: Larger than the 25, with Garrett turbofans. 36A has 4202 liters of fuel and a standard gross weight of 18,300 lb (8300 kg). Special missions versions are the EC-35A calibration,

electronic warfare training and other duty model; PC-35A sea patrol model with Litton AN/APS-504(V)3 surveillance radar and much other equipment (Finnish examples are used to tow targets in support of the Hawk trainers and undertake mapping, photography, patrol, medevac and other duties); RC-35A survey, photography and reconnaissance model with side-looking airborne radar and other equipment; and UC-35A utility model. JMSDF U-36As are used for target towing, ECM and simulating antiship missiles, and carry among much equipment long-range surveillance radar. *C-21A:* USAF designation for 80 Learjet 35As, as detailed above.

Operators: Argentina, Bolivia, Chile, Ecuador (army), Finland, Iraq, Japan (navy), Mexico (navy), Peru, Saudi Arabia, United States and Uruguay.

General Dynamics F-16 Fighting Falcon
United States

General Dynamics was one of five companies that proposed designs for the USAF's Lightweight Fighter program, and it and Northrop were contracted to build prototypes for evaluation. These were not merely to fly in competition with each other but prove the very concept of a low-cost and lightweight air superiority fighter being suitable for USAF deployment. The first YF-16 prototype made its maiden flight on 2 February 1974, its blended wings and fuselage being as recognizable as its 'yawning' underfuselage air intake. After nearly a year of flight evaluation, the F-16 was announced the winner. Although intended merely as a day fighter, the requirement was updated to take in an attack capability, which included allowance for radar and all-weather navigation equipment. Thus began the course of added

Below: Special Missions Gates Learjet 35A.

sophistication that greatly raised the capability of the aircraft as well as its weight and cost. Conversely, however, NATO requires aircraft that can operate in all weathers and it was by enhancing this aspect that the F-16 also interested Belgium, Denmark, the Netherlands and Norway as a Starfighter replacement, with final assembly of these European aircraft taking place in Belgium and the Netherlands. To date these European nations have ordered 160, 70, 213 and 72 F-16s (including two-seat trainers) respectively.

The first production F-16 for the USAF, of what stands at a current expected total of 2795, joined the 388th Tactical Fighter Wing in January 1979. This eventual total includes those going to Air Force Reserve and Air National Guard units. The first European nation to receive F-16s was Belgium, the air force receiving its first two in January 1979.

The original F-16A version was fitted with Westinghouse AN/APG-66 pulse-Doppler radar. As an interim step toward upgrading the aircraft to allow attack missions at night, beyond-vision interceptions and pinpoint strikes, aircraft delivered after November 1981 were given the structural and wiring changes necessary to allow new equipment to be fitted at a later date. However, on 14 December 1982 the first F-16 flew with new radar to enable the delivery of weapons in all weather conditions (including the AMRAAM

Below: Venezuelan General Dynamics F-16A Fighting Falcon.

air-to-air missile), an upgraded cockpit with multifunction displays, a GEC Avionics wide-angle head-up display and other modifications. Production aircraft to this standard are known as F-16Cs and Ds (single- and two-seat respectively), the first F-16C joining the USAF in July 1984. All manufacture is now to these standards. Further revisions have brought changes to the engine. The original 25,000-lb (11,340-kg) thrust with afterburning Pratt & Whitney F100-PW-200 turbofan of the F-16 has recently given way to the improved F100-PW-220 and, as an alternative, the General Electric F110-GE-100.

Other versions of the F-16 are given below, but special mention should be made of the US Navy's F-16Ns, which are being acquired as 'aggressor' aircraft to replace Kfirs. Fourteen have been ordered from a requirement for 26.

Specifications (F-16C data unless otherwise stated)
Radar: Westinghouse APG-68 pulse-Doppler range and angle track radar.
Weapons: One 20-mm General Electric M61A-1 Vulcan 6-barrel cannon, with 515 rounds of ammunition. 2 wingtip air-to-air missile launchers, 6 underwing stores attachment points and one under the fuselage for weapons and drop-tanks, etc. 6 air-to-air missiles of Sidewinder type is usual for a fighter role, though missile choices are many and include Magic (as used by Belgium) and AMRAAM. Attack weapons include missiles (Norwegian

Above: General Dynamics F-16R Fighting Falcon reconnaissance aircraft under test. Developed from the two-seat F-16D, it could become the replacement aircraft for the RF-4C.

aircraft can carry Penguin from antiship missions), bombs and the normal very wide range of other armaments, up to a total weight of 12,000 lb (5443 kg).
Accommodation: The pilot.
Wingspan: 31 ft 0 in (9.45 m).
Length: 49 ft 3 in (15.01 m).
Maximum take-off weight: 37,500 lb (17,010 kg).
Maximum speed: Over Mach 2.
Combat radius: Over 575 miles (925 km) for the F-16A.
Mission performance: Ceiling over 50,000 ft (15,240 m) for the F-16A; G limit +9 design.
Engine: As above.

Versions in service
F-16A: Initial single-seat air combat fighter version, only with an F100-PW-200 engine. Maximum take-off weight 35,400 lb (16,057 kg). AN/APG-66 radar. Israeli F-16As were used during the attack on the nuclear reactor in mid-1981, the first actual mission of any F-16s.
F-16B: Initial 2-seat operational trainer version, based on the F-16A.
F-16C: Much improved single-seater, the first going to the USAF on 19 July 1984. Improved AN/APG-68 radar, engine choices as given and advanced cockpit with up-front controls, multifunction displays, a new head-up display, and much else.
F-16D: 2-seat operational trainer version of the F-16C, received by the USAF from September 1984.
F-16N: US Navy 'aggressor' version to perform as enemy aircraft during front-line training, squadron readiness exercises, etc. Based on the F-16C but with F-16A radar, the General Electric engine and structural changes. The first was received in spring 1987.
F-16R: Reconnaissance version of the F-16D, expected to eventually supersede McDonnell Douglas RF-4C Phantoms.
(F-16XL: Advanced version of the F-16, with a 'cranked arrow' delta-type wing replacing the usual wings and tailplane. This is no longer an active project.)
Operators: Belgium, Denmark, Egypt, Greece, Indonesia, Israel, South Korea, Netherlands, Norway, Pakistan, Singapore, Thailand, Turkey, United States (air force and navy) and Venezuela.

Left: USAF General Dynamics F-111F with wings spread.

Below: Cutaway drawing of an F-111E.

General Dynamics F-111, FB-111A and EF-111A
United States

Originally known in 1960 as the TFX (Tactical Fighter Experimental), the F-111 was planned to replace almost all fighter and attack aircraft in the USAF and Navy, and be built in thousands. For various reasons, including a giant rise in weight and cost, only 562 were built (including development aircraft) and these were not used as fighters but as attack bombers and, in the case of the FB-111A, as a strategic bomber. The original F-111A (141 built) no longer equips a combat unit, but 42 have been withdrawn and have been totally rebuilt by Grumman (which was the F-111 associate contractor on the cancelled Navy version) to serve as EW (electronic warfare) and ECM tactical jamming aircraft. The resulting EF-111A Raven is serving in Britain and the United States with USAF squadrons tasked with helping other kinds of aircraft get through enemy ground defenses safely in order to carry out attack missions. The EF version still seats only two crew, a pilot and an EWO (electronic-warfare officer), though the aircraft carries the comprehensive ALQ-99 series receiving and jamming system which in older aircraft needed a crew of four.

The chief attack versions in service are listed below. Under a basic six-year contract priced at well over $1 billion, General Dynamics is gutting all surviving USAF attack F-111s and fitting them with completely new avionics and displays. The airframes are considered to be suitable for frontline use until at least 2010.

Spoilers/lift dumpers

Leading-edge slats

Swivelling inboard stores pylons

Crew's jettisonable escape capsule

Center-hinged canopy

General Electric AN/APQ-113 terrain following and attack radar

Twin-wheel nose undercarriage unit

750-lb bomb

Specifications (F-111F data)

Radar: General Electric AN/APQ-144 attack radar.

Weapons: One 20-mm General Electric M61A-1 Vulcan multibarrel cannon, plus bombs or other weapons carried in the weapon bay and on 6 underwing pylons.

Accommodation: 2 crew side-by-side.

Wingspan: Spread 63 ft 0 in (19.20 m); swept 31 ft 11½ in (9.74 m).

Maximum take-off weight: 100,000 lb (45,360 kg).

Maximum speed: Mach 2.5.

Range: 2925 miles (4707 km).

Mission performance: Ceiling above 59,000 ft (17,980 m).

Engines: Two 25,100-lb (11,385-kg) thrust with afterburning Pratt & Whitney TF30-P-100 turbofans.

Versions in service

F-111A: No longer an operational version. Four ex-USAF aircraft delivered to Australia in 1982 with F-111C avionics to make up for attrition. (See EF-111A below).

F-111C: Long-span wings and strengthened undercarriage. 24 aircraft for the Royal Australian Air Force, with 18,500-lb (8391-kg) thrust with afterburning TF30-P-3 engines. 15 remaining as strike aircraft, plus 4 converted to RF-111C reconnaissance aircraft with cameras, infrared linescan and TV but retaining strike capability. F-111Cs carry avionics for over-the-horizon attack, and some reportedly have Pave Tack systems (See F-111F).

F-111D: 19,600-lb (8890-kg) thrust with afterburning TF30-P-9 engines. Improved navigation and weapon-delivery avionics.

96 delivered to the USAF, based at Cannon, New Mexico.

F-111E: USAFE version, of which 94 were built. Modified engine air intakes for the TF30-P-3 engines. Based at Upper Heyford, England.

F-111F: 106 delivered by 1976 to the USAF with greatly uprated TF30-P-100 engines, improved avionics, and the Pave Tack infrared/laser sensor for enhanced all-weather attack capability. Based at Lakenheath, England.

FB-111A: 2-seat strategic bomber derivative of the F-111, first flown on 30 July 1967. Long-span wings and strengthened undercarriage. 76 built for Strategic Air Command. Two 20,350-lb (9230-kg) thrust with afterburning TF30-P-7 turbofan engines, bestowing Mach 2.5 performance

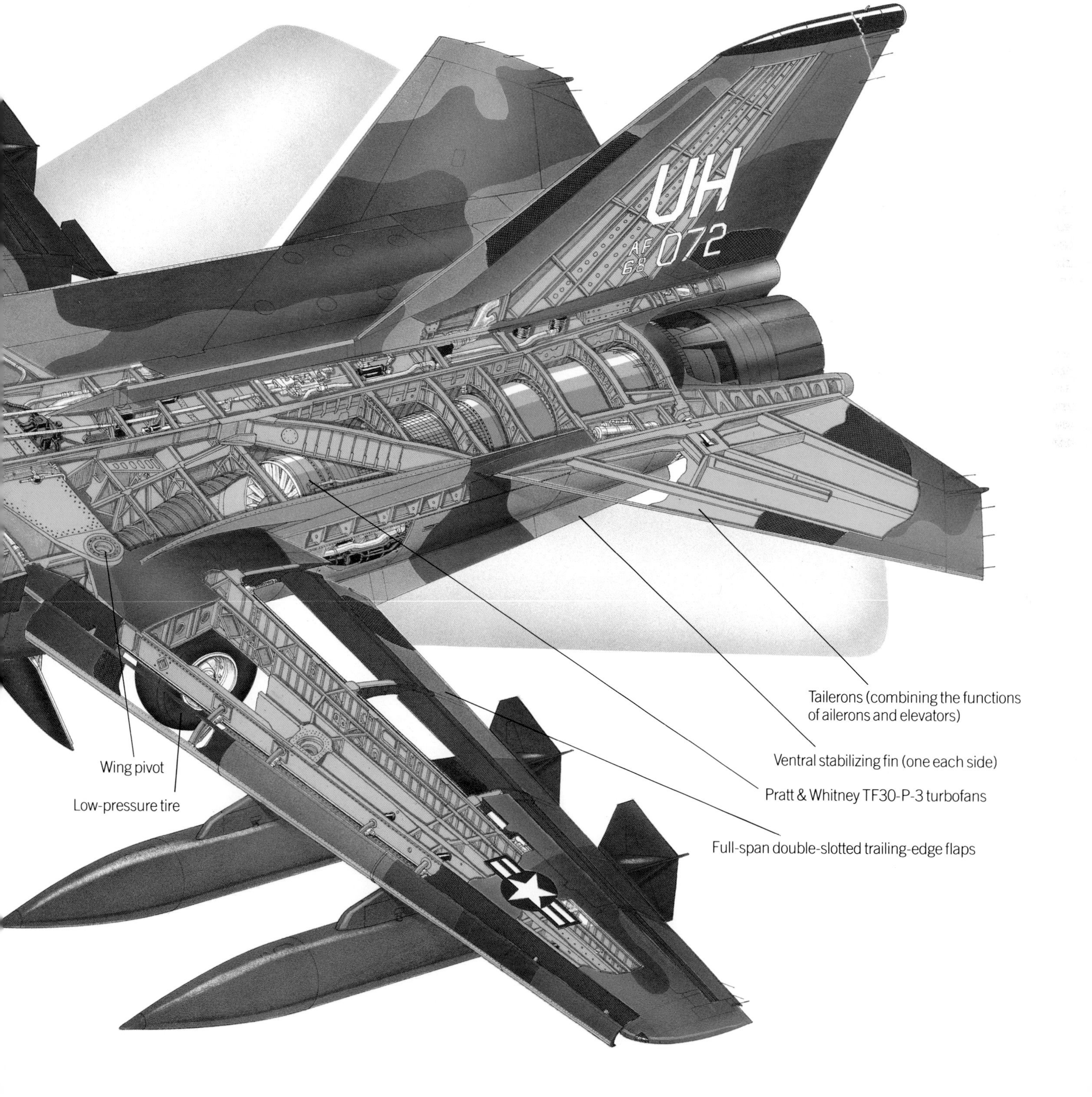

Wing pivot

Low-pressure tire

Tailerons (combining the functions of ailerons and elevators)

Ventral stabilizing fin (one each side)

Pratt & Whitney TF30-P-3 turbofans

Full-span double-slotted trailing-edge flaps

Above: EF-111A Raven tactical jamming aircraft of the 390th Electronic Combat Squadron.

at 36,000 ft (10,795 m) altitude. 2 SRAM short-range nuclear missiles in the weapon bay and 4 more under the wings, 6 nuclear bombs or 31,500 lb (14,290 kg) of conventional weapons (typically forty-two 750-lb bombs). Capable of accurate low-altitude attacks by day or night and in poor weather conditions. Deliveries began to the 340th Bomb Group in October 1969. 56 are still active, with five in reserve. Wingspan 70 ft 0 in (21.34 m) spread and 33 ft 11 in (10.34 m) swept; length 73 ft 6 in (22.40 m); range 4100 miles (6598 km). General Electric AN/APQ-114 attack radar.

EF-111A: 42 F-111As converted by Grumman into ECM tactical jamming aircraft. Delivery began in November 1981 and the 390th Electronic Combat Squadron became operational in December 1983. Now also with the USAFE, based at Upper Heyford, England.
Operators: Australia and United States.

Grumman A-6 Intruder, KA-6D and EA-6B Prowler
United States

The Intruder is an all-weather carrier-borne bomber, able to strike deep into enemy territory or fly close support missions by day or night, and can be armed with conventional or nuclear weapons. Originally designated A2F-1 but later A-6A, the first Intruder flew initially on 19 April 1960 and in 1963 US Navy Squadron VA-42 received the first operational examples. A-6As provided the US Navy/Marine Corps with its only all-weather bomber during the Vietnam War, some becoming A-6Bs when modified to carry AGM-78A Standard ARM antiradiation missiles to home onto the emissions of enemy radar sites and radar-controlled anti-aircraft systems. The A-6A, A-6B and improved night-attack A-6C are no longer operational. However, as early as 23 May 1966 a flight-refuelling tanker conversion of the A-6A had flown and eventually 66 A-6As were similarly

modified with drogue equipment as KA-6Ds. In 1986, 52 of these were still active.

The current operational version of Intruder is the A-6E, originally a conversion of the A-6A but also built as new. The first A-6E flew on 10 November 1970 and deployment began in September 1972. These differ from previous versions by having improved navigation and attack radar and an IBM AN/ASQ-133 computer. TRAM (target recognition and attack multisensor) equipment has been added progressively to the fleet of aircraft since 1978, introducing a sensor package with infrared and laser equipment and much else to help detect and identify targets in bad weather conditions and attack them with great accuracy using conventional or laser-guided weapons. The ability to launch the Harpoon antiship missile was retrofitted to 50 existing A-6E/TRAMS from 1981. All new and converted aircraft are Harpoon-capable.

In 1989 deliveries are scheduled to start of

Below: US Navy Grumman EA-6B Prowler tactical jamming aircraft accompanying Intruder bombers.

the latest Intruder version, the A-6F. Four of the five development aircraft flew in 1987. This version features many avionics and engine changes, as detailed below.

An electronic countermeasures derivative of the Intruder was first flown in 1963 as the EA-6A Prowler, and 27 went into USN/USMC service. On 25 May 1968 an advanced version flew as the EA-6B and this is the currently deployed model. Although longer than the Intruder by 4 ft 6 in (1.37 m), with a pod on the tailfin and a different cockpit arrangement that gives a clue to its increased crew of four, the airframes are almost identical. Many US Navy and Marine Corps squadrons are so equipped. The Prowler can undertake both defensive and offensive missions and can even be armed with HARM antiradar missiles. It is what is termed a 'force multiplier', greatly enhancing the capabilities of the USN/USMC's fighter and attack forces. In a defensive role, it can help secure the safety of the aircraft carrier and supporting vessels by jamming the radar emissions of attacking enemy aircraft carriers or mislead them. In an offensive role, Prowler can accompany a strike force to help it elude enemy defenses by suppressing radars, while also collecting electronic intelligence. A strike mission could therefore see Intruders, Hornets or Tomcats accompanied by Prowlers and the Hawkeyes, the latter to keep guard for enemy fighters while the attack aircraft and Prowlers do their job.

Specifications (A-6E/TRAM Intruder data)
Radar: Norden AN/APQ-148 multimode radar, for navigation (ground mapping and terrain avoidance/following) and identification/tracking/rangefinding of enemy targets.
Weapons: Up to 18,000 lb (8165 kg) of weapons on 5 pylons, typically twenty-eight 500-lb high-explosive bombs or Harpoon antiship missiles. Sidewinder air-to-air missiles can be carrried.
Accommodation: 2 crew

Wingspan: 53 ft 0 in (16.15 m).
Length: 54 ft 9 in (16.69 m).
Maximum take-off weight: 58,600 lb (26,580 kg) for carrier operations.
Maximum speed: 644 mph (1037 km/h).
Range: 1011 miles (1627 km) with full weapon load.
Mission performance: Rate of climb at sea level 7620 ft (2323 m); ceiling 42,400 ft (12,920 m).
Engines: Two 9300-lb (4218-kg) thrust Pratt & Whitney J52-P-8B turbojets, with 8873 liters of fuel standard.
Versions in service
A-6E/TRAM Intruder: Attack bomber, as detailed above.
A-6F Intruder: Version for service in the 1990s. 150 aircraft planned. New radar with increased detection range and stand-off weapon capability, long-range ship classification, and air-to-air mode compatible with AMRAAM as well as Sidewinder missiles. Many other avionics updates. Engines will be two 10,807-lb (4900-kg) thrust General Electric F404-GE-400D turbofans.
EA-6B Prowler: ECM aircraft with a length of 59 ft 10 in (18.24 m), maximum take-off weight of 65,000 lb (29,483 kg), and maximum speed of 610 mph (982 km/h) in mission configuration on the power of two 11,200-lb (5080-kg) thrust J52-P-408 turbojets. Flight crew plus 2 ECM operators for the Eaton AN/ALQ-99F tactical jamming system. Tailfin pod contains surveillance receivers to detect enemy radars.
KA-6D: Flight refuelling tanker.
Operator: United States (navy and marine corps).

Grumman C-2A Greyhound
United States

Derived from the Hawkeye but without the AEW radar/rotodome and associated avionics, the Greyhound is a carrier on-board delivery (COD) transport, tasked with car-

rying important freight or personnel from land to aircraft carriers. Because of its close relationship to the Hawkeye, it is naturally compatible with carrier elevators and hangars and can make the normal arrester-hook landings and catapult take-offs. The first pre-series Greyhound made its maiden flight on 18 November 1964 and the US Navy received 19, all based upon the then-current E-2A version of the Hawkeye.

Just 12 of the original C-2As remain active, and to supplement/supersede this fleet a new order was placed for 39 C-2As based on the latest E-2C Hawkeye. The first of these flew initially on 4 February 1985 and by 1986 two squadrons were already active with new C-2As, these based at Sigonella, Sicily, and Cubi Point, the Philippines. The last will be delivered in 1988.

Specifications (New production C-2A data)
Radar: Doppler and weather radar.
Accommodation: Flight crew of 2 plus loadmaster, and up to 10,000 lb (4536 kg) of freight for deck landing or a 50 percent increase in this for a land-to-land mission. Alternatively 28 passengers or 12 stretchers and medical attendants.
Wingspan: 80 ft 7 in (24.56 m).
Length: 56 ft 10 in (17.32 m).
Maximum take-off weight: 54,354 lb (24,654 kg).
Maximum speed: 357 mph (574 km/h).
Range: 1200 miles (1930 km).
Mission performance: Rate of climb at sea level 2610 ft (796 m) per min; ceiling 33,500 ft (10,210 m).
Engines: Two 4910-ehp Allison T56-A-425 turboprops, with 6905 liters of fuel.
Versions in service
C-2A: 2 production series, the original based upon the E-2A Hawkeye and the second on the E-2C.
Operator: United States (navy).

Below: The first reprocured Grumman C-2A Greyhound COD aircraft.

Grumman E-2 Hawkeye
United States

On 21 October 1960 the first prototype was flown of a new carrier-borne airborne early warning (AEW) aircraft to supersede the E-1 Tracer. This was the E-2 Hawkeye, 56 E-2A production examples of which joined the US Navy. The E-2A was first deployed on board USS *Kitty Hawk* in 1966. By 1971 all remaining E-2As had been upgraded to E-2B standard by the installation of the Litton Industries L-304 computer, the AN/APS-96 surveillance radar inside the revolving overfuselage rotodome remaining unchanged.

Meanwhile, on 20 January 1971 the prototype of a new version flew, designated E-2C. The first sea deployment of this model took place on board USS *Saratoga* in 1974. More than 100 of the 128 E-2Cs planned for the US Navy have been delivered, the radars carried being updated progressively during the E-2C production run but all with the ability to detect air targets in a ground clutter environment, making the aircraft equally suited to land operations. Indeed, four other nations operate E-2Cs from land bases. Flying at an altitude of 30,000 ft (9145 m), the

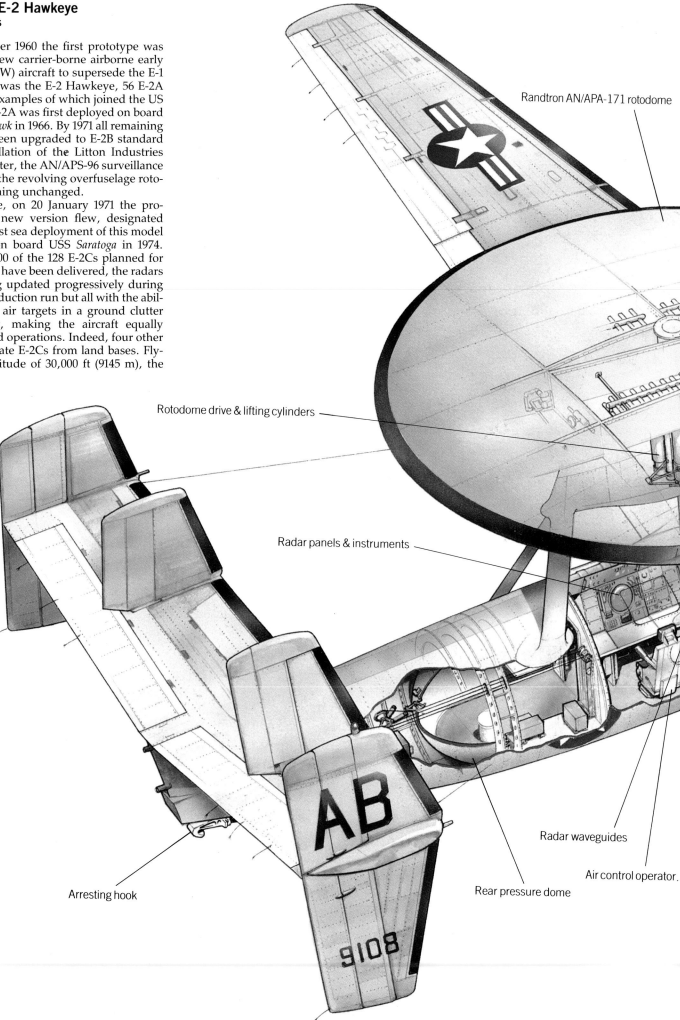

Randtron AN/APA-171 rotodome

Rotodome drive & lifting cylinders

Radar panels & instruments

Radar waveguides

Air control operator

Rear pressure dome

Arresting hook

Right: Grumman E-2C Hawkeye in Japanese service.
Below: A cutaway drawing of a US Navy Grumman E-2C Hawkeye of VAW.125.

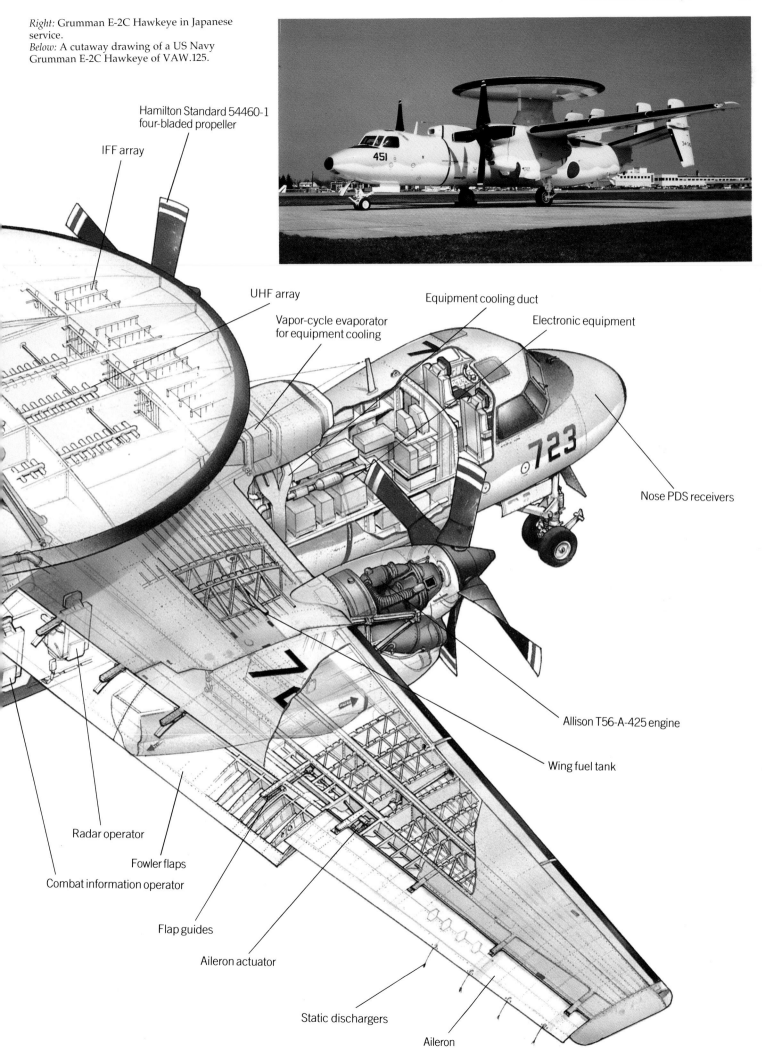

Hamilton Standard 54460-1 four-bladed propeller

IFF array

UHF array

Equipment cooling duct

Electronic equipment

Vapor-cycle evaporator for equipment cooling

Nose PDS receivers

Allison T56-A-425 engine

Wing fuel tank

Radar operator

Fowler flaps

Combat information operator

Flap guides

Aileron actuator

Static dischargers

Aileron

all-weather E-2C can detect targets to a range of 260 nautical miles, although small targets, such as cruise missiles, at about 145 nm. Air, land and sea targets are all detectable. More than 600 targets can be tracked simultaneously and over 40 intercepts can be controlled by each E-2C.

Specifications (E-2C data)

Radar: E-2Cs have been given either a General Electric AN/APS-125 (now being replaced) or AN/APS-138 surveillance radar system. From 1988 to 1990 respectively, the AN/APS-139 and AN/APS-145 systems will be installed in aircraft on the production line, leading eventually to all E-2Cs having the APS-145.
Accommodation: 5 crew, including those in the ATDS (airborne tactical data system) compartment.
Wingspan: 80 ft 7 in (24.56 m).
Length: 57 ft 6¾ in (17.54 m).
Maximum take-off weight: 51,933 lb (23,556 kg).
Maximum speed: 372 mph (598 km/h).
Mission performance: Ceiling 30,800 ft (9385 m); endurance 6 h 6 min.
Engines: Two 4910-ehp Allison T56-A-425 turboprops.
Versions in service
E-2B: US Navy's oldest version.
E-2C: Current advanced version, with APS-138 radar system normally. Also used by the US Naval Reserve and exported.
TE-2C: Training version with the US Navy.
Operators: Egypt, Israel, Japan, Singapore and United States (navy).

Grumman F-14 Tomcat
United States

When the unhappy Grumman/General Dynamics F-111B was finally cancelled in July 1968, Grumman was already well ahead with studies for a far superior and uncompromised carrier-based fighter using the same engines, radar and weapons known as the Model 303. This finally flew as the F-14A prototype on 21 December 1970. It was intended

Below: US Navy Grumman F-14A Tomcats.

that the TF30 should be only an interim engine, but the planned definitive power plant, the F401, was never funded. This proved a great mistake, and for 17 years the TF30 has been the only serious problem in what is otherwise a fabulous multirole fighter, with many qualities no other aircraft built since can equal. This is proved by the fact that later F-14s, with new engines but otherwise looking just the same, are likely to remain in production until the end of the century.

Like the F-111, the F-14 has variable-sweep 'swing-wings'. It is of especially great power and versatility, with advanced high-lift systems and a computer-controlled programmer which automatically swings the wings to front and rear, constantly seeking the best angle, whenever combat is engaged. Most F-14s are unlikely to need to engage in close combat, because the mighty Hughes radar can spot intruders from great distances, pick out particular targets and then, while continuing to search and add fresh targets in strict priority of the threat they pose, guide Sparrow or Phoenix missiles to attack them in sequence. The F-14A also has a large attack capability, but this is not part of its mission in the US Navy carrier air wings.

As well as having two engines (installed in such an effective way that the same arrangement has been used in today's MiG-29 and Su-27) and two fins, the F-14 also has a crew of two, the NFO (naval flight officer) in the back handling the difficult tasks in overwater navigation, all-weather interception and recovery to the carrier. Most missions, including deck-launched intercept over extreme radius, and Barcap (barrier combat air power) and Forcap (cover for the task force), can be flown without using drop tanks or the retractable in-flight refuelling probe. Some F-14s have a Northrop TCS (TV camera set) in a chin pod which, replacing earlier chin pods, gives a detailed visual picture of air targets from extreme ranges, for early positive identification. Another add-on is the TARPS (tactical air reconnaissance pod system) which contains cameras and infrared linescan sensors. About 50 F-14As with TARPS are the only replacements so far for the Navy's RF-8G and RA-5C in the reconnaissance role.

In 1987 production switched to the F-14A (Plus), powered by the vastly superior F110-GE-400 engine. Grumman is now well advanced with development of what will at last be the definitive Tomcat, the F-14D, with the F110 engine and a totally upgraded suite of radar (AN/APG-71), EW (electronic warfare) systems, navigation avionics and cockpit displays, as well as the computer-controlled Martin-Baker NACES (Navy aircrew common ejection seat). The final 300 of some 900 Tomcats will be F-14Ds.

Specifications (F-14A data)
Radar: Hughes AN/AWG-9 weapons control system, capable of detection to a range of over 75 to 195 miles (120 to 315 km), depending upon the size of the enemy target, tracking 24 targets and engaging 6 simultaneously.
Weapons: One 20-mm General Electric M61A-1 Vulcan six-barrel cannon, plus 6 long-range Phoenix and 2 close-range Sidewinder air-to-air missiles, 6 medium-range Sparrow and 2 Sidewinder, 4 Phoenix or Sparrow and 4 Sidewinder, or up to 14,500 lb (6577 kg) of attack weapons. AIM-54 Phoenix, originally developed for the F-111B, has a cruising speed of over Mach 4 and a range of 124 miles (200 km).
Accommodation: 2 crew in tandem.
Wingspan: Spread 64 ft 1½ in (19.54 m); swept 38 ft 2½ in (11.65 m); overswept 33 ft 3½ in (10.15 m).
Length: 62 ft 8 in (19.10 m).
Maximum take-off weight: 74,349 lb (33,724 kg).
Maximum speed: Mach 2.34.
Range: 2000 miles (3220 km) with auxiliary fuel.
Mission performance: Rate of climb at sea level more than 30,000 ft (9140 m) per min; ceiling more than 50,000 ft (15,250 m).
Engines: Two 20,900-lb (9480-kg) thrust with afterburning Pratt & Whitney TF30-P-412A or -414A turbofans, with 9028 liters of fuel standard.
Versions in service
F-14A: Carrier-borne multirole fighter. 531 delivered to the US Navy by March 1986, with deployment beginning in 1972. Iran received 80 for land operation during 1976-78, of which reports suggest only 10-15 are serviceable.
F-14A Plus and F-14D: See above.
Operators: Iran and United States (navy).

Grumman HU-16 Albatross and Convair PBY-5A Catalina
United States

As a utility amphibian, the prototype Albatross made its maiden flight on 24 October 1947. The US forces took in various models for search and rescue (SAR) and general purpose/utility duties, and in 1961 Grumman also produced an armed antisubmarine version with full detection equipment. While the aircraft flying with the Hellenic Air Force represent the ASW version and undertake maritime patrol work, Albatross amphibians in service today are mainly concerned with SAR.

Just a single example of the World War II vintage Convair Catalina amphibian remains in service today, with Paraguay as a utility transport.

Above: Hellenic Air Force Grumman HU-16B Albatross.

Specifications (HU-16B data)
Accommodation: 5 crew in SAR version. Up to 22 passengers.
Wingspan: 96 ft 8 in (29.46 m).
Length: 62 ft 10 in (19.18 m).
Maximum take-off weight: 37,500 lb (17,010 kg).
Maximum speed: 236 mph (380 km/h).
Range: 2850 miles (4586 km).
Mission performance: Rate of climb at sea level 1450 ft (440 m) per min; ceiling 21,000 ft (6400 m).
Engines: Two 1425-hp Wright R-1820-76A/B radial pistons, with 2555 liters of fuel standard.

Versions in service
HU-16A: Original SAR model for the USAF. Currently flown by Indonesia for SAR and patrol.

HU-16B: Improved and higher performance version, having first flown as a prototype on 16 January 1956. Serves with Greece (maritime patrol) and Taiwan (SAR).
HU-16D: Ex-US Navy utility model, used today by Mexico for SAR.
HU-16E: Ex-US Coast Guard model. Used by the Philippines for SAR.
Catalina: Two 1200-hp Pratt & Whitney R-1930-92 radial piston engines.
Operators: Greece, Indonesia, Mexico (navy), Paraguay (Catalina), Philippines and Taiwan.

Grumman OV-1 and RV-1 Mohawk
United States

The OV-1 Mohawk is the US Army's standard fixed-wing observation aircraft, first flown on 14 April 1959. It was the first turboprop-powered aircraft to enter US Army service when OV-1As began equipping units, this basically photographic model being followed by the OV-1B with side-looking airborne radar (SLAR) and the OV-1C with infrared mapping sensor and a camera. While some examples of early versions remain on strength, 72 OV-1Bs and Cs were subsequently brought up to OV-1D standard which, with new production, increased the OV-1D strength to 110 aircraft. The Army also uses 28 electronic intelligence and emitter-locating RV-1Ds.

Specifications (OV-1D data)
Equipment: Able to carry either a Motorola AN/APS-94D SLAR or AN/AAS-24 infrared system, in addition to three cameras.
Accommodation: 2 crew, seated side by side.
Wingspan: 48 ft 0 in (14.63 m).
Length: 41 ft 0 in (12.50 m).
Maximum take-off weight: 18,000 lb (8164 kg).
Maximum speed: 305 mph (465 km/h) with IR equipment.
Range: 1080 miles (1738 km) with IR equipment.
Mission performance: Rate of climb at sea level 3465 ft (1056 m) per min; ceiling 25,000 ft (7620 m).
Engines: Two 1400-shp Avco Lycoming T53-L-701 turboprops, with 1045 liters of fuel standard.

Versions in service
OV-1C: IR surveillance sensor and camera version, with T53-L-3 turboprops. Wingspan, like the OV-1A, of 42 ft (12.80 m), gross weight of 19,230 lb (8723 kg), and maximum speed of 308 mph (496 km/h).
OV-1D: Main US Army version, as detailed above.
RV-1D: The latest in a line of electronic reconnaissance versions, modified from OV-1s.
Operator: United States (army).

Below: US Army Grumman OV-1D Mohawk.

Above: US Navy Grumman C-1A Trader.

Grumman S-2 Tracker and C-1A Trader
United States

The Tracker was designed as a carrier-borne antisubmarine aircraft for the US Navy, with the ability to detect and attack submarines, the equipment carried (according to the version) including underfuselage search radar, a Jezebel passive acoustic search system, Julie active acoustic ranging system, sonobuoys carried in the engine nacelles, ECM direction finder, Sniffer submarine exhaust detector, MAD and a searchlight. The prototype flew for the first time on 4 December 1952, and by the close of production in 1964 over 1000 had been delivered to the Navy and for export. Neither the US Navy, Italy, Japan, nor some other original operators remain users, but most versions can still be found within the forces of the 10 remaining operators. It is reported that Canada may fit Pratt & Whitney Canada PT6A-67R turboprops to its CP-121s to maintain them into the next century. Avionics updates are also likely.

The C-1A Trader was developed from the S-2D Tracker as a carrier transport-trainer, first flying in early 1955. About 30 remain in the inventory of the US Navy.

Specifications (S-2E Tracker data)
Radar: Search radar carried under the fuselage.
Weapons: 60 echo-sounding explosive charges in a fuselage bay for use with Julie. 2 torpedoes, 4 depth charges or one depth bomb in the weapons bay, plus torpedoes, 250-lb (113-kg) bombs, air-to-surface missiles or rockets on 6 underwing pylons.
Wingspan: 72 ft 7 in (22.13 m).
Length: 43 ft 6 in (13.26 m).
Maximum take-off weight: 29,150 lb (13,200 kg).
Maximum speed: 265 mph (426 km/h).
Ferry range: 1300 miles (2090 km).
Mission performance: Ceiling 21,000 ft (6400m); patrol speed 150 mph (241 km/h).
Engines: Two 1525-hp Wright R-1820-82WA pistons.

Versions in service
S-2A: Initial and major production version, with similar engines to the S-2E. Wingspan 69 ft 8 in (21.23 m) and length 42 ft (12.80 m). Canadian examples are designated CP-121s. Some became S-2Bs when retrofitted with Jezebel and Julie.
S-2E: Advanced ASW version, as detailed above. Delivered from October 1962.
S-2F: Upgraded S-2Bs, themselves originating as S-2As.
S-2G: 49 earlier Trackers upgraded with Martin Marietta kits to continue service with the US Navy until superseded by the Viking. Withdrawn from USN front-line units in 1976.
TS-2A: Trainer derivative of the S-2A.
C-1A Trader: Carrier on-board delivery (COD) transport and all-weather trainer, based on the S-2D and accommodating 9 passengers or freight. A cage system secures freight during deck landings.
Operators: Argentina (navy, A and E), Brazil (marines, E), Canada (CP-121), South Korea (navy, A and F), Peru (navy, E), Taiwan (A), Thailand (navy, F), Turkey (E and TS-2A), United States (navy, Trader), Uruguay (navy, A and G) and Venezuela (navy, E).

Grumman/Gulfstream Aerospace Gulfstream I, II, III and IV
United States

Before Grumman relinquished its Gulfstream series of twin-jet commuter and executive transports in 1978 to Gulfstream American (later Gulfsteam Aerospace), it had delivered a VC-4A VIP transport to the US Coast Guard (Gulfstream I) and a VC-11A (Gulfstream II) to the same force. More importantly, the US Navy had taken into service TC-4C Academe bombardier/navigator flying classrooms based on the Gulfstream I, to train Intruder crews, each with a distinctive bulged nose housing search and tracking radar. Nine were ordered, the first taking to the air on 14 June 1967.

Apart from Special Mission aircraft based on the Gulfstream III and IV that can undertake maritime and fishery patrol, surveillance, antisubmarine warfare, electronic warfare, medevac, command control and many other duties, that have entered foreign military service, the USAF operates four C-20A and seven C-20B versions of the Gulfstream III for VIP transport duties, each with a crew of five and seats for 14 passengers. These are replacing C-140Bs and serve with the 89th Military Airlift Wing.

Specifications (C-20 data)
Radar: Weather radar.
Accommodation: As given above.
Wingspan: 77ft 10 in (23.72 m).
Length: 83 ft 1 in (25.32 m).
Maximum take-off weight: 69,700 lb (31,615 kg).
Cruising speed: 508-561 mph (818-903 km/h).
Range: 4718 miles (7593 km).
Mission performance: Rate of climb at sea level 4270 ft (450 m) per min; ceiling 45,000 ft (13,715 m).
Engines: Two 11,400-lb (5171-kg) thrust Rolls-Royce F113-RR-100 turbofans, with 15,868 liters of fuel.

Below: US Navy TC-4C Academe Intruder crew trainer.

Versions in service
Gulfstream I: Two 2185-ehp Rolls-Royce Dart Mk 529-8X turboprops. Used by the USCG as the VC-4A, and USN as the TC-4C Academe Intruder crew trainer with accommodation for a student pilot, student bombardier/navigator and four further students at radar/computer consoles.
Gulfstream II: Twin turbofan transport, with Spey Mk 511-8 engines (F113-RR-100) and accommodating 19 passengers. Military examples are used as VIP transports. The first Gulfstream II flew on 2 October 1966.
Gulfstream III: Military examples include VIP transports, as detailed above. The Royal Danish Air Force was the initial customer for Special Missions SRA-1 versions. The first Gulfstream III flew on 2 December 1979.
Gulfstream IV: Latest twin-turbofan version, first flown on 19 September 1985. Also available in Special Missions SRA-4 forms. Two 12,420-lb (5634-kg) thrust Rolls-Royce Tay Mk 610-8 engines. Accommodation for the crew of 2 or 3 plus 14 to 19 passengers.
Operators: Denmark (SRA-1), Egypt (III), Gabon (III), Greece (I), Italy (III), Ivory Coast (II and III), Morocco (II), United States (air force, C-20; navy, TC-4C; coast guard VC-4A/VC-11A) and Venezuela (II).

HAL Ajeet and Ajeet Trainer
India

In Britain on 18 July 1955 the prototype of a new lightweight single-seat fighter flew as the Folland Gnat, this being about half the size and a third of the weight of a conventional first-line fighter. A two-seat trainer version followed, the latter entering RAF service and became best known as the mount of the Red Arrows aerobatic display team. The single-seater, however, did achieve service with India, Finland and Yugoslavia, being built under license also in the former.

Below: HAL Ajeet lightweight combat aircraft, armed with rockets and bombs.

From the Gnat, HAL developed an upgraded version as the Ajeet (Invincible), which flew as a prototype on 5 March 1975. Apart from improvements to the navigation and communications systems, longitudinal control was improved and wing fuel tanks were introduced to free the wings to carry more armament. Eighty single-seat Ajeets had been acquired by the Indian Air Force by 1982 and these remain in use as attack fighters.

On 20 September 1982 the prototype lengthened two-seat Ajeet Trainer flew for the first time, having less fuel but retaining combat capability. Eighteen are earmarked for the Indian Air Force and 12 for the Navy.

Specifications (Ajeet data)
Weapons: Two 30-mm Aden Mk 4 cannon plus bombs, rockets or other stores on four underwing pylons.
Accommodation: The pilot.
Wingspan: 22 ft 1 in (6.73 m).
Length: 29 ft 8 in (9.04 m).
Maximum take-off weight: 9200 lb (4173 kg).
Maximum speed: 716 mph (1152 km/h).
Combat radius: 107 miles (172 km) with two 551-lb (250-kg) bombs.
Mission performance: Time to 39,370 ft (12,000 m) 6 min 2 sec without external weapons; ceiling 45,000 ft (13,720 m).
Engine: One 4500-lb (2041-kg) thrust Rolls-Royce Orpheus 701-01 turbojet, with 1350 liters of fuel standard.

Above: HAL HF-24 Marut.

Versions in service
Ajeet: Single-seat attack fighter.
Ajeet Trainer: Lengthened 2-seat operational trainer, with 4850-lb (2200-kg) thrust Orpheus 701-01AT turbojet. 1874 lb (850 kg) of weapons. In production in 1986.
Operator: India (air force, Ajeet and Ajeet Trainer; navy, Ajeet Trainer).

HAL HF-24 Marut
India

The Marut (Wind Spirit) has several historic claims: it was the first supersonic combat aircraft to be designed and built in Asia other than by the Soviet Union; it was designed under the direction of the designer of the World War II German Focke-Wulf aircraft, Professor Kurt Tank; and it fought without loss during the conflict between India and Pakistan in late 1971.

A swept-wing strike fighter, the Marut prototype made its maiden flight on 17 June 1961 and altogether 129 were built in single-seat Mk 1 form. Eighteen Mk 1T tandem two-seat trainers were also produced during the 1970s, the main change as a result of the second cockpit being the deletion of the retractable rocket pack. Of these two versions, at the time of writing it was believed that one squadron of the Indian Air Force still flew Mk 1s and 10 to 15 trainers remained active. Marut Mk 1s are being superseded by MiG-23BNs.

Specifications (Marut Mk 1 data)
Weapons: Four 30-mm Aden Mk 2 single-barrel cannon in the fuselage nose, each with 120 rounds of ammunition, plus 50 68-mm SNEB air-to-air rockets in a retractable lower-fuselage pack, and underwing pylons for other weapons including four 1000-lb (454-kg) bombs.
Accommodation: The pilot.
Wingspan: 29 ft 6¼ in (9.00 m).
Length: 52 ft 0¾ in (15.87 m).
Maximum take-off weight: 24,048 lb (10,908 kg).
Maximum speed: Mach 1.02.
Range: 746 miles (1200 km).
Mission performance: G limit +9.34.
Engines: Two 4850-lb (2200-kg) HAL-produced Rolls-Royce Bristol Orpheus 703 nonafterburning turbojets, with 2491 liters of fuel standard.
Versions in service
Marut Mk 1: As detailed above.
Marut Mk 1T: 2-seat operational trainer version. First flew on 30 April 1970.
Operator: India.

HAL HJT-16 Kiran
India

The Kiran was designed for the indigenous Air Force as a basic jet trainer, using the British Viper turbojet as power plant. It also adopted the British Jet Provost general layout, providing side-by-side seating for the two pilots. The prototype made its maiden flight on 4 September 1964 and progressive production versions introduced heavier armament (as detailed below). A total of 247 Kirans had been ordered at the time of writing (mostly Mk Is and IAs), of which a few were taken into Navy service.

Specifications (Kiran Mk II data)
Armament: Two 7.62-mm machine-guns in the fuselage nose, with 150 rounds of ammunition each. 4 underwing pylons for four 551-lb (250-kg) bombs, practice bombs, four pods of 18 68-mm SNEB rockets, etc, or two 227-liter drop tanks.
Accommodation: Student copilot and instructor/pilot side by side.
Wingspan: 35 ft 1¼ in (10.70 m).
Length: 34 ft 9½ in (10.60 m).
Maximum take-off weight: 11,023 lb (5000 kg).
Maximum speed: 418 mph (672 km/h).
Range: 457 miles (735 km).
Mission performance: Rate of climb at sea level 5250 ft (1600 m) per min; ceiling 39,370 ft (12,000 m).
Engine: One 4200-lb (1905-kg) thrust Rolls-Royce Orpheus 701-01 turbojet, with 1345 liters of fuel standard.

Versions in service
Kiran Mk I: Initial production version without armament. 118 aircraft built. 2500-lb (1134-kg) thrust Viper 11 engine.
Kiran Mk IA: 72 aircraft, similar to the Mk I but with 2 underwing pylons for 551-lb (250-kg) bombs, gun and rocket pods, or drop tanks, thereby expanding roles to include weapons training and light attack.
Kiran Mk II: Latest standard, still in production for weapons training and COIN. First flown in 1976 and featuring also improved avionics.
Operator: India (air force and navy).

Below: HAL Kiran Mk II jet trainer.

HAL HPT-32 and HTT-34
India

The first prototype of the HPT-32 aerobatic trainer flew initially on 6 January 1977. Offering side-by-side seating for two, it can be used for instructing pupil pilots with no previous experience, for night flying, and formation, instrument and navigation training. By early 1986, the Indian Air Force had received 32. A turboprop-powered derivative for ab initio training has been developed as the HTT-34. First flown in 1984, it had not been taken into service by 1986. Power is provided by a 420-shp Allison 250-B17D engine.

Specifications (HPT-32 data)
Accommodation: Pupil and instructor side by side.
Wingspan: 31 ft 2 in (9.50 m).
Length: 25 ft 4 in (7.72 m).
Maximum take-off weight: 2756 lb (1250 kg).
Maximum speed: 164 mph (265 km/h) IAS.
Range: 462 miles (744 km).
Mission performance: Rate of climb at sea level 1100 ft (335 m) per min; ceiling 18,050 ft (5500 m); G limits +6, −3.
Engine: One 260-hp Avco Lycoming AEIO-540-D4B5 piston, with 229 liters of fuel.

Above: By replacing the piston engine of an HPT-32 with an Allison 250—B17D turboprop, HAL has produced the HTT-34. The prototype seen here first flew in mid-1984.

Version in service
HPT-32: Other roles to which this aircraft can be put include ground attack, patrol, reconnaissance, and search and rescue.
Operator: India.

Handley Page Victor K.Mk 2
United Kingdom

This RAf flight-refuelling tanker began life as one of three types of so-called V-bombers, which entered RAF service during the 1950s and early 1960s to carry Britain's nuclear deterrent. By 1968, however, the Victor had passed out of service as a bomber and many became strategic reconnaissance aircraft and flight refuelling tankers. The Victor K.Mk 2 improved tanker entered RAF service from May 1974 and during the Falklands conflict performed nearly 600 missions of which 594 were entirely successful. During one operation, Victors flying from Ascension Island refuelled Vulcans used on the longest-range bombing missions in aviation history. Interestingly, the Vulcan was, itself, about to pass out of service when the conflict began, and during that war other Vulcans were quickly converted into tankers to supplement the Victors. The Vulcan is no longer in use.

Specifications (Victor K.Mk 2 data)
Equipment: 3 flight refuelling Mk 20 pods.
Wingspan: 117 ft 0 in (35.66 m).
Length: 114 ft 11 in (35.03 m).
Maximum take-off weight: 223,000 lb (101,150 kg).
Maximum speed: More than 600 mph (966 km/h).
Range: 4600 miles (7400 km).
Engines: Four 20,600-lb (9344-kg) thrust Rolls-Royce Conway RCo.17 Mk 201 turbojets.

Version in service
Victor K.Mk 2: Flight refuelling tanker. Ex-British Airways Super VC10s (Model 1151s) have been suggested as replacements for Victors once suitably modified. The Victor bomber prototype first flew on 24 December 1952. Only operator is No 55 RAF Sqn.
Operator: United Kingdom.

Harbin PS-5
China

Although few details are available, one of the most significant military aircraft of recent appearance is the PS-5, a large long-range antisubmarine and maritime patrol amphibian of Chinese design. PS-5s are already operational with the Aviation of the People's Navy. Believed to have first flown in prototype form in 1980, it has the appearance of a Soviet Be-12 but with much greater span wings. Power could be provided by four 3150-shp Shanghai WJ-5 turboprops. The V-shaped hull has a single step, with circular depressions in the sides into which the main undercarriage units retract; the nose gear retracts into the forward hull itself. Various spray-suppressing features appear on the hull to keep the spray from the propellers during take-off and landing. A radome is carried at the nose, above the observation station.

Specifications (PS-5 data)
Weapons: Typical armament for antisubmarine and antishipping warfare. No details are available. Options could include air-to-surface missiles.
Wingspan: 110 ft (33.5 m) estimated.
Length: 96 ft 9 in (29.5 m) estimated.
Engines: As detailed above.
Version in service
PS-5: Designed to supersede the Be-6s in service.
Operator: China (navy).

Below: Harbin PS-5 patrol and ASW amphibian.

Hawker Hunter
United Kingdom

More than 35 years after its first flight as a prototype (on 20 July 1951), the Hunter remains a much-prized first-line combat aircraft with no signs of retirement. Indeed, the Swiss Air Force alone has 132 F.Mk 58 single-seat fighter-bombers (and seven trainers in

Above: Royal Navy Hawker Hunter GA.Mk 11s of the Fleet Requirements and Air Direction Unit.
Top: Handley Page Victor K.Mk 2 operating from Ascension Island.

the typical side-by-side two-seat arrangement), having taken in 60 during the 1970s that had been assembled after refurbishment at the Swiss Federal Aircraft Factory.

Originating as an RAF swept-wing cannon fighter and designed under the leadership of the legendary Sydney Camm, the Hunter was probably the most beautiful of the early 1950s fighters and found favor with other nations too. It joined the RAF in 1954, having in the previous year taken the world speed record from the United States, which had held it with an F-86D Sabre. But such was the furious pace of fighter development that by the end of the 1950s the Hunter had been left behind in speed, rate of climb and modern air-to-air armament. However, by then the FGA.Mk 9 fighter-bomber was appearing as a Venom replacement for tropical deployment and this brought new life to the warbird.

Specifications (Hunter FGA.Mk 9 data)

Weapons: Four 30-mm Aden cannon in the nose. Underwing pylons for bombs of up to 1000-lb (454-kg) weight each (2) or 74 2-in rockets, plus 48 3-in rockets on the outer pylons.
Accommodation: The pilot.
Wingspan: 33 ft 8 in (10.26 m).
Length: 45 ft 10½ in (13.98 m).
Maximum take-off weight: 24,000 lb (10,886 kg).
Maximum speed: 710 mph (1142 km/h).
Range: 1840 miles (2961 km) with auxiliary fuel.
Mission performance: Rate of climb at sea level about 17,500 ft (5335 m) per min; ceiling over 50,000 ft (15,240 m).
Engine: One 10,000-lb (4536-kg) thrust Rolls-Royce Avon Mk 207 turbojet.

Versions in service

Hunter single-seaters: Many of the Hunters still in use were based on the F.Mk 6, with an Avon 203 engine (including the similar F.Mk 56, Mk 58, Mk 70 and Mk 73), or the FGA.Mk 9 ground attack model as detailed above (including the Mk 59, Mk 71 and Mk 73). GA.Mk 11 is a ground attack trainer conversion of the F.Mk 4 for the Royal Navy.
Hunter trainers: Side-by-side 2-seaters with T designations.
Operators: Chile (FGA.Mk 71 and T.Mk 77), India (FGA.Mk 56 and T.Mk 66), Iraq (FGA.Mk 59 and T.Mk 69), Lebanon (F.Mk 70 and T.Mk 69), Oman (FGA.Mk 73 and T-66B), Qatar (FGA.Mk 78 and T.Mk 79), Singapore (FGA.Mk 74, FR.Mk 74 and T.Mk 75), Somali Republic (FGA.Mk 76 and T.Mk 77), Switzerland (F.Mk 58 and T.Mk 68), United Kingdom (air force, FGA.Mk 9 and T.Mk 7; navy, GA.Mk 11 and T.Mk 8) and Zimbabwe (FGA.Mk 9).

Below: RAF Hawker Siddeley Buccaneer S.Mk 2.

Hawker Siddeley Buccaneer
United Kingdom

Conceived as a carrier-borne transonic low-level strike aircraft and first flown on 30 April 1958, the Buccaneer joined the Royal Navy from 1962 in S.Mk 1 form, superseded in production from 1964 by the S.Mk 2, S.Mk 2C and S.Mk 2D, the latter with the ability to launch Martel tactical missiles. It remained in service until the Royal Navy gave up its last large aircraft carrier, those left being transferred to the RAF for land operations, joining the RAF's own Martel-carrying S.Mk 2Bs ordered in 1968. Those Navy aircraft unable to carry Martel became S.Mk 2As in RAF service.

Such is the continuing potential of the Buccaneer that British Aerospace is currently updating 60 RAF aircraft for many more years of service in a maritime strike role in a $40 million program. Apart from fatigue testing of the airframe, the Buccaneer will have its Ferranti Blue Parrot attack radar optimized for use of Sea Eagle and TV-guided Martel anti-shipping missiles, and the radar warning and ESM avionics will be updated. New avionics include the Ferranti FIN 1063 inertial navigation system. The South African Air Force continues to deploy its six Buccaneer S.Mk 50s in a land-based role.

Specifications (S.Mk 2B data)

Radar: Ferranti Blue Parrot attack radar.
Weapons: Bay and four underwing pylons for up to 16,000 lb (7257 kg) of weapons, including Sea Eagle and Martel missiles.
Accommodation: 2 crew in tandem.
Wingspan: 44 ft 0 in (13.41 m).
Length: 63 ft 5 in (19.33 m).
Maximum take-off weight: 62,000 lb (28,123 kg).
Maximum speed: 646 mph (1040 km/h).
Range: 2300 miles (3700 km).
Engines: Two 11,100-lb (5035-kg) thrust

Rolls-Royce RB.168.1A Spey Mk 101 turbofans, with 7092 liters of fuel standard.

Versions in service

S.Mk 2A: RAF version without Martel.
S.Mk 2B: RAF version with Martel and Sea Eagle. Update, as detailed above.
S.Mk 50: SAAF version, based on the S.Mk 2 but with an 8000-lb (3629-kg) Bristol Siddeley BS.605 rocket motor in the fuselage to boost power during take-off.
Operators: South Africa and United Kingdom.

Hawker Siddeley Shackleton AEW.Mk2
United Kingdom

Looking like something left over from World War II, and indeed developed by Avro who gave the Allies the famous Lancaster bomber, the Shackleton has been the RAF's standard airborne early warning aircraft since the early 1970s and now, with the demise of the Nimrod AEW.Mk 3 program, will have to continue for some years more.

The Shackleton was first flown in March 1949 as a prototype long-range maritime reconnaissance aircraft, and the RAF acquired 188 and the South African Air Force eight. The only remaining examples today are those Shackleton MR.Mk 2s specially converted to the AEW role, 12 of which were produced with all former armament deleted and AN/APS-20 search radar from decommissioned Fairey Gannet AEW Mk.3s installed in each in an underfuselage radome. Five or six remain operational, with others in store.

Specifications (Shackleton AEW.Mk 2 data)

Radar: As detailed above.
Accommodation: 10 crew.
Wingspan: 119 ft 10 in (36.52 m).
Length: 87 ft 4 in (26.62 m).
Maximum take-off weight: 98,000 lb (44,452 kg).
Maximum speed: 260 mph (418 km/h).
Range: 2900 miles (4667 km).
Mission performance: Patrol endurance 10 h.
Engines: Four 2455-ehp Rolls-Royce Griffon 57A pistons.

Version in service

Shackleton AEW.Mk 2: As detailed above.
Operator: United Kingdom.

Hughes Model 269A and 300/TH-55A Osage, and Schweizer Model 300C
United States

As the Model 269 two-seat light helicopter, the first prototype to this series made its maiden flight in October 1956. It later entered production in Model 269A form, five going to the US Army for evaluation as YHO-2HUs, followed by 792 TH-55A Osage helicopter primary trainers (180-hp Avco Lycoming HIO-360-B1A piston engines). Kawasaki also constructed TH-55Js for its indigenous army. From the Model 269A was developed the three-seat Model 300, which itself entered production in 1964. Then in 1983 Hughes

Above right: Hawker Siddeley Shackleton AEW.Mk 2 flies alongside the now-abandoned Nimrod AEW.Mk 3.
Right: US Army Hughes TH-55A Osage.

transferred Model 300 production to the Schweizer Aircraft Corporation, which offers the Model 300C. Up to that time Hughes had built over 2800 Model 269/300 helicopters for civil and military operation. The latest military sales are 24 TH-300C trainers to the Royal Thai Army. BredaNardi in Italy has also built similar helicopters over the years, among the most recent military customers being the Hellenic Air Force.

Specifications (Model 300C data)
Accommodation: 3 persons.
Diameter of rotor: 26 ft 10 in (8.18 m).
Length with rotors: 30 ft 10 in (9.40 m).
Maximum take-off weight: 2150 lb (975 kg).
Cruising speed: 95 mph (153 km/h).
Range: 224 miles (360 km).
Mission performance: Rate of climb at sea level 750 ft (229 m) per min; ceiling 10,200 ft (3110 m); hovering ceiling in ground effect 5900 ft (1800 m); hovering ceiling out of ground effect 2750 ft (840 m); endurance 3 h 24 min.
Engine: One 225-hp Avco Lycoming HIO-360-D1A piston (derated to 190 hp), with 114 liters of fuel standard.
Versions in service
Model 269A: Production 2-seat light helicopter. Formed the basis for the Osage.
TH-55A Osage: US Army 2-seat helicopter primary trainer. Engine as given above. Production ended in 1969. Similar TH-55Js for the JGSDF. Maximum speed 86 mph (138 km/h). Range 204 miles (328 km). Under half of the TH-55As remain in use.
Model 300: Civil and military three-seaters. The initial Model 300 version was built with a 180-hp HIO-360-A1A engine.
BredaNardi NH-300: Italian license-built version.
Operators: Algeria, Colombia, Costa Rica (air force?), Greece, Haiti, Indonesia (army), Iraq, Japan (army), Nigeria, Spain, Sweden (army, as HKp-5), Thailand (army), Turkey (army) and United States (army).

IAI 1123 and 1124 Westwind
Israel

Israel Aircraft Industries built a total of 36 Jet Commander business jets from 1968, based on the original design by Ted Smith in the United States, under the names 1121 Commodore Jet and 1123 Westwind. The latter

Above: IAI Arava STOL light transport.

represented a longer and modified model, as detailed below. Although basically civil, both Israel and Ciskei operate the early Westwind in military guise. From the 1123 Westwind IAI developed the turbofan 1124 Westwind 1, made available in 1975, followed in 1979 by the 1124A Westwind 2. A maritime patrol derivative of the Westwind is the 1124N Sea Scan, with Litton APS-504(V)2 search radar and other equipment. The Israeli Navy uses three Sea Scans, while Honduras and Panama may be operators of single examples for reconnaissance.

Specifications (Westwind 1 data)
Radar: RCA Primus 400 weather radar.
Accommodation: 2 crew plus 7 to 10 passengers.
Wingspan: 44 ft 9½ in (13.65 m) with wingtip tanks.
Length: 52 ft 3 in (15.93 m).
Maximum take-off weight: 22,850 lb (10,365 kg).
Maximum speed: 542 mph (872 km/h).
Range: 2475 miles (3983 km) with 7 passengers.
Mission performance: Rate of climb at sea level 5000 ft (1524 m) per min; ceiling 45,000 ft (13,715 m).
Engines: Two 3700-lb (1678-kg) thrust Garrett TFE731-3-100G turbofans, with 4920 liters of fuel.
Versions in service
1121A/B Commodore Jet: Initial IAI models, the latter with two 2950-lb (1338-kg) thrust

General Electric CJ610-5 turbojets.
1123 Westwind: IAI-developed model, with 3100-lb (1405-kg) thrust CJ610-9 engines, a 1 ft 8 in (0.51 m) longer cabin (10 passengers), double-slotted flaps, drooped wing leading-edges, and much else.
1124 Westwind 1: First turbofan version. Rhein-Flugzeugbau flies four in support of the West German forces as target-towing aircraft.
1124A Westwind 2: Better 'hot and high' performance, improved range and operational costs. Modified wings with winglets, and cabin improvements.
1124N Sea Scan: Maritime version, with an endurance of between 6½ and 8 hours. Range 1588-2878 miles (2555-4633 km).
Operators: Ciskei (1123), West Germany (1124 Westwind), Honduras (1124N?), Israel (air force, 1123/1124 Westwind; navy, 1124N) and Panama (1124N?).

IAI Arava
Israel

The Arava is a STOL light transport, built for both the civil and military markets. It is of pod-and-boom configuration, with a large section of the fuselage tailcone able to be swung to one side to provide clear access to the main cabin. The first prototype flew initially on 27 November 1969. In addition to the

Below: IAI 1124N Sea Scan maritime patrol derivative of the Westwind business jet.

transport role, the Arava can undertake other missions including reconnaissance, maritime patrol and electronic warfare, with Elta supplying electronic surveillance and elint avionics, radomes, etc. The Israeli Air Force includes electronic models in its inventory.

Specifications (Model 201 data)
Radar: Provision for weather radar.
Weapons: Optional armament is two 0.50-in Browning machine-guns and two packs each containing six 82-mm rockets.
Accommodation: One or 2 crew plus up to 24 armed troops, 16 paratroops plus dispatchers, 12 stretchers and 2 attendants, or up to 5184 lb (2351 kg) of freight which can include vehicles.
Wingspan: 68 ft 9 in (20.96 m).
Length: 30 ft 7 in (9.33 m).
Maximum take-off weight: 15,000 lb (6804 kg).
Maximum speed: 203 mph (326 km/h).
Range: 656 miles (1056 km) with reserves.
Mission performance: Rate of climb at sea level 1290 ft (393 m) per min; ceiling 25,000 ft (7620 m).
Engines: Two 750-shp Pratt & Whitney Canada PT6A-34 turboprops, with 1663 liters of fuel standard.

Versions in service
Arava 201: Military version used in transport, reconnaissance, maritime patrol and electronic warfare roles.
Arava 202: Larger military version, with a wingspan and length of 70 ft 11½ in (21.63 m) and 44 ft 2 in (13.47 m) respectively. Two 750-shp PT6A-36 turboprops, with increased fuel. Maximum load increased to 5510 lb (2500 kg), with accommodation for 30 troops. Winglets.
Operators: Bolivia, Colombia, Ecuador (army and navy), El Salvador, Guatemala, Honduras, Israel, Liberia, Mexico, Nicaragua, Papua New Guinea, Paraguay, Swaziland, Thailand and Venezuela (army).

IAI Lavi
Israel

The complications of politics, affecting the supply from outside sources of major items of equipment for its armed services, has quickened Israeli determination to make itself as independent as possible. The length to which the nation has gone in this direction is exemplified by the Lavi (Young Lion), a single-seat multirole combat aircraft, the design of which was initiated in the late 1970s. Being required to supersede the large number of Douglas A-4 Skyhawks and later Kfirs in service with the Heyl Ha' A-vir, it needed to be a capable aircraft of high performmace.

The Lavi clearly incorporates some of the design features of the General Dynamics F-16 Fighting Falcon; it is, however, a smaller aircraft and to achieve the desired high maneuverability it combines close-coupled 'swept delta' main wings with all-moving foreplanes (or canard surfaces) of similar planform. Extensive use is made of advanced weight-saving composite materials, these representing some 22 percent of the total structural weight. A go-ahead for the program was given in 1980 and construction of six flight development aircraft (two of them two-seat trainers) allowed a maiden flight to be recorded on 31 December 1986 by one of the two-seaters. However, it has been reported

that Israel's economic problems have cast doubts on the future of the Lavi. Initial operational capability is scheduled for 1992.

Specifications
Radar: Elta multimode pulse-Doppler radar which in the air-to-air mode will provide track-while-scan and automatic target acquisition, and in the air-to-surface mode high-resolution ground mapping, terrain avoidance and sea search.
Weapons: Excluding air-to-air missiles on wingtip launch rails, a maximum weapon load of 6000 lb (2722 kg) can be carried on seven underfuselage and four underwing attachments; this can include air-to-surface missiles, bombs, rockets and auxiliary fuel tanks. Internally-mounted 30-mm cannon.
Accommodation: The pilot.
Wingspan: 28 ft 9¾ in (8.78 m).
Length: 47 ft 9½ in (14.57 m).
Maximum take-off weight: 42,500 lb (19,278 kg).
Maximum speed: 1188 mph (1912 km/h) estimated.
Combat radius (estimated): 1324 miles (2131 km), with a 3000-lb (1361-kg) weapon load.
Mission performance (estimated): Sustained turn rate 13.2 degrees per sec at Mach 0.8; maximum turn rate 24.3 degrees per sec at Mach 0.8; G limit +9.
Engine: One 20,620-lb (9353-kg) thrust with afterburning Pratt & Whitney PW1120 turbojet, with 3330 liters of fuel standard.
Operator: Perhaps Israel eventually.

IAI Nesher and Kfir
Israel

In 1962 the Israeli Air Force received its first Mirage III fighters from France and these were to be followed by 50 Mirage 5 fighter-bombers from 1967. However, a French embargo put a stop to the arrival of Mirage 5s, leaving Israel with an unfulfilled requirement. Having got hold of some Mirage 5 production drawings, IAI began the two-stage development of its own aircraft to satisfy the role, initially producing the Nesher. This, which first flew in September 1969, was little more than an indigenously built Mirage III airframe fitted with an Atar 9C turbojet and

Above: Israel's latest fighter, the multirole IAI Lavi on its first flight on 31 December 1986.

Israeli avionics and equipment. Delivery of about 100 started in 1972 and 40 took part in the Yom Kippur war of October 1973 with notable operational success. During 1978-79 26 Neshers were sold to the Argentine Air Force, going to the No VI Brigade Aérea and known locally as Daggers. Some of these were encountered by British Forces during the Falklands conflict of 1982.

Having also test-flown a US General Electric J79 turbojet installed in a modified Mirage under project Black Curtain on 19 October 1970, work on a ground attack and fighter aircraft based on this engine produced the Kfir, which first flew in mid-1973. The Kfir adopted the basic Mirage 5/Nesher airframe but was flatter under the forward section of the fuselage and with a shortened and wider-diameter aft section to accommodate the new engine. Five new airscoops were added to deliver cooling air to the afterburner (one forward of the tailfin and four smaller scoops on the fuselage) and the undercarriage was modified and strengthened. Inside the revised cockpit, new Israeli avionics were evident. Two IAF squadrons were given the early Kfir. In mid-1976 the new Kfir-C2 was shown in public, the most obvious changes being the adoption of modified wings with extended leading edges and swept canards, these changes improving take-off performance and maneuverability. The canards could be removed for attack missions when maneuverability was not the main consideration. A great many C2s were built and earlier aircraft were brought up to this general standard, later production aircraft featuring longer noses to house new Elta EL/M-2001B range-only radar. A two-seat combat-capable trainer appeared in 1981 as the TC2. In 1983 deliveries switched to the Kfir-C7 and trainers became TC7s, the main updates being greater engine power, new avionics to allow HOTAS (hands on throttle and stick) and so giving the pilot his switches/triggers on these controls to make operation easier, and two more weapon pylons. C2s are being modified to C7 standard.

Kfirs have been exported to a small number of air forces, including the US Navy which is leasing 12 early-built Kfirs as 'aggressor' aircraft (simulating enemy fighters) to fly with VF-43 Squadron under the designation F-21A, while a similar role is undertaken by 13 Kfirs now in US Marine Corps hands. US Navy Kfirs will be returned when F-16Ns are received into service.

Specifications (Kfir-C7 data)
Radar: Elta EL/M-2001B range-only radar.
Weapons: Two 30-mm IAI/DEFA 552 cannon in the fuselage, each with 140 rounds of ammunition, plus 5 underfuselage and 4 underwing pylons for up to 12,730 lb (5775 kg) of weapons. For air defense, 2 Shafrir, Sidewinder of Python 3 air-to-air missiles is usual. Ground attack weapons can include the normal range of bombs, rocket launchers, etc, plus Shrike, Maverick or other guided weapons.
Accommodation: The pilot.
Wingspan: 26 ft 11½ in (8.22 m).
Length: 51 ft 4 in (15.65 m).
Maximum take-off weight: 36,375 lb (16,500 kg).
Maximum speed: More than Mach 2.3.
Combat radius: 737 miles (1186 km) with 4700 liters of auxiliary fuel in drop tanks plus 2 AA missiles and 2600 lb (1179 kg) of bombs.
Mission performance: Rate of climb at sea level 45,925 ft (14,000 m) per min; ceiling 58,000 ft (17,680 m).
Engine: One 18,750-lb (8505-kg) thrust with afterburning General Electric J79-J1E turbojet, with 3243 liters of fuel standard.
Versions in service
Nesher/Dagger: One SNECMA Atar 9C turbojet, as detailed above.
Kfir-C2: One 17,900-lb (8120-kg) thrust with afterburning J79-GE-17 turbojet.
Kfir-C7: Latest production version, as detailed above.
Kfir-TC2 and TC7: Lengthened tandem 2-seat operational trainers, relating to the Kfir-C2 and C7 respectively.
F-21A: US Navy and US Marine Corps Kfirs, leased for operation as 'aggressor' training aircraft.

Below: Israeli IAI Kfir-C2s.

Operators: Argentina (Dagger), Ecuador (Kfir-C2), Israel (Kfir-C2, C7, TC2 and TC7) and United States (navy and marine corps, F-21A).

ICA IAR-28MA
Rumania

This is a side-by-side 2-seat trainer used by the Rumanian Air Force, which received 10 as the first production batch in 1984. It is a development of the IAR-28M2 powered glider, the main changes being the adoption of the powered glider's optional engine as the standard power plant and new wings with split flaps and ailerons.

Specifications
Accommodation: Student pilot and instructor side by side.
Wingspan: 34 ft 1½ in (10.40 m).
Length: 24 ft 7¼ in (7.50 m).
Maximum take-off weight: 1675 lb (760 kg).
Maximum speed: 118 mph (190 km/h).
Range: 435 miles (700 km).
Mission performance: Rate of climb at sea

Above: ICA IAR-28MA in Rumanian Air Force markings.

level 395 ft (120 m) per min; ceiling 16,400 ft (5000 m); G limits +5.3m, −2.65.
Engine: One 80-hp Limbach L2000 EOI piston.
Version in service
IAR-28MA: 2-seat training lightplane, as described above.
Operator: Rumania.

ICA IAR-823
Rumania

It is believed that 40 IAR-823s serve with the Rumanian Air Force as 2-seat fully aerobatic primary trainers. The design also allows for up to 5 seats in the cabin, or ambulance or photographic layouts. The prototype flew initially in 1973.

Specifications
Weapons: 2 stations under the wings allow for the carriage of practice weapons or auxiliary fuel tanks.
Accommodation: As above.
Wingspan: 32 ft 9¾ in (10.00 m).
Length: 27 ft 3½ in (8.31 m).
Maximum take-off weight, aerobatic: 2623 lb (1190 kg).
Maximum speed: 186 knots (300 km/h).
Range at aerobatic weight: 807 miles (1300 km).
Mission performance, aerobatic weight: Rate of climb at sea level 1380 ft (420 m) per min; ceiling 18,375 ft (5600 m); G limits +6, −3.
Engine: One 290-hp Avco Lycoming IO-540-G1D5 piston, with 360 liters of fuel standard.
Version in service
IAR-823: Trainer and utility aircraft.
Operator: Rumania.

ICA IAR-825TP Triumf
Rumania

The latest trainer for the Rumanian Air Force is the Triumf, a turboprop basic flying and multirole trainer which entered production in 1986. It uses the wings of the IAR-823, which have been strengthened and other components. In most other respects it is a new design, which made its maiden flight on

Above: ICA IAR-823.

12 June 1982. It has been reported that the Rumanian Air Force has a total requirement for 85 Triumfs, of which the first 15 have been ordered.

Specifications (IAR-825TP Triumf data)

Weapons: Practice weapons carried underwing.
Accommodation: Student pilot and instructor in tandem cockpits.
Wingspan: 32 ft 9¾ in (10.00 m).
Length: 29 ft 6 in (8.99 m).
Maximum take-off weight, utility: 5070 lb (2300 kg).
Maximum take-off weight, aerobatic: 3748 lb (1700 kg).
Maximum speed: 292 mph (470 km/h).
Range: 870 miles (1400 km).
Mission performance: Rate of climb at sea level 3150 ft (960 m) per min; ceiling 29,530 ft (9000 m); G limits +6, −3; endurance 3h.
Engine: One 750-shp Pratt & Whitney Canada PT6A-25C turboprop.

Version in service
IAR-825TP: Basic flying and multirole trainer. The aerobatic maximum take-off weight is 3747 lb (1700 kg).
Operator: Rumania.

Right: ICA IAR-825TP Triumf.
Below: The Ilyushin Il-14 is approaching the end of its military career.

Ilyushin Il-14 (NATO name Crate)
Soviet Union

The Il-14 appeared in 1953 as a more powerful and refined development of the Il-12 (NATO Coach) which is almost certainly out of military use. Contemporary of the US Convair-Liner, many thousands of Il-14s were constructed for civil and military operation, including a license-built model in Czechoslovakia as the Avia 14. However, the Czech Air Force is superseding its remaining Avia 14s with Antonov An-26s.

Specifications (Il-14M data)
Accommodation: 3 crew and 32 passengers or freight. A small number were adapted for an ECM role.

Wingspan: 103 ft 11 in (31.67 m).
Length: 73 ft 3½ in (22.34 m).
Maximum take-off weight: 38,030 lb (17,250 kg).
Maximum speed: 258 mph (416 km/h).
Range: 937 miles (1508 km).
Mission performance: Rate of climb at sea level 950 ft (288 m) per min.
Engines: Two 1900-hp Shvetsov ASh-82T radial pistons.

Versions in service
Il-14: Initial version for 28 passengers.
Il-14M: Developed model of 1956 appearance, with a longer fuselage for 32 passengers.
Il-14P: Preceded the Il-14M. Better performance during take-off and climb by a weight reduction to 36,376 lb (16,500 kg). 18 to 26 passengers only, or freight.
Avia 14: Czech license-built model, probably out of military use.
Operators: Albania, Bulgaria, China, Congo, Cuba, Czechoslovakia (?), East Germany (?), Guinea, Hungary, Iraq, North Korea, Poland, Rumania and Vietnam.

Ilyushin Il-18, Il-20 and Il-38
(NATO names Coot, Coot-A and May)
Soviet Union

A contemporary of the Antonov An-10, the four-turboprop Ilyushin Il-18 was designed to serve as a 75- or 98-passenger airliner on domestic and international air routes. The prototype flew initially on 4 July 1957 and the same month made its first public appearance at Vnukovo airport in Moscow. An exceedingly successful airliner, more than 700 were produced over many years, some of which

Above: The Soviet Ilyushin Il-38 (May) ASW aircraft.

found their way into military service as VIP transports. Airline operations began in 1959. Today passenger or freighter-converted Il-18s are to be found flying with several air forces, as detailed below.

Two specialized military aircraft were developed from the Il-18 for the Soviet forces, namely the Il-20 and Il-38. The first is unique to the Soviet Air Force and is used as an elint aircraft for electronic intelligence and reconnaissance missions. With many externally visible sensor housings, radomes and antennae, little is known of the equipment it carries; the largest pod found under the fuselage is thought to contain side-looking radar.

The Il-38 (NATO May) is the standard land-based antisubmarine and maritime patrol aircraft of the Soviet Navy, a force which has been increasing its field of activity by the use of new bases, including that in South Yemen from which patrols are made over the Indian Ocean, Red Sea and other important areas. Each May carries search radar under the forward fuselage and MAD equipment in a tail 'sting'. Of the 50 to 60 Mays in Soviet use, some have a second, larger radome over one weapon bay, the purpose of which is uncertain. Three Mays are also flown by the Indian Navy, based at Dabolim, Goa, having been supplied by the Soviet Union as refurbished aircraft in a deal which allowed for the possible future delivery of two more.

Specifications (Il-38 data)
Weapons: Range of antisubmarine and antishipping weapons, including missiles, torpedoes, mines and sonobuoys normally in two weapon bays.
Accommodation: 9 crew.
Wingspan: 122 ft 9 in (37.42 m).
Length: 117 ft 9 in (35.90 m).
Maximum take-off weight: 139,995 lb (63,500 kg).
Maximum speed: 449 mph (722 km/h).
Range: 4475 miles (7200 km).
Mission performance: Speed for sea patrolling

Right: Air Force of the People's Liberation Army Harbin H-5 bombers.

249 mph (400 km/h); endurance 12 h.
Engines: Four 4250-shp Ivchenko AI-20M turboprops, with 30,000 liters of fuel.
Versions in service
Il-18: Operated by several air forces as military transport. The Il-18V model accommodates 110 passengers or freight and is powered by four 4000-ehp AI-20K turboprops. Numbers in service are, however, small when compared to the older twin-engined Soviet-designed transports remaining in military use.
Il-18D ORR: Conversion of Il-18D airliner (141,095-lb/64,000-kg normal maximum weight) for fishery protection duties.
Il-20: Coot-A elint aircraft, in service only with the Soviet Air Force.
Il-38: Land-based ASW and maritime patrol aircraft, similar in concept to US Lockheed Orion. Soviet Mays have sometimes been based in Libya, Mozambique, Syria and South Yemen. Only other user is Indian Navy.
Operators: Afghanistan (Il-18), China (Il-18), Guinea (Il-18), India (navy, Il-38), North Korea (Il-18), Poland (Il-18), Soviet Union (air force, Il-18 and Il-20; navy Il-38), Syria (Il-18) and Vietnam (Il-18).

Ilyushin Il-28
(NATO name Beagle)
Soviet Union and China

First flown as a prototype light bomber on 8 August 1948 on the power of engines derived from British Nenes, the Il-28 became the first jet bomber in Soviet Air Force service. Apart from Afghanistan and North Korea, which appear to use them in their intended role, it is believed that all other remaining Soviet-built Il-28s undertake reconnaissance and similar noncombat tasks.

The North Korean fleet of between 60 and 80 Il-28s is by far the largest outside of China, and undoubtedly includes supplies from Harbin in China. Chinese production of the Il-28, under the Harbin designation of H-5, began in 1966 and continued for some 16 years. Remarkably for such an old design, the Air Force of the People's Liberation Army is thought still to operate about 500 H-5s, with a further 130 in the Aviation of the People's Navy. A number could be equipped with nuclear bombs.

Specifications (Harbin H-5 data)
Weapons: Two 23-mm cannon in the fuselage, with 100 rounds of ammunition each, and two 23-mm cannon in a tail turret, with 225 rounds of ammunition each, plus up to 6615 lb (3000 kg) of weapons in the bay. The bay can house conventional bombs and possibly nuclear bombs in some aircraft, torpedoes, depth charges or mines. A camera can be carried.
Accommodation: 3 crew.
Wingspan: 70 ft 4½ in (21.45 m).
Length: 57 ft 11 in (17.65 m).
Maximum take-off weight: 46,740 lb (21,200 kg).
Maximum speed: 560 mph (902 km/h).
Range: 705-1490 miles (1135-2400 km).
Mission performance: Rate of climb at sea level 2950 ft (900 m) per min; ceiling 40,355 ft (12,300 m).
Engines: Two 5950-lb (2700-kg) thrust Wopen-5 or WP-5 turbojets, with 7908 liters of fuel. JATO can be used during take-off.
Versions in service
Il-28: Several Soviet versions were produced, including the Il-28R tactical

reconnaissance aircraft and the Il-28U 2-seat trainer (NATO Mascot) which remain in use. Powered by Klimov VK-1A engines, upon which the Chinese Wopens are based.

H-5: Chinese light bomber and torpedo-bomber, the latter carrying one or two torpedoes in the bay.

HJ-5: Chinese equivalent of the Il-28U Mascot.

HZ-5: 3-seat reconnaissance aircraft with 3 to 5 cameras, equivalent to the Soviet Il-28R.

Operators: Afghanistan, China (air force and navy), Egypt, North Korea, Poland (navy) and Rumania.

Ilyushin Il-76 and variants (NATO names Candid, Mainstay and Midas)
Soviet Union

The history of this heavy freight transport aircraft offers a good example of the close relationship between squadrons of Soviet Transport Aviation and the national airline Aeroflot in its capacity as a military reserve organization. Indeed, many of the airline's Il-76s are of the Il-76M military version which can carry two 23-mm Nudelman-Rikter NR-23 cannon in a gun turret at the rear of the fuselage, though for normal civil operation the armament is removed.

Designed as an Antonov An-12 replacement and intended to be capable of carrying a 40-tonne load over 3107 miles (5000 km) in under six hours, specifications also called for the ability to operate in any weather conditions throughout the harsh regions of the Soviet Union, to be independent of the normal ground facilities when flying into remote regions, and yet be easier to maintain than its predecessor. The first prototype Il-76 flew initially on 25 March 1971 and it soon became clear that it would be capable of meeting all the conditions. Evaluation by the Air Force had been completed before the aircraft went into major production in 1975.

Loading of the pressurized main freight cabin, which is 65 ft 7 in (20.00 m) in length, 11 ft 2 in (3.40 m) wide and 11 ft 4 in (3.46 m)

Below: Ilyushin Il-76MD in civil registration but used by the Iraqi Air Force.

high, is via clamshell doors under the upward swept 'beaver' rear fuselage. Through these doors can be loaded freight containers or items using overhead cranes and floor rollers, civil construction or military vehicles, weapons, or quickchange modules with passenger seats, stretchers or other layouts to increase the aircraft's usefulness.

In addition to the transport role, the Il-76 has formed the basis of the Soviet Air Force's latest and best airborne early warning and control system (AEW&C) aircraft, known to NATO by the name Mainstay. Developed to supersede the Tupolev Tu-126 Moss, though at present complementing Moss in service while production builds up, it serves with the Voyska PVO home defense force to detect incoming hostile aircraft and cruise missiles and direct the huge Soviet interceptor force on to them, and it can control the aircraft of the tactical air forces in their operations of both a defensive and offensive nature. The importance of Mainstay is that it is thought to be fully effective over land as well as water, something that Moss is not.

From the outset, experts in the West believed that the Il-76 would form the basis of an advanced probe-and-drogue flight refuelling tanker to extend the ranges of strategic and tactical supersonic Backfire bombers operating with the Soviet Air Force and Naval Aviation (Aviatsiya-Voenno-Morskovo Flota), superseding the Myasishchev M-4. This assumption has proved correct and, after trials that started in the 1970s, the tanker entered service in or around 1986. This version of the Il-76 is known to NATO as Midas. It is, of course, suited to refuelling other aircraft as well, including the latest and most formidable strategic bomber yet, the supersonic Tupolev Blackjack.

Specifications (Il-76T data unless otherwise stated)
Radar: Mainstay carries surveillance radar in an elliptical rotating radome above the fuselage.
Weapons: Military versions of Candid, plus Mainstay and Midas are armed with two 23-mm NR-23 cannon in a rear fuselage turret.
Accommodation: Approximately 88,200 lb (40,000 kg) of freight or vehicles for Il-76M

and 105,800 lb (48,000 kg) for Il-76MD, or 125 paratroops, 140 armed troops, or stretchers and medical attendants.
Wingspan: 165 ft 8 in (50.50 m).
Length: 152 ft 0 in (46.59 m).
Maximum take-off weight: 374,785 lb (170,000 kg).
Maximum speed: 528 mph (850 km/h).
Range: 4165 miles (6700 km).
Mission performance: Ceiling about 50,800 ft (15,500 m).
Engines: Four 26,455-lb (12,000-kg) thrust Soloviev D-30KP turbofans, with 81,830 liters of fuel.

Versions in service
Il-76: Military versions of the first production version are in Soviet service.
Il-76M: Known to NATO as Candid-B, this is the military transport equivalent of the Il-76T, with guns and ECM fitted as standard. Indian Air Force aircraft (20 ordered) are known as Gajarajs.
Il-76MD: Also known to NATO as Candid-B, with Soloviev D-30KP-1 engines for improved hot weather operation. A heavier load can be carried, and range is increased by 746 miles (1200 km) due to a larger fuel capacity.
Il-76T: Civil equivalent of Il-76M, without cannon.
Mainstay: NATO name for the AEW&C version of the Il-76, now in production and service.
Midas: NATO name for the flight refuelling tanker version of the Il-76.
Operators:* Czechoslovakia (Il-76 type), India (Il-76M – some might become AEW&C-modified), Iraq (civil-registered Il-76M and Il-76T), Libya (civil-registered Il-76T), Poland, Soviet Union (Il-76, Il-76M Il-76MD, Mainstay and Midas) and Syria (civil-registered Il-76M and Il-76T).
*Civil-registered Il-76Ms have cannon removed.

Kaman SH-2 Seasprite
United States

Intended to remain in US Navy and Reserve strength into the twenty-first century, the SH-2F Seasprite is a standard ship-borne antisubmarine helicopter, with antiship surveillance and targeting, search and rescue, observation, and utility as other areas of operation in keeping with its LAMPS Mk I category (Light Airborne Multi-Purpose System); there is no LAMPS Mk II, but the Mk III is the new Sikorsky Seahawk. The current fleet of around 130 SH-2Fs includes a number used by the Navy Reserve, and is made up of upgraded SH-2Ds and SH-2Fs built as such, with production continuing in 1987.

Specifications (SH-2F data)
Radar: Canadian Marconi LN-66HP surveillance radar. Other equipment includes electronic support measures, MAD, and sonobuoys/receiver/recorder/data link.
Weapons: One or two torpedoes.
Accommodation: 3 crew. 4 passengers, cargo or 2 stretchers can be carried with the sonobuoy launcher deleted; one passenger or stretcher otherwise. Rescue hoist carried.
Diameter of rotor: 44 ft 0 in (13.41 m).
Fuselage length: 40 ft 6 in (12.35 m).

Above: Kaman SH-2F LAMPS Mk I helicopter deploying a flare.

Maximum take-off weight: 13,500 lb (6123 kg).
Maximum speed: 150 mph (241 km/h).
Mission performance: Rate of climb at sea level 2440 ft (744 m) per min; ceiling 22,500 ft (6855 m); hovering ceiling in ground effect 18,600 ft (5670 m); hovering ceiling out of ground effect 15,400 ft (4700 m); endurance on station, 70 nm from ship 2 h 5 min.
Engines: Two 1350-shp General Electric T58-GE-8F turboshafts, with 1802 liters of fuel.

Versions in service
SH-2F: LAMPS Mk I helicopter, detailed above.
HH-2D: Single oceanographic helicopter, modified from an SH-2D.
NHH-2D: Test helicopter, modified from an SH-2D.
Operator: United States (navy).

Kamov Ka-25 (NATO name Hormone)
Soviet Union

The Ka-25 was a vitally important helicopter to the Soviet Navy, superseding the old piston-engined Mil Mi-4 in the antisubmarine role. Typically a Kamov design by virtue of its two coaxial contra-rotating rotors and multi-fin tail unit (no tail rotor, as contra-rotating designs have no need for torque compensation), it was first seen publicly in 1961. Now itself being superseded by the more capable Ka-27 (NATO name Helix), one drawback of Hormone had been its lack of proper ship-shore assault capability, something Helix has. Today some 150 Hormones remain with the Soviet Navy on board ship and on land, while four other nations also deploy the helicopter, the Indian helicopters to be found aboard destroyers.

Right: Soviet Navy Kamov Ka-25 (Hormone-A) helicopter.

Specifications (Hormone-A data)
Radar: Search radar in a chin radome. Other equipment includes dipping sonar, sonobuoys and ESM.
Weapons: Weapons bay houses 2 torpedoes, nuclear depth charges, etc.
Accommodation: 5 crew.

Diameter of each rotor: 51 ft 7¾ in (15.74 m).
Fuselage length: 32 ft 0 in (9.75 m).
Maximum take-off weight: 16,534 lb (7500 kg).
Maximum speed: 136 mph (220 km/h).
Range: 249 miles (400 km).
Mission performance: Ceiling 11,480 ft (3500 m).
Engines: Two 900-shp Glushenkov GTD-3F

or 990 shp GTD-3BM turboshafts.
Versions in service
Hormone-A: Ship-borne antisubmarine
helicopter.
Hormone-B: Version to locate over-the-
horizon enemy ships to be attacked by
Soviet Navy ship-launched missiles. Soviet
use only.
Hormone-C: SAR and utility helicopter,
accommodating up to 12 passengers.
Operators: India (navy), Soviet Union
(navy), Syria (air force, but navy-flown),
Vietnam and Yugoslavia (navy).

Kamov Ka-26 (NATO name Hoodlum)
Soviet Union

First flown as a prototype in 1965, the Ka-26 is
a very clever little general-purpose helicopter. It has two main design features: the
contra-rotating coaxial rotors so readily associated with Kamov helicopters, and the airframe, comprising the cockpit area and a slim
upper fuselage/twin-boom arrangement.
Behind or under the latter a detachable passenger pod, a flat freight platform or agricultural equipment can be secured, or the space
can be left unoccupied to allow the helicopter
to operate as a flying-crane. The Ka-26 is,
therefore, a highly adaptable helicopter,
though not a great many are in military use.

Specifications (Ka-26 data)
Accommodation: Pilot and up to 2
passengers, up to 2425 lb (1100 kg) of cargo
as a flying-crane, 2 stretchers and 3
attendants/sitting casualties as an
ambulance, or equipped for SAR or other
missions.
Diameter of each rotor: 42 ft 8 in (13.00 m).
Fuselage length: 25 ft 5 in (7.75 m).
Maximum take-off weight: 7165 lb (3250 kg).
Maximum speed: 105 mph (170 km/h).
Range: 248 miles (400 km) with full
passenger load and reserves.
Mission performance: Ceiling 9840 ft (3000 m);
hovering ceiling in ground effect 4265 ft
(1300 m) at 6614-lb (3000-kg) AUW; hovering

Below: Kamov Ka-26 in ambulance configuration.
Aeroflot forms a reserve for the active Soviet
forces.

ceiling out of ground effect 2625 ft (800 m)
at 6614-lb (3000-kg) AUW; endurance
3 h 42 min.
Engines: Two 325-hp Vedeneyev M-14V-26
radial pistons.
Version in service
Ka-26: Described above.
Operators: Benin, Hungary and Poland.

Kamov Ka-27 (NATO name Helix)
Soviet Union

First seen in 1981 in its Ka-32 civil variant, the
very similar military Ka-27 was developed as
a modern replacement for the Ka-25 as the
standard Soviet Navy ship-borne antisubmarine and SAR helicopter. Three versions have
so far been identified by the West, one as an
assault transport. This explains the purpose
of the larger main cabin, and yet the Kamov
bureau has managed to keep the overall size
of the helicopter much the same as the Ka-25,
enabling the existing facilities on board ship
to be used.
Operationally, the extra capacity and
vastly more powerful engines of the Ka-27
give the Soviet Navy its first full marine
assault capability from ship to shore which,
when viewed alongside the building of huge
aircraft carriers to match any in the US

Above: Kamov Ka-27 Helix-A ASW helicopter.

Navy, shows its interest in US-style power
projection. A version of the Ka-27 which has
not yet been identified is one for over-the-
horizon targeting for long-range cruise missiles launched from Soviet ships, but this
must be assumed a role for the Ka-27.

Specifications (Ka-27 data)
Radar: Search radar is carried in an
undernose radome, of improved type to
that carried by the Ka-25. Electronic support
measures, IFF (identification friend or foe)
and radar warning antennae are carried by
the Ka-27; the maritime version of the Ka-32
also carries radar and the equipment
detailed above. Dipping sonar and
sonobuoys for submarine detection.
Weapons: Will include the usual ASW stores
housed in a fuselage bay.
Accommodation: Crew of 2 or 3 plus up to 16
assault troops, or internal or 11,020 lb
(5000 kg) of externally slung cargo.
Diameter of each rotor: 52 ft 2 in (15.90 m).
Fuselage length: 37 ft 1 in (11.30 m).
Maximum take-off weight: 24,250 lb
(11,000 kg).
Maximum speed: 155 mph (250 km/h).
Range: 497 miles (800 km).
Mission performance: Ceiling 19,675 ft
(6000 m); hovering ceiling out of ground
effect 11,475 ft (3500 m).
Engines: Two 2225-shp Isotov TV3-117V
turboshafts.
Versions in service
Helix-A: NATO name for the antisubmarine
version of the Ka-27. This became
operational with the Soviet Navy in or
around 1982. Helix-A has been seen on
board various Soviet ships, including Kirov
class battle cruisers, Sovremenny and
Udaloy class guided missile destroyers, and
the Kiev class aircraft carriers which can
carry 16 each.
Helix-B: NATO name for the assault
transport version.
Helix-C: NATO name for the SAR version.
It also undertakes plane guard duties.
Equipment includes a hoist of 661-lb
(300-kg) capacity.
Ka-32: Civil variant, but the Ka-32S
maritime version in particular could have
military potential.
Operators: India (navy, Helix-A) and Soviet
Union (navy, all versions of the Ka-27).

Above: Impression of the Kamov Hokum attack and air-to-air combat helicopter armed with AAMs.

Kamov air superiority helicopter
(NATO name Hokum)
Soviet Union

In recent years significant endeavors have focussed on increasing the battlefield potential of the helicopter, introducing such tasks as AEW, airborne command post and electronic jamming to the more traditional roles. Another mission that has interested both East and West is that of air superiority over other helicopters and low-flying fixed-wing aircraft. The United States has produced several interesting designs but as yet no prototype for actual testing. The Soviet Union, on the other hand, having recognized the same future requirement, rapidly had a design approved and put prototypes into the air. In the words of the US Department of Defense, 'Hokum helicopter, which has no Western counterpart, may give the Soviets a significant rotary-wing air-superiority capability'.

Typically a Kamov helicopter, by having two three-blade contra-rotating rotors and a multifin tail unit (two endplate fins on the horizontal stabilizer and a marginally swept-back fin and rudder at the fuselage tail), it has a narrow cross-section fuselage with tandem cockpits for the two crew, anhedral stub wings with six pylons for air-to-air or air-to-surface missiles or other weapons, an under-nose cannon, a retractable undercarriage, and various survivability features. These include cockpit armor, infrared suppressors and jammers, and IR decoy dispensers. The current status of the helicopter is not known, though flight testing began back in 1984. It is therefore entirely possible that Hokums are already in initial operational service.

Specifications (Hokum data)
Weapons: Single-barrel cannon beneath the fuselage nose and missiles, rockets or other stores carried under the stub wings.
Accommodation: Copilot/gunner and pilot in tandem cockpits.

Diameter of each rotor: 45 ft 10 in (14.00 m).
Fuselage length: 44 ft 3 in (13.50 m).
Maximum take-off weight: About 11,900 lb (5400 kg).
Maximum speed: 217 mph (350 km/h) estimated.
Combat radius: 155 miles (250 km).
Mission performance: Unknown.
Engines: 2 turboshafts of unidentified type, but possibly 2200-shp Isotov TV3-117s.
Version in service
Hokum: NATO name for a category of combat helicopter with no Western equivalent.
Operator: Soviet Union (status unknown).

Kawasaki C-1 and C-1ECM
Japan

The C-1 was designed to supersede Curtiss C-46 Commando transports serving with the JASDF, and flew initially on 12 November 1970. Twenty-nine C-1s were received between 1974 and 1981 (including two pre-series aircraft), the final five each with 4732 liters of additional fuel to increase range. Of these, three have since been modified for different programs. One involves development of a quiet STOL transport with four turbofan engines carried ahead of the wings, known as the NAL Asuka. Another, and more important program from the military standpoint, has seen the installation of a TRDI/Mitsubishi Electric XJ/ALQ-5 ECM system in the C-1ECM, with nose and tail radomes and other blisters and antennae. This serves with the Electronic Warfare Training Unit.

Specifications (C-1 data)
Accommodation: 5 crew plus 26,235 lb (11,900 kg) of freight including vehicles, howitzer, etc, or 60 troops, 45 paratroops, 36 stretchers plus attendants.
Wingspan: 100 ft 4¾ in (30.60 m).
Length: 95 ft 1¾ in (29.00 m).
Maximum take-off weight: 99,208 lb (45,000 kg).
Maximum speed: 500 mph (806 km/h) at 78,154-lb (35,450-kg) AUW.
Range: 807 miles (1300 km) with a 17,416-lb (7900-kg) load.
Mission performance: Rate of climb at sea level 3500 ft (1065 m) per min; ceiling 38,000 ft (11,580 m).
Engines: Two 14,500-lb (6577-kg) thrust

Below: NAL Asuka, derived from a Kawasaki C-1.

Above: Camouflaged JASDF Kawasaki C-1 transports.

Mitsubishi/Pratt & Whitney JT8D-M-9 turbofans, with 15,200 liters of fuel standard.
Versions in service
C-1 and C-1ECM: As described above.
Operator: Japan.

Kawasaki P-2J
Japan

The Lockheed P-2 Neptune land-based anti-submarine and maritime patrol aircraft had been designed during World War II and first flew in 1945. It enjoyed a long service life with the US Navy and many others, the last two in service (SP-2Hs operated by Argentina) being retired in the 1980s.

Meanwhile, Kawasaki of Japan had developed the P-2J from the piston-engined P-2H Neptune, encompassing so many changes as to leave virtually nothing original. The prototype P-2J flew on 21 July 1966 and deliveries to the JMSDF began in October 1969. Today at least 55 remain in the original role, flying alongside the aircraft that generally displaced the Neptune, the P-3 Orion, while other P-2J types serve for different purposes.

Specifications (P-2J data)
Radar: AN/APS-80-N search radar and AN/APN-187B-N Doppler radar.
Equipment includes MAD, sonobuoy indicator and receiver, AN/ASA-20B Julie recorder, AN/AQA-5-N Jezebel recorder, and electronic support measures.

Weapons: Up to 8000 lb (3629 kg) of torpedoes, bombs or depth charges in the weapon bay and underwing pylons for 16 5-in rockets.
Accommodation: 12 crew.
Wingspan: 101 ft 3½ in (30.87 m).
Length: 95 ft 10¾ in (29.23 m).
Maximum weight: 75,000 lb (34,020 kg).
Cruising speed: 250 mph (402 km/h).
Range: 2765 miles (4450 km).
Mission performance: Rate of climb at sea level 1800 ft (550 m) per min; ceiling 30,000 ft (9145 m).
Engines: Two 2850-ehp General Electric/Ishikawajima-Harima T64-IHI-10 turboprops, plus two 3085-lb (1400-kg) thrust J3-IHI-7C auxiliary turbojets.
Versions in service
P-2J: Antisubmarine and patrol aircraft.
EP-2J: Small number of electronic countermeasures (ECM) aircraft.
UP-2J: Utility model. Very few used.
Operator: Japan (navy).

Kawasaki T-4
Japan

Intended to supersede the Lockheed T-33As and Fuji T-1As/T-1Bs flying with the JASDF, the T-4 is a typical modern jet trainer suited also to target towing and liaison. Its design emphasizes maneuverability and a high subsonic speed. The new IHI XF3-30 engine was chosen for the trainer in 1982. The initial prototype XT-4 flew for the first time on 29 July 1985 and, although production has started, operational evaluation was not scheduled for completion until 1988. About 200 are required for JASDF use. Mitsubishi and Fuji are both involved in major work-sharing programs.

Specification
Weapons: 4 underwing and one underfuselage pylons for weapons including air-to-air missiles, gun pods, or up to four 500-lb (227-kg) practice bombs. ECM pods and chaff dispensers are among optional equipment.
Accommodation: Student pilot and instructor in tandem, the rear raised to improve forward view. Baggage compartment in fuselage centersection.
Wingspan: 32 ft 5¾ in (9.90 m).
Length: 42 ft 8 in (13.00 m).
Maximum take-off weight: 16,535 lb (7500 kg).
Maximum speed: 645 mph (1038 km/h).
Range: 806 miles (1297 km).
Mission performance: Rate of climb at sea level 10,000 ft (3050 m) per min; ceiling 50,000 ft (15,240 m); G limits +7.33, −3.
Engines: Two 3660-lb (1660-kg) thrust Ishikawajima-Harima XF3-30 turbofans, with 2271 liters of fuel standard.
Version in service
T-4: Not yet operational.
Operator: Japan (air force later).

Below: Kawasaki P-2J.
Bottom: Prototype Kawasaki T-4 jet trainer.

Lockheed C-5 Galaxy
United States

Until the recent appearance of the Soviet Antonov An-124 Condor, the Galaxy was the world's largest aircraft. It is Military Airlift Command's principal heavy logistics transport. Though a design of the early 1960s, the general conception proved so efficient that basically identical aircraft are currently in production for the USAF to relieve its chronic shortage of heavy airlift capacity (in C-5B form), and the Antonov uses an extremely similar layout that is a far departure from the previous Soviet An-22.

The Galaxy flew for the first time on 30 June 1968 and deliveries to MAC began on 17 December 1969. In total 81 C-5As were received, of which 76 remained by 1986. Various improvements have been introduced to these over the years, the most important being the installation of strengthened wings and uprating of the engines. The new C-5Bs currently being constructed for MAC incorporate all improvements to the C-5A but otherwise are similar. Fifty are wanted for service. The first C-5B flew on 10 September

1985 and the 443rd Military Airlift Wing (MAW) received its first example in January 1986. All should be in service by 1989. C-5Bs have allowed the release of some C-5As into Air Force Reserve and National Guard units, with the 433rd MAW and 105th MAG receiving their first C-5As respectively.

The massive main cargo cabin of the Galaxy is 121 ft 1 in (36.91 m) long, 19 ft (5.79 m) wide and 13 ft 6 in (4.11 m) high, with an upper deck reserved for the crew, a relief

crew and others totalling 15 persons, and 75 troops. Loading and unloading of the main cabin is via a rear loading ramp under the rear fuselage and the nose of the fuselage which lifts up like the visor on a helmet.

Specifications (C-5B data)
Radar: Bendix AN/APS-133 weather and terrain mapping radar.
Accommodation: Up to a 261,000-lb (118,388-kg) payload. Main cabin loads can

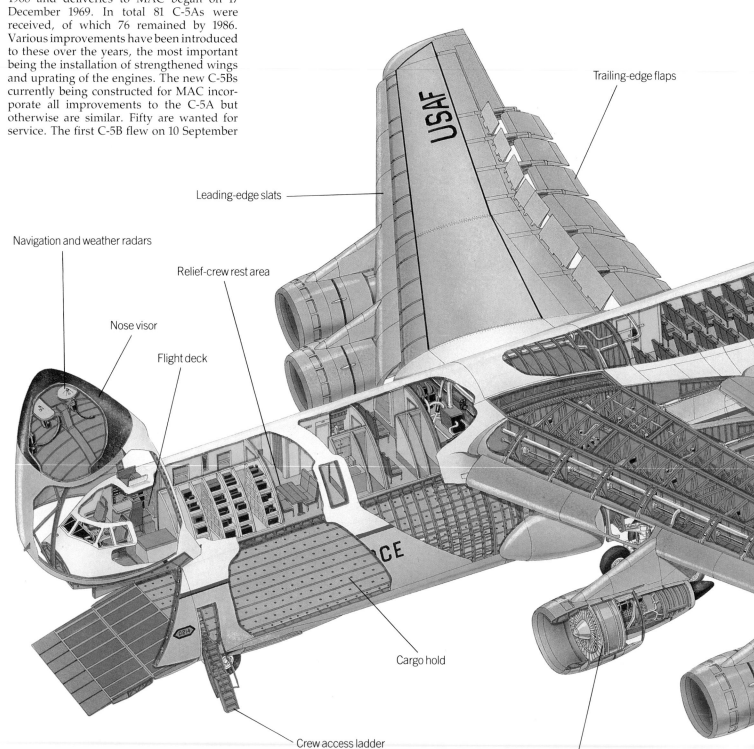

Trailing-edge flaps

Leading-edge slats

Navigation and weather radars

Relief-crew rest area

Nose visor

Flight deck

Cargo hold

Crew access ladder

General Electric TF39-GE-1 turbofan

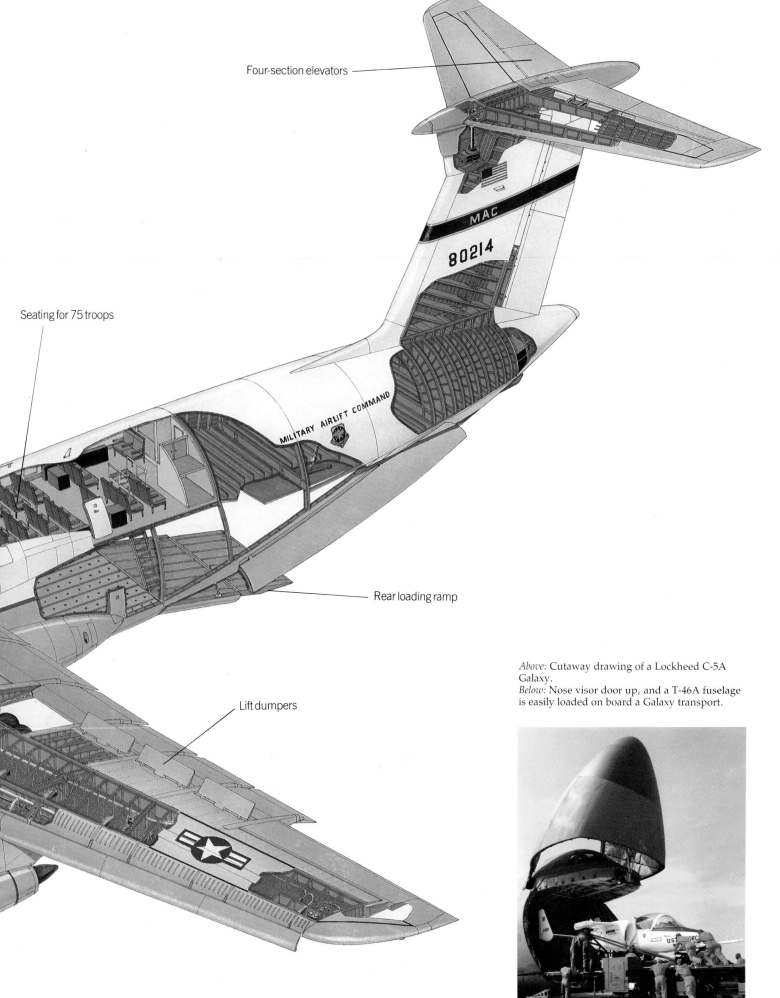

Four-section elevators

MAC

80214

Seating for 75 troops

MILITARY AIRLIFT COMMAND

Rear loading ramp

Lift dumpers

Above: Cutaway drawing of a Lockheed C-5A Galaxy.
Below: Nose visor door up, and a T-46A fuselage is easily loaded on board a Galaxy transport.

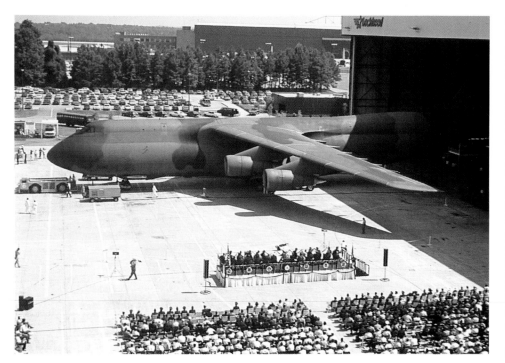

Above: Roll-out of the first Lockheed C-5B Galaxy.

include 270 troops, palleted freight, or a great variety of vehicles and weapon systems including choices of 2 main battle tanks, 10 Pershing missiles with vehicles, 6 Apache attack helicopters, 16 ¾-ton trucks.
Wingspan: 222 ft 8½ in (67.88 m).
Length: 247 ft 10 in (75.54 m).
Maximum take-off weight: 837,000 lb (379,655 kg).
Maximum speed: 571 mph (919 km/h).
Range: 3434-6469 miles (5525-10,410 km) depending on payload/fuel arrangement.
Mission performance: Rate of climb at sea level 1725 ft (525 m) per min; ceiling 35,750 ft (10,900 m).
Engines: Four 43,000-lb (19,500-kg) thrust General Electric TF39-GE-1C turbofans, with 193,624 liters of fuel.
Versions in service
C-5A: Four 41,000-lb (18,600-kg) thrust TF39-GE-1 engines fitted originally, of which the majority have been converted to 1C standard (as given above).
C-5B: New production model, as detailed above.
Operator: United States (air force AFRES and ANG).

Lockheed C-130 and L-100 Hercules
United States

The Hercules must be one of the greatest success stories in military aviation history. Designed originally as a medium transport for Tactical Air Command of the USAF and first flown in prototype form on 23 August 1954, deliveries of the initial production C-130A began in 1956 and more than 30 years later the Hercules is still in production. Today 52 nations count Hercules transports in their military inventories, in a few cases represented by examples of the L-100 Commercial Hercules. The latter include Saudi Arabia's L-100-30HS hospital aircraft, flown by that country's Air Force, with operating theaters and even X-ray equipment. But this is only one of a myriad of nontransport roles undertaken by specialized models of the Hercules,

some of the others including satellite midair recovery, RPV launcher, gunship (Spectres), weather reconnaissance, electronic surveillance, ECM jamming, flight refuelling tanker, and so on.

Specifications (C-130H data)
Radar: Bendix RDR-1F weather, beacon homing and terrain mapping radar.
Accommodation: 4 crew plus 92 troops, 64 paratroops, 74 stretchers, or up to 42,673 lb (19,356 kg) of freight or vehicles.
Wingspan: 132 ft 7 in (40.41 m).
Length: 97 ft 9 in (29.79 m).
Maximum take-off weight: 155,000 lb (70,310 kg) normal.
Cruising speed: 374 mph (602 km/h).
Range: 2356 miles (3791 km) with full load.
Mission performance: Rate of climb at sea level 1900 ft (580 m) per min; ceiling 33,000 ft (10,060 m).
Engines: Four 4508-ehp Allison T56-A-15 turboprops, with 26,346 liters of fuel standard.

Below: Tunisian Air Force Lockheed C-130H.

Versions in service

AC-130A Spectre: US Air Force Reserve gunship, used during the Grenada operation and armed with two 40-mm and two 20-mm cannon and two 7.62-mm machine-guns.

AC-130H Spectre: Used by the Special Operations Wing of MAC (USAF). Similar equipment to the AC-130A but with a 105-mm howitzer replacing a 40-mm cannon.

C-130A: Original production transport model, with 3750-eshp Allison T56-A-1A or A-9 engines. A photographic derivative was also produced for the USAF as the RC-130A.

C-130B: Longer range transport version, with a strengthened undercarriage. 4050-eshp T56-A-7 engines.

C-130D: Designation of 12 C-130As with wheel/ski undercarriages for operation by the USAF in the Antarctic. JATO can be used to boost take-off performance.

C-130E: Longer-range transport model, with two 5148-liter auxiliary tanks carried under the wings.

C-130F: US Navy transport. Only seven completed. See KC-130F.

C-130H: Transport version with upgraded avionics, changes to the wings and uprated engines. As detailed above.

C-130H-30: 'Stretched' model of the C-130H, with a length of 112 ft 9 in (34.37 m). Payload reduced to 38,900 lb (17,645 kg) but with accommodation for 128 troops, 92 paratroops, or 97 stretchers and 2 attendants.

C-130H-MP: Maritime patrol and SAR derivative of the C-130H, used by Indonesia and Malaysia.

C-130K: RAF version of the C-130H, known in service as the Hercules C.Mk 1. Of 66 ordered, one has become the W.Mk 2 meteorological aircraft and 30 have been 'stretched' to accommodate 128 troops, etc.

DC-130H: USAF RPV launch and control aircraft, similar in mission to the earlier DC-130A.

EC-130E: USAF battlefield command and control aircraft.

EC-130E Coronet Solo II: USAF electronic surveillance aircraft.

EC-130H Compass Call: USAF communications jamming aircraft.

EC-130Q Tacamo: US Navy command communications aircraft, providing a survivable airborne link between command authorities and ballistic submarines.

HC-130G: US Coast Guard SAR model.

HC-130H: USAF Aerospace Rescue and Recovery Service version. Also used by the US Coast Guard.

HC-130N: USAF SAR version with direction-finding avionics for space vehicle and astronaut retrieval.

HC-130P: USAF Aerospace Rescue and Recovery Service version, for retrieving parachute-borne loads while airborne, and flight refuelling tanker for helicopters.

JHC-130H: USAF Aerospace Rescue and Recovery Service version for retrieving parachute-borne space vehicles in midair.

KC-130F: US Marine Corps flight refuelling tanker, with probe and drogue equipment.

KC-130H: Exported flight refuelling tanker. Users include Argentina, Israel, Morocco, Saudi Arabia and Spain.

KC-130R: USMC flight refuelling tanker.

KC-130T: USMC flight refuelling tanker for combat aircraft and helicopters alike, but in Reserve service.

LC-130E/H/R: US Navy, Air Force Reserve and ANG wheel/ski transports for Antarctic use.

MC-130E Combat Talon I: USAF version for penetration missions at low level.

MC-130H Combat Talon II: Similar to the MC-130E but based on the C-130H version of Hercules. Terrain-following radar and other avionics for precision airdrops.

Above: An RAF Hercules makes an air-drop during the Ethiopian mercy operations.

WC-130E/H: USAF weather reconnaissance versions.

C-130AEW: Proposed airborne early warning version with GEC radar and scanners at the nose and tail.

L-100-20/-30: Versions of the Commercial Hercules, used by Dubai, Ecuador, Gabon, Indonesia, Kuwait, the Philippines and Saudi Arabia. L-100-30HS is a hospital version for Saudi Arabia.

Operators: Abu Dhabi, Algeria, Argentina, Australia, Belgium, Bolivia, Brazil, Cameroon, Canada, Chad, Chile, Colombia, Denmark, Dubai, Ecuador, Egypt, Gabon, Greece, Indonesia, Iran, Italy, Japan, Jordan, South Korea, Kuwait, Libya, Malaysia, Morocco, New Zealand, Nigeria, Norway, Oman, Pakistan, Peru, Philippines, Portugal, Saudi Arabia, Singapore, South Africa, Spain, Sudan, Sweden, Taiwan, Thailand, Tunisia, Turkey, United Kingdom, United States (air force, navy, marine corps and coast guard), Venezuela, Vietnam, North Yemen and Zaire.

Lockheed C-140 JetStar
United States

Although also used by West Germany, Indonesia and Saudi Arabia the JetStar light jet transport remains most prominently operated by the USAF as the C-140, having entered that service in 1961 following the first flight of the prototype on 4 September 1957. Four C-140Bs are used by the USAFE for airlift support and a similar number by the 89th MAW of Military Airlift Command. A further five JetStars, in C-140A form, are with Communications Command, USAF, to check air navigation aids worldwide.

Above: USAF Lockheed C-140A JetStar.

Specifications (JetStar data unless otherwise stated)
Accommodation: C-140B has a flight crew of 3 plus seven passengers.
Wingspan: 54 ft 5 in (16.60 m).
Length: 60 ft 5 in (18.42 m).
Maximum take-off weight: 40,920 lb (18,561 kg).
Cruising speed: 550 mph (885 km/h).
Range: 2280 miles (3670 km).
Mission performance: Rate of climb at sea level approx 5200 ft (1585 m) per min; ceiling 45,000 ft (13,715 m).
Engines: Four 3000-lb (1360-kg) thrust Pratt & Whitney J60-P-5A turbojets.
Versions in service
JetStar: Utility jet transport, seating up to 13 passengers.
C-140A: Used by the US Air Force Communications Command. Five crew.
C-140B: Transport model, with MAC
Operators: West Germany, Indonesia, Saudi Arabia and United States.

Lockheed C-141B StarLifter
United States

Second only in size and capacity to the C-5 Galaxy within the USAF's Military Airlift Command, the StarLifter is an older aircraft that first flew in 1963 and began operations in April 1965. All 285 were originally of the C-141A type, although some were modified to carry Minuteman intercontinental ballistic missiles, but operating experience showed that the aircraft was capable of lifting a heavier payload than its fuselage would hold. This led to the decision to lengthen the fuselage by 23 ft 4 in (7.11 m) by the insertion of two 'plugs' into each of the remaining 270 C-141As, also adding in-flight refuelling equipment. The fleet of lengthened and redesignated C-141Bs was returned between December 1979 and June 1982. Since then avionics updates have been carried out, including the latest to fit electroluminescent light panels in the flight cabin of 20 C-141Bs of the 437th military airlift wing for its SOLL (special operations low level) missions. In

1986, 267 C-141Bs remained operational, with the first 16 (of a planned 80 by the mid-1990s) being transferred to ANG and AFRES units.

Specifications
Accommodation: 5 crew plus 90,000 lb (40,823 kg) of freight, vehicles, 200 troops, 155 paratroops, or 103 stretchers and attendants.
Wingspan: 159 ft 11 in (48.74 m).
Length: 168 ft 3½ in (51.29 m).
Maximum take-off weight: 343,000 lb (155,582 kg).
Cruising speed: 566 mph (911 km/h).
Range: 1970 miles (3170 km) with full payload.
Mission performance: Rate of climb at sea level 2920 ft (890 m) per min.
Engines: Four 21,000-lb (9525-kg) thrust Pratt & Whitney TF33-P-7 turbofans.
Version in service
C-141B: As detailed above.
Operator: United States.

Lockheed RF-19 CSIRS
United States

Undoubtedly the most secret aircraft in service today, the RF-19 is the world's first fully stealth small combat aircraft and is largely unknown to all outside of the USAF, US government and Lockheed. Its acronym, CSIRS, indicates its purpose, that of Covert Survivable In-weather Reconnaissance-Strike aircraft, though it should also be said that production is likely to have been extremely small and that the 4450th Tactical Test Group at Nellis Air Force Base is the only assumed operator.

First flown in 1982 and developed from the XST concept demonstrator of 1977 appearance, the RF-19 has as its principal aim that of remaining undetected by an enemy. This is achieved using stealth technology. The airframe is a blended wing-fuselage design, with possibly retractable canards on the fuselage chines each side of the specially tinted cockpit canopy that reduces sun-glint and so

Below: USAF Lockheed C-141B StarLifter.

Above: Will the Lockheed RF-19 look anything like this stealth reconnaissance-fighter concept when revealed?

infrared signature. The tailfins are likely to be small and canted inward, themselves helping to shield the special engine exhaust nozzles from IR detection. As IR signature is one of the major problems when attempting to remain undetected, the engines have no afterburners. This means the RF-19 almost certainly cruises at high subsonic speed and reportedly makes almost zero exhaust noise. The airframe is painted in a special finish that is said to minimize radar and infrared signatures. During a mission, the pilot is required not to allow electromagnetic emissions.

Specifications (RF-19 CSIRS estimated data)

Accommodation: The pilot.
Wingspan: 31 ft 8 in (9.65 m).
Length: 59 ft 0 in (18.00 m).

Below: Japanese F-104J Starfighters.

Maximum take-off weight: 33,050 lb (15,000 kg).
Cruising speed at low altitude: 645 mph (1040 km/h).
Combat radius: 460 miles (740 km).
Engines: Four 10,800-lb (4900-kg) thrust General Electric F404-GE-400 turbofans.
Version in service
RF-19: As detailed above.
Operator: United States.

Lockheed F-104 Starfighter and Aeritalia F-104S
United States and Italy

When Aeritalia ended series manufacture of 246 F-104Ss in March 1979, production finally came to a close of the Starfighter which had begun as Lockheed's contribution to the USAF's so-called 'Century Series' of fighters. Drawing from the design concept of the experimental Douglas X-3, with a very slim and pointed fuselage and short-span thin wings, the F-104 was first flown as a pro-

totype on 7 February 1954 but went on to enjoy far less acceptance by the USAF than some of its fellow Century Series fighters. However, an important redesign brought about the F-104G multimission fighter, which became a hit with many European air forces and Japan (as the Mitsubishi-built F-104J). Japan was not alone in production and assembly outside of the USA, with similar lines in Canada, Belgium, West Germany, Italy and the Netherlands. Today F-104Gs are still flown, but many have been replaced by aircraft like the General Dynamics F-16 and Panavia Tornado.

In December 1966 the first F-104S flew, as a Lockheed-built modernized multimission fighter. Aeritalia took over production, the first of more than 200 entering the Italian Air Force in early 1969. Forty also went to the Turkish Air Force. A current program is underway to upgrade the F-104S Starfighters in Italian service, to improve interception by installing the FIAR R21G/M1 Setter radar and defense by using advanced electronic countermeasures. Modified aircraft have better weapons delivery, and lookdown capability to engage low-flying aircraft. Equipment to modify the Starfighters has been delivered since 1986.

Specifications (F-104S data)
Radar: FIAR R21G/H radar before upgrading.
Weapons: 9 stations under the fuselage and wings and at the wingtips for up to 2 Sparrow and 4 Sidewinder air-to-air missiles or a 20-mm M61 Vulcan multibarrel cannon plus attack weapons. Maximum weapon load is 7500 lb (3402 kg).
Accommodation: The pilot.
Wingspan: 21 ft 11 in (6.68 m).
Length: 54 ft 9 in (16.69 m).
Maximum take-off weight: 31,000 lb (14,060 kg).
Maximum speed: Mach 2.2.
Combat radius: 775 miles (1247 km).
Mission performance: Time to 35,000 ft (10,670 m) 1 min 20 sec; ceiling 58,000 ft (17,680 m).
Engine: One 17,900-lb (8120-kg) thrust with afterburning General Electric J79-GE-19 turbojet, with 3392 liters of fuel standard.
Versions in service
F-104G: First multirole version, powered by a 15,800-lb (7166-kg) thrust with afterburning General Electric J79-GE-11A turbojet. First model with an upward-ejecting seat.
RF-104G: Reconnaissance version of F-104G.
TF-104G: Tandem two-seat trainer, based on the F-104G.
F-104J: Japanese-produced F-104G.
F-104S: Aeritalia multirole version.
Operators: West Germany (F-104G), Greece (F-104G and TF-104G), Italy (F-104G, RF-104G, TF-104G and F-104S), Japan (F-104J), Taiwan (F-104G, RF-104G and TF-104G) and Turkey (F-104G, TF-104G and F-104S).

Lockheed L-188 Electra, P-3 Orion and CP-140 Aurora
United States

On 6 December 1957 the first flight took place of the L-188 Electra, a four-turboprop medium-range airliner in the same general

Above: Kawasaki-assembled Lockheed P-3C
Orion for the JMSDF.

class as the British Vickers Viscount and
Soviet Ilyushin Il-18. Some Electras are today
in military service as transports, though the
Argentine Navy also uses a number for maritime reconnaissance and elint.

When the US Navy held a competition for a
shore-based antisubmarine warfare aircraft to
supersede the P-2 Neptune, to be based on
an existing aircraft, Lockheed developed the
Electra into the specialist Orion, which first
flew with a complete ASW avionics suite on
25 November 1959. Several versions subsequently went into US Navy service, beginning with the P-3A in August 1962, and have
been exported. The latter include the CP-140
Aurora for the Canadian Armed Forces,
which has a different avionics suite to the
Orion but is based on the same airframe and
engines as the P-3C.

Specifications (P-3C data)
Radar: The extensive avionics suite includes
AN/APS-115 radar, sonar receivers,
sonobuoys and associated equipment,
MAD, magnetic compensator, ECM, etc. A
passive radar detection system is being
tested for future use, to be carried in
wingtip pods.
Weapons: Weapons bay for mines, depth
charges, conventional or nuclear depth
bombs, 8 torpedoes, or a combination. 10
pylons under the wings for further
weapons, including Harpoon antiship
missiles. Total weapons load is
approximately 20,000 lb (9070 kg).
Accommodation: 10 crew.
Wingspan: 99 ft 8 in (30.37 m).
Length: 116 ft 10 in (35.61 m).
Maximum take-off weight: 135,000 lb
(61,235 kg).
Maximum speed: 473 mph (761 km/h).
Combat radius: 2383 miles (3835 km)
maximum.
Mission performance: Rate of climb at sea
level 1950 ft (595 m) per min; ceiling
28,300 ft (8625 m); on-station patrolling
speed 237 mph (381 km/h).
Engines: Four 4910-ehp Allison T56-A-14
turboprops, with 34,825 liters of fuel.
Versions in service
P-3A/CP-3A: The P-3A was the initial

production version, powered by four
4500-ehp T56-A-10W engines. Of those that
remain, and not being converted to EP-3Es,
most are reportedly being modified into
CP-3A transports.
P-3B: Follow-on version to the P-3A, with
4910-ehp T56-A-14 engines. US Navy
examples were modified to allow Bullpup
missiles to be carried. Some converted into
EP-3B elint aircraft. 6 of the 10 P-3Bs
delivered to the Royal Australian Air Force
in 1968 are currently being upgraded for
service with Portugal.
P-3C: Current production version, as
detailed above. Delivery to the US Navy
began in 1969. Three 'Update' programs
have been introduced successively to
aircraft on the production line since 1975 to
enhance the avionics and weapon systems,
with a fourth currently undergoing trials to
meet the latest challenges in the ASW role.
P-3D: New version of the Orion with
Allison 501-M80C engines, still at the
planning stage.
P-3F: P-3Cs for Iran, received in 1975.
EP-3E: 2 EP-3Bs and 10 P-3As converted to
this latest electronic warfare version, with
much equipment including Texas

Instruments AN/APS-115 search radar, an
infrared detector, jamming systems and
ESM.
CP-140 Aurora: First flown on 22 March
1979, this ASW and patrol aircraft for the
Canadian Armed Forces represents the
P-3C with a Lockheed S-3A Viking avionics
suite.
P-3 AEW&C: Proposed AWACS version,
using Hawkeye radar.
L-188 Electra: Medium range transport with
four 3750-ehp Allison 501-D13A turboprop
engines. Seating for up to 99 passengers or
freight. Some Argentine examples have
been modified to perform maritime
reconnaissance and elint roles.
Operators: Argentina (navy, Electra),
Australia (P-3C), Bolivia (Electra), Canada
(Aurora), Ecuador (Electra), Honduras
(Electra), Iran (P-3F), Japan (navy, P-3C),
Mexico (Electra), Netherlands (navy, P-3C),
New Zealand (P-3B), Norway (air force and
coast guard, P-3B), Panama (Electra),
Portugal (P-3B modified) and United States
(navy, P-3A, P-3B, P-3C/CI/CII/CIII, CP-3A
and EP-3).

Lockheed S-3A and S-3B Viking
United States

First flown as a prototype on 21 January 1972,
the S-3A Viking introduced an entirely new
shape to the decks of US Navy aircraft carriers from the time of its initial deployment
on board USS *John F Kennedy* in July 1975.
Superseding the piston-engined Tracker, the
Viking became the standard carrier-borne
antisubmarine aircraft of the US Navy, its
pleasing lines – with two podded turbofan
engines under shoulder-mounted wings and
weapons bays – disguising a very sophisticated avionics suite for the intended role
and an arsenal of lethal armaments. Production of 187 S-3As ended in 1978. Evaluation of
a COD version as the US-3A and dedicated
tanker as the KS-3A came to little, although a
'buddy' system which allows the Viking to
adopt the tanker role when required proved

Below: Lockheed S-3A Viking ASW aircraft comes
in to land with its arrester hook lowered.

successful and may become available on an operational basis.

In the meantime, to enhance the S-3A's ASW role, the US Navy awarded Lockheed a contract in 1980 to work on a WSIP (weapons systems improvement program). With the new avionics, equipment and weapon options, any modified S-3As become S-3Bs. The first S-3B-standard aircraft made its maiden flight on 28 April 1986 and to date the US Navy has ordered 22 kits for installation by the Navy at its Cecil Field air station. Reports suggest that 160 S-3As might be so modified from 1988, with perhaps the eventual backup of newly built S-3Bs to equip the Navy's expanding fleet of modern aircraft carriers.

Specifications (S-3A data)
Radar: Texas Instruments AN/APS-116 antisubmarine search radar, designed to be capable of detecting periscope targets with short exposure times in rough seas. Other equipment for its ASW missions include FLIR in a retractable turret, MAD, passive ECM receiving and frequency measuring system, and sonobuoys with the associated processing systems.
Weapons: Include four Mk-46 torpedoes, or a similar number of depth charges, destructors, bombs or mines carried in the bays, and weapons of a similar type plus rocket pods on 2 underwing pylons with multiple racks.
Accommodation: 4 crew.
Wingspan: 68 ft 8 in (20.93 m).
Length: 53 ft 4 in (16.26 m).
Normal take-off weight: 42,500 lb (19,277 kg).
Maximum speed: 518 mph (834 km/h).
Range: Over 2300 miles (3700 km).
Mission performance: Rate of climb at sea level more than 4200 ft (1280 m) per min; ceiling more than 35,000 ft (10,670 m).
Engines: Two 9275-lb (4207-kg) thrust General Electric TF34-GE-2 turbofans, with about 7192 liters of fuel standard.
Versions in service
S-3A: Current standard version, as detailed above.

Below: The fastest military aircraft in service is the Lockheed SR-71A Blackbird.

S-3B: Modified S-3As under the WSIP program, for service from about 1988 onward, with perhaps 24 S-3Bs rejoining units per year thereafter. Many avionics updates, including Texas Instruments AN/APS-137(V)1 with inverse synthetic aperture radar (ISAR) imaging to allow classification of ships at long range, better ESM, and updated computer and sonobuoy receiver system. Weapon improvements center on the S-3B's ability to launch the Harpoon antiship missile.
Operator: United States (navy).

Lockheed SR-71 Blackbird
United States

This truly remarkable product of Lockheed's secretive so-called 'Skunk Works' first flew on 22 December 1964 and entered USAF service with the 9th Strategic Reconnaissance Wing at Beale Air Force Base in early 1966. Available also to respond to the requirements of tactical commanders, the SR-71A can give reconnaissance coverage of up to 100,000 sq miles (259,000 sq km) of territory in an hour, in all weathers and by day or night. It is also the fastest and highest operating military aircraft in use today, currently holding the world height record for sustained horizontal flight at 85,069 ft (25,929 m) and world speed in a straight line record at 2193.17 mph (3529.56 km/h), both established on 28 July 1976. It holds the closed circuit speed record.

Unarmed and built in small numbers, the SR-71A was the first 'production' aircraft designed with true stealth technology to enhance performance and avoid detection. This is all the more remarkable when one appreciates that its design began in the 1950s. To ensure that strong radar waves from an enemy are not returned, the SR-71 was designed without deep angles, leaving an aircraft with a flat undersurface, sharp chines along the sides and blended wing-fuselage junctures. Under the skin covering, which itself is finished in a blue paint containing millions of microscopic iron balls to conduct electricity and so prevent strong radar reflection, the structure has V angles which allow the radar signals to bounce back and forth

and thereby only a very weak signal is returned. A two-seat training version is the SR-71B, having a raised rear cockpit.

Specifications (SR-71A data)
Radar: Synthetic aperture radar (SAR I).
Accommodation: 2 crew.
Wingspan: 55 ft 7 in (16.95 m).
Length: 107 ft 5 in (32.74 m).
Maximum take-off weight: 170,000 lb (77,111 kg) estimated.
Maximum speed: Over Mach 3.
Range: 2982 miles (4800 km) estimated at Mach 3.
Mission performance: Operational ceiling over 80,000 ft (24,385 m).
Engines: Two 34,000-lb (15,422-kg) thrust with afterburning Pratt & Whitney JT11D-20B (J58 type) turbojets.
Versions in service
SR-71A: Strategic reconnaissance aircraft, with many sensor systems ranging from the SAR I to simple battlefield surveillance equipment.
SR-71B: 2-seat (tandem) training version of the SR-71A, received by the 4200th Strategic Reconnaissance Wing of SAC from early 1966.
Operator: United States.

Lockheed T-33A and Boeing Skyfox
United States

The T-33A is a tandem two-seat jet trainer that first flew as a prototype lengthened and modified F-80C Shooting Star fighter on 22 March 1948 (designated TF-80C). Lockheed went on to build 5691 T-33As and basically similar TV-2s for the US Navy (which in 1962 were redesignated as T-33 models), while Canadair constructed more than 650 as CT-133 Silver Stars and Kawasaki in Japan added a further 210. A substantial number of T-33A types remain in use today (perhaps as many as 700) for training and other duties, including some RT-33A tactical reconnaissance aircraft and AT-33As for counter-insurgency. Twenty-five USAF T-33As are the subject of a current upgrading program, T-33As with this service being used for proficiency training, combat support missions

Above: Boeing Skyfox prototype, a twin-turbofan modernized conversion of the Lockheed T-33A.

and radar target evaluation training, most having their machine-guns deleted.

Boeing is currently evaluating the market for a much modified version of the T-33A, known as the Skyfox, as a high performance combat trainer. Apart from airframe changes which offer an entirely new configuration, although the refurbished airframe is said to be about 70 percent original, the most obvious change is the adoption of two 3700-lb (1678-kg) thrust Garrett TFE731-3A turbofans, pod-mounted on the fuselage sides.

Specifications (T-33A data)

Weapons: Sometimes two 0.50-in machine guns.
Accommodation: Student pilot and instructor in tandem.
Wingspan: 38 ft 10½ in (11.85 m).
Length: 37 ft 9 in (11.51 m).
Maximum take-off weight: 14,440 lb (6550 kg).
Maximum speed: 543 mph (874 km/h).
Range: 1345 miles (2165 km).

Mission performance: Ceiling 47,500 ft (14,475 m).
Engine: One 5200-lb (2359-kg) thrust Allison J33-A-35 turbojet.
Versions in service
T-33A: 2-seat trainer. As detailed above.
AT-33A: COIN conversion of the T-33A.
RT-33A: Reconnaissance derivative of the T-33A, with cameras in the nose and avionics in the rear cockpit. Operators include Colombia, Pakistan, the Philippines and Thailand.
CT-133 Silver Star: Canadair derivative of the T-33A, with a 5100-lb (2313-kg) thrust Rolls-Royce Nene 10 turbojet engine.
Boeing Skyfox: Much modified and twin-turbofan modification of the T-33A, proposed for production and capable of carrying 6000 lb (2720 kg) of weapons under the wings. Maximum speed is 581 mph (935 km/h).
Operators: Bolivia, Burma, Canada, Colombia, Ecuador, Greece, Guatemala, Iran, Japan, South Korea, Mexico, Pakistan, Philippines, Singapore, Taiwan, Thailand, Turkey, United States and Uruguay.

Lockheed TriStar K.Mk 1 and BAe VC10
United States and United Kingdom

Marshall of Cambridge (Engineering) in the UK is currently converting six ex-British Airways L-1011-500 and three ex-Pan Am TriStar airliners into flight refuelling tankers for the RAF. Each aircraft will have two hose drum units and fuel tanks in the baggage compartments and a Flight Refuelling Mk 32 pod under each wing (later installation), plus a receiving refuelling probe. Seven will be able to carry passengers in a dual role, while the remainder will have passenger and freight options. The first TriStar K.Mk 1 flew on 9 July 1985.

The RAF's No 10 Squadron is equipped with 13 VC10 C.Mk 1 transports. In addition, nine commercial VC10 Model 1101s and 1154s were purchased for conversion into flight refuelling tankers for the RAF, as K.Mk 2s and K.Mk 3s respectively. The first K.Mk 2 was flown on 22 June 1982 and the first for

Below: BAe VC10 K.Mk 3 flight refuelling tanker.

service went to No 101 Squadron on 20 February 1985. All had been delivered by the following year.

Specifications (VC10 K.Mk 2 data)
Radar: Weather radar.
Equipment: Flight Refuelling Mk 17B hose drum unit in the fuselage and 2 detachable Flight Refuelling Mk 32/2800 refuelling pods under the wings. Total fuel capacity, including the aircraft's own fuel, is 94,270 liters.
Wingspan: 146 ft 2 in (44.55 m).
Length: 166 ft 1 in (50.62 m) including probe.
Maximum take-off weight: Approximately 314,000 lb (142,430 kg).
Engines: Four 21,800-lb (9888-kg) thrust Rolls-Royce Conway Mk 301/Mk 550B turbofans.

Versions in service
VC10 C.Mk 1: 4 crew plus 150 passengers, 76 stretchers and six attendants, or 57,400 lb (26,036 kg) of freight. Cruising speed 581 mph (935 km/h), and range 3900 miles (6275 km). Mk 301 turbofans.
VC10 K.Mk 2: Refuelling tanker conversion of the Model 1101, as detailed above.
VC10 K.Mk 3: Refuelling tanker conversion of the Model 1154, with 102,780 liters of fuel (total).
TriStar K.Mk 1: Gross take-off weight 540,000 lb (244,940 kg).
Operator: United Kingdom.

Lockheed U-2 and TR-1, and Soviet RAM-M
United States and Soviet Union

The world was stunned on 1 May 1960 when, during the height of the 'Cold War', Soviet long-range surface-to-air missiles brought down a USAF U-2 strategic reconnaissance aircraft flying at extreme altitude over the Soviet Union. Until then U-2s had had a free hand to gather reconnaissance, Soviet fighters being unable to reach sufficient altitude to offer any opposition. The U-2, of which a number of the 55 or thereabouts built from

Below: Lockheed TR-1B tandem cockpit trainer.

about 1954 are still operating, had been designed for the very purpose of high-altitude strategic reconnaissance, relying on very wide-span high-aspect ratio wings to attain height and cruise when necessary with the engine shut down to extend range. For the pilot, the speed margin between cruising speed and stall is so small that it requires precise flying, especially during take-off and landing. This remains so also for the TR-1 tactical reconnaissance derivative, which is still in production to meet the USAF's requirement for 26 operational TR-1As and two TR-1B tandem two-set trainers. TR-1As can undertake stand-off surveillance missions and are particularly used in Europe. The first TR-1A made its maiden flight on 1 August 1981 and by early 1983 the first of 14 for basing in the UK had arrived in Europe. Some TR-1As may undertake at a future time the PLSS (precision location strike system) role, working in groups of three to locate enemy defense systems for attack by other forces. It is also interesting to note that photographs have been published of a TR-1A carrying what appears to be an AWACS type surveillance radar in a radome above the fuselage. A Soviet reconnaissance aircraft of similar type to the TR-1, but with a multifin tail unit has been undergoing trials.

Above: Max Holste Broussard.

Specifications (TR-1A data)
Equipment: The aircraft's special reconnaissance equipment is carried in a detachable and interchangeable nose section, a bay and underwing pods. Its equipment includes SLAR and a tracking camera.
Accommodation: The pilot.
Wingspan: About 103 ft 0 in (31.39 m).
Length: 63 ft 0 in (19.20 m).
Maximum take-off weight: 40,000 lb (18,143 kg).
Cruising speed: Over 430 mph (692 km/h).
Range: Over 3000 miles (4830 km).
Mission performance: Operational ceiling 90,000 ft (27,435 m); G limit +2.5; endurance 12h.
Engine: One 17,000-lb (7711-kg) thrust Pratt & Whitney J75-P-13B turbojet, with about 4448 liters of fuel standard.
Versions in service
U-2: Strategic reconnaissance aircraft. Several versions were built, with a wingspan of about 80 ft (24.39 m) and length of 49 ft 7 in (15.11 m), except for the U-2R which has TR-1A dimensions. The J75 turbojet powered the original U-2A version, which is no longer in service.
TR-1A: Tactical reconnaissance aircraft.
TR-1B: Tandem cockpit two-seat training version of the TR-1A.
RAM-M: Provisional NATO designation of a Soviet TR-1 type reconnaissance aircraft that was undergoing trials in the early 1980s.
Operator: United States (U-2/TR-1 models).

Max Holste M.H.1521 Broussard
France

Although the Société des Avions Max Holste company had a relatively short lifespan before becoming part of Nord Aviation, it enjoyed great success with a sturdy strut-braced high-wing utility transport known as the Broussard. This was a 'no nonsense' aircraft of virtually all-metal construction, with a fixed tailwheel undercarriage and twin fin/rudders. It could accommodate six persons in three rows within the square-section fuselage or, as an ambulance, two stretchers and two sitting casualties in addition to the pilot. Another possible use was as an agricultural spraying aircraft.

The majority of the Broussards ordered during the 1950s were destined for the French Air Force and Army (335) and could be operated in and out of areas without proper airfields or facilities, especially in French colonies; it was to these colonies that some were passed after independence. Today, those still flying are used in light transport and liaison roles.

Specifications (Broussard data)

Accommodation: 6 persons, freight, or 2 stretchers and 2 sitting casualties in ambulance role.
Wingspan: 45 ft 1 in (13.75 m).
Length: 28 ft 4½ in (8.65 m).
Maximum take-off weight: 5953 lb (2700 kg).
Maximum speed: 168 mph (270 km/h).
Range: 746 miles (1200 km).
Mission performance: Rate of climb at sea level 1080 ft (330 m) per min; ceiling 18,045 ft (5500 m).
Engines: One 450-hp Pratt & Whitney R-985-AN-1 radial piston, with 440 liters of fuel.

Version in service

M.H.1521: Production version, first flown in June 1954. Recently passed out of service with several smaller air forces.
Operators: Burkina-Faso, Central African Republic and France (air force, army and navy).

MBB BO 105
West Germany

Messerschmitt-Bölkow-Blohm Gmbh began the design of this normally five-seat pod-and-boom utility helicopter in 1962. The second prototype, which first flew on 16 February 1967, featured what became the standard rotor system of a rigid hub and hingeless glassfiber blades, the prototype with only feathering hinges. Many of the BO 105s in military service are for utility duties, but also included are West German Army VBH observation and PAH 1 anti-armor models, while

Above: Federal German Army Air Corps MBB BO 105 PAH 1s armed with Hot missiles.

the Swedish and Iraqi armies both deploy anti-armor versions (with TOW and SS-11 missiles respectively), as does the Spanish Army. The Swedish Air Force has BO 105s for search and rescue, Mexican Navy examples adding to this fishery protection and anti-smuggling duties. Assembly of BO 105s is also undertaken by IPTN in Indonesia and by MBB in Canada.

Specifications (BO 105 CB data)

Weapons: Can carry 8 TOW or 6 Hot anti-armor missiles.
Accommodation: The pilot and 4 passengers, freight or 2 stretchers.
Diameter of rotor: 32 ft 3½ in (9.84 m).
Fuselage length: 28 ft 1 in (8.56 m).
Maximum take-off weight: 5510 lb (2500 kg).
Cruising speed: 150 mph (242 km/h).
Range: 370 miles (596 km) at maximum gross weight.
Mission performance (at maximum weight unless otherwise stated): Rate of climb at sea level 1375 ft (419 m) per min; operating ceiling 16,990 ft (5180 m) at 5291-lb (2400-kg) AUW; hovering ceiling in ground effect 5000 ft (1525 m); hovering ceiling out of ground effect 1500 ft (457 m).
Engines: Two 420-shp Allison 250-C20B turboshafts, with 580 liters of fuel standard.

Versions in service

BO 105: Initial version with 400-shp 250-C20 turboshafts.
BO 105 CB: Basic version from 1975, as detailed above. Includes Swedish anti-armor examples.
BO 105 CBS: 28 ft 11 in (8.81 m) length, permitting a sixth person. Includes Swedish SAR examples.
BO 105 LS: Canadian-built version, combining the fuselage of the CBS with two 550-shp 250-C28C engines, offering improved 'hot and high' performance.
BO 105 PAH 1: West German Army anti-armor model, carrying six Hot missiles on outriggers. 212 acquired between 1980 and 1984. Singer Kearfott AN/ASN-128 Doppler navigation system (also used in Spanish Army BO 105s).
BO 105 VBH: Observation and liaison helicopter, 100 acquired by the West

German Army by 1984.
Operators: Bahrain, Colombia (navy), Dubai, West Germany (army), Iraq (army), Lesotho, Mexico (navy), Netherlands (army), Nigeria, Peru, Philippines, Spain (army) and Sweden (army and air force).

MBB HFB 320 Hansa
West Germany

The Hansa was designed by HFB (Hamburger Flugzeugbau GmbH) which, in 1969, merged with Messerschmitt-Bölkow to become Messerschmitt-Bölkow-Blohm (MBB). Before this, on 21 April 1964, the first prototype of an unusual 7- to 12-seat executive jet had flown as the HFB 320 Hansa, featuring wings that swept forward at 15 degrees to remove the necessity of taking the main spar through the passenger cabin and thereby made best use of available space. This wing layout also offered unimpaired downward vision for the passengers. The Luftwaffe became the only military customer for the Hansa, receiving six as VIP transports, seven as ECM trainers, and a small number for calibration and other duties. The final four aircraft, in ECM form, were not delivered until the early 1980s.

Specifications (320 Hansa data)

Radar: The Hansa was fitted with RCA AVQ-20 weather radar.
Equipment: At least the final 4 ECM Hansas for the Luftwaffe carry Elettronica SpA electronic warfare equipment.
Accommodation: 2 crew and 12 passengers in VIP form.
Wingspan: 47 ft 6 in (14.49 m).
Length: 54 ft 6 in (16.61 m).
Maximum take-off weight: 20,283 lb (9200 kg).
Maximum speed: 513 mph (825 km/h).
Range: 1472 miles (2370 km) with 6 passengers.
Mission performance: Rate of climb at sea level 4250 ft (1295 m) per min; ceiling 40,025 ft (12,200 m).
Engines: Two 3100-lb (1405-kg) thrust General Electric CJ610-9 turbojets, with 4140 liters of fuel when including wingtip tanks.

Above: MBB HFB 320 Hansa in electronic countermeasures form.

Versions in service
Hansa: VIP transport, ECM training and calibration aircraft remain in Luftwaffe service. The ECM aircraft can be identified by their long nose radomes.
Operator: West Germany.

MBB/Kawasaki BK 117 A
West Germany and Japan

This international multipurpose helicopter first flew as a prototype on 13 June 1979 and production deliveries started in 1983. It uses some components from the BO 105. At the 1985 Paris Air Show a German military derivative of the BK 117 was displayed, designated BK 117 A-3M. However, military customers are few so far and almost certainly are only for the basically civil model.

Specifications (BK 117 A-3 data)
Accommodation: The pilot, and 6 to 10 passengers or freight. Can be equipped for SAR, stretcher carrying, firefighting, etc.
Diameter of rotor: 36 ft 1 in (11.00 m).
Fuselage length: 32 ft 6¼ in (9.91 m).
Maximum take-off weight: 7055 lb (3200 kg).
Cruising speed: 157 mph (252 km/h).
Range: 314 miles (505 km).
Mission performance: Maximum operating height 15,000 ft (4575 m); hovering ceiling in ground effect 10,000 ft (3050 m); hovering ceiling out of ground effect 11,500 ft (3505 m); endurance up to 3 h.
Engines: Two 592-shp Avco Lycoming LTS 101-650B-1 turboshafts, with 608 liters of fuel standard.
Versions in service
BK 117 A: The initial production version was the BK 117 A-1 with a gross take-off weight

Right: MBB BK 117 A-3M multirole helicopter with roof- and mast-mounted sights, eight Hot antiarmor missiles and an underfuselage gun.

of 6614 lb (3000 kg) with an external sling load. Follow-on heavier A-3 model is described above. The new 1987 model is the A-4, with more fuel and improved performance.
BK 117 A-3M: German-developed military version with a 12.7-mm Browning gun in an underfuselage turret, weapons on outriggers (options can include antitank missiles and much else), roof-mounted sight and a tall undercarriage. In a transport role, 11 troops or cargo can be accommodated.
Operators: Ciskei and Indonesia.

McDonnell Douglas DC-8 and DC-9
United States

The DC-8 was Douglas's first jet airliner and rival to the Boeing Model 707. The first Series 10 took to the air on 30 May 1958 and began a production run that lasted until 556 DC-8s had been built up to the early 1970s. This covered Series 10 to Series Super 60. The subsequent Super 70 series, with CFM56 turbofan engines, was produced by modification of 60s. Today small numbers of DC-8s are in military service, the Series 50s of France

Above: McDonnell Douglas C-9A Nightingale
aeromedical airlift aircraft.

including an electronic warfare testbed aircraft flown by Escadron Electronique 51
based at Evreux. Both of Spain's DC-8-52s are
used as VIP transports but are scheduled for
replacement in 1987. Super 60s are flown by
Peru and Thailand as transports, while
France also uses DC-8-72s as freighters.

While the DC-8 was designed with four
podded underwing engines, the company's
follow-on airliner, the short/medium-range
DC-9, used just two mounted on the rear of
the fuselage ahead and below of the T-tail.
The first DC-9 flew initially on 25 February
1965 and production continues today under
the new MD-80 designation. Military
examples of the DC-9 include the USAF's
C-9A Nightingale, an aeromedical transport
for up to 40 stretchers or more than that number of sitting casualties. All USAF/USN
versions are based on the Series 30.

Specifications (C-9B Skytrain II data)
Accommodation: Pilot, copilot and crew
chief, plus 107 passengers; 32,444 lb
(14,716 kg) of freight only or a mixture of
passengers and freight that might comprise
45 persons and three standard military
freight pallets.
Wingspan: 93 ft 5 in (28.47 m).
Length: 119 ft 3½ in (36.37 m).
Maximum take-off weight: 110,000 lb
(49,895 kg).
Cruising speed: 576 mph (926 km/h).
Range: 2923 miles (4704 km) with 10,000-lb
(4536-kg) load.
Engines: Two 14,500-lb (6577-kg) thrust
Pratt & Whitney JT8D-9 turbofans, with
22,444 liters of fuel standard.
Versions in service:
DC-8: As described above. The Series 50 has
four 18,000-lb (8164-kg) thrust Pratt &
Whitney JT3D-3/3B turbofans, a wingspan
of 142 ft 5 in (43.41 m), length 150 ft 6 in
(45.87 m), maximum take-off weight
325,000 lb (147,417 kg), freight payload
34,360 lb (15,585 kg), cruising speed
580 mph (933 km/h) and range of 5720 miles
(9200 km).

DC-9: Airliners used by Italy are VIP
transports. Kuwait aircraft are similar to the
C-9B, and Venezuela has or had one DC-9
used by the Presidential squadron.
C-9A Nightingale: USAF aeromedical
transport with JT8D-9 turbofans, delivered
between 1968 and 1973.
C-9B: US Navy logistic support transport.
VC-9C: USAF VIP transport delivered to the
Special Air Missions Wing.
Operators: France (DC-8), Italy (DC-9),
Kuwait (DC-9), Peru (DC-8), Spain (DC-8),
Thailand (DC-8), United States (air force
C-9A and VC-9C; navy, C-9B) and
Venezuela (DC-9?).

McDonnell Douglas F-4 Phantom II
United States

Nearly three decades after the first prototype
flew, on 27 May 1958 (under the original designation F4H-1), the Phantom II remains so
important among air forces around the world
that even now new improvements are being
introduced. For example, to reduce aircraft
losses and crew injury McDonnell Douglas
and Goodyear have conceived a one-piece
bird-resistant windshield made of layers of
polycarbonate and acrylic plastics for retrofit-
ting; 75 Luftwaffe F-4Fs are being given look-
down/shootdown capability under a German
program; Israeli F-4s are undergoing airframe
and avionics improvements; and modernization of the USAF/Air National Guard's F-4s
covers the navigation and weapons delivery
systems. Also, on 24 April 1987 an Israel F-4E
was flown powered by two Pratt & Whitney
PW1120 engines. This installation greatly
increases thrust.

Intended originally as a long-range, all-
weather fleet fighter to supersede the F3H
Demon with the US Navy, the Phantom's
role was changed to that of missile fighter
well before the prototype appeared with its
unusual upturned dogtooth outer wing panels and anhedral tail. The first version, the
F-4A, comprised 23 pre-production and 24
production aircraft but the initial major production version for the US Navy and Marine
Corps was the F-4B, of which 649 were built.

The first squadron to receive a production F-4
was US Navy VF-101, in December 1960.

Meanwhile, interest shown by the USAF in
the F-4A's fighter-bomber capabilities led to
the Phantom's adoption by this service in
F-4C form. Thereafter the aircraft quickly
established itself as a classic, able to deliver
an attack load similar in weight to that managed by four-engined bombers of World War
II era and including nuclear bombs. By the
end of production in October 1979 a total of
5057 F-4s had been built in the United States
for domestic use and export (1196 delivered
for service abroad), and Mitsubishi of Japan
constructed 127 more after assembling eleven
from knockdown components.

Specifications (F-4E Phantom II data)
Radar: Westinghouse AN/APQ-120 fire-
control radar for the guns and missiles,
with computer-aided target acquisition.
(This has solid-state circuitry, a feature that
was first introduced to the F-4 in 1966 with
the AWG-10 interceptor radar, which was
subsequently also improved to become the
first multimode radar with a pulse-Doppler
lookdown facility.)
Weapons: Up to 16,000 lb (7257 kg) of air-to-
air and attack weapons on 8 stations under
the fuselage and wings, including Sparrow
and Sidewinder missiles, air-to-surface
missiles, conventional and nuclear bombs,
rockets, gun pods and spray tanks. ECM
pods can be carried for self-defense. One
20-mm M61A-1 Vulcan 6-barrel cannon with
1020 rounds of ammunition.
Accommodation: 2 crew in tandem.
Wingspan: 38 ft 7½ in (11.77 m).
Length: 63 ft 0 in (19.20 m).
Maximum take-off weight: 61,795 lb
(28,030 kg).
Maximum speed: 1454 mph (2340 km/h).
Combat radius: 786 miles (1266 km) as an
interceptor.
Mission performance: Rate of climb at sea
level 49,500 ft (15,085 m) as an interceptor;
rate of climb at sea level at 53,814-lb
(24,410-kg) AUW 9340 ft (2847 m) per min;
ceiling 54,400 ft (16,580 m).
Engines: Two 17,900-lb (8120-kg) thrust with
afterburning General Electric J79-GE-17A

Above: JASDF McDonnell Douglas F-4EJ
Phantom II.

turbojets, with 7022 liters fuel standard.
Versions in service
F-4A: First pre-production/production
model for US Navy operation.
F-4B: Original US Navy/Marine Corps
version, with two J79-GE-8 turbojets.
RF-4B: First appearing in 1965, this was
developed as a multisensor reconnaissance
aircraft for the USMC, based on the F-4B
but without armament or dual controls.
F-4C: Original USAF version with J79-GE-15
turbojets, APQ-100 radar and other avionics
and equipment changes in comparison with
the F-4B. Naval folding wings and arrester
gear were retained for simplicity of
production.
RF-4C: Multisensor reconnaissance version
for the USAF, with a fuselage 2 ft 9 in
longer to accommodate the radar and
photographic equipment in a changed nose.
First flown in 1963, and thereby the first
reconnaissance version in service, it was
given side-looking radar, an infrared
detector, and forward- and side-looking
cameras. Production of this very important
version exceeded 500.
F-4D: Development of the F-4C initially for
the USAF, with the APQ-109 radar and
other avionics changes.
F-4E: The first true multirole version for the
USAF, with an AN/APQ-120 radar to allow
computer-aided target acquisition, leading-
edge maneuvering slats, additional internal
fuel, and an integral cannon. Deliveries
began in 1967. To help F-4E crews identify
targets at long range, a TV camera with
zoom lens was later fitted to the port wing
under the USAF/Northrop's TISEO (target
identification system electro-optical)
program.
RF-4E: Multisensor reconnaissance version
of the F-4E, delivered to several foreign air
forces.
F-4EJ: F-4E built by Mitsubishi in Japan for
the JASDF, with tail warning radar. Missiles
can include Mitsubishi AAM-2s.
F-4F: Fighter for the West German
Luftwaffe, with some avionics changes and

leading-edge slats to enhance
maneuverability. 175 delivered.
F-4G: The so-called 'Wild Weasel' variant,
produced by modifying F-4Es, to suppress
enemy radar early warning and weapon
guidance systems. Five regular USAF
tactical squadrons and one Air National
Guard squadron are so equipped.
F-4J: Development of the F-4B for the US
Navy/Marine Corps, with 16 degree 30
minute drooping ailerons and a slotted tail
to attain a lower landing speed. This model
was conceived to serve mainly as a fighter,
but with a secondary attack capability.
AN/AWG-10 pulse-Doppler fire-control
radar with lookdown capability and built-in
test system. AJB-7 bombing system fitted.
F-4K: Development of the F-4B for the Royal
Navy, with F-4J and other updates
including some British equipment, 2 Rolls-
Royce Spey RB.168-25R Mk 202/3 turbofan
engines, and a folding nose radome to
shorten its length to suit British aircraft
carrier deck-lifts. When the Royal Navy
gave up its last large aircraft carrier in favor
of Invincible-class 'jump-jet' carriers,
Phantom FG.Mk 1s were handed to RAF.
F-4M: RAF version, delivered from 1968.
Similar to the F-4K but without the leading-
edge fixed slot in the tailplane. Service
designation FGR.Mk 2.
F-4N: Some US Navy F-4Bs were updated to
this model and redelivered from 1973.
F-4S: Modified US Navy F-4Js to include a
strengthened structure to lengthen the
service life, use of leading-edge slats,
installation of the reliability-improved
AN/AWG-10A weapon-control radar with a
solid-state transmitter and digital computer,
and modified J79-GE-10B turbojets.
Operators: Egypt (F-4E), West Germany
(F-4E, F-4F and RF-4E), Greece (F-4E and
RF-4E), Iran (F-4D, F-4E and RF-4E), Israel
(F-4E and RF-4E), Japan (F-4EJ and RF-4EJ),
South Korea (F-4D and F-4E), Spain (F-4C),
Turkey (F-4E and RF-4E), United Kingdom
(F-4K and F-4M) and United States (air
force, F-4C, F-4D, F-4E, F-4G and RF-4C;
navy/marine corps, including F-4N, F-4S
and RF-4B)*.

*Including reserve forces.

McDonnell Douglas F-15 Eagle and F-15 STOL
United States

Regarded by most observers as the world's
No 1 fighter, the F-15 was planned as the FX in
1968 (following the USAF's disappointing
experience with the F-111) and the first prototype flew on 27 July 1972. The USAF
planned to buy 729, but the total has now
risen to 1266, of which almost 900 have been
delivered. Despite the aircraft's high price
and extremely high operating cost, F-15s
have also been sold to Israel (51) and Saudi
Arabia (62), and in Japan Mitsubishi is leading a team building 86 F-15Js under license
(Japan also bought two F-15Js and 12 dual-
control F-15DJ trainers from the USA).

To power the F-15 Pratt & Whitney developed the F100 engine, which after years of
problems has now matured as the slightly
less powerful but otherwise infinitely superior F100-220 version, which may set new
high standards in long trouble-free life. The
engines are fairly close together at the nozzles but the inlets are separated by the fuselage, and each can be rotated downward to
match inlet airflow to take-off, landing and
low-speed flight. The giant wing has no slats
or droops on the leading edge, and has ordinary ailerons instead of spoilers. Much of the
structure is metal honeycomb, and in 1986
McDonnell flew an F-15 with wings made of
new aluminum-lithium alloy. The horizontal
and vertical tails are attached to beams canti-
levered back on each side of the engines.
The wing is mounted high, and in the center
of the wide upper surface of the aircraft is a
huge door-type airbrake. All three units of
the undercarriage have single wheels with
high-pressure tires needing strong paved
runways.

The radar was one of the best in the world
when the first F-15s reached Tactical Air
Command in November 1974, giving sharp
and clear cockpit pictures with all unwanted
detail or interference eliminated. The radar
has since been upgraded in the F-15C, now in
production, and this version also has a pro-
grammable signal processor and the ability to
carry conformal fuel tanks (CFTs) or FAST

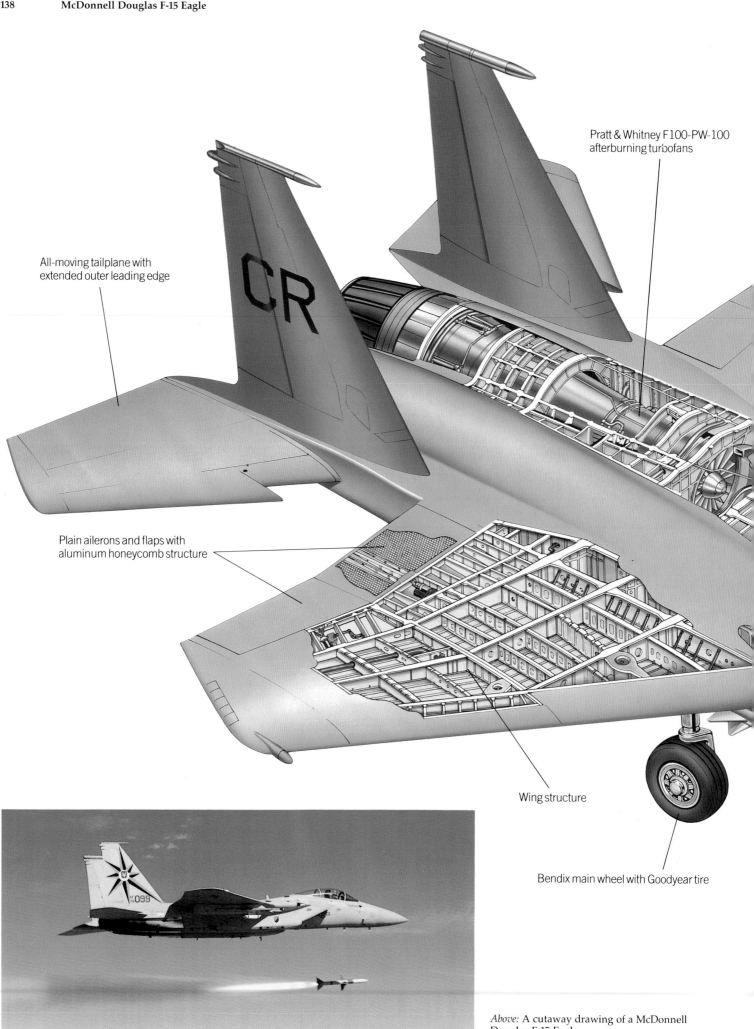

Pratt & Whitney F100-PW-100
afterburning turbofans

All-moving tailplane with
extended outer leading edge

Plain ailerons and flaps with
aluminum honeycomb structure

Wing structure

Bendix main wheel with Goodyear tire

Above: A cutaway drawing of a McDonnell
Douglas F-15 Eagle.
Left: USAF McDonnell Douglas F-15C Eagle firing
a Sparrow missile.

packs. The latter, meaning Fuel And Sensor Tactical, add 2839 liters of fuel 'scabbed' closely beside each side of the fuselage, where they cause virtually no extra drag. The packs also provide so-called tangential attachments for additional external stores including attack missiles. The gun is inside the right wing, the ammunition being fed across the inlet duct from a 940-round drum in the fuselage. The F-15B and D are dual-pilot training versions of the A and C.

The latest model is the F-15E, which adds all-weather ground attack capability (this was anathema when the F-15 was first developed). Carrying extremely heavy loads of fuel and ordnance, the E model will carry all the sensors and other aids needed to make blind attacks on point targets. The first of 392 of this version is expected to be delivered in late 1988.

Specifications (F-15C data)

Radar: Hughes Aircraft AN/APG-63 X-band pulse-Doppler all-digital radar, with long-range detection and tracking of targets flying at all altitudes, automatic close-in detection, and with the tracking and steering guidance data displayed on a HUD to enable the pilot to keep his eyes 'up' during a dogfight.
Weapons: One 20-mm General Electric M61A-1 6-barrel cannon, with 940 rounds of ammunition, plus up to 8 air-to-air missiles of AMRAAM, Sparrow or Sidewinder types. Three attachment points for up to 23,600 lb (10,705 kg) of attack weapons, plus 2 more with FAST packs fitted.
Accommodation: The pilot.
Wingspan: 42 ft 9¾ in (13.05 m)
Length: 63 ft 9 in (19.43 m).
Maximum take-off weight: 68,000 lb (30,844 kg).
Maximum speed: Mach 2.5
Ferry range: 3570 miles (5745 km).
Mission performance: Ceiling 60,000 ft (18,290 m); G limits +9 design, −3 design; endurance 5 h 15 min with CFT/FASTs.
Engines: Two 23,830-lb (10,810-kg) thrust with afterburning Pratt & Whitney F100-PW-100 turbofans, with 7836 liters of fuel standard. The F100-PW-220 turbofan will power F-15C/Ds of 23,450-lb (10,637-kg) thrust with afterburning.

Versions in service

F-15A: Original single-seat air superiority fighter, with attack capability.
F-15B: 2-seat training version of the F-15A.
F-15C: Production version since 1979.
F-15D: 2-seat trainer version of the F-15C.
F-15E: Actual prototype first flew in late 1986, following evaluation of a demonstrator. Attack and air superiority are both principal roles, by day or night and in all weathers, and missions can include long-range interdiction.
F-15J and DJ: Single- and 2-seat Eagles for the JASDF.
F-15 STOL: Proposed advanced technology Eagle, with STOL performance to shorten the length of the runways needed in wartime in case of airfield attack, and with perhaps rough and soft field operating capability. Features include two-dimensional thrust vectoring/reversing engine nozzles. A demonstrator should fly in 1988.
Operators: Israel, Japan, Saudi Arabia and United States.

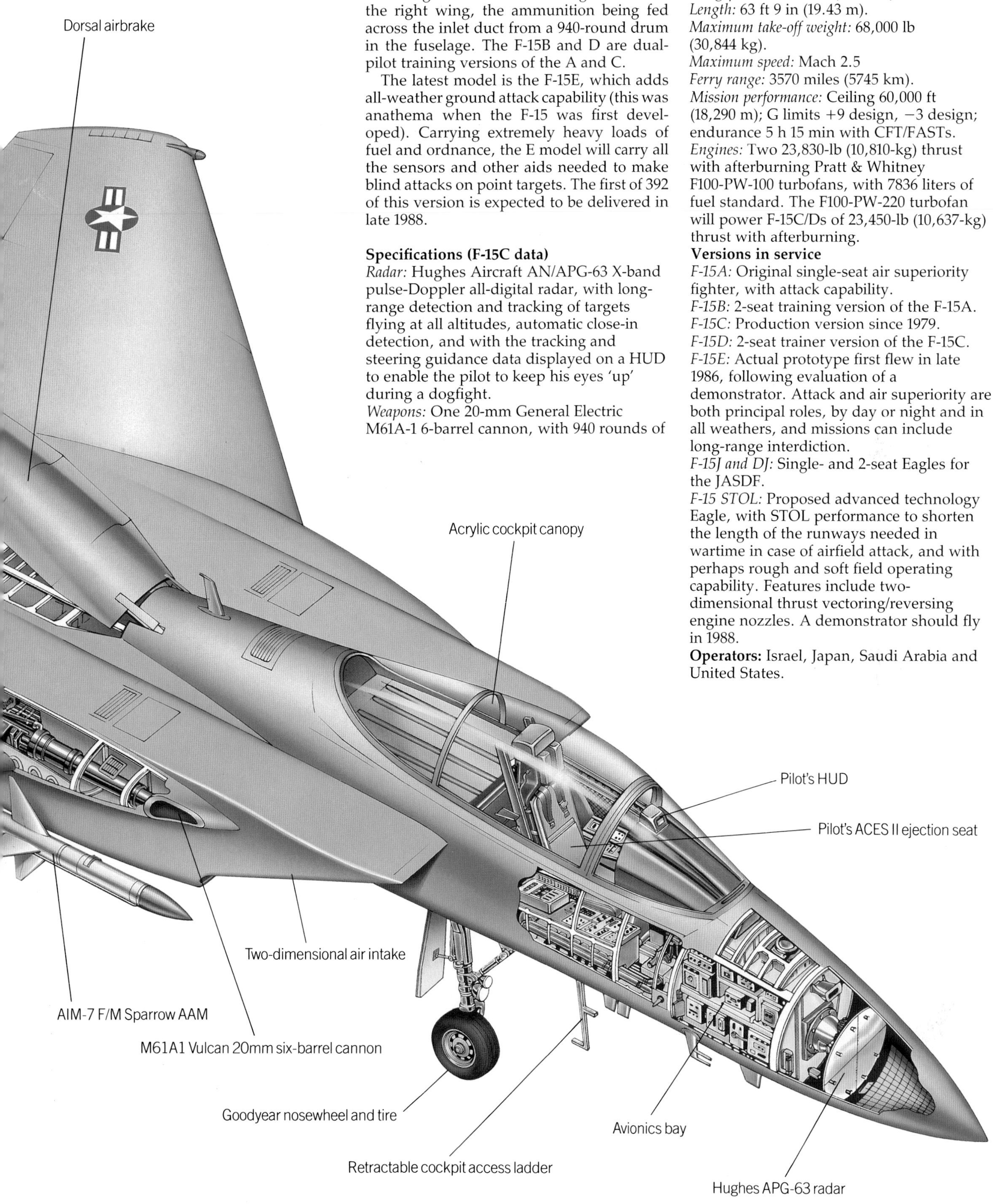

Dorsal airbrake

Acrylic cockpit canopy

Pilot's HUD

Pilot's ACES II ejection seat

Two-dimensional air intake

AIM-7 F/M Sparrow AAM

M61A1 Vulcan 20mm six-barrel cannon

Goodyear nosewheel and tire

Retractable cockpit access ladder

Avionics bay

Hughes APG-63 radar

McDonnell Douglas F/A-18 Hornet
United States

The US Navy holds a unique position among the world's navies by its operational deployment of 15 large aircraft carriers, the latest of which, the USS *Theodore Roosevelt*, was launched in 1984 and was commissioned recently; one of these carriers, the USS *Independence*, is currently undergoing a service life extension program. The few aircraft carriers commissioned by other navies (excepting the new Soviet 65,000-tonne carriers soon to begin sea trials) are either of much smaller size and suited only to the operation of helicopters or 'jump jets' or are of fairly old design. So it appears incongruous that not only will the US Navy take delivery of a further two Nimitz-class supercarriers in the early 1990s as replacements for older vessels but that it continues to deploy new fixed-wing, conventionally powered aircraft at least equal in fighting capability to their land-based counterparts.

No better example of Navy air power can be found than the F/A-18 Hornet, which began its service career in early 1983 with US Marine fighter/attack squadron 314 and went to sea on its first major deployment on board USS *Constellation* two years later. The squadrons forming the strike fighter detachment on this historic occasion were 'Fist of the Fleet' VFA-25 and 'Stingers' VFA-113.

The Hornet was developed to supersede the F-4 Phantom II fighter, the A-4 Skyhawk and A-7 Corsair II attack aircraft with US Navy and Marine squadrons. It has greatly enhanced naval fighting capability in both air superiority and ground attack scenarios. As a fighter it is marginally less powerful in terms of engine thrust than the Phantom but to compensate it is a very much lighter single-seater, with the maximum speed sacrificed slightly for an incredible climb rate and excellent maneuverability. In a strike role, which is one of its two intended functions in combat, its warload is far superior to the replaced aircraft and with the added bonus that it requires no fighter escort; for the outward journey of an attack mission it can carry air-to-air missiles as well as its strike weapons and when returning in 'light' condition it becomes a fully maneuverable fighter once again.

The first Hornet prototype flew initially on 18 November 1978 and by early 1986 the US Navy/Marine Corps had received 287 aircraft of a planned 1377. This includes a number of F/A-18B tandem two-seat trainers which retain full combat capability. In addition to domestic sales, the Hornet has attracted orders from Australia (75), Canada (138) and Spain (72), all for operation from land.

The design of the Hornet includes most of the latest technologies, though composite structures, such as graphite/epoxy, are

Below: A cutaway drawing of the McDonnell Douglas F/A-18A Hornet.

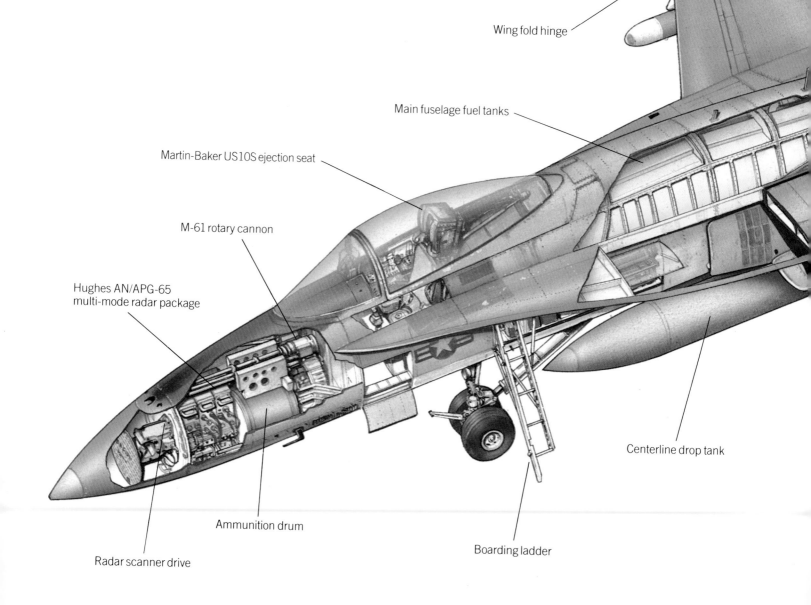

Wing fold hinge

Main fuselage fuel tanks

Martin-Baker US10S ejection seat

M-61 rotary cannon

Hughes AN/APG-65 multi-mode radar package

Centerline drop tank

Ammunition drum

Boarding ladder

Radar scanner drive

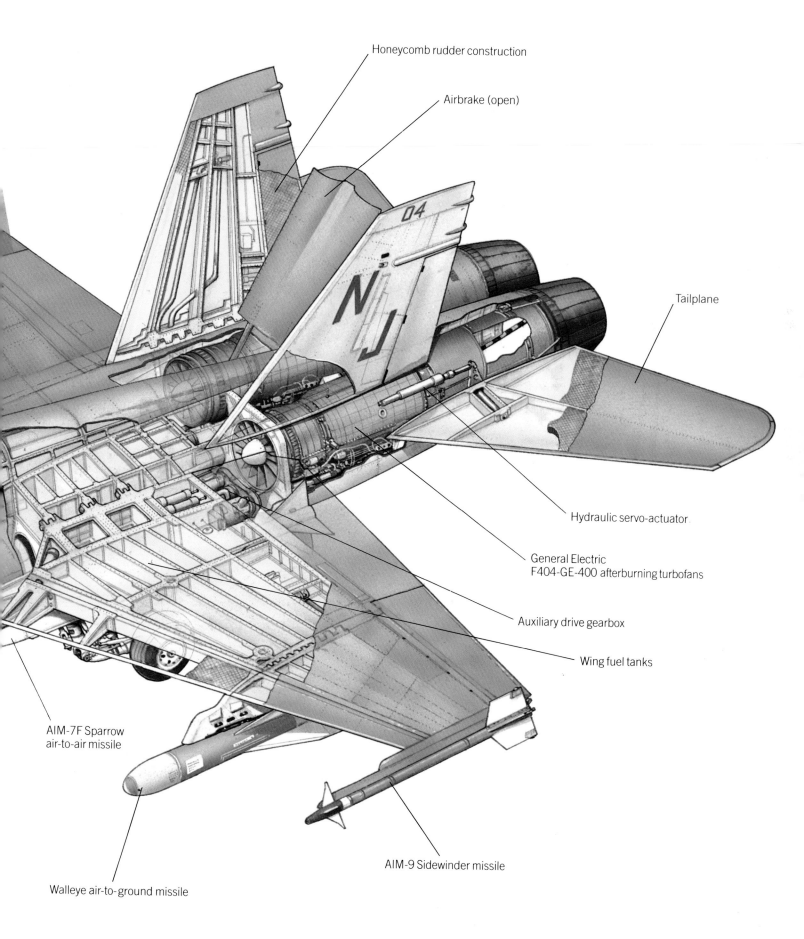

Honeycomb rudder construction

Airbrake (open)

Tailplane

Hydraulic servo-actuator

General Electric
F404-GE-400 afterburning turbofans

Auxiliary drive gearbox

Wing fuel tanks

AIM-7F Sparrow
air-to-air missile

AIM-9 Sidewinder missile

Walleye air-to-ground missile

Above: McDonnell Douglas F/A-18A Hornets of USN VFA-113 and VFA-25.

combined with conventional light alloy to form the airframe. The 'straight' wings have marked sweepback on the leading edges and carry wing-root slots, full-span leading-edge maneuvering flaps, single-slotted trailing-edge flaps and ailerons. The latter can be drooped by 45 degrees, thereby giving the known benefits of full-span flaps with regard to maintaining the low approach speed desirable when attempting to land on deck. The leading and trailing flaps are computer-controlled to provide the best lift and lowest drag conditions for maneuvering in combat and cruising'.

Conventional systems to actuate the moving control surfaces have all but disappeared from the Hornet, superseded by a quadruplex digital fly-by-wire system which links the pilot's controls with the surfaces via electronic signals. This gives the benefit of lighter weight and greater battle survivability. Conventional instrumentation is another casualty of modern technology, with three cathode-ray tubes and a head-up display showing the information on screens.

Specifications

Radar: Hughes Aircraft AN/APG-65 multimode digital tracking radar with air-to-air and air-to-ground modes including velocity search, range-while-search and track-while-scan. It can track 10 targets and display 8.

Weapons: An impressive 17,000 lb (7711 kg) can include 2 Sidewinder air-to-air missiles at the wingtips, 2 more, or Sparrows, on the outer underwing pylons, and 2 Sparrows or a laser tracker/strike camera and FLIR pods on air-intake pylons. The F/A-18C and D can carry new generation AMRAAM fire-and-forget air-to-air missiles. Attack weapons include air-to-surface missiles (infrared Maverick for the F/A-18C and D, which also carries jammers), bombs, rockets, etc. One 20-mm M61 Vulcan 6-barrel cannon is mounted in the nose.

Accommodation: The pilot, except on training models which have a crew of 2 in tandem.

Wingspan: 37 ft 6 in (11.43 m).

Length: 56 ft 0 in (17.07 m).

Maximum take-off weight: 49,224 lb (22,328 kg) in attack configuration, 36,710 lb (16,651 kg) in fighter configuration.

Maximum speed: Over Mach 1.8.

Combat radius: 662 miles (1065 km) in attack configuration; 460 miles (740 km) in fighter configuration.

Mission performance: Combat ceiling 50,000 ft (15,240 m).

Engines: Two 16,000-lb (7257-kg) thrust General Electric F404-GE-400 turbofans.

Versions in service

C-15: Spanish Air Force designation of the single-seat EF-18 Hornet, with which initial operational capability was achieved in 1987.

CE.15: Spanish Air Force designation of the 2-seat training model of the EF-18 Hornet.

CF-18A: Canadian Armed Forces version of the F/A-18A, received to supersede the CF-5, CF-101 Voodoo and CF-104 Starfighter. The first examples were received in 1982. These have minor equipment changes compared to the US Navy versions.

CF-18B: Canadian Armed Forces 2-seat version, of which forty are wanted.

F/A-18A: Initial US Navy/Marine Corps version for carrier and shore operations.

F/A-18B: 2-seat training version for US Navy/Marine Corps. Known previously as the TF/A-18A.

F/A-18C: New production model for 1987 delivery to the US Navy/Marine Corps, with an improved computer. Weapon updates include the ability to launch AMRAAM and infrared Maverick. Jammers and reconnaissance equipment are also available. Aircraft delivered after October 1989 will be further updated to enhance all-weather night attack.

F/A-18D: 2-seat training version of the F/A-18C.

F/A-18R: Proposed reconnaissance model, under test. Can be changed back into a weapon-carrying combat aircraft 'in the field' if required.

GAF F/A-18A: Hornets for the Royal Australian Air Force are mostly being built in Australia at the Government Aircraft Factories. The first GAF-built Hornet flew in mid-1985. Acquired to supersede the RAAF's Dassault-Breguet Mirage IIIs.

GAF F/A-18B: RAAF 2-seat model, of which 18 are required.

Operators: Australia, Canada, Spain and United States (navy and marine corps).

McDonnell Douglas KC-10A Extender
United States

Developed from the commercial DC-10-30CF, the Extender is the USAF's latest combined flight refuelling tanker and cargo aircraft. The first Extender entered service in 1981 and by mid-1986 45 had been received. Its roles are similar to the KC-135; but it has a greater capacity and is more economical.

The main function of the Extender is that of a tanker, with the seven rubberized fabric cells carried in the lower fuselage compartments containing about 68,600 liters of transferable fuel. This is linked to the aircraft's own fuel system, providing for the transfer of fuel from both systems if required or the use of both for very long-range ferry flights of up to 11,500 miles (18,507 km). A flight refuelling probe also allows the aircraft to top up, which is especially important on cargo-carrying missions. The refuelling operation is managed by the boom operator, who occupies a ventral station in the lower aft fuselage and can view through a rearward-facing window and a periscope. Apart from the boom through which fuel is transferred to the receiving aircraft, a secondary probe and drogue refuelling system allows the tanker to serve aircraft that only have this type of facility, which includes many older warplanes, types in use with the US Navy and Marine Corps, and aircraft of other nations.

Seats provided in the front of the main cabin are essentially to transport the ground personnel accompanying squadrons being deployed away from their home bases, while as a cargo carrier the Extender can accommodate up to twenty-seven 463L pallets or other goods up to a weight of 169,409 lb (76,842 kg).

Specifications
Accommodation: Flight crew of 3, a boom operator, optional student and instructor if required for training, ground personnel, fuel and cargo as detailed above.
Wingspan: 165 ft 4½ in (50.40 m).
Length: 181 ft 7 in (55.35 m).
Maximum take-off weight: 590,000 lb (267,619 kg).
Maximum speed: Approx 610 mph (982 km/h).
Range with full payload: 4370 miles (7030 km).
Engines: Three 52,500-lb (23,810-kg) thrust General Electric CF6-50C2 turbofans, with 132,141 liters of fuel standard. Tanker cells hold approx 68,600 liters of fuel.
Version in service
KC-10A: First deployed by SAC at Barksdale Air Force Base.
Operator: United States

McDonnell Douglas AH-64A Apache
United States

Originating as a Hughes design, the Apache is the US Army's latest and most formidable attack helicopter. 675 are expected to enter service by early 1990. Retaining the basic slim fuselage/tandem stepped cockpit arrangement conceived by Bell with its HueyCobra, Apache is the heavyweight companion to the Cobra. It is capable of anti-armor or other missions by day or night and in adverse weather, long-range self-deployment by the use of ferry tanks to a distance of more than 1000 miles (1600 km), and can operate from and be maintained at forward fighting positions. If the deployment is beyond the helicopter's ferry range, then six can be carried by a Galaxy transport.

The first Apache prototype flew initially on 30 September 1975. The helicopter went on to win the US Army's AAH (advanced attack helicopter) competition against the Bell YAH-63, and operational capability with production examples was achieved in 1986, initially by the 1/6 Cav, 6th Air Cavalry Combat Brigade. The first Army National Guard unit to acquire Apaches was the 28th Aviation Battalion in North Carolina, in 1987. Apache uses the Singer-Kearfott AN/ASN-128 Doppler navigation system and Litton strapdown attitude and heading reference system to fly nap-of-the-earth missions and store the locations of targets. Survivability is enhanced by the use of the 'Black Hole' system which reduces the engine exhaust and nozzle temperatures and so makes them less vulnerable to heat-seeking missiles, while other methods to confuse an attacking enemy are an infrared jammer, radar jammer and chaff dispenser. The crew is protected by boron armor around the cockpits that can resist 23-mm ammunition. A radar warning receiver is also carried. Naval versions of the Apache have also been proposed for roles that could include air-to-air combat and antishipping, each fitted with T700-GE-401 engines.

Specifications (AH-64A Apache data)
Equipment: Avionics and equipment as given in the introduction and much more, including a target acquisition and designation sight and night vision sensor for the pilot (both carried on the fuselage nose).
Weapons: One 30-mm McDonnell Douglas M230 Chain Gun cannon on an

Below: USAF McDonnell Douglas KC-10A Extender.

underfuselage mounting, with up to 1200 rounds of ammunition. Under stub-wing pylons for 16 Hellfire anti-armor missiles, 76 2.75-in rockets carried in launchers, or a number of each. Sidewinder air-to-air missiles could be carried on stub-wing tip launchers of the proposed naval Apache, which could presumably also become a feature of Army helicopters at a future date.
Accommodation: The pilot in the rear cockpit and the gunner/copilot in the forward lower cockpit.
Diameter of rotor: 48 ft 0 in (14.63 m).
Length, including the rotors: 58 ft 3 in (17.76 m).
Maximum take-off weight: 21,000 lb (9525 kg).
Maximum speed: 184 mph (296 km/h).
Range: 300 miles (482 km).
Mission performance: Rate of climb at sea level 2500 ft (762 m) per min; ceiling

21,000 ft (6400 m); hovering ceiling in ground effect 15,000 ft (4570 m); hovering ceiling out of ground effect 11,500 ft (3500 m); endurance up to 3 h 9 min.
Engines: Two 1696-shp General Electric T700-GE-701 turboshafts, with 1423 liters of fuel standard.
Versions in service
AH-64A Apache: As detailed above.
US Marine Corps Apache: Proposed anti-armor and air-to-air version, without the 30-mm cannon and with TOW as an alternative to Hellfire. Other new weapons could be Sidewinder AAMs and 5-in rockets.
Sea Apache: Proposed US Navy version with search and acquisition radar, antiship or perhaps 6 Sidewinder air-to-air missiles, and a folding tail for ship-borne operation.
Operator: United States (army).

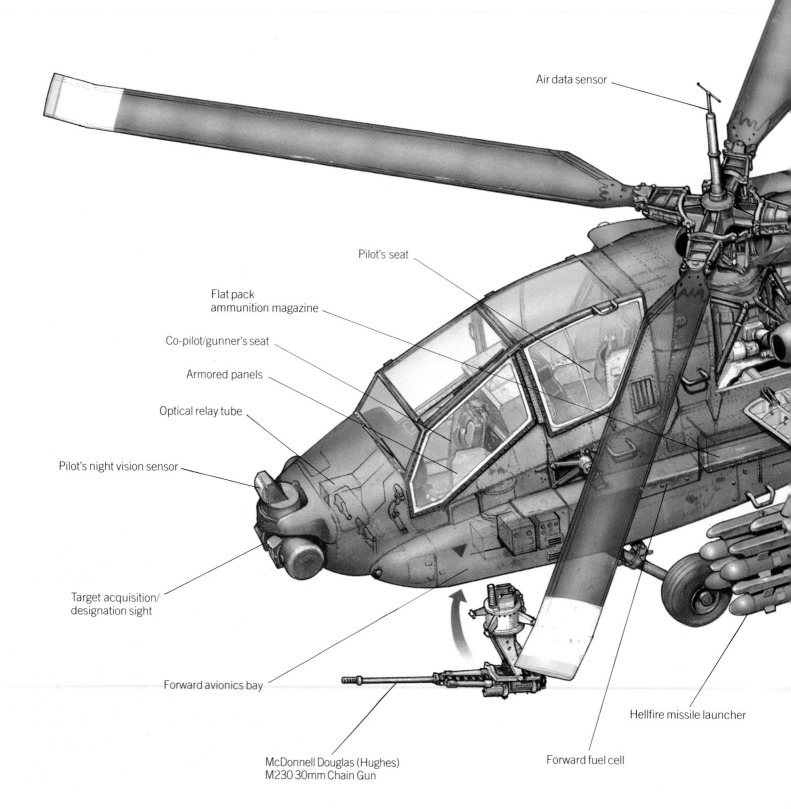

Air data sensor

Pilot's seat

Flat pack ammunition magazine

Co-pilot/gunner's seat

Armored panels

Optical relay tube

Pilot's night vision sensor

Target acquisition/ designation sight

Forward avionics bay

McDonnell Douglas (Hughes) M230 30mm Chain Gun

Forward fuel cell

Hellfire missile launcher

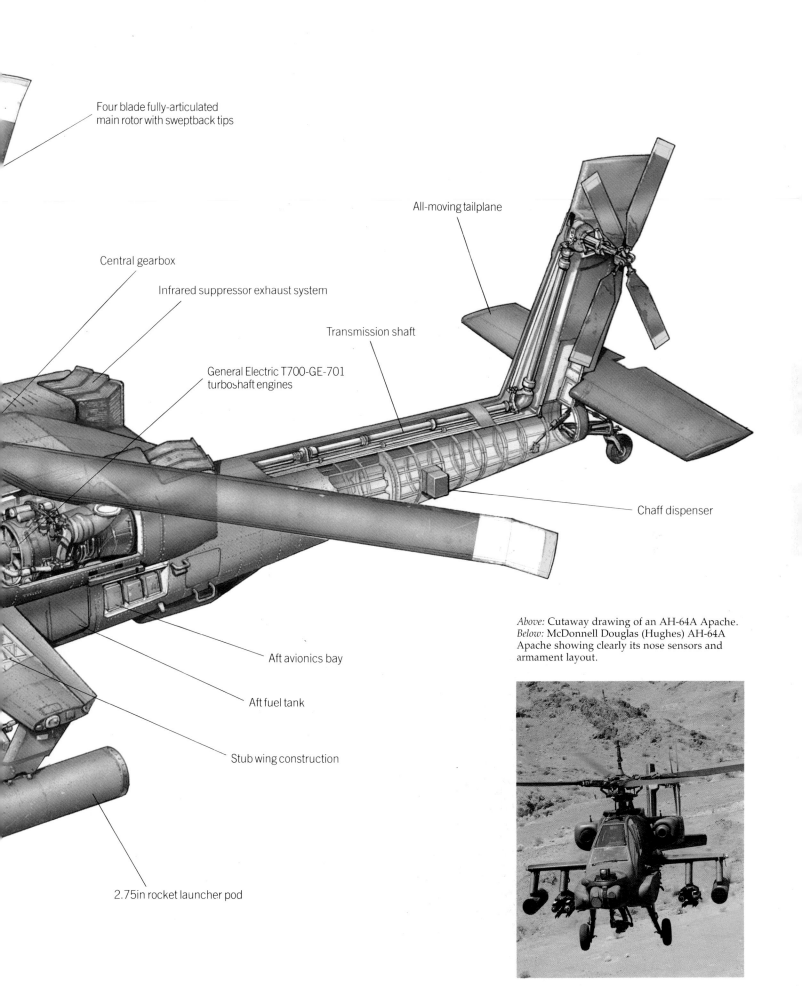

Four blade fully-articulated
main rotor with sweptback tips

All-moving tailplane

Central gearbox

Infrared suppressor exhaust system

Transmission shaft

General Electric T700-GE-701
turboshaft engines

Chaff dispenser

Aft avionics bay

Aft fuel tank

Stub wing construction

2.75in rocket launcher pod

Above: Cutaway drawing of an AH-64A Apache.
Below: McDonnell Douglas (Hughes) AH-64A
Apache showing clearly its nose sensors and
armament layout.

McDonnell Douglas (Hughes) Model 500/530 Defender and OH-6A Cayuse series
United States

First flown as a prototype on 27 February 1963, the four-seat Hughes OH-6A light observation helicopter was chosen for service by the US Army as the Cayuse. By 1970 1434 had been delivered. The civil version of this helicopter was known as the Model 500, with production also taking place in Argentina, Italy, Japan and South Korea, some of which have passed into military service. However, a specific military version was developed as the Model 500M, representing an improved OH-6A type that could undertake varied roles from observation to antisubmarine; the Spanish Navy became a customer for the 500M in ASW form. The 500M has since been superseded by the Model 500MD Defender series.

Specifications (Model 500MD/TOW Defender data)
Weapons: 4 TOW anti-armor missiles carried on fuselage outriggers.
Accommodation: 2 crew for armed missions. Up to 7 persons can be carried in Defenders if required.
Diameter of rotor: 26 ft 4 in (8.03 m).
Fuselage length: 25 ft 0 in (7.62 m).
Maximum take-off weight: 3000 lb (1361 kg).
Cruising speed: 137 mph (221 km/h).
Range: 242 miles (389 km).
Mission performance: Rate of climb at sea

Below: McDonnell Douglas (Hughes) 500MD Defender carrying two TOW antitank missiles and a gun pod.

level 1650 ft (503 m) per min; ceiling 13,800 ft (4200 m); hovering ceiling in ground effect 7600 ft (2315 m); hovering ceiling out of ground effect 5800 ft (1770 m); endurance 2 h 47 min.
Engine: One 420-hp Allison 250-C20B turboshaft (derated to 375 shp).

Versions in service
OH-6A Cayuse: US Army light observation helicopter, powered by a 252-shp Allison T63-A-5A turboshaft engine. 2 crew plus 2 passengers or up to 4 troops on the cabin floor. Maximum speed 160 mph (257 km/h).
Model 500: Basically the civil version but some in military service, such as the 500Ds used by Jordan and South Korea.
Model 500M: Original military export version, also built by Argentina and Japan. Spanish ASW examples carry MAD and two torpedoes.
500MD Defender: Multirole military helicopter, available as the armed Scout Defender (fourteen 2.75-in rockets plus 7.62-mm machine-guns or other light attack weapons), ASW Defender for antisubmarine and search missions (carrying search radar, MAD and other equipment, plus two torpedoes), TOW Defender for anti-armor missions (as detailed above), MMS-TOW Defender (anti-armor version with a mast-mounted sight), Defender II with a five-blade main rotor and a wider variety of avionics and equipment options (including infrared suppression system and Stinger or similar missiles for an air-to-air role), MG Defender which combines the 530MG with the 420-shp 250-C20B engine and rotor, and the Nightfox which is an armed and FLIR-carrying night surveillance and night

mission helicopter.
530MG Defender: 650-shp Allison 250-C30 turboshaft (derated to 425 shp), first flown in 1984. Basically an attack and antitank helicopter, but suited also to a wide range of missions. A Nightfox version is available. Rotor diameter is 27 ft 4 in (8.33 m), maximum weight is 3550 lb (1610 kg), and cruising speed is 140 mph (226 km/h). This helicopter is particularly suited to high temperature or high altitude operation.
Operators: Argentina, Bolivia, Brazil, Colombia, Denmark (navy), Dominican Republic, El Salvador, Finland, Haiti, Indonesia, Iraq, Israel, Japan (navy and army), Kenya, South Korea, Mexico, Morocco, Nicaragua, Philippines, Spain (navy), Taiwan (navy) and United States (army).

McDonnell Douglas/BAe Harrier II
United States and United Kingdom

Although a brilliantly simple design, the Harrier suffers from various deficiencies. No money was available to uprate the engine, but McDonnell Douglas (assisted in some areas by BAe) found that by redesigning the wing, jet nozzles (and their relationship to the wing) and other areas it would be possible to make the same engine thrust lift much greater loads and fly further. By rebuilding an AV-8A, McDonnell Douglas and the US Marine Corps got an aerodynamic prototype into the air on 9 November 1978, and the first FSD (full-scale development) AV-8B flew on 5 November 1981. Today the two partners are in full production against requirements of the USMC for 300 AV-8B Harrier IIs and 28 two-seat TAV-8Bs (first flight 21 October 1986), 12 EAV-8Bs for the Spanish Navy and 89 Harrier GR.Mk 5s for the RAF in Germany.

The obviously new feature is the long-span high-lift wing, made entirely of carbon composite material, which also has giant flaps and drooped ailerons used in the jet-lift mode. LERX (leading-edge root extensions) developed by BAe improve the instantaneous turn rate. Another obvious change is the bigger nose and raised cockpit, with a huge bulged canopy. Less obvious is a new computerized stability system which removes dangerous problems during transition to and from the hover. In the nose is an ARBS (angle-rate bombing system) with an FLIR and laser; in the future McDonnell Douglas will fly an AV-8B with a lightweight radar. On the wingtips and tail is an inbuilt radar warning system, and a chaff/flare dispenser is inside the rear fuselage. Under the belly are lift-improvement devices, part of which are the guns in twin pods. In the GR.Mk 5 each pod houses a 25-mm gun, while in the AV-8B one houses a 25-mm GAU-12 gun and the other its ammunition. The new wings carry 50 percent more fuel than in the Harrier, and also enable more weapon pylons to be attached; there are six under the wings on the AV-8B and eight on the GR.Mk 5.

Specifications
Weapons: Two 25-mm Royal Ordnance Factory cannon in the GR.Mk 5, with 200 rounds of ammunition; one 25-mm General Electric 5-barrel cannon on the AV-8B, with 300 rounds of ammunition. 9200 lb (4173 kg)

Above: RAF Harrier GR.Mk 5.

of underwing and underfuselage weapons, which can include among many options 16 500-lb (227-kg) bombs, ten Paveway laser-guided bombs, Maverick missiles or two/four Sidewinder or Magic air-to-air missiles (the GR.Mk 5 can carry 4 Sidewinders, the extra 2 on two additional pylons, while equipment includes a nose-mounted IR reconnaissance sensor, Marconi ECM system with a radar warning receiver and a multimode jammer). AV-8B has provision for ECM.
Accommodation: The pilot.
Wingspan: 30 ft 4 in (9.25 m).
Length: 46 ft 4 in (14.12 m).
Maximum take-off weight: 31,000 lb (14,061 kg) for short take-off (not vertical).
Maximum speed: 647 mph (1041 km/h) at sea level.
Combat radius: 103 miles (167 km) with 12 Snakeye bombs and one-hour loiter,

standard fuel; 553 miles (889 km) with 4000-lb (1814-kg) load and auxiliary fuel.
Mission performance: Short take-off run 1640 ft (500 m); G limits +7, −3.
Engine: One 21,750-lb (9865-kg) thrust Rolls-Royce Pegasus Mk 105 vectored-thrust turbofan, with 4160 liters of fuel standard for GR.Mk 5. One 21,500-lb (9775 kg) thrust Pegasus F402-RR-406 vectored-thrust turbofan in AV-8B with 4164 liters of fuel.
Versions in service
AV-8B: US Marine Corps version. Initial operational squadron was VMA-331 based in North Carolina, in 1985. Eventually AV-8Bs will supersede Skyhawks with 5 squadrons, 3 fleet squadrons now using Harrier and one training squadron.
TAV-8B: 2-seat trainer.
EAV-8B: Spanish Navy designation.
GR.Mk 5: RAF version, for basing in West Germany. Deliveries began in 1987.
Operators: Spain (navy), United Kingdom and United States (marine corps).

Microjet 200 B
France

Microturbo SA, a French producer of small jet engines, conceived the idea of using its own engines in a new lightweight trainer that would be both less expensive to purchase and cheaper to operate than more conventional jet trainers. As for other trainers, the Microjet also has some combat potential, roles possibly including light strike and anti-helicopter.

To initiate development, Microjet SA was founded and the first prototype (with a wooden structure) made its maiden flight on 24 June 1980. Other Microjets have since flown, the airframe now established as a light alloy fuselage and composites (carbonfiber, glassfiber and epoxy) wings and tail unit. The first pre-production Microjet achieved its

Below: McDonnell Douglas/BAe AV-8B of US Marine Corps squadron VMA-331.

Above: Pre-series examples of the Mircojet 200 B jet trainer.

first flight in 1983. The planned production version is the 200 B. No orders had been announced by 1986.

Specifications

Weapons: Training, light attack and air-to-air weapons.
Accommodation: Student pilot and instructor
Wingspan: 24 ft 9¾ in (7.56 m).
Length: 21 ft 10½ in (6.67 m).
Maximum take-off weight: 2866 lb (1300 kg).
Maximum speed: 287 mph (463 km/h).
Range: 541 miles (870 km).
Mission performance: Rate of climb at sea level 1705 ft (520 m) per min; ceiling 30,000 ft (9150 m); G limits +7 aerobatic, −3.5 aerobatic, +4 utility, −1.8 utility; endurance 2 h.
Engines: Two 293-lb (133-kg) thrust Microturbo TRS 18-1 turbojets, with 440 liters of fuel. Engine ratings will increase to 405-lb (184-kg) thrust in stages as production builds up.
Version in service
Microjet 200 B: Production version, as detailed above.
Operators: None at time of writing.

Mikoyan-Gurevich MiG-15 and MiG-15UTI
(NATO names Fagot and Midget)
Soviet Union

The single-seat MiG-15 is viewed by aviation historians as one of the all-time classic fighters, though its success lay as much in the adoption of a Soviet engine based upon the British Rolls-Royce Nene turbojet (25 Nenes were exported to the Soviet Union along with 30 Derwents in 1947) as in its well-designed airframe. Indeed, the prototype, known as the I-310, actually flew for the first time with one of the British Nene engines, on 30 December 1947.

The Soviet RD-45 was the original power plant for the production MiG fighter, superseded by the 5952-lb (2700-kg) thrust Klimov VK-1 on the MiG-15bis (both Nene developments), and these aircraft gave United Nations forces effective opposition during the Korean War of the early 1950s, having been supplied to North Korea and China. Fighter versions of the swept-wing MiG-15 received the NATO name Fagot, and apart from Soviet production the type was built also in Czechoslovakia, Poland and China. It was China's first production jet aircraft (known sometimes as the J-2). It is interesting to note that the only avionics carried by the early MiGs were a high-frequency radio and a homing receiver, simplicity being a feature of MiG fighters right up to the MiG-21 and in this respect guaranteeing high serviceability. Today, it is believed that only Albania, Congo Republic and perhaps North Korea still operate Fagots in a high fighter-bomber role, although until recently Algeria, China, Mali and the Somali Republic were also users. A tandem two-seat operational advan-

ced training variant became the MiG-15UTI, which was manufactured in the Soviet Union, Czechoslovakia (as the CS-102), Poland (as the SBLiM-1) and China (at Shenyang). Known to NATO as Midget, the MiG-15UTI remains active with a great many air forces.

Specifications (MiG-15UTI data unless otherwise stated)
Accommodation: Student pilot and instructor in tandem under a long canopy.
Wingspan: 33 ft 1½ in (10.08 m).
Length: 32 ft 11¼ in (10.04 m).
Maximum take-off weight: 11,905 lb (5400 kg).
Maximum speed: 630 mph (1015 km/h).
Range: 885 miles (1425 km).
Mission performance: Rate of climb at sea level (MiG-15bis) 10,400 ft (3170 m) per min; ceiling (MiG-15bis) 50,855 ft (15,500 m).
Engine: One 5445-lb (2470-kg) thrust RD-45 turbojet.
Versions in service
MiG-15bis: Developed version of the fighter, with a more powerful Klimov engine. Has been used also in a training role.
MiG-15UTI: Dedicated operational trainer.
Shenyang J-2: MiG-15UTI built in China.
Operators: All MiG-15UTI or J-2 trainers, except where indicated. Afghanistan, Albania (MiG-15bis/J-2), Algeria, Angola, Bangladesh, Bulgaria, China (air force and navy, J-2s and possibly single-seat Fagots as fighter-bombers?), Congo Republic (MiG-15), East Germany, Guinea, Guinea-Bissau, Hungary, Iraq, North Korea (MiG-15UTI and possibly fighter-bombers?), Mali, Mozambique, Pakistan, Rumania, Somali Republic, Soviet Union, Tanzania, Uganda, Vietnam, North Yemen, South Yemen and Yugoslavia.

Mikoyan-Gurevich MiG-17 and Shenyang J-5 (NATO name Fresco)
Soviet Union and China

A logical development of the highly successful MiG-15 was to refine the airframe in an attempt to boost performance to supersonic level while retaining initially the VK-1

Below: Chinese-built MiG-15, sometimes known as the J-2.

Above: Shenyang JJ-5 tandem two-seat trainers, based on the J-5/MiG-17.

engine. The rear fuselage was lengthened, the tail unit modified to improve handling and, most importantly, the wings were changed to have a thinner section and rounded tips. However, sweepback remained at 42 degrees along part of the wing leading-edges, though the center section leading-edges were given greater sweep than the outer panels, and this is the reason for the often-quoted and misleading assertion that the later fighter had much sharper swept wings.

The cannon-armed first production version, known to NATO as Fresco-A, began to enter Soviet units in 1953, followed by the refined MiG-17P (Fresco-B) and then the major production day fighter version, the MiG-17F (Fresco-C). The MiG-17F was a milestone, the adoption of an afterburner to the engine giving the VK-1A a thrust of 7451 lb (3380 kg) and the aircraft a maximum speed of more than 700 mph (1127 km/h) at an altitude of 9850 ft (3000 m). Armament changes saw the deletion of the large 37-mm N-37 cannon, replaced by an extra NR-23, while pylons were provided under the wings for fighter-bomber missions and for carrying drop tanks.

The fighter still had another obvious step to take before being superseded by a later design, and with the MiG-17PF (Fresco-D) came limited all-weather capability. A non-afterburning variant was Fresco-E, which had the ability to carry four first-generation AA-1 Alkali air-to-air missiles, as did some MiG-17PFs. The radar fitted to the all-weather MiG was carried in a 'bullet' radome at the center of the air intake, which allowed neither a wide scanning angle nor a large antenna. It is thought that the radar fitted was an E/F-band version of 'Scan Fix' (NATO name), which can be regarded today as obsolescent.

In addition to Soviet production, the MiG-17 was produced in Czechoslovakia, Poland and China, the latter country's air-craft known as Shenyang J-5s in MiG-17F and J-5 Jias or J-5As in MiG-17PF forms. Without doubt, China currently operates the greatest number of MiG-17s, with an estimated 300 to 400 in the Air Force of the People's Liberation Army and several hundred with the Aviation of the People's Navy. However, as a fighter-bomber the MiG-17 remains a strong element of the Warsaw Pact forces outside of the Soviet Union, with Poland and Rumania alone having a combined strength of between 150 and 190.

Specifications (MiG-17F data)

Weapons: Three 23-mm NR-23 cannon, plus two 551-lb (250-kg) bombs or 4 pods each containing 8 rockets on underwing pylons.
Accommodation: The pilot.
Wingspan: 31 ft 7 in (9.63 m).
Length: 37 ft 3¼ in (11.36 m).
Maximum take-off weight: 13,379 lb (6069 kg).
Maximum speed: 711 mph (1145 km/h).
Range: 870 miles (1400 km).
Mission performance: Rate of climb at sea level 12,795 ft (3900 m) per min; ceiling 54,460 ft (16,600 m).
Engine: One 7451-lb (3380-kg) with afterburning Klimov VK-1A turbojet.

Versions in service

MiG-17F: Day fighter version, known to NATO as Fresco-C. Polish-built examples were given the designation LiM-6.
MiG-17PF: Limited all-weather version with Scan Fix radar. Known to NATO as Fresco-D.
J-5: Chinese designation for its own production series of MiG-17s beginning in 1956. This series includes the unique JJ-5 tandem 2-seat conversion trainer, which brought together the MiG-17PF airframe and the tandem cockpit arrangement of the MiG-15UTI. Powered by a nonafterburning Wopen engine (Chinese Klimov) with 1500 liters of fuel as standard, and armed with just one cannon in a removable underfuselage pack, it has a take-off weight of 13,700 lb (6215 kg) and a maximum speed of 651 mph (1048 km/h). Exported J-5 series aircraft designated as F-5 and FT-5 (the latter the JJ-5).
Operators: Afghanistan, Albania, Algeria, Bulgaria, China (air force and navy), Congo Republic, Equatorial Guinea, Ethiopia, Guinea, Malagasy Republic, Mali, Mozambique, Pakistan, Poland, Rumania, Somali Republic, Soviet Union (training?), Syria, Tanzania, Uganda, North Yemen and South Yemen.

Mikoyan MiG-19 and Shenyang J-6
(NATO name Farmer)
Soviet Union and China

First flown in 1953, the MiG-19 was the last of the early generation Soviet swept-wing fighters that included the MiG-15 and 17, and the first to give true supersonic performance while flying level (not just in a dive). The initial Farmer-A day fighter began equipping Soviet units in 1955 and was quickly followed by a succession of improved models that introduced some all-weather capability (Farmer-B) and missile armament (Farmer-D). Indeed, the late 1950s were important years in the strengthening of the Soviet air defense capabilities, as shown on 1 May 1960 when newly deployed surface-to-air missiles brought down a USAF reconnaissance aircraft as well as (unintentionally) a MiG-19 scrambled to intercept it.

Before the ideological rift between the

Below: Shenyang J-6s of various models operated by the Air Force of the People's Liberation Army.

Soviet Union and China, the latter had received MiG-19s for assembly. Thereafter, China put the MiG into production as a fighter, fighter-bomber and reconnaissance aircraft, and from 1962 began equipping its indigenous forces with its own J-6. This first model was based on the MiG-19S (Farmer-C) day fighter but others followed, as detailed below. Today the J-6 is the more important of the two basic types, operating with 13 air forces when including the F-6 export models. However, there is some confusion over the Iranian F-6s, which might have come from China, and not via North Korea as originally believed, but these were not thought operational by the close of 1986. This gives rise to speculation that Iran might also have received a number of older MiG-19s.

Specifications (F-6 data)

Radar: Izumrud interception radar in the J-6A and an indigenous radar in the J-6Xin.
Weapons: Three 30-mm NR-30 cannon in the wings and fuselage nose (in all versions except for the J-6A and JZ-6, which have only the wing guns). Air-to-air missiles or rockets, air-to-surface rockets, bombs, and so on carried on underwing pylons.
Accommodation: The pilot.
Wingspan: 30 ft 2 in (9.20 m).
Length: 48 ft 10½ in (14.90 m) with probe.
Maximum take-off weight: About 22,050 lb (10,000 kg).
Maximum speed: 957 mph (1540 km/h).
Range: 863 miles (1390 km).
Mission performance: Rate of climb at sea level more than 30,000 ft (9150 m) per min; ceiling 58,730 ft (17,900 m); endurance 2 h 38 min.
Engines: Two 7165-lb (3250-kg) thrust with afterburning Shenyang Wopen-6 turbojets, with 2170 liters of fuel standard.

Versions in service

MiG-19S/SF: NATO name Farmer-C. Day fighter-bomber, powered by two 7165-lb (3250-kg) thrust Klimov RD-9B turbojets. Maximum speed 902 mph (1452 km/h).
MiG-19PF: Farmer-D. Some all-weather capability bestowed by the addition of Izumrud interception radar. 2 cannon armament.
MiG-19PM: Also Farmer-D, differing from the PF in having no cannon but carrying 4 Alkali (NATO name) air-to-air missiles.
MiG-19R: Fighter-reconnaissance aircraft, carrying cameras and cannon.

Below: Xian F-7M Airguard, the Chinese export model of the Mikoyan MiG-21 featuring advanced Western avionics.

J-6: Chinese version of the MiG-19S/SF, and also known to NATO as Farmer-D.
J-6A: Chinese version of the MiG-19PF but with cannon and rockets.
J-6B: Chinese version of the MiG-19PM.
J-6C: Improved version of the J-6, with resited pneumatically deployed braking parachute.
J-6Xin: Similar to the J-6A but with indigenous radar in a very pointed conical radome in the nose intake.
JJ-6: Tandem 2-seat operational trainer, for which there is no Soviet equivalent.
JZ-6: Chinese version of the MiG-19R. 2 cannon.
F-6: Export versions of the J-6, with the ability to carry an underfuselage auxiliary fuel tank.
FT-6: Export 2-seat trainer version of the F-6.
Operators: Afghanistan (MiG-19), Albania (F-6), Bangladesh (F-6), China (air force and navy, MiG-19 and J-6), Cuba (MiG-19), Egypt (F-6), Iran (MiG-19 and F-6?), Iraq (F-6), Kampuchea (F-6), North Korea (MiG-19 and F-6), Pakistan (F-6), Somali Republic (F-6), Soviet Union (MiG-19?), Tanzania (F-6), Vietnam (F-6) and Zambia (F-6)

Mikoyan MiG-21 and Xian J-7
(NATO name Fishbed)
Soviet Union and China

The design of the MiG-17 and 19 had been established before the conclusion of the Korean War in the early 1950s, and were of similar basic configuration (substantially improved) to the MiG-15 that proved such a rival for US Sabres and other jets. From the experience of MiG-15s in combat, Mikoyan was able to formulate a totally new and improved fighter as the MiG-21. The most important factors were considered to be small size and light weight, a high rate of climb and good handling at higher speeds. As the Ye-4, a prototype of the MiG-21 flew for the first time on 16 June 1956, and subsequently the first production aircraft appeared as day fighters with cannon armament only and modest range. Known to NATO as Fishbed-As, these entered service but the numbers were small. Subsequent deployment of the Atoll (NATO name) air-to-air missile, the installation of the necessary avionics for all-weather capability and longer range brought much improved versions, of which the first was the MiG-21F (Fishbed-C), although this major service version added little to the

earlier fighters except for missile armament (only one cannon). Limited all-weather capability came with the MiG-21PF (Fishbed-D), the MiG-21PFM (Fishbed-F) introducing many improvements and the MiG-21PFMA a multi-role capability. However, although a very large number of countries still operate MiG-21s, the Soviet Air Force only retains about 720 fighters and 60 Fishbed-H reconnaissance aircraft, the MiG-23 being its major replacement type.

As the most-produced fighter in the world, the MiG-21 established itself with a great many air forces. It was also manufactured in Czechoslovakia and India, while China has been producing fairly modest numbers of a version known as the Xian J-7 for its indigenous forces and export (F-7 designation). There are also reports that Pakistan is looking into licensed production of the Xian F-7M at a future date, but in very altered form. With Grumman assistance, Pakistan is studying a version with a modern US turbofan engine, side air-intakes and a 'solid' nose for a new multimode radar.

Specifications (MiG-21MF Fishbed-J data)

Radar: 'Jay Bird' (NATO name) air-to-air search and tracking interception radar, carried in the shock-cone centerbody of the air intake. Tracking range is said to be 12.4 miles (20 km).
Weapons: One 23-mm GSh-23 cannon in the fuselage plus four air-to-air missiles of Atoll or Advanced Atoll type or rocket packs and/or bombs for ground attack.
Accommodation: The pilot.
Wingspan: 23 ft 5½ in (7.15 m).
Length: 51 ft 8½ in (15.76 m).
Maximum take-off weight: 20,723 lb (9400 kg).
Maximum speed: Mach 2.1.
Range: About 684 miles (1100 km).
Mission performance: Ceiling 59,000 ft (18,000 m; instantaneous turn rate at Mach 0.9 for the MiG-21US 13.4 degrees per sec.
Engine: One 14,550-lb (6600-kg) thrust with afterburning Tumansky R-13-300 turbojet, with 2600 liters of fuel standard.

Versions in service

MiG-21 Fishbed-C: First major service version and the oldest model still in use, suited to day operation only. 2 missiles and one cannon. One 12,675-lb (5750-kg) thrust with afterburning Tumansky R-11 engine.
MiG-21PF Fishbed-D: This represented the start of a new series, with a more contoured fuselage and 'Spin Scan A' radar for some all-weather capability. 13,117-lb (5950-kg) thrust with afterburning R-11 engine.
MiG-21 Fishbed-E: Similar to Fishbed-C but with a broader fin and allowance for an underfuselage pack containing a 23-mm cannon.
MiG-21FL Fishbed-D: Export version of the MiG-21PF. Can use the gun pack of Fishbed-E type.
MiG-21PFS: Similar to the MiG-21PF but with flap blowing as a standard design feature rather than a late introduction.
MiG-21 PFM Fishbed-F: Follow-on to the MiG-21PFS, with a broader fin, sideways-opening canopy, R2L radar and other changes.
MiG-21PFMA Fishbed-J: Multirole aircraft with 'Jay Bird' radar, four underwing pylons for AA and attack weapons, and a 13,669-lb (6200-kg) thrust with afterburning R-11-300 turbojet.

MiG-21R Fishbed-J: Reconnaissance version of the MiG-21PFMA, with 3 cameras or electronic intelligence sensors.

MiG-21MF Fishbed-J: This version entered service from 1969 as a MiG-21PFMA type with a more powerful engine. See above.

MiG-21M Fishbed-J: Export version, with an R-11F2S-300 turbojet.

MiG-21RF Fishbed-H: Improved reconnaissance aircraft, based on the MiG-21MF.

MiG-21SMB Fishbed-K: Longer-range aircraft based on the MiG-21MF but with additional fuel in a dorsal spine.

MiG-21bis Fishbed-L: Engine change to a 16,535-lb (7500-kg) thrust with afterburning Tumansky R-25 turbojet, improved avionics and better manufacturing standards typify this multirole aircraft.

MiG-21bis Fishbed-N: Much improved late model, with upgraded avionics and the ability to carry Atoll and Aphid missiles. Rate of climb is an amazing 58,070 ft (17,200 m) per min.

MiG-21U, US and UM: 2-seat operational trainers, known to NATO as Mongol and Mongol-B.

Xian J-7 and F-7: Chinese versions of the MiG-21, the F-7 as the export model. The original J-7 model used a Wopen-7 version of the Tumansky R-11 and was based on Fishbed-C. Later examples used the 11,245-lb (5100-kg) thrust with afterburning Wopen-7B. The J-7 II also has two 30-mm cannon and many other changes, and is known as the F-7B in export form.

Xian F-7M Airguard: Improved Chinese version, using a Wopen-7B(BM) engine and western avionics, such as the GEC Avionics Skyranger 226 lightweight radar, a head-up display, ECCM, etc.

Operators: All MiGs, unless otherwise stated. Afghanistan, Albania (F-7), Algeria, Angola, Bulgaria, China (air force and navy, J-7 series), Cuba, Czechoslovakia, Egypt (MiG-21 and F-7), Ethiopia, Finland, East Germany, Guinea, Hungary, India, Iraq, North Korea, Laos, Libya, Malagasy, Mongolia, Mozambique, Nigeria, Pakistan (F-7), Poland, Rumania, Somali Republic (F-7), Soviet Union, Sudan (F-7), Syria, Tanzania, Uganda, Vietnam, North Yemen, South Yemen, Yugoslavia and Zambia.

Mikoyan MiG-23 and MiG-27
(NATO name Flogger)
Soviet Union

Probably built in larger numbers than any other combat aircraft during the past 15 years, these swing-wing machines stem from a prototype demonstrated in 1967. They each have a single large and powerful afterburning turbojet engine, fed by lateral inlets, a high-mounted wing and slab tailplanes (the latter providing both pitch and roll control, roll being augmented by wing spoilers whenever the wings are not at the sharpest 72-degree sweep angle), large internal fuel capacity, and a very good main undercarriage which, despite folding into the fuselage (an action which extends an underfin at the tail), has wide track and very long-stroke 'soft' travel.

The last-mentioned feature is a help in operations from unsurfaced airstrips, and to this end the MiG-27 and MiG-23BN versions also have large low-pressure tires which

need a bulged fuselage when retracted. All MiG-23s have fully variable air inlets, a large engine afterburner and divergent nozzle for high supersonic performance at high altitudes, and most are fitted with radar and air-to-air missiles for the fighter mission. The MiG-27 is a dedicated ground attack model with plain inlets and a simple nozzle tailored to low-level (mainly subsonic) performance. MiG-27 versions have a shorter 'ducknose', giving improved downward view over the nose, packed with attack sensors but no main radar. The weapon pylons on the fuselage are moved out under the inlet ducts, and extra pylons are added on the flanks of the rear fuselage. The MiG-27 also has a different gun, slabs of side armor to protect the pilot, and a raised seat and canopy. The 23BNs are hybrids, similar to the MiG-27 in the nose and cockpit areas but resembling the other MiG-23s in propulsion system, gun and pylons. The Soviet Air Force alone is thought to include about 2200 MiG-23s in its inventory, some 400 or more on air defense duty and the remainder with tactical units, plus nearly 800 MiG-27s.

Specifications (Flogger-G data)
Radar: 'High Lark' (NATO name) J-band radar, with a search range of about 53 miles (85 km) and reportedly similar in capability to the US F-4J Phantom's Westinghouse radar. Other equipment includes a radar warning system.
Weapons: One 23-mm GSh-23L 2-barrel cannon plus up to 4410 lb (2000 kg) of weapons on 3 fuselage (2 as twin missile launchers) and 2 underwing pylons, normally comprising 2 Apex and 4 Aphid (NATO names) air-to-air missiles.
Accommodation: The pilot.
Wingspan: Spread 46 ft 9 in (14.25 m), swept 26 ft 9½ in (8.17 m).
Length: 59 ft 6½ in (18.15 m).
Maximum take-off weight: About 41,670 lb (18,900 kg).
Maximum speed: Mach 2.35.
Combat radius: 560-800 miles (900-1300 km).
Mission performance: Ceiling 65,620 ft (20,000 m).
Engine: One 27,550-lb (12,500-kg) thrust

Above: Mikoyan MiG-27 Flogger-D.

with afterburning Tumansky R-29B turbojet on Soviet examples, with 5750 liters of fuel standard.

Versions in service
MiG-23, S and SM Flogger-A: Prototypes, pre-production and early production aircraft with Lyulka AL-7F-1 engines.
MiG-23M Flogger-B: First major version, with a 22,487-lb (10,200-kg) thrust with afterburning R-27 engine. Deployed from 1972.
MiG-23MF Flogger-B: Much improved version, deployed from about 175. Higher rated R-29 engine and improved avionics including the addition of an IF sensor pod.
MiG-23U and UM Flogger-C: Tandem 2-seat trainers, relating to the MiG-23S and M respectively.
MiG-23MS Flogger-E: Export counterpart of Flogger-B, with Atoll missiles, 'Jay Bird' (NATO name) radar with a search range of only about 18.5 miles (30 km) and tracking range of 12.5 miles (20 km) and with no lookdown capability. No IR sensor pod. Operators include Algeria, Cuba, Iraq, North Korea and Libya.
MiG-23BN Flogger-F: Hybrid export fighter-bomber, with the general airframe of the MiG-27 matched to Flogger-B's engine, variable air intakes and gun. Laser rangefinder carried and no search radar. Operators include Algeria, Cuba, Egypt(?), Ethiopia, Iraq, Libya, Syria and Vietnam.
MiG-23 Flogger-G: Similar to Flogger-B but with changes to the fin (without the usual long leading edge), the radar and IR sensor pod. Exported to East Germany and Syria as well as in Soviet use.
MiG-23BN Flogger-H: Soviet service and export model, similar to Flogger-F but with added avionics. Export countries include Bulgaria, Czechoslovakia, India and Poland.
MiG-23 Flogger-K: Identified by the West in 1986, this very much improved and capable model has 'dogtooth' notches in the wing gloves to enhance stability at high angles of attack, smaller dorsal (of Flogger-G type) and ventral fins, some new avionics,

Braking-parachute housing

All-moving tailplane

Tumansky R-29B turbojet with afterburning

Two position ventral fin

Full-span three-section single-slotted flap

Leading-edge flap

pivoting weapon pylons under the variable outer panels of the wings, and the new and much improved AA-11 air-to-air missiles.
MiG-27 Flogger-D: First attack derivative of the MiG-23, with differences as noted above. Length 52 ft 6 in (16.00 m). Six-barrel 30-mm cannon and pylons for up to 9921 lb (4500 kg) of attack weapons, including Kerry (NATO name) tactical missiles. Maximum speed is thought to be around Mach 1.7 at high altitude and Mach 1.1 at low level. One 25,353-lb (11,500-kg) thrust with afterburning R-29B turbojet. Combat radius is about 242 miles (390 km).
MiG-27 Flogger-J: New avionics in slightly reshaped nose. 2 gun pods on underwing pylons.
MiG-27M Flogger-J: Export version, also being built by HAL in India (165 aircraft). IAF deployment started in 1986.
Operators: All MiG-23s, unless otherwise stated. Algeria, Bulgaria, Cuba, Czechoslovakia, Ethiopia, East Germany (MiG-23 and 27), Hungary, India (MiG-23 and 27), Iraq, North Korea, Libya, Poland, Rumania, Soviet Union (MiG-23 and 27), Syria, United States (perhaps three MiG-23s obtained from another country for nonoperational use) and Vietnam.

Above: Cutaway drawing showing internal detail of the MiG-23.
Below: Mikoyan MiG-23 Flogger-E, an export Flogger-B type used by Libya and others.

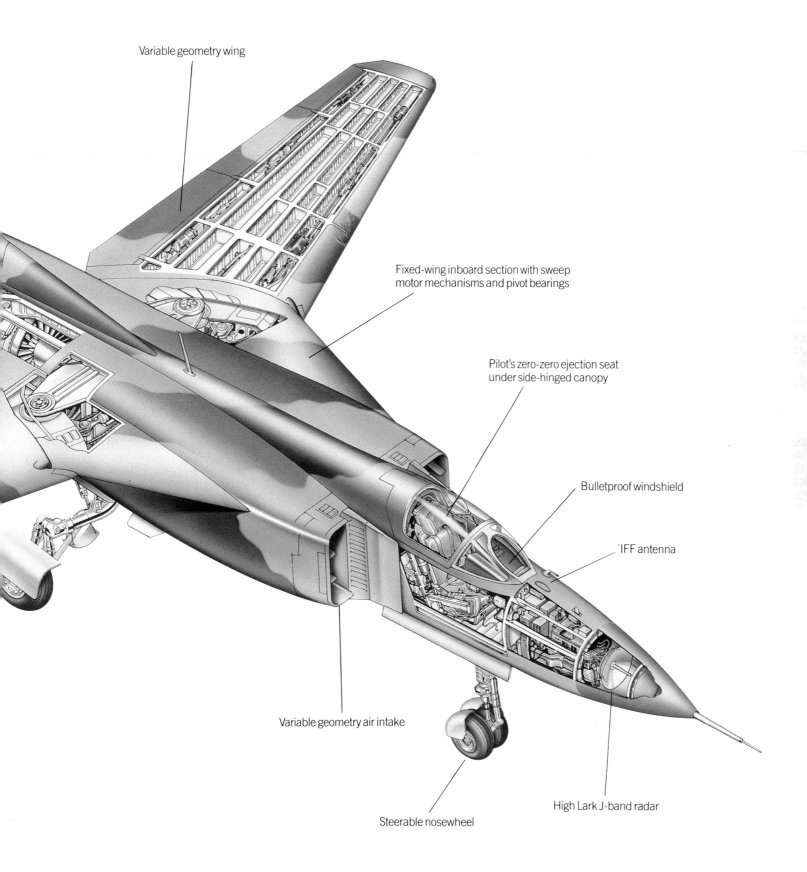

Variable geometry wing

Fixed-wing inboard section with sweep
motor mechanisms and pivot bearings

Pilot's zero-zero ejection seat
under side-hinged canopy

Bulletproof windshield

IFF antenna

Variable geometry air intake

High Lark J-band radar

Steerable nosewheel

Mikoyan MiG-25
(NATO name Foxbat)
Soviet Union

It is probably true to say that no modern Soviet Jet fighter/interceptor caused as much interest in the West as Foxbat, which appeared to be greatly superior to anything else when it was made public in 1967 during the Aviation Day flypast at Domodedovo. By then its existence had already been confirmed by the setting of a world speed record by a new aircraft in 1965 known as the Ye-266. Subsequent records established by the Ye-266 between 1967 and 1977 included the setting of an absolute altitude record of 123,523 ft (37,650 m) on 31 August 1977 by the Ye-266M, which remains unbeaten. The specially-prepared record-breaking MiG had also set new time-to-height records, of which many of the lower altitude ones were subsequently captured by the US F-15 Streak Eagle, though some have recently gone back to the Soviet Union by the efforts of the new Sukhoi Su-27. This showed that while Foxbat had the highest speed and operating altitude of any first-line combat aircraft in the world, its initial rate of acceleration was not as good, something confirmed by a defecting Soviet pilot who flew a Foxbat under Japanese radar to land in that country on 6 September 1976. Examination of this aircraft showed it to be mainly of steel construction, with titanium in areas of extreme temperatures, and that Mach 2.8 was probably the maximum speed with missiles carried.

The MiG-25 had been designed to counter the US North American B-70 Valkyrie Mach 3 strategic cruise bomber, intended to supersede the B-52. (Design of the Valkyrie had started in the 1950s and the first flew on 21 September 1964, but by then the bomber program had been cancelled and the huge Valkyrie became a research aircraft only.) So good

Below: Libyan Arab Air Force Mikoyan MiG-25 Foxbat-A, armed with two Acrid AAMs.

was the MiG that development continued anyway, with as much emphasis on reconnaissance as air defense as an interceptor. Today about 300 Foxbats serve with the Soviet Voyska PVO air defense interceptor force, with a similar number flying with tactical units as interceptors and reconnaissance aircraft. Enhanced capability has been given to Foxbat-As by conversion of many to Foxbat-E standard, which is nearer in capability to the derived and superior MiG-31 Foxhound. Exports of Foxbat have been made.

Specifications (Foxbat-A data)
Radar: 'Fox Fire' (NATO name) fire control radar, with a range of about 52 miles (85 km). Other equipment includes a radar warning system, ECCM, jammers and decoys.
Weapons: 2 Apex and 4 Aphid or new AA-11, or four Acrid air-to-air missiles (NATO names) on underwing pylons.
Accommodation: The pilot.
Wingspan: 45 ft 9 in (13.95 m).
Length: 78 ft 1¾ in (23.82 m).
Maximum take-off weight: 82,500 lb (37,425 kg).
Maximum speed: Mach 3.2.
Combat radius: 900 miles (1450 km).
Mission performance: Rate of climb at sea level 40,950 ft (12,480 m) per min; ceiling 80,000 ft (24,400 m).
Engines: Two 27,007-lb (12,250-kg) thrust with afterburning Tumansky R-31 turbojets, with about 17,410 liters of fuel standard.
Versions in service
MiG-25 Foxbat-A: Interceptor, as detailed above. Also exported to Algeria, Iraq, Libya and Syria.
MiG-25M Foxbat-E: Modified Foxbat-A, mainly to improve the radar which has lookdown/shootdown capability, and increase the thrust of each engine to 30,864-lb (14,000-kg) with afterburning. These and other improvements may assist in combating low-flying cruise missiles as well as manned aircraft. A number of

Libyan Foxbat-As have also been upgraded to this form.
MiG-25R: This designation applies to 2 models, known to NATO as Foxbat-B and D, serving as tactical and strategic reconnaissance aircraft. Both are unarmed and both carry SLAR, Foxbat-B having 5 cameras among its other equipment. Wingspan 44 ft 0 in (13.40 m). Also exported to India (B) and Libya (D).
MiG-25U: 2-seat trainer, with a second cockpit in a lengthened nose. Also exported to India.
Operators: Algeria, India, Iraq, Libya, Soviet Union and Syria.

Mikoyan MiG-29
(NATO name Fulcrum)
Soviet Union

With the MiG-31 Foxhound and Sukhoi Su-27 Flanker, Fulcrum represents the latest in Soviet fighter technology, indeed designed and equipped to end any technology failings compared to its Western counterparts. First flown during the late 1970s and operational with the Soviet air forces since 1985, Fulcrum is roughly comparable with the US Hornet, though more powerful, faster and with better air-to-air missiles, but with a more restricted view for the pilot and a rather unsophisticated HUD. It has a mostly metal airframe of blended design, with huge wingroot extensions that end level but well below the front of the canopy. The engines are fed with air from two huge low-slung underfuselage intakes, which have the unique feature of blanking off doors (activated automatically when the nosewheel touches down) to prevent ingestion of snow or objects off the runway, whereupon air is passed via louvers in the wingroots. This gives some indication of the poor conditions Warsaw Pact aircraft sometimes have to operate in, because of bad weather or in order to deploy in the widest manner. The radar is said to be roughly equivalent in capability to the US AN/APG-68, offering all-weather day-and-night operation against low targets and the ability to fly independently of ground control during air defense interceptions.

Production of Fulcrum is on a massive scale, and in 1986 it was estimated that more than 150 were already operational with Soviet forces. In addition, Syria has received a number against its requirement for 80, and in early 1987 India too had begun receiving examples. Eventually, license production will take place in India.

Specifications
Radar: Pulse-Doppler multimode radar with lookdown/shootdown capability. Other equipment includes an IF search and tracking sensor, and a radar warning system.
Weapons: One 30-mm 6-barrel cannon plus 6 AA-10 and/or AA-11 air-to-air missiles under the wings, or attack weapons in a secondary role.
Accommodation: The pilot.
Wingspan: 37 ft 9 in (11.50 m).
Length: 56 ft 5 in (17.20 m).
Take-off weight with AAMs: 36,376 lb (16,500 kg) estimated.
Maximum speed: Mach 2.2 estimated.
Combat radius: 714 miles (1150 km) estimated.

Above: The new Mikoyan MiG-29 Fulcrum counter-air fighter, carrying the latest AAMs.

Engines: Two 18,298-lb (8300-kg) thrust with afterburning Tumansky R-33D turbofans.

Versions in service

MiG-29: Apart from the single-seat counter-air fighter, a 2-seat training version with full combat capability is in production and service.

Operators: India, Soviet Union and Syria. Other operators will undoubtedly follow.

Mikoyan MiG-31
(NATO name Foxhound)
Soviet Union

Deployment of the MiG-25 Foxbat gave the Soviet Air Force an interceptor and reconnaissance aircraft that could fly faster and higher than Western contemporaries. This capability was particularly exploited in the reconnaissance role. To build upon this success, in the 1970s Mikoyan began developing a follow-on of lower maximum speed but far more formidable in capability and firepower, with the ability to fly at supersonic speeds at low altitude and thereby making it an interceptor of cruise missiles as well as aircraft. This was the MiG-31, deployment of which began in 1983 with the Voyska PVO home defense force and then with strategic recon-

Right: The formidable Mikoyan MiG-31 Foxhound, photographed by an intercepting Royal Norwegian Air Force fighter.
Below: Harbin Z-5, a Chinese-built Mil Mi-4.

naissance units. To date well over 100 are operational, mostly as interceptors but some 24 in reconnaissance form. Production continues at a high rate.

Compared to the MiG-25, the MiG-31 has more powerful engines, leading-edge extensions to the wings, a crew of two, much improved radar with full lookdown/shootdown capability and provision for six or eight air-to-air missiles.

Specifications

Radar: New long-range pulse-Doppler radar, the first Soviet type with full lookdown/shootdown, and multitarget tracking/engagement capabilities. Other operational equipment includes infrared search/active tracker, ECM, and radar warning receivers.

Weapons: Could be up to eight Amos long-range air-to-air missiles or a mix of Amos and Aphid missiles.

Accommodation: 2 crew under a low flush canopy.

Wingspan: 45 ft 11 in (14.00 m).

Length: 70 ft 6 in (21.50 m).

Maximum take-off weight: 90,700 lb (41,150 kg).

Maximum speed: Mach 2.4.

Combat radius: 1305 miles (2100 km).

Engines: Two 30,865-lb (14,000-kg) thrust with afterburning Tumansky turbojets, possibly related to the R-266/R-31, with perhaps 17,410 liters of fuel standard.

Versions in service

MiG-31: Already operational in interceptor and strategic reconnaissance forms.

Operator: Soviet Union.

Mil Mi-4 and Harbin Z-5
(NATO name Hound)
Soviet Union and China

Often compared to the Sikorsky S-55, the Mil Mi-4 was in fact larger than the US helicopter, with clamshell doors in the rear of the fuselage through which even vehicles could be loaded, and military versions had an under-fuselage gondola for an observer. The true successor to the Mi-1, it was first flown in May 1952 and entered military service from 1953. Soviet production up to 1969 is believed to have totalled around 3500, while about another 1000 were constructed in China for 20 years from 1959 as Harbin Z-5s; the Z-5 was the first helicopter built in China by Harbin. Mi-4 variants included one for land-based antisubmarine warfare, but this has been superseded by the Mi-14 Haze, while a communications-jamming model with many antennae on the fuselage was not identified until 1977 and represents an ECM type by conversion.

Specifications (Mi-4 data)

Weapons: One machine-gun and rockets can be carried.
Accommodation: 2 crew plus 14 troops, 8 stretchers and an attendant, 3527 lb (1600 kg) of freight, a vehicle or large gun.
Diameter of rotor: 68 ft 11 in (21.00 m).
Fuselage length: 55 ft 1 in (16.80 m).
Maximum take-off weight: 17,196 lb (7800 kg).
Maximum speed: 130 mph (210 km/h).
Range: 249 miles (400 km).
Mission performance: Ceiling 18,050 ft (5500 m).
Engine: One 1700-hp Shvetsov ASh-82V radial piston.

Versions in service

Mi-4: Currently operated versions include the Hound-A basic transport helicopter and the ECM Hound-C. The Hound-B for ASW and carrying search radar is probably not used for this purpose any longer. SAR might be a current Mi-4 role.
Harbin Z-5: Chinese version of the Mi-4, with Huosai-5A (Chinese ASh-82Vs) engines. Perhaps 300 may remain with the Air Force of the People's Liberation Army and 40 with the Aviation of the People's Navy.
Operators: Afghanistan, Albania, Algeria, Bulgaria (air force and navy), China (air force and navy), Cuba, Iraq, North Korea, Mali, Mongolia, Poland (air force and navy), Rumania, Somali Republic, Soviet Union and Vietnam.

Below: Mil Mi-6 heavy transport helicopters.

Mil Mi-6 (NATO name Hook)
Soviet Union

The Mi-6 is the mainstay heavy lift helicopter of the Soviet forces, an estimated 350 to 450 of the approximately 600 delivered remaining operational. Though its payload is now dwarfed by that of the Mi-26, the Mi-6 was the largest helicopter in the world at the time of its appearance in the late 1950s. Apart from its size, special design features are its clamshell rear fuselage doors for straight-in loading and large wings which give about 20 percent of the 'lift' for cruising. The wings are removable when the helicopter is operating as a flying-crane.

Specifications

Weapons: One 12.7-mm machine-gun in the glazed nose of some examples.
Accommodation: 5 crew plus 70 equipped troops, 26,455 lb (12,000 kg) of internal or 17,635 lb (8000 kg) of external freight, or 41 stretchers and 2 attendants.
Wingspan: 50 ft 2 in (15.30 m).
Diameter of rotor: 114 ft 10 in (35.00 m).
Fuselage length: 108 ft 10 in (33.18 m).
Maximum take-off weight: 93,700 lb (42,500 kg).
Maximum speed: 186 mph (300 km/h).
Range: 621 miles (1000 km) with a 9921-lb (4500-kg) load.
Mission performance: Ceiling 14,760 ft (4500 m).
Engines: Two 5500-shp Soloviev D-25V turboshafts.

Version in service

Mi-6: As detailed above.
Operators: Algeria, Iraq (army), Peru, Soviet Union and Vietnam.

Mil Mi-8, Mi-14 and Mi-17
(NATO names Hip, Haze and Hip-H)
Soviet Union

First seen publicly in 1961, the Mi-8 medium transport helicopter has been the subject of truly massive production, with well over 10,000 built (including the derived Mi-17). Of those for military use, the bulk have gone into Soviet service, although 37 other countries deploy Mi-8s (and some Mi-17s also). Among the versions, distinguished by their NATO code names, is the Hip-E, recognized as one of the most heavily armed helicopters in the world and standard to Soviet army support units.

The Mi-17 is a refined and more-powerful new version of the Mi-8, with two 1900-shp TV3-117MT turboshafts; Mi-8s can be upgraded to Mi-17 standard if required.

The Mi-14, also an Mi-8 variant, is an important land-based antisubmarine and mine-countermeasures helicopter, of which the Soviet Navy alone has more than one hundred. With a watertight hull and sponsons to bestow amphibious qualities, it carries Doppler radar, search radar, sonar, sonobuoys and MAD. If a submarine or surface vessel is located, an attack can be mounted with torpedoes or depth charges from the hull bay.

Specifications (Mi-8 data)

Radar: Doppler radar. Infrared suppressors and IR decoy dispensers carried.
Weapons: Antiarmor missiles, rockets and guns, as detailed below.
Accommodation: 2/3 crew plus 32 troops, 12 stretchers and an attendant, or 8818 lb (4000 kg) of internal or 6614 lb (3000 kg) of slung freight.
Diameter of rotor: 69 ft 10 in (21.29 m).
Fuselage length: 59 ft 7½ in (18.17 m).
Maximum take-off weight: 26,455 lb (12,000 kg).
Maximum speed: 161 mph (260 km/h).
Range: 289 miles (465 km).
Mission performance: Ceiling 14,765 ft (4500 m); hovering ceiling in ground effect 6235 ft (1900 m); hovering ceiling out of ground effect 2625 ft (800 m).
Engines: Two 1700-shp Isotov TV2-117A turboshafts, with 1870 liters of fuel standard.

Versions in service

Hip-C: Assault helicopter, carrying troops and with provision for 128 57-mm rockets or other armament to suppress enemy fire while operating in forward areas.
Hip-D: Communications helicopter, with antennae and special equipment.
Hip-E: Fire support helicopter, carrying perhaps a nose-mounted 12.7-mm gun, 4 Swatter (NATO name) anti-armor missiles, and 192 rockets.
Hip-F: Export Hip-E, with 6 Sagger (NATO name) anti-armor missiles plus rockets.
Hip-G: Improved communications helicopter.
Hip-H: Mi-17, with more powerful engines and other changes. See above.
Hip-J: ECM helicopter.

Above: Mil Mi-8 in Peruvian Air Force service.

Hip-K: ECM helicopter, for communications jamming.
Mi-14: Land-based ASW (Haze-A) and mine-countermeasures (Haze-B) helicopters, with two TV3-117 turboshafts. Maximum speed 143 mph (230 km/h); range 575 miles (925 km). An estimated 10 Haze-Bs are in Soviet Navy use.
Operators: All Mi-8 operators, unless otherwise stated. Afghanistan, Algeria, Angola (-8, -14 and -17), Bangladesh, Bulgaria (-8 and -14), China, Cuba (-8, -14 and -17), Czechoslovakia, Egypt, Ethiopia, Finland, East Germany (air force and navy, -8 and -14), Guinea-Bissau, Hungary, India (-8 and -17), Iraq (army), Kampuchea, North Korea, Laos, Libya (-8 and -14), Malagasy, Mali, Mongolia, Mozambique, Nicaragua (-8 and -17), Pakistan (army), Peru (-8 and -17), Poland (air force and navy, -8 and -14), Rumania (-8 and -14), Somali Republic, Soviet Union (air force and navy, -8, -14 and -17), Syria (-8 and -17), Uganda, Vietnam, North Yemen, South Yemen, Yugoslavia and Zambia.

Below: An early example of the Mil Mi-10 demonstrating its capabilities.

Mil Mi-10 (NATO name Harke)
Soviet Union

First seen publicly in 1961, the Mi-10 is a large flying-crane helicopter with a tall quadricycle undercarriage that has a wheel track of 6.01 meters on the nose units to allow it to stand over its cargo. A more specialized model followed as the Mi-10K, with a lower undercarriage and other changes but for a similar role. It is believed some ten Mi-10s are in Soviet Air Force use.

Specifications
Accommodation: Flight crew of 3, 28 passengers in the main cabin, and up to a 17,637-lb (8000-kg) sling load. A freight platform can be carried.
Diameter of rotor: 114 ft 10 in (35.00 m).
Fuselage length: 107 ft 10 in (32.86 m).
Maximum take-off weight: 96,342 lb (43,700 kg).
Maximum speed: 124 mph (200 km/h).
Range: 155 miles (250 km).
Mission performance: Ceiling 9840 ft (3000 m).
Engines: Two 5500-shp Soloviev D-25V turboshafts.
Version in service
Mi-10: As described above.
Operator: Soviet Union.

Mil Mi-24 and Mi-25
(NATO name Hind)
Soviet Union

Design of the Mil Mi-24 seems to have originated in the mid-1960s, probably at a time when all development work on the Mil Mi-8 had been completed. The resulting multirole military combat helicopter combines a dedicated gunship with the main cabin as an assault transport, seating up to eight armed troops. The slender forward fuselage originally seated a crew of three, but now provides tandem accommodation for a weapons operator and the pilot who has a raised position to give an unobstructed forward field of view. Incorporating features borrowed from the Mil Mi-8/Mi-14 family, and with a dynamic system based on that of the Mi-8, the Mi-24's reduced size and the installation of turboshaft engines developing some 30 percent more power than those of the Mi-8, mean that this helicopter is more maneuverable and much faster. In fact it has a maximum speed some 31 mph (50 km/h) greater than the Mi-8, and this is undoubtedly due in part to stub wings which span an estimated 24 ft (7.32 m) and help to offload the main rotor in high-speed flight. The wings also incorporate four underwing pylons that can carry a weapon load of up to 3307 lb (1500 kg), as well as twin launch rails at each wingtip for AT-2 Swatter antitank missiles.

Undoubtedly a formidable military helicopter, the Mi-24's existence became known to Western sources during 1972, approximately a year before it entered service (with the initial deployment being made in East Germany). Since that time several variants of the Mi-24 have been developed for such roles as armed assault, anti-armor attack and for helicopter escort with the capability to take on enemy helicopters in air-to-air combat. Involvement in Afghanistan has emphasized that in the Mi-24 the Soviet Union has a weapon that complements fixed-wing aircraft of Su-25 Frogfoot type in heavy ground attack roles, a factor underlined by production figures that in 1987 must be approaching the 2500 mark in a number of variants. Such capability has proved attractive to nations that rely on the Soviet Union for their major equipment supplies and some versions with somewhat altered equipment have been exported; some of those exported are believed to carry the designation Mil Mi-25.

Specifications (Mi-24 Hind-D data, estimated)

Weapons: One 12.7-mm 4-barrel machine-gun in an undernose turret. 4 pylons on the stub wings for up to 3307 lb (1500 kg) of weapons, including rocket pods, conventional bombs, and other stores; wingtip launcher rails for four AT-2 Swatter antitank missiles.
Accommodation: Pilot and gunner in tandem stepped cockpits.
Diameter of rotor: 55 ft 9 in (17.00 m).
Length with rotors: 70 ft 6½ in (21.50 m).
Maximum take-off weight: 24,250 lb (11,000 kg).
Maximum speed: 193 mph (310 km/h).

Combat radius: 99 miles (160 km) with full load.
Mission performance: Rate of climb at sea level 2460 ft (750 m) per min; ceiling 14,765 ft (4500 m).
Engines: Two 2200-shp Isotov TV3-117 turboshafts.

Versions in service
Hind-A: Original assault version identified easily by its large enclosed flight deck for a crew of 3 and stub wings with pronounced anhedral. Early production models had TV2-117 turboshafts; late production TV3-117s tail rotor repositioned on port side of tailfin.
Hind-B: Generally similar to Hind-A except for level stub wings. No wingtip launch rails.
Hind-C: Training version of late production Hind-A, without the nose gun. Undernose fairing and wingtip launch rails for antitank missiles.
Hind-D: Generally similar to late production

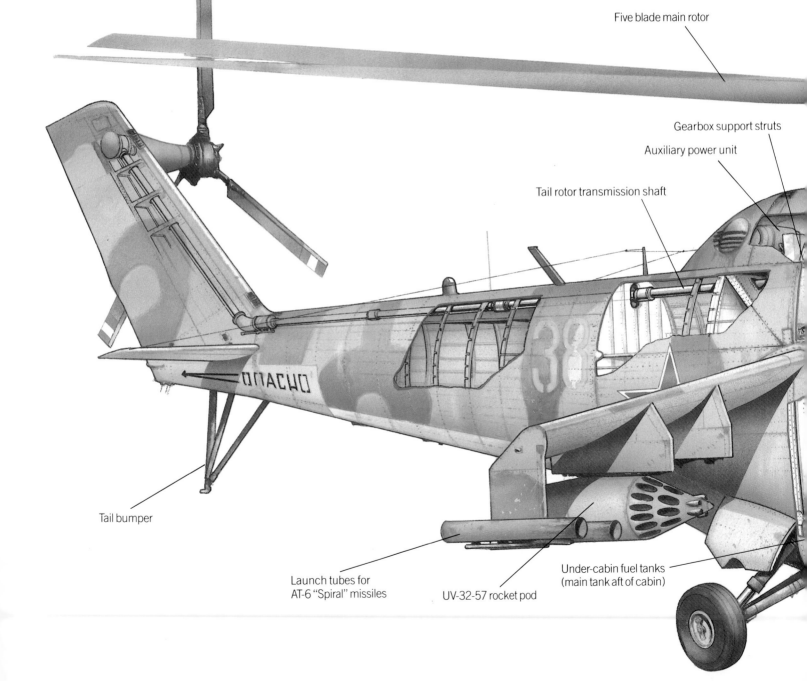

Five blade main rotor

Gearbox support struts

Auxiliary power unit

Tail rotor transmission shaft

Tail bumper

Launch tubes for
AT-6 "Spiral" missiles

UV-32-57 rocket pod

Under-cabin fuel tanks
(main tank aft of cabin)

Hind-A but introducing tandem gunship-type cockpits for crew of two. Nosewheels partly exposed when 'up'.
Hind-E: Generally as Hind-D but with wingtip and underwing pylons suitable for the carriage of twelve AT-6 Spiral antitank missiles.
Hind-F: Generally as Hind-E but with the nose gun turret removed and replaced by twin 30-mm cannon in a pack on the starboard side of the fuselage.
Mi-25: Export version of the Mi-24 although some Mi-24s have also been exported.
Operators: Afghanistan, Algeria, Angola, Bulgaria, Cuba, Czechoslovakia, Ethiopia, East Germany, Hungary, India, Iraq, Libya, Mozambique, Nicaragua, Poland, Soviet Union, Syria, Vietnam and South Yemen.

Left: US Department of Defense impression of Mil Mi-24 Hind-D gunship helicopters being used to spray chemicals from pylon tanks.
Below: Cutaway drawing of a Mil Mi-24 Hind-F helicopter.

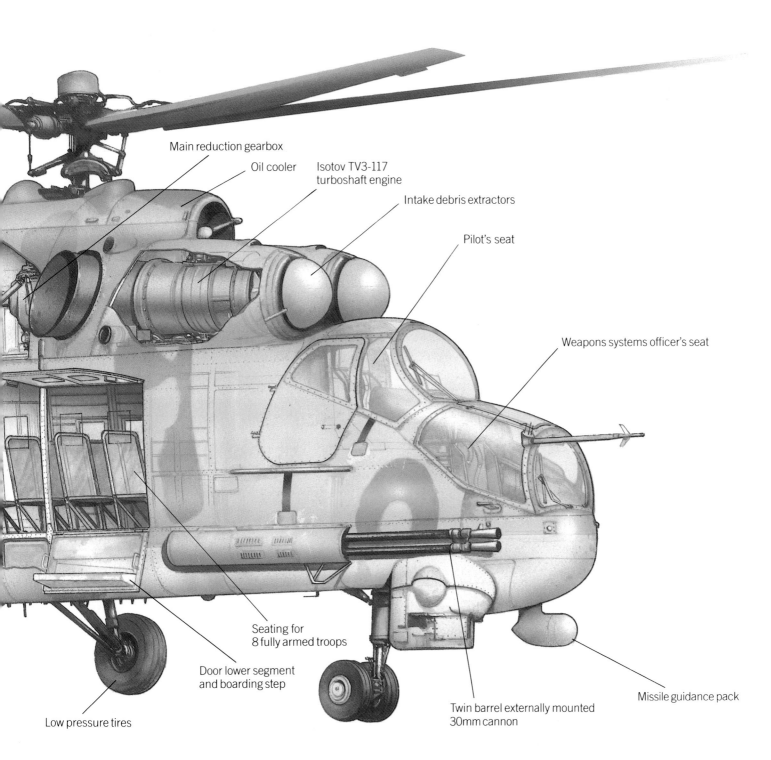

Main reduction gearbox

Oil cooler

Isotov TV3-117 turboshaft engine

Intake debris extractors

Pilot's seat

Weapons systems officer's seat

Seating for 8 fully armed troops

Door lower segment and boarding step

Low pressure tires

Twin barrel externally mounted 30mm cannon

Missile guidance pack

Mil Mi-26 (NATO name Halo)
Soviet Union

The Mi-26 combines the cargo-carrying potential of a fixed-wing transport aircraft of Antonov An-12 Cub class with the flight capabilities of a helicopter, suited to day/night and all-weather flying: it is therefore a heavy lift helicopter with enormous operational possibilities. Apart from being the largest operational (civil and military) helicopter in the world, only second in size to the Mil Mi-12 twin-rotor machine that remained a prototype, it is the heaviest and most powerful, and the first to operate using an eight-blade main rotor to keep the diameter moderate. It currently holds five world payload-to-height records for helicopters, including lifting a 20,000-kg load to 15,090 ft (4600 m), set in February 1982. The initial prototype Mi-26 must have flown in the late 1970s and military examples became operational in 1985. The first export Halos went to India in June 1986.

Specifications
Radar: Weather radar in the nose.
Accommodation: 5 crew and up to 20,000 kg (44,090 lb) of freight in a cabin 39 ft 4 in (12.00 m) long, 10 ft 8 in (3.25 m) wide and up to 10 ft 5 in (3.17 m) high. Small compartment to the rear of the flight deck for 4 persons accompanying the mission. Some 40 tip-up troop seats along the main cabin walls, though the maximum troop capacity is 85. Loads can include vehicles, driven into the cabin through clamshell doors under the boom via a ramp.
Diameter of rotor: 105 ft 0 in (32.00 m).
Fuselage length: 110 ft 8 in (33.73 m).
Maximum take-off weight: 123,460 lb (56,000 kg).
Maximum speed: 183 mph (295 km/h).
Range: 497 miles (800 km) with reserves.

Below: Seen here in Aeroflot colors, the Soviet Mil Mi-26 is the world's largest operational helicopter.

Mission performance: Ceiling 15,090 ft (4600 m); hovering ceiling out of ground effect 5900 ft (1800 m).
Engines: Two 11,400-shp Lotarev D-136 turboshafts.
Version in service
Mi-26: Being produced in civil and military forms, undoubtedly in substantial numbers.
Operators: India and Soviet Union.

Mil Mi-28 (NATO name Havoc)
Soviet Union

In a shift away from the bulky attack helicopter of Hind-D/E/F type, Mil has recently put into production a new combat helicopter much more closely akin to the US Army's Apache. Without any troop-carrying capability, it has the gunner/copilot and pilot seated in tandem height-staggered cockpits protected by fuselage armor. A nose radome

Above: US Department of Defense impression of the new Mil Mi-28 combat helicopter.

houses radar, and glazed panels in the lower fuselage nose probably contain a laser designator and marked target seeker or low light level TV. Survivability in the battle area is enhanced by the narrow frontal area and low silhouette of the fuselage, aided by IR decoy dispensers, IR jammers and suppressors. The exhaust from the engines is directed upward to reduce the IR signature.

Specifications
Radar: Radar is carried in a nose radome.
Weapons: A large-caliber single-barrel cannon is carried in an underfuselage turret. The anhedral stub wings have two pylons each, the inboard for a rocket pack or other armament and the tip pylon for twin-round missile launchers (air-to-air or air-to-surface).
Accommodation: Pilot and gunner/copilot in tandem, the former in a much raised rear cockpit.
Diameter of rotor: 55 ft 9 in (17.00 m) estimated.
Fuselage length: 57 ft 1 in (17.40 m) estimated.
Maximum take-off weight: Unknown.
Maximum speed: 186 mph (300 km/h).
Combat radius: 149 miles (240 km).
Mission performance: Unknown.
Engines: 2 turboshaft engines of unidentified type; the Mi-14, Mi-17 and Mi-24 use examples of the 2200-shp Isotov TV3-117, and therefore it is possible that the Mi-28 also adopts 2 similar engines.
Version in service
Mi-28: 2-seat attack helicopter, first made known publicly by the US Department of Defense in 1984.
Operator: Soviet Union.

Mitsubishi F-1 and T-2
Japan

These are respectively a single-seat close-support fighter and a two-seat trainer, grouped together for this single entry as the fighter was a direct development of the trainer and thereby has the same airframe and engines.

Above: Mitsubishi F-1 close support fighter.
Right: Mitsubishi T-2 supersonic trainer in the colors of the JASDF's Blue Impulse aerobatic team, its braking parachute streamed.

The T-2, Japan's first indigenous supersonic jet, first flew as a prototype on 20 July 1971. Ninety have been acquired by the JASDF as two-seat T-2 advanced and T-2A combat trainers. The latter carries a 20-mm Vulcan JM61 multibarrel cannon in the fuselage and has seven weapons stations which include wingtip points for Sidewinder air-to-air missiles.

First flying as a prototype on 3 June 1975, the F-1 close-support fighter entered JASDF service in production form in 1977 and deliveries of the 77 aircraft ordered ended in 1986. These serve with units at Tsuiki and Misawa. Both the F-1 and T-2 types have cockpit HUDs, but the radars differ (as detailed below).

Specifications (F-1 data)
Radar: Mitsubishi Electric J/AWG-12 multimode radar with air-to-air and air-to-ground capabilities.
Weapons: Cannon plus attachment stations as for T-2, for up to 6000 lb (2722 kg) of weapons. These can include 4 Sidewinder air-to-air missiles, 2 Type 80 (ASM-1) antiship missiles, or twelve 500-lb (227-kg) bombs, rocket pods, etc.
Accommodation: The pilot.
Wingspan: 25 ft 10¼ in (7.88 m).
Length: 58 ft 7 in (17.86 m).
Maximum take-off weight: 30,203 lb (13,700 kg).
Maximum speed: Mach 1.6.
Mission performance: Rate of climb at sea level 35,000 ft (10,670 m) per min; ceiling 50,000 ft (15,240 m).
Engines: Two 7305-lb (3313-kg) thrust with afterburning Rolls-Royce/Turboméca Adour Mk 801A turbofans, with 3823 liters of fuel standard.
Versions in service
T-2/2A: 2-seat trainers. Operated by the 4th Air Wing based at Matsushima. The radar fitted is the J/AWG-11 search and ranging type. The T-2A is armed for combat training.
F-1: Single-seat close-support fighter, developed from the T-2.
Operator: Japan.

Mudry CAP 10B
France

Constructed of wood, with wood and fabric covering, this side-by-side two-seat aerobatic aircraft has found some success as an unarmed military basic trainer, although the majority have gone into civil use. Derived from the French Piel Emeraude homebuilt aircraft, it has a fixed-tailwheel undercarriage and provision for equipment options that can include IFR standard instrumentation. Instructor and pupil have parachutes.

Specifications
Accommodation: Instructor and pupil.
Wingspan: 26 ft 5¼ in (8.06 m).
Length: 23 ft 6 in (7.16 m).
Take-off weight for aerobatics: 1675 lb (760 kg).
Maximum speed: 168 mph (270 km/h).
Range: 745 miles (1200 km).
Mission performance: Rate of climb at sea level 1180 ft (360 m) per min; ceiling 16,400 ft (5000 m); G limits +6, −4.5.
Engine: One 180-hp Avco Lycoming AEIO-360-B2F piston, with 72 liters of fuel standard.
Version in service
CAP 10B: With 1829 lb (830 kg) alternative utility maximum weight.
Operators: France (air force and navy), Mexico and Morocco.

Below: French Air Force CAP 10B.

Above: Equipe de Voltige Aérienne (EVA) CAP 20s.

Mudry CAP 20 and 230
France

The CAP 20 is a single-seater of all-wood construction except for the plastic engine cowling. Power is provided by a 200-hp Avco Lycoming AIO-360 piston engine with a fuel system to allow inverted flight. Six are in French Air Force service with the Equipe de Voltige Aérienne aerobatic team at Salon-de-Provence alongside some CAP 10Bs.

Using the engine of the Epsilon trainer, the CAP 230 is of similar, but not identical, overall dimensions to the CAP 20, but is a considerably more powerful aircraft. It was derived from the CAP 21. First flown in October 1985, at the time of writing small numbers had been ordered for aerobatic use with the teams of France and Morocco.

Specifications (CAP 230 data)
Accommodation: Pilot only.
Wingspan: 26 ft 6 in (8.08 m).
Length: 22 ft 1¾ in (6.75 m).
Take-off weight: 1543 lb (700 kg).
Maximum cruising speed: 198 mph (320 km/h).
Range: 465 miles (750 km).
Mission performance: G limits +10, −10.
Engine: One 300-hp Avco Lycoming AEIO-540 piston.
Versions in service
CAP 20: Being replaced by CAP 230s in Equipe de Voltige Aérienne.
CAP 230: Deliveries began in mid-1986.
Operators: France and Morocco.

Below: Myasishchev M-4 Bison.

Myasishchev M-4
(NATO name Bison)
Soviet Union

The huge M-4 strategic bomber was a complementary design to the Tupolev Tu-95, using four turbojet engines carried in the wingroots rather than the turboprops of the Tupolev. But although this engine choice made the M-4 a more modern-looking bomber and nearer in conception to the US Stratofortress, it could not match the Tupolev in mission performance as a carrier of thermonuclear free-fall bombs over intercontinental ranges. Most particularly, its service ceiling was too low and thereby required heavy defensive armament even by Soviet standards.

A prototype of the M-4 was first displayed over Moscow in May 1954. In operational service it was always eclipsed by the Tu-95, and although today about 75 remain in active use they are flown mainly for tasks other than those for which the aircraft was designed. All versions use tandem main bogie and outrigger undercarriage units (of Boeing B-47 type). Bison-A bombers concentrate on missions over Europe and Asia, both land and maritime, while others have specific maritime reconnaissance roles or act as flight refuelling tankers. The last can be regarded as the aircraft's most important role today, serving to extend the ranges of the Soviet strategic bomber force and tactical attack-bombers. As M-4s are superseded even in these roles, by such types as the Il-76 Midas, they are put into reserve store. This is in marked contrast to the Tu-95, which is still manufactured to keep up the numbers flying operationally and are more than ever found flying over international waters towards the United States making what are judged to be mock missile-launch attacks.

Specifications (Bison-A unless otherwise stated)
Radar: The radar carried by the M-4 maritime aircraft is believed to be Puff Ball (NATO name) and I-band search radar that can scan over large areas for the detection of shipping.
Weapons: See 'Versions in service.'
Wingspan: 165 ft 7 in (50.48 m).
Length: 154 ft 10 in (47.20 m).
Maximum take-off weight: 350,000 lb (158,750 kg).
Maximum speed: 621 mph (1000 km/h).
Range: 4971 miles (8000 km) with 12,000 lb (5443 kg) of bombs, unrefuelled.
Mission performance: Ceiling 45,000 ft (13,715 m).
Engines: Four 19,180-lb (8700-kg) thrust Mikulin AM-3D turbojets.
Versions in service
Bison-A: NATO name for the original and only strategic bomber version. 8 to 10 23-mm NR-23s are carried in twin-cannon turrets above and below the fuselage and at the tail. 3 bays for nuclear or conventional weapons.
Bison-B: First maritime reconnaissance version with specialized electronics, identifiable by a radome in place of the glazed nose of the bomber. Self-defense armament is reduced to 6 cannon. Not many remain active.
Bison-C: Improved version of Bison-B, with a longer nose housing a large surveillance radar. The C has also become the carrier aircraft for the Soviet space shuttle orbiter during the initial test phases, as was a Boeing 747 for the US orbiter.
Bison-A tanker: Bombers converted into flight refuelling tankers with probe-and-drogue systems operate in support of Backfire, Bison, Bear and Blinder bombers.
Operator: Soviet Union.

NAMC YS-11
Japan

The YS-11 was designed as a short/medium-range turboprop airliner and many went into commercial service. The prototype made its maiden flight on 30 August 1962. The JASDF and JMSDF also received examples for various roles and were the only military operators until the Hellenic Air Force took over six ex-Olympic Airways airliners in 1980 as transports.

Above: JASDF NAMC YS-11 multimission air transport.

Specifications (YS-11A-218 data)

Accommodation: 2 crew plus 60 passengers.
Wingspan: 104 ft 11¾ in (32.00 m).
Length: 86 ft 3½ in (26.30 m).
Maximum take-off weight: 54,013 lb (24,500 kg).
Cruising speed: 291 mph (469 km/h).
Range: 677-1998 miles (1090-3215 km).
Mission performance: Rate of climb at sea level 1220 ft (372 m) per min; ceiling 22,900 ft (6980 m).
Engines: Four 3060-ehp Rolls-Royce Dart RDa 10/1 Mk 542-10K turboprops, with 7270 liters of fuel.

Versions in service
YS-11-103: VIP transport operated by JASDF.
YS-11-105: VIP transport operated by JASDF.
YS-11A-206: JMSDF ASW training model, carrying radar.
YS-11A-218: JASDF transport.
YS-11A-305: JASDF transport for 46 passengers and freight as a mixed payload.
YS-11A-400: JMSDF cargo transport, of which four are flown by one squadron as YS-11Ms.
YS-11A-402: JASDF cargo transport.
YS-11E: JASDF electronic warfare trainer.
YS-11T: Training version.
Operators: Greece (YS-11A) and Japan (air force, YS-11, A and E; navy YS-11, A, M and T).

Nanchang Q-5 (NATO name Fantan)
China

Because of the design age of some of the aircraft in production in China, it is easy to believe that only recently has the indigenous aircraft industry had the courage to develop its own aircraft. But this is not strictly the case. As far back as 1958 the design began of an attack aircraft intended for first-line service, which first flew on 5 June 1965 and entered service around 1970 as the Q-5. Of course this was based heavily on the J-6 fighter, itself a MiG-19 type, but with substantial differences to suit its changed role. Although modified J-6 wings were adopted, the fuselage was made considerably longer in comparison to accommodate an internal weapons bay. This feature has been deleted from the second and subsequent production models, the room enabling more fuel to be carried and thereby leaving all weaponry (except for the guns) to be externally mounted. With the anticipation of retrospectively fitting an attack radar, the Q-5's nose was made 'solid,' the F-6-type nose air-intake giving way to fuselage side intakes level with the cockpit.

With production of the latest Q-5III and export A-5C continuing, it is believed that the Air Force of the People's Liberation Army operates about 500 Q-5s, while the Aviation of the People's Navy has some 100 equipped as interceptors. Pakistan is a recent export customer, with more than 40 A-5Bs in service against a reported A-5 requirement of 140 to arm eight first-line squadrons and an operational conversion unit. Subsequent A-5s will be of the latest A-5C standard.

Below: Chinese Nanchang Q-5s on a low-flying training exercise.

Specifications (Q-5III data)

Radar: Q-5 interceptors may have 'High Fix' (NATO name) I-band ranging radar.
Weapons: Two 23-mm cannon in the wingroots, each with 100 rounds of ammunition, plus up to 4409 lb (2000 kg) of weapons (normally bombs) carried on eight pylons under the fuselage and wings. As an interceptor, PL-2, PL-7, Matra Magic or Sidewinder air-to-air missiles can be carried.
Accommodation: The pilot.
Wingspan: 31 ft 10 in (9.70 m).
Length: 53 ft 4 in (16.26 m) with probe.
Maximum take-off weight: 26,455 lb (12,000 kg).
Maximum speed: 752 mph (1210 km/h).
Range: 1243 miles (2000 km) with auxiliary fuel.
Mission performance: Rate of climb at sea level 20,275 ft (6180 m) per min; ceiling 52,000 ft (15,850 m); G limit 7.5 without external stores.
Engines: Two 7165-lb (3250-kg) thrust with afterburning Shenyang Wopen-6 turbojets, with 3720 liters of fuel standard.

Versions in service
Q-5: Production version for the indigenous forces, used in attack and interceptor configurations.
A-5: Export version, of which the A-5C is current.
Q-5M and A-5M: These are future improved versions for the home air forces and export, incorporating new avionics supplied by Aeritalia (including a nav/attack system with a HUD) and 8267-lb (3500-kg) thrust with afterburning Wopen-6A engines.
Operators: China (air force and navy), North Korea and Pakistan.

Neiva N-621 Universal
Brazil

The Universal was designed as an aerobatic two- or three-seat basic trainer and it entered Brazilian Air Force service in this role under the designation T-25. However, some of the 140 aircraft delivered were of the T-25A version for observation and light attack duties with the EMRAs (reconnaissance and attack squadrons). Approximately 87 T-25/T-25As remain in Brazilian service, together with a small number flown by Paraguay. The latter are represented by five ex-Chilean Air Force T-25s handed over in 1983. It appears that the remaining five of the 10 supplied to Chile are still in use, while Brazilian aircraft are being superseded by Tucanos.

Specifications
Weapons: 2 pods for 7.62-mm machine-guns are carried on underwing pylons.
Accommodation: Student pilot/copilot and pilot side by side, with optional rear seat.
Wingspan: 36 ft 1 in (11.00 m).
Length: 28 ft 2½ in (8.60 m).
Maximum take-off weight: 3747 lb (1700 kg).
Maximum speed: 186 mph (300 km/h).
Range: 932 miles (1500 km).
Mission performance at aerobatic weight of 3307 lb (1500 kg): Rate of climb at sea level 1315 ft (400 m) per min; ceiling 20,000 ft (6100 m).
Engine: One 300-hp Avco Lycoming IO-540-K1D5 piston, with 332 liters of fuel.
Versions in service
T-25: Basic trainer.
T-25A: Designation of aircraft still used by one Brazilian Air Force EMRA squadron.
Operators: Brazil, Chile and Paraguay.

Neiva Regente
Brazil

The Regente strut-braced high-wing light aircraft entered military service with the Brazilian Air Force for liaison, observation and utility duties, the former tasks undertaken by the L-42 three-seat model and the latter by the four-seat C-42 model. The prototype had flown initially on 7 September 1961.

Specifications (L-42 data)
Weapons: 4 underwing pylons for a light load of bombs or rockets.
Accommodation: 3 seats, the single rear seat for the observer/navigator.
Wingspan: 29 ft 11½ in (9.13 m).
Length: 23 ft 8 in (7.21 m).
Maximum take-off weight: 2469 lb (1120 kg).
Maximum speed: 153 mph (246 km/h).
Range: 590 miles (950 km).
Mission performance: Rate of climb at sea level 920 ft (280 m) per min; ceiling 15,800 ft (4820 m); G limits +4, −2.5.
Engine: One 210-hp Continental IO-360-D piston, with 172 liters of fuel.
Versions in service
C-42: Initial production version for utility tasks, originally designated U-42. Accommodates 4 persons and is powered by a 180-hp O-360-A1D engine.
L-42: First flown in 1967, this more powerful 3-seater introduced a new rear window for improved visibility, with the effect of stepping the rear fuselage aft of the cabin. L-42s replaced Brazilian O-1 Bird Dogs.
Operator: Brazil.

Below: Neiva T-25 Universal trainer.

Above: Neiva L-42 Regente.

Nord 2501 Noratlas
France

One of the oldest transport aircraft in military service today, the Noratlas was developed into several versions of which only the 2501 remains active. Its long service life, especially with the French Air Force which has approximately 60 (although these are being replaced), can be attributed to the clever design of the main cabin, which provided for a level reinforced floor and a hinged rear fuselage for direct loading of vehicles and other bulky cargoes into the 32 ft 6 in (9.90 m) hold between and under the twin tail booms. Most other Noratlas transports in use are ex-German Luftwaffe, which formerly operated a large number but now has none.

Specifications (2501 Noratlas data)
Accommodation: Up to 14,991 lb (6800 kg) of freight, using optional 2-ton winch, or vehicles. In troop transport configuration can carry 45 troops or paratroops.
Wingspan: 106 ft 7½ in (32.50 m).
Length: 72 ft 0 in (21.96 m)
Maximum take-off weight: 48,502 lb (22,000 kg).
Maximum speed: 251 mph (405 km/h).

Below: Nord Noratlas transport, photographed in 1982.

Range: 1553 miles (2500 km).
Mission performance: Rate of climb at sea level 1180 ft (360 m) per min; ceiling 23,290 ft (7100 m).
Engines: Two 2040-hp Bristol/SNECMA Hercules 738 or 758 radial pistons, with 5090 liters fuel.
Versions in service
N 2501: As described above. Prototype (Nord 2500) was first flown on 10 September 1949. Second largest user today is Greece, with 20. Other operating nations have very few.

N 2502: Variant of N 2501 with 2 Turboméca Marboré turbojet engines carried at wingtips for improved take-off performance. Very small number of civil examples available to Mozambique.
Operators: Congo, Djibouti, France, Greece, Mozambique and Niger.

North American T-6 Texan
United States

The AT-6 basic combat trainer was the subject of massive production during World War II and this included Harvards sent to the RAF from 1938. From 1949 more than 2000 Texans were updated to T-6G standard, the main service version today. This was mainly for USAF considerations, thereby avoiding the need for a costly total replacement type. Changes included simplifying the pilot's cockpit to make it closer to that of the new T-28 advanced trainer and fitting instrument training equipment into the rear cockpit. Incredibly, the Texan has shown itself to be so rugged and competent that even today at least seven air forces still have some in their inventories for training, light attack and even reconnaissance. These aircraft are mainly with South

Below: Spanish North American T-6 Texan, known in service as the E.16.

American and African forces, where unusual operational requirements often favor aircraft of this type. The list of forces, though, should be treated as a guide, as it is almost impossible to be sure which of the 22 nations holding Texan/Harvards in 1980 still have any.

Specifications (T-6G data)
Weapons: Provision for attack weapons carried on underwing attachments, including bombs and rockets.
Accommodation: Student pilot and instructor in tandem under a long canopy.
Wingspan: 42 ft 0 in (12.80 m).
Length: 29 ft 6 in (8.99 m).
Maximum take-off weight: 5617 lb (2548 kg).
Maximum speed: 212 mph (341 km/h).
Range: 870 miles (1400 km).
Mission performance: Rate of climb at sea level 1650 ft (500 m) per min; ceiling 24,750 ft (7550 m).
Engine: One 550-hp Pratt & Whitney R-1340-AN-1 radial piston.
Versions in service
Texan: Most Texans, but probably not all, are of the T-6G type.
Operators: Bolivia, Dominican Republic, Paraguay, Spain, Tunisia, Uruguay and Zaire.

North American T-28 Trojan
United States

The T-28 was designed as a basic trainer to supersede T-6 Texans serving with the USAF. It flew for the first time in 1949 and entered production the following year. After a decision to standardize trainers throughout the US military forces, the T-28 was adopted also by the US Navy, initially in T-28B form. This model introduced the two-section sliding bubble canopy that subsequently became standard for the model range. Including the

Right: Will the new Northrop Advanced Technology Bomber look anything like this Northrop YB-49 of 1949?
Below: North American T-28C Trojan.

T-28C, 1948 Trojans were completed by 1957. There had always been provision for light armament but many surplus T-28As were eventually modified into T-28D light attack aircraft for use during the Vietnam war and the Congo where multimillion-dollar jets proved impracticable. A French T-28D-type attack conversion by Sud-Aviation produced the Fennec, which fought in Algeria. Today the T-28D is the most commonly flown variant of the Trojan, of which many remain.

Specifications (T-28D data)
Weapons: Two 0.50-in machine-guns and two 1000-lb (454-kg) bombs, or six 2.25-in rockets, napalm, etc, on 6 wing pylons.
Accommodation: 2 crew.
Wingspan: 40 ft 7½ in (12.38 m).
Length: 32 ft 10 in (10.00 m).
Maximum take-off weight: 8495 lb (3853 kg).
Maximum speed: 380 mph (610 km/h).
Range: 500 miles (804 km) with full load.
Engine: One 1425-hp Wright R-1820-56S radial piston.
Versions in service
T-28A: Initial production version, with an 800-hp Wright R-1300-1 radial piston engine.
T-28B and C: T-28B was the first US Navy version, with a 1425 hp Wright R-1820-86 engine and two-piece sliding cockpit canopy. The USN T-28C had also deck landing equipment. Four remain active.
T-28D: Light attack aircraft by modification.
Fennec: French-produced attack version.
Operators: South Korea (T-28A and D), Laos (T-28D), Mexico (T-28A), Philippines (T-28D), Taiwan (T-28A), Thailand(T-28D), United States (navy, T-28B/C?) and Uruguay (navy, Fennec).

Northrop Advanced Technology Bomber (ATB)
United States

Undoubtedly the most secret military aircraft currently under development in the West, the ATB is intended to supersede the Rockwell International B-1B as the USAF's (and thus NATO's) strategic penetration bomber at the end of the 1990s. Very few hard facts are available at present, although it has been reported that a scale vehicle has been under-

going flight tests since 1982. Speculation has centred upon the ATB being of 'flying-wing' configuration, a concept Northrop successfully developed in both fighter and strategic bomber forms during the 1940s but was not able to press beyond the pre-production stage. However, as any future bomber will have to take advantage of every known 'stealth/low observable' feature and technology to mask itself from radar, infrared and other forms of detection, the flying-wing appears to be a strong possibility.

Under the reported $36,600 million program, with $7300 million already allocated for the prototypes, 132 ATBs are to be purchased for service with the USAF. The first prototype could be flying by the end of 1987. Though it is difficult and almost pointless to compare a flying-wing aircraft with a more conventional type, it is thought the ATB will be both smaller and lighter than the current B-1B, the prototypes at least powered by perhaps four augmented turbofan engines of probably F101 type that are used in the B-1B, General Electric being one of the known contributors to the program.

Northrop F-5, F-5E/F Tiger II, RF-5E TigerEye and T-38A Talon
United States

As the N-156, the first prototype of Northrop's low-cost and lightweight tactical fighter flew for the first time on 30 July 1959, exceeding the speed of sound on this occasion. Ideal for air forces not requiring or unable to afford the very high-performance heavyweights built for US front-line service, the Department of Defense placed orders on behalf of Greece, Taiwan, Thailand, Turkey, South Korea, South Vietnam and others, principally under mutual aid programs. Initial versions were the F-5A single-seat fighter, F-5B two-seat combat capable trainer and single-seat RF-5A reconnaissance aircraft. Other nations placed their own orders, while production or assembly also took place in Canada and Spain.

On 11 August 1972 Northrop flew the first F-5E, an upgraded new version of the F-5 that had won a US government competition as the IFA (International Fighter Aircraft) to super-

sede the F-5A. As Tiger IIs, single-seat F-5Es and two-seat F-5Fs offered more powerful engines and several other important features, the most notable being auto-maneuvering flaps, with the leading-edge and trailing-edge flaps working together and automatically in accordance to airspeed and the angle of attack. In addition to US production, manufacturing lines were also set up in South Korea, Switzerland and Taiwan. Interestingly, the USAF took in examples of the F-5E to help train foreign crews and technicians, while also using the type as an 'aggressor,' simulating enemy fighters to 'bounce' front-line squadrons. F-5E/Fs are used as 'aggressors' by the Navy also. In 1983 the Royal Malaysian Air Force received the first production example of a reconnaissance derivative of the F-5E, known as the RF-5E TigerEye. However, all production of the F-5 series has now ended. It has been reported that Honduras is to receive 12 ex-USAF F-5Es and Fs as replacements for Super Mystère B.2s. This will end the service life of the old French fighter.

Way back in 1974 Northrop had proudly announced delivery of its 2500th F-5 type, a figure which included the T-38 Talon, a purpose-designed supersonic jet trainer that had first flown on 10 April 1959. Virtually identical in structure to the F-5, it filled the gap between primary trainers and front-line jets. Over 1100 went into USAF service, of which about 900 remain. This number includes a few also used as 'aggressors', a role to which the US Navy also puts a small number. Most Talons are operated by Air Training Command, but some are with Strategic Air Command and the 479th Tactical Training Wing which has AT-38s fitted with practice bomb dispensers and gunsights for FLIT (Fighter Lead-In Training).

Further development of the F-5 design has led to the much improved F-20 Tigershark (originally designated F-5G) but at the time of writing no purchasers had been found.

Specifications (F-5E Tiger II data)
Radar: Emerson AN/APQ-159 radar with search and tracking functions. USAF F-5s

Below: USAF Northrop T-38A Talon supersonic jet trainer.

Above: Northrop F-5E Tiger II, built in Switzerland by the Federal Aircraft Factory for the Swiss Air Force.

have AN/APQ-153, but its F-5Es will be updated with AN/APQ-159(V)5 and F-5Fs with (V)6.

Weapons: Two 20-mm M39A2 cannon in the fuselage, 2 Sidewinder air-to-air missiles at the wingtips, and up to 7000 lb (3175 kg) of attack weapons on 4 underwing and one underfuselage pylons.

Accommodation: The pilot.

Wingspan: 26 ft 8 in (8.13 m).

Length: 47 ft 4¾ in (14.45 m).

Maximum take-off weight: 24,722 lb (11,214 kg).

Maximum speed: Mach 1.64.

Range: Up to 1779 miles (2863 km) with drop tanks.

Mission performance: Rate of climb at sea level 34,500 ft (10,515 m) per min; ceiling 51,800 ft (15,790 m).

Engines: Two 5000-lb (2268-kg) thrust with afterburning General Electric J85-GE-21B turbojets, with 2563 liters of fuel standard.

Versions in service

F-5A: Initial single-seat tactical fighter, with two 4080-lb (1850-kg) thrust with afterburning J85-GE-13 engines. 6200-lb (2812-kg) weapon load.

F-5B: Initial 2-seat combat-capable trainer, first flown in production form on 24 February 1964.

CF-5A and D: Canadair-built F-5A and B for the indigenous armed forces and export.

NF-5A and B: Royal Netherlands Air Force F-5A and B. NF-5As are being superseded by F-16s.

RF-5A: Single-seat reconnaissance version of the F-5A, with four KS-92 cameras.

SF-5A and B: CASA-produced Spanish Air Force F-5A and B, service designated C.9 and CE.9. The CR.9 is the SRF-5A reconnaissance aircraft.

F-5E Tiger II: Higher performance and improved maneuvering development of the F-5A, as detailed above.

F-5B TigerII: 2-seat combat-capable trainer version of the F-5E.

F-5G and RF-5G: Norwegian F-5A, B and RF-5A.

RF-5E TigerEye: Reconnaissance derivative of the F-5E, with a modified forward fuselage. Can carry medium- and low-altitude cameras and an IR linescanner pallet or a low-altitude and wide-scan angle cameras pallet.

T-38A Talon: USAF and US Navy 2-seat jet trainer and 'aggressor'. Also used by 4 other nations. Two 3850-lb (1746-kg) thrust with afterburning J85-GE-5 turbojets. Maximum speed is over Mach 1.23.

AT-38: FLIT version of Talon, as above.

Operators: Bahrain (E and F), Brazil (B and E), Canada (A and D), Chile (E and F), Ecuador (Tiger II), Ethiopia (Tiger II), West Germany (Talon), Greece (A, B, RF-5A), Honduras (E and F), Indonesia (E and F), Iran (E and F), Jordan (E and F), Kenya (E and F), South Korea (A, B, E, F, RF-5A), Malaysia (E, F and TigerEye), Mexico (E and F), Morocco (A, B, E, F and RF-5A), Netherlands (A? and B), Norway (A, B and RF-5A), Philippines (A, B and Tiger II), Portugal (Talon), Saudi Arabia (E and TigerEye), Singapore (E and F), Spain (A, B and RF-5A – as G types), Sudan (E), Switzerland (E and F), Taiwan (E, F and Talon), Thailand (A, B, E, F and RF-5A), Tunisia (E and F), Turkey (A, B, RF-5A and Talon), United States (air force, E, F and Talon; navy, E, F and Talon), Venezuela (A and D) and North Yemen (B and E).

Panavia Tornado
United Kingdom, West Germany and Italy

In the past there have been some superb examples of aircraft that have resulted from international collaboration. However, the technological triumph of the Tornado multi-role combat aircraft must be regarded as among the greatest of these successes by meeting, as it does in a single airframe/power plant combination, the differing requirements of four European air arms. Originating as the MRCA (multirole combat aircraft) with a variable-geometry wing, to serve with the West German air force and navy, and the air forces of Italy and the United Kingdom, the common aircraft was required to fulfill the roles of air superiority, battlefield interdic-

tion, close air support, counter-air strike/interdiction, naval strike and reconnaissance. The two additional roles of interception/air defense required by the Royal Air Force were to be met by a separate configuration known as the ADV.

The consortium to design and ultimately produce the MRCA, subsequently named the Panavia Tornado, was formed by the manufacturers now known as Aeritalia, British Aerospace and Messerschmitt-Bölkow-Blohm (MBB), with Panavia GmbH being formed on 26 March 1969 to oversee the activities of these companies. Although the user nations had each decided the need to be able to deploy their full standard range of weapons, Panavia was also successful in meeting this requirement.

The first of nine prototypes was flown on 14 August 1974 and the first production aircraft for use by the Tri-national Tornado Training Establishment at RAF Cottesmore were delivered on 1 July 1980. Initial deliveries to the air arms of West Germany, Italy and the United Kingdom were made in the period 1982-83, these being the first of a planned total of 809. Since the original production requirements were planned new orders include nine more for the RAF, 35 of an ECR (electronic combat and reconnaissance) version for the Luftwaffe, 72 for the Royal Saudi Air Force and eight for the Sultan of Oman's air force.

Tornado is of conventional construction, mainly aluminum alloy, with wings that can vary between 25 and 67 degrees of sweepback. The tailplane is all-moving and a huge single fin/rudder is adopted. Among the avionics are a laser rangefinder and marked target seeker for the IDS.

Specifications (Tornado IDS data)

Radar: Texas Instruments multimode forward-looking ground-mapping radar, Decca Type 72 Doppler nav radar, a flight control system using inputs from the radars and a GEC Avionics terrain-following E-scope to give automatic approach and terrain-following modes.

Weapons: Fixed armament of 2 IWKA-Mauser 27-mm cannon, each with 180 rounds of ammunition, plus about

19,840 lb (9000 kg) of external stores on 3 underfuselage attachments and up to 4 swivelling pylons beneath the wings. Loads can comprise all non-nuclear weapons in the inventory of the user nations and include free-fall, retarded and guided bombs, air-to-air and air-to-surface missiles and a variety of ECM and reconnaissance pods.

Accommodation: 2 crew.
Wingspan: Spread 45 ft 7½ in (13.91 m); swept 28 ft 2½ in (8.60 m).
Length: 54 ft 10¼ in (16.72 m).
Maximum take-off weight: Approximately 60,000 lb (27,216 kg).
Maximum speed: 1452 mph (2337 km/h) 'clean' at altitude.
Combat radius: 864 miles (1390 km) with heavy load.
Mission performance: Climb to 30,000 ft

Right: RAF Panavia Tornado F.Mk 2 from 229 OCU Coningsby.
Below: Royal Saudi Air Force Panavia Tornado IDS.

(9145 m) from brake release less than 2 min;
G limit +7.5.
Engines: Two 16,000-lb (7257-kg) thrust
Turbo-Union RB199-34R Mk 101
afterburning turbofans.
Versions in service
IDS: Basic multipurpose 2-seat combat
aircraft, available also as a dual control
trainer retaining full operational capability.
In RAF service it is designated Tornado
GR.Mk 1, and the trainer Tornado
GR.Mk 1T. Production orders for the 3
European nations total 653, comprising
Luftwaffe (212), Marineflieger (112),
Aeronautica Militare Italiana (100) and
RAF (229).
ADV: Air defense variant specifically for
service with the RAF, which ordered a total
of 165. It differs structurally by having the
forward fuselage lengthened to house AI-24
Foxhunter multimode Doppler radar, and a
lightly lengthened rear fuselage to allow the
underfuselage carriage of 2 tandem pairs of
Sky Flash air-to-air missiles. Other
armament comprises only one IWKA-
Mauser cannon, and up to 4 AIM-9
Sidewinders can be carried on underwing
pylons in addition to drop tanks. The first
18 ADVs, which have RB 199 Mk 103
engines, are designated Tornado F.Mk 2;
subsequent production with Mk 104 engines
which have some seven percent more
reheat thrust, automatic wing sweep and a
number of avionics and equipment
improvements are designated Tornado
F.Mk 3. The F.Mk 2s are to be upgraded to
F.Mk 3 standard with the exception of the
Mk 104 engine installation, and will then be
redesignated F.Mk 2A.
ECR: Luftwaffe electronic combat and
reconnaissance derivative of the IDS, for
delivery from 1989.
Operators: West Germany (air force and
navy), Italy, Oman, Saudi Arabia and
United Kingdom.

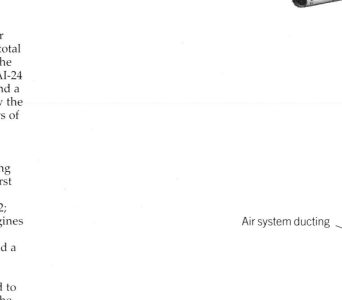

Cerebus jamming pod

Air system ducting

Wing sweep control actuator

Forward fuselage fuel tank

Intake by-pass air spill ducts

IFF antenna

Ground mapping and attack radar antenna

Variable area
intake ramp doors

Intake suction relief doors

Avionics equipment bay

MW-1 multipurpose munitions dispenser

Radar processing avionics

Terrain following radar antenna

IWKA-Mauser 27mm cannon

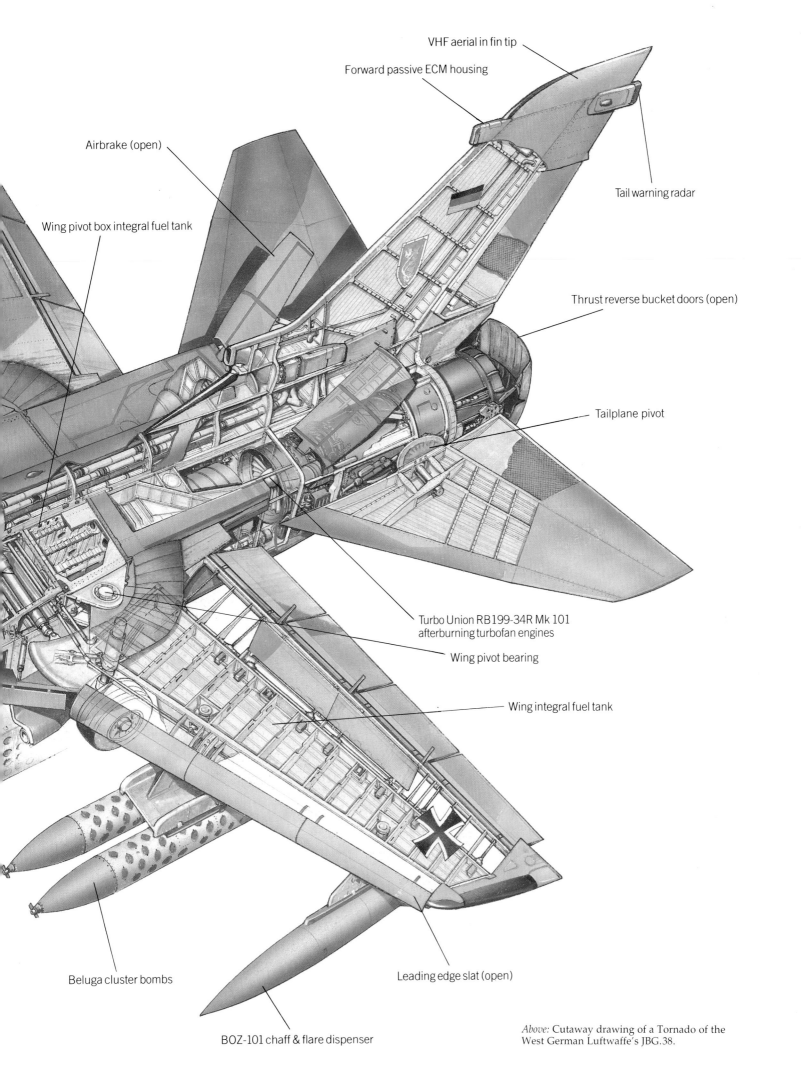

VHF aerial in fin tip

Forward passive ECM housing

Airbrake (open)

Wing pivot box integral fuel tank

Tail warning radar

Thrust reverse bucket doors (open)

Tailplane pivot

Turbo Union RB199-34R Mk 101 afterburning turbofan engines

Wing pivot bearing

Wing integral fuel tank

Beluga cluster bombs

Leading edge slat (open)

BOZ-101 chaff & flare dispenser

Above: Cutaway drawing of a Tornado of the West German Luftwaffe's JBG.38.

Above: Piaggio P.149D in Luftwaffe markings.

Piaggio P.149D
Italy

First flown in July 1953, the P.149D is still used as a trainer and liaison aircraft by the Federal German Luftwaffe and in the former role by Uganda. However, the status of the Ugandan aircraft is uncertain and the Luftwaffe has been looking at the RFB Fantrainer as a replacement. The P.149D, developed from the P.148, is entirely conventional, with an all-metal structure and a retractable tricycle undercarriage.

Specifications
Accommodation: Student pilot and instructor in side-by-side seats, with 2 or 3 persons accommodated behind.
Wingspan: 38 ft 5¾ in (11.12 m).
Length: 28 ft 10 in (8.80 m).
Maximum take-off weight: 3703 lb (1680 kg).
Maximum speed: 180 mph (304 km/h).
Range: 677 miles (1090 km).
Mission performance: Rate of climb at sea level 985 ft (300 m) per min; ceiling 19,850 ft (6050 m).
Engine: One 270-hp Avco Lycoming GO-480 piston, with 240 liters of fuel.

Below: Italian Air Force Piaggio PD-808.

Version in service
P.149D: 75 were built by Piaggio for German service and others were built under license by Focke-Wulf.
Operators: Germany and Uganda (army).

Piaggio PD-808
Italy

The PD-808 was designed as a jet utility aircraft, suitable for various civil and military tasks including that of a six- to eight-seat VIP transport. The only military order came from the Italian Defense Ministry, which required a small number for Air Force service in four versions as detailed below.

Specifications
Radar: Weather radar was offered as an option.
Accommodation: Flight crew of one or two. The Italian Air Force VIP version seats 6 passengers. The PD-808 TA seats 9 passengers as a transport and the training version has the pilot plus one student in the copilot's seat and up to three more in the cabin. 2 pilots and 3 systems operators are accommodated in the ECM model.
Wingspan: 43 ft 3½ in (13.20 m).
Length: 42 ft 2 in (12.85 m).
Maximum take-off weight: 18,000 lb (8165 kg).
Maximum speed: 529 mph (852 km/h).

Range: 1322 miles (2128 km) with a 840-lb (381-kg) payload.
Mission performance: Rate of climb at sea level 5415 ft (1680 m) per min; ceiling 45,000 ft (13,715 m).
Engines: Two 3360-lb (1524-kg) thrust Rolls-Royce Viper Mk 526 turbojets, with 3727 liters of fuel.
Versions in service
PD-808 ECM: Electronic countermeasures model.
PD-808 RM: Radio calibration model for navigation aids.
PD-808 TA: Transport and navigation trainer.
PD-808 VIP: Transport for government and military VIPs.
Operator: Italy.

Pilatus P-3, PC-7 Turbo-Trainer and PC-9
Switzerland

This series of tandem two-seat trainers spans a period of more than 30 years, during which the transition from piston to turboprop power has been the greatest change. The PC-3, first flown in 1953, was built for the Swiss Air Force for ab initio, basic and intermediate training, including aerobatic, instrument, night- and blind-flying, and weapon training. Seventy-two were built, of which well over 60 remain in use.

The PC-7 Turbo-Trainer is, as its name indicates, a turboprop development; deliveries to customers started in December 1978. Including civil examples, 380 had been sold by September 1986. The crew sit on lightweight ejection seats beneath a clear-view canopy without the PC-3's frames.

The latest Pilatus, the PC-9, differs greatly from the PC-7. It is a far more powerful advanced trainer with a raised rear cockpit, and various airframe improvements including a ventral airbrake. The first PC-9 made its maiden flight on 7 May 1984 and to date Burma has ordered four, Australia 67, Saudi Arabia 30 and two other undisclosed customers have selected it. Forty-eight of the Australian PC-9s will be built entirely in that country.

Specifications (PC-9 data)
Accommodation: Student pilot and instructor in tandem cockpits.

Above: Pilatus PC-7 Turbo-Trainers belonging to the Burma Air Force.

Wingspan: 33 ft 5¼ in (10.19 m).
Length: 33 ft 4¾ in (10.17 m).
Maximum take-off weight: 7055 lb (3200 kg).
Maximum speed: 345 mph (556 km/h).
Range: 955 miles (1538 km) with reserves.
Mission performance: Rate of climb at sea level 4090 ft (1247 m) per min; ceiling 38,000 ft (11,580 m); G limits +7 aerobatic, −3.5 aerobatic, +4.5 utility, −2.25 utility.
Engine: One 1150-shp Pratt & Whitney Canada PT6A-62 turboprop, with 508 liters of fuel standard.

Versions in service
PC-3: Powered by one 260-hp Avco Lycoming GO-435-C2A piston engine. Can carry one machine-gun, 2 rocket launchers, practice bombs, etc. Maximum speed 193 mph (310 km/h).
PC-7 Turbo-Trainer: The internationally best-selling trainer of the 3, powered by a 650-shp Pratt & Whitney Canada PT6A-25A turboprop. Maximum weight 5952 lb (2700 kg); maximum speed 310 mph (500 km/h). Can carry 2293 lb (1040 kg) of weapons on 6 underwing stations.
PC-9: Can carry weapons for tactical training.
Operators: Include Abu Dhabi (PC-7), Angola (PC-7), Australia (PC-9), Austria (PC-7), Bolivia (PC-7), Burma (PC-7 and PC-9), Chile (navy, PC-7), Guatemala (PC-7), Iraq (PC-7), Iran (PC-7), Mexico (PC-7), Saudi Arabia (PC-9) and Switzerland (PC-3 and PC-7).

Pilatus PC-6 Porter and Turbo-Porter, and Fairchild AU-23A Peacemaker
Switzerland and United States

The piston-engined Porter first flew as a prototype STOL multipurpose utility aircraft on 4 May 1959. Production aircraft were followed by Turbo-Porters introducing turboprop power, the latter representing the current type. In configuration they are rugged 'go anywhere' transports, with the strut-braced high wings having double-slotted flaps and single-slotted ailerons along the entire trailing edges. The short take-off/landing distances and sturdy undercarriage with wheels, wheel/skis or floats, mean that few places are inaccessible, while the main cabin can be quickly converted from passenger to freight or ambulance layouts. Fairchild in the United States also evolved a counter-insurgency model as the AU-23A Peacemaker, which went only to the Royal Thai Air Force and Police.

Specifications (Current PC-6/B2-H4 Turbo-Porter data)
Accommodation: The pilot plus 10 passengers, 8 paratroops, 2 stretchers and 3 attendants/sitting casualties, or freight.
Wingspan: 52 ft 0¾ in (15.87 m).
Length: 36 ft 1 in (11.00 m).
Maximum take-off weight: 6173 lb (2800 kg).

Cruising speed: 161 mph (259 km/h).
Range: 934 miles (1503 km).
Mission performance: Rate of climb at sea level 940 ft (287 m) per min; operating ceiling 25,000 ft (7620 m); take-off run at sea level 645 ft (197 m); landing run at sea level 420 ft (127 m); G limits +3.72, −1.5.
Engine: One 680-shp Pratt & Whitney Canada PT6A-27 turboprop, with 480-644 liters of fuel standard.

Versions in service
Porter: Original piston-engined version, with a 340-hp Avco Lycoming GSO-480-B1A6 or 350-hp IGO-540-A1A engine.
Turbo-Porter: Turboprop versions, previously built also in PC-6A form with a 523-573-shp Turboméca Astazou and PC-6C form with a 575-shp AiResearch TPE-331 engine. The current version is the PC-6B2-H4.
AU-23A Peacemaker: 650-shp TPE331-1-101F engine. Armed with two 20-mm M-197 guns, fired from the cabin door, and light attack weapons carried on 4 underwing and one underfuselage pylon.
Operators: (P=Porter, T-P=Turbo-Porter). Angola (T-P), Argentina (army and navy, T-P), Australia (army, T-P), Austria (T-P), Bolivia (T-P), Burma (P and T-P), Chad (T-P), Colombia (T-P), Ecuador (army, T-P), Iran (T-P), Oman (T-P), Peru (T-P), Sudan (T-P), Switzerland (P and T-P), Thailand (T-P and Peacemaker) and United States (army, T-P as the UV-20A Chiricahua).

Pilatus Britten-Norman BN-2 Islander and Defender series
United Kingdom

The prototype Islander twin piston-engined feederline commercial transport flew initially on 13 June 1965. Including examples of the BN-2T Turbine Islander that introduced turboprop power as an alternative in 1980, and specific armed military versions known as Defenders, well over 1000 have been

Below: Pilatus PC-6/B2-H2 Turbo-Porter, used by Colombia's SATENA military airline.

delivered to military and civil customers in around 120 countries.

Specifications (BN-2B Islander with 300-hp engines data)

Accommodation: Pilot and up to 9 passengers, 8 paratroops and a dispatcher, 3 stretchers and 2 attendants, or up to 2048 lb (929 kg) of freight.
Wingspan: 49 ft 0 in (14.94 m).
Length: 35 ft 7¾ in (10.86 m).
Maximum take-off weight: 6600 lb (2993 kg).
Maximum speed: 173 mph (280 km/h).
Range: Up to 706 miles (1136 km).
Mission performance: Rate of climb at sea level 1130 ft (344 m) per min; ceiling 17,200 ft (5245 m).
Engines: Two 300-hp Avco Lycoming IO-540-K1B5 pistons, with 518 liters of fuel standard. Alternatively, two 260-hp O-540-E4C5 engines; 855-liter fuel capacity with optional wingtip tanks, which can be further increased with underwing tanks.

Versions in service

Islander: Piston-engined version, currently manufactured in BN-2B form.
BN-2T Turbine Islander: two 400-shp Allison 250-B17C turboprops, with 814 liters of fuel. Maximum cruising speed 196 mph (315 km/h).
Defender: Military version of the Islander, with 300-hp engines as standard. Optional weather radar, allowing maritime search role. 4 underwing pylons for optional bombs (up to 500-lb/227-kg weight each), 7.62-mm gun pods, anti-armor missiles, rockets, antipersonnel grenades, etc. Possible roles include SAR, armed and unarmed land and sea patrol, security, FAC (forward air control), troop/paratroop/freight transport and casualty evacuation.
Turbine-Defender: Turboprop version of the Defender.
Maritime Defender: All-weather day or night derivative of the Defender for coastal patrol, fishery protection, etc. Bendix RDR-1400 weather/multifunction search radar and a crew of 5. Searchlight and

Below: Pilatus Britten-Norman ASV Maritime Defender, equipped with Seaspray radar in the underfuselage radome and armed with Sea Skua antiship missiles.

camera. 4 underwing pylons optional for weapons and such other equipment as dinghy packs dropped by parachute.
AEW Defender: Version with Thorn EMI Skymaster multimode early warning and maritime reconnaissance radar in a bulged nose.
AEW/MR Defender: More capable version of the AEW Defender, with a second console to enhance missions and target-handling capacity. ESM, IFF, data links and navigation systems can be integrated with the radar display and control equipment.
ASW/ASV Maritime Defender: Latest variant with optionally a 360 degree scanning radar, FLIR, MAD, sonobuoys and associated processing equipment, and underwing pylons for depth charges, 4 Sea Skua antiship missiles or 2 lightweight Sting Ray torpedoes or other weapons/equipment.
CASTOR Islander: British Ministry of Defence experimental battlefield surveillance model, operating with the Phoenix RPV.

Operators: All Defenders unless otherwise stated. Abu Dhabi, Belgium (army), Belize, Botswana, Ciskei, Cyprus (national guard*), Ghana, Guyana, Hong Kong (auxiliary air force), India (navy*), Indonesia (army), Iraq (Islander), Israel (Islander), Jamaica,

Above: Piper PA-23-250 Aztec, known in Spanish Air Force service as the E.19.

Malagasy, Malawi (army), Mauritania, Mexico, Oman, Panama, Philippines (navy*), Qatar (Islander), Rwanda, Seychelles (Ministry of Agriculture and Fisheries), Somali Republic, Surinam, Venezuela (army) and Zimbabwe.
*Maritime Defender.

Piper Aztec, Twin Comanche, Navajo, Chieftain, Cheyenne, Seneca and Seminole
United States

This series of Piper twin-engined light transports is best known in its civil form, but a considerable number have also entered military service over the years for various duties ranging from transport, liaison and training to maritime reconnaissance. The data below applies to the early PA-23-250 Aztec, which was taken into service by the United States Navy from 1960 as the UO-1 (later redesignated U-11A).

Specifications (Aztec data)

Accommodation: The pilot and 4 passengers. Can carry, alternatively, a stretcher, up to 1600 lb (726 kg) of freight, or a survey camera.
Wingspan: 37 ft 0 in (11.28 m).
Length: 27 ft 7 in (8.41 m).
Maximum take-off weight: 4800 lb (2177 kg).
Maximum speed: 215 mph (346 km/h).
Range: 1200 miles (1930 km).
Mission performance: Rate of climb at sea level 1650 ft (505 m) per min; ceiling 22,500 ft (6860 m).
Engines: Two 250-hp Avco Lycoming O-540-A1A pistons, with 545 liters of fuel.

Versions in service and Operators

PA-23 Aztec: Earliest of the 'twins' in service, later examples having slightly greater dimensions and updated engines. The 6-seat Aztec E, for example, has a wingspan of 37 ft 2½ in (11.34 m) and length of 31 ft 2¾ in (9.52 m), and is powered by 2 TIO-540-C1As of 250 hp. The Aztec was first flown in 1959. Current operators are Colombia, Costa Rica, Malagasy, Senegal, Spain, Uganda and United States (navy).
PA-30 Twin Comanche: The 4-seat Twin Comanche first flew in 1962. A typical

version is powered by two 160-hp Avco Lycoming IO-320-B piston engines, has a wingspan and length of 36 ft (10.97 m) and 25 ft 2 in (7.67 m) respectively, a maximum speed of 205 mph (330 km/h) and a range of 830-1200 miles (1336-1931 km). The Spanish Navy uses it for liaison under the designation E.31.

PA-31 Navajo: First flown in 1964, the Navajo is a 6/9-seat transport, typically with 300-hp Avco Lycoming IO-540-M piston engines. Later models used 310-hp TIO-540s. Wingspan and length are 40 ft 8 in (12.40 m) and 32 ft 7½ in (9.94 m) respectively, with a maximum speed of 261 mph (420 km/h) and a range of 1157 miles (1860 km). Operators are Chile (army), Colombia, France (navy), Kenya (army), Panama and Spain.

PA-31 Chieftain: Lengthened Navajo of 1972 appearance, with 350-hp TIO-540-J2BD engines. Up to 10 seats. Length 34 ft 7½ in (10.55 m). Maximum speed 266 mph (428 km/h) and range 1019 miles (1640 km). This version is employed by the Finnish Air Force.

PA-31T Cheyenne: Versions of this 6- to 8-seat turboprop transport included the Cheyenne II, with 620-ehp Pratt & Whitney Canada PT6A-28 engines, made available also in maritime patrol form with a radar pod under the wing and other equipment,

which found favor with the Mauritanian Islamic Republic Air Force in 1981. Wingspan and length are 42 ft 8¼ in (13.01 m) and 34 ft 8 in (10.57 m) respectively, with a cruising speed of 325 mph (523 km/h) and a range of 1254 miles (2018 km) in Cheyenne II form. Other operators of the Cheyenne are Bolivia (army?), Panama and Peru (?).

PA-34 Seneca: Announced in 1971 as a six-seat transport. Seneca II and III models followed in 1975 and 1981 respectively. The current Seneca III, of which six joined the Royal Jordanian Air Academy, is powered by two 220-hp Continental L/TSIO-360-KB piston engines, has a wingspan and length of 38 ft 10¾ in (11.85 m) and 28 ft 7½ in (8.72 m) respectively, a maximum speed of 226 mph (363 km/h) and a range of typically 633 miles (1018 km). Operators are (Argentina for calibration), Brazil, Colombia, Costa Rica and Jordan.

PA-44 Seminole: The least important Piper twin from a military standpoint, it is believed only Colombia operates any. A four-seater of 1976 first flight, it is powered by two 180-hp Avco Lycoming LO/O-360-E1A6D piston engines, has a wingspan and length of 38 ft 7¼ in (11.77 m) and 27 ft 7¼ in (8.41 m) respectively, a maximum speed of 193 mph (311 km/h) and a typical range of 834 miles (1343 km).

Piper Super Cub, Comanche, Cherokee, Cherokee Arrow, Cherokee Six, Dakota and Warrior II
United States

This series of Piper single-engined light-planes fulfill mainly training, liaison and utility roles with the armed forces detailed below. The PA-18 Super Cubs differ from all the others in being strut-braced high-wing monoplanes and often carry the service designations L-18 and L-21.

Specifications (PA-28-236 Dakota data)
Accommodation: 4 persons.
Wingspan: 35 ft 0 in (10.67 m).
Length: 24 ft 8¾ in (7.54 m).
Maximum take-off weight: 3000 lb (1361 kg).
Maximum speed: 170 mph (274 km/h).
Range: Up to 933 miles (1500 km).
Mission performance: Rate of climb at sea level 1110 ft (338 m) per min; ceiling 17,500 ft (5335 m).
Engine: One 235-hp Avco Lycoming O-540-J3A5D piston, with 291 liters of fuel.
Versions in service
PA-18 Super Cub: As a more powerful derivative of the Cub (L-4), the Super Cub often carries the military designations L-18

Below: Prototype Chincul Cherokee Arrow trainer.

(1949 appearance, with a 90-hp Continental C90 piston engine) and L-21 (1951 appearance, with a 125- or 135-hp Avco Lycoming O-290 piston engine or 150-hp O-320). Wingspan 35 ft 3 in (10.73 m) and length 22 ft 7 in (6.88 m). Maximum speed of the 125-hp L-21A is 123 mph (198 km/h) and range 770 miles (1240 km).

P-24 Comanche: 4/6-seat cantilever low-wing cabin trainer, first flown in 1956 and powered by a 260-hp Avco Lycoming IO-540-A1A piston engine. Wingspan 36 ft (10.97 m) and length 25 ft (7.62 m). Cruising speed 185 mph (298 km/h). Range up to 1225 miles (1970 km).

PA-28-140 Cherokee 140: Two- to four-seat cantilever low-wing cabin lightplane of 1964 appearance, used for liaison by Tanzania. 140-hp Avco Lycoming O-320-A2B piston engine. Wingspan 30 ft (9.14 m) and length 23 ft 6 in (7.16 m).

PA-28R Cherokee Arrow: 4-seat cantilever low-wing cabin monoplane of 1977 appearance. One 200-hp Avco Lycoming O-360-C1C piston engine. Also produced in Argentina as the Chincul Cherokee Arrow Trainer, with a 260-hp AEIO-540 engine, a 2-seat cabin with a canopy and allowance for a 7.62-mm machine-gun and light weapons under the wings. Wingspan, length, maximum speed and range for the Chincul version are 35 ft (10.67 m), 23 ft 9½ in (7.25 m), 195 mph (314 km/h) and 840 miles (1352 km) respectively.

PA-32 Cherokee Six: 6/7-seat cantilever low-wing monoplane of 1963 appearance, powered by a 300-hp Avco Lycoming O-360 piston engine. Wingspan 32 ft 9½ in (9.99 m) and length 27 ft 8¾ in (8.45 m). Maximum speed 174 mph (279 km/h) and range up to 1060 miles (1700 km).

PA-28-236 Dakota: 1978 model, as detailed above. Used as a trainer by Chile.

PA-28-161 Warrior II: Four-seat cantilever low-wing cabin monoplane, powered by a 160-hp Avco Lycoming O-320-D3G piston engine. First flown in 1976. Wingspan and length as for Dakota. Maximum speed 146 mph (235 km/h).

Below: Polish Air Force PZL-104 Wilga 35.

Above: Prototype PZL-130 Orlik trainer.

Operators: Argentina (Chincul Cherokee Arrow), Belgium (L-21B), Chile (air force and army, Dakota), Colombia (Cherokee Six), Costa Rica (Cherokee Six), Finland (Cherokee Arrow), Israel (Super Cub), Jordan (Warrior II), Mexico (Cherokee Six?), Spain (navy, Comanche), Tanzania (Cherokee 140 and Cherokee Six), Turkey (army, L-18 and Cherokee Six), Uganda (Super Cub) and Uruguay (navy, Super Cub).

PZL-104 Wilga
Poland

The Wilga (Thrush) is an extremely useful and unique-looking light general-purpose aircraft of all-metal construction, features including a cantilever high-mounted wing, ailerons that can be drooped to complement the flaps during landing, and a forward projecting tail and fixed undercarriage with low-pressure tires for operation from unprepared strips; it can take off from grass with only 397 ft (121 m) run and land in less distance. The prototype first flew on 24 April 1962 and nearly 850 had been built by 1986 for military and civil use. Those in current military service are used in liaison roles.

Specifications (Wilga 35 data)
Accommodation: 4 seats in the enclosed cabin. An ambulance layout is optional, and the aircraft can be used for glider-towing.
Wingspan: 36 ft 5¾ in (11.12 m).
Length: 26 ft 6¾ in (8.10 m).
Maximum take-off weight: 2755 lb (1250 kg).
Maximum speed: 125 mph (201 km/h).
Range: 422 miles (680 km) with spare fuel.
Mission performance: Rate of climb at sea level 1245 ft (380 m) per min; ceiling 15,025 ft (4580 m).
Engine: One 260-hp PZL AI-14RA radial piston, with 195 liters of fuel.
Versions in service
Wilga 32: 230-hp Continental O-470-K/L/R engine. Higher standard of passenger comfort and shorter undercarriage (with glassfiber tailwheel unit leg) than previous models. First appeared in 1967.
Wilga 35: Similar to Wilga 32, also of 1967 appearance, but with a more powerful engine.
Lipnur Gelatik: This version of the Wilga was built in Indonesia by Lipnur under the new name, meaning Rice Bird. Production totalled 39 aircraft, built between 1964 and 1975, mostly for military use. Later production aircraft were based on the Wilga 32. Engines fitted to Gelatiks were 225-hp Continental O-470-13As, and 230-hp O-470-L and Rs.
Operators: Egypt, Indonesia (air force and navy, Gelatiks), Mongolia and Poland.

PZL-130 Orlik and PZL-130T Turbo Orlik
Poland

Surprise shown in the West at the new Polish multipurpose trainer being given a radial piston engine of the well-used M-14P series has been muted by the first flight in 1986 of the Turbo Orlik, developed with the assistance of Airtech Canada and powered by a 550-shp Pratt & Whitney Canada PT6A-25 turboprop.

The Orlik is the flying element of a three-part system, the other two comprising an electronic diagnostic system and a flight simulator. It can be used for primary and basic flying, and other training roles from navigation to combat, or for light strike, target acquisition, reconnaissance, target towing, etc. The use of modular instrumentation also allows the aircraft's avionics to be changed for yet another training role, that of a flying simulator for pilots of jet aircraft.

The first two prototype Orliks were flying in 1984 and production of a pre-series batch began in 1985.

Specifications (PZL-130 Orlik data)
Weapons: 2 underwing pylons for gun pods, bombs or other training and light attack weapons.
Accommodation: Student pilot and instructor in tandem stepped cockpits.
Wingspan: 26 ft 3 in (8.00 m).
Length: 27 ft 8¾ in (8.45 m).
Maximum take-off weight: 3527 lb (1600 kg).
Maximum speed: 227 mph (365 km/h).
Range: 881 miles (1417 km).
Mission performance: Rate of climb at sea level 1575 ft (480 m) per min; ceiling 17,060 ft (5200 m); G limits +6 aerobatic, −3 aerobatic; endurance 6 h 6 min.
Engine: One 360-hp Vedeneyev M-14Pm radial piston, with 430 liters of fuel.
Versions in service
PZL-130 Orlik: Standard radial-engined version for use as a military and civil trainer.
PZL-130T Turbo Orlik: Turboprop-engined version, as mentioned above with a hydraulically actuated retractable tricycle undercarriage (instead of pneumatic). First flown in 1986 it has avionics and equipment changes including the provision for up to 1411 lb (640 kg) of weapons on 4 underwing pylons. Maximum speed is increased to about 272 mph (438 km/h).
Operator: Poland.

Above: PZL Swidnik Mi-2s.

PZL Mielec TS-11 Iskra and IL I-22
Poland

Designed as a jet trainer to supersede the TS-8 Bies, which it did not entirely do, the Iskra first flew as a prototype on 5 February 1960. Today it looks rather dated, yet the aircraft re-entered production in 1982 (after a three-year suspension) in its latest Iskra-Bis DF form. Since the start of production in the 1960s, some 500 Iskras have been built.

The Iskra is of all-metal construction, with the fuselage forming a boom as it passes over the turbojet nozzle. Both India and Poland have substantial numbers in service.

In October 1986 Poland made public details of a new jet trainer and light attack aircraft as the Instytut Lotnictwa I-22. Presumed an Iskra replacement, it has the general appearance of an Alpha Jet and has a twin-barrel 23-mm underbelly gun and wing pylons.

Specifications (Iskra-Bis DF data)
Weapons: One 23-mm cannon in the nose, plus bombs (up to 221-lb/100-kg) weight each), rocket and/or machine-gun pods on 4 underwing pylons. Three reconnaissance cameras can be carried.
Accommodation: Student pilot and instructor in tandem.
Wingspan: 33 ft 0 in (10.06 m).
Length: 36 ft 7 in (11.15 m).
Maximum take-off weight: 8465 lb (3840 kg).
Maximum speed: 478 mph (770 km/h).
Range: 783 miles (1260 km).
Mission performance: Rate of climb at sea level 3820 ft (1164 m) per min; ceiling 37,730 ft (11,500 m); G limits +8 ultimate, −4 ultimate.

Engine: One 2425-lb (1100-kg) thrust SO-3W turbojet, with 1200 liters of fuel.
Versions in service
TS-11 Iskra: Initial production version, installed successively with a 1720-lb (780-kg) thrust HO-10, 2205-lb (1000-kg) thrust SO-1 and SO-3 turbojet. Entered Polish Air Force service in 1964.
Iskra 100: Version with underwing pylons for weapons training. A single-seat variant was developed for ground attack.
Iskra-Bis DF: Latest model, in production, as detailed above.
IL I-22: See above.
Operators: India (Iskra 100) and Poland (Iskra, Iskra 100 and Iskra-Bis DF).

PZL Swidnik (Mil) Mi-2
(NATO name Hoplite)
Poland

In September 1948 the Soviet bureau led by Mikhail Mil flew the prototype four-seat Mi-1, which became the first Soviet helicopter to go into large-scale production. Subsequent development of an enlarged twin-turbine derivative produced the Mi-2, which first flew a full 11 years after the Mi-1. After flight testing, the Mi-2 was given to Poland for manufacture and production there started in 1965. Over the ensuing years well over 4700 Mi-2s have been built for military and civil use, the great majority of military examples going to the

Below: PZL TS-11 Iskra demonstrator at Farnborough.

indigenous forces and the Soviet Union, where hundreds remain operational. As for the Mi-1 (NATO name Hare), the final user was probably China, though some may still remain serviceable elsewhere.

Specifications (Mi-2 data)

Weapons: A number of Polish Air Force Mi-2s each carry rocket pods or four Sagger (NATO name) anti-armor missiles on fuselage outriggers.
Accommodation: The pilot plus up to eight passengers, four stretchers and an attendant, or 1543-lb (700-kg) of freight.
Diameter of rotor: 47 ft 7 in (14.50 m).
Fuselage length: 37 ft 4¾ in (11.40 m).
Maximum take-off weight: 8157 lb (3700 kg).
Cruising speed: 124 mph (200 km/h).
Range: 273 miles (440 km).
Mission performance: Rate of climb at sea level 885 ft (270 m) per min; ceiling 13,125 ft (4000 m); hovering ceiling in ground effect about 6550 ft (2000 m); hovering ceiling out of ground effect about 3280 ft (1000 m); endurance 2 h 45 min.
Engines: Two 400-shp Polish-constructed Isotov GTD-350 turboshafts, with 600 liters of fuel standard.

Versions in service

Mi-2 series: Many versions of the Mi-2 have been produced to suit particular roles. These include weapon carrier, troop and freight transport, ambulance, SAR, trainer and photography types.
Operators: Bulgaria, Czechoslovakia, Lesotho, Nicaragua, Poland, Soviet Union and Syria.

Below: RFB Fantrainer ducted-fan trainer.

RFB Fantrainer 400 and 600
West Germany

Development of these unusual primary and basic trainers was to Federal German Defense Ministry contract, with the first prototype making its maiden flight on 27 October 1977. Constructed of light alloy, glassfiber and plastics, the Fantrainer has midmounted wings that sweep forward at an angle of 2 degrees 30 minutes and a cruciform rear fuselage that is joined to the main fuselage pod at three points, thereby allowing for the engine and pusher ducted-fan that are carried at the junction of the two fuselage sections. The duct for the five-blade fan is an integral part of the fuselage but carries no structural loads.

The only country to receive Fantrainers at the time of writing was Thailand, which ordered 31 400s and 16 600s. Of these, only two were built and assembled in West Germany. The remainder are being assembled in Thailand, the first few with glassfiber/plastics wings and the bulk with all-metal wings. It has been reported that the Luftwaffe has considered the Fantrainer as a replacement for its Piaggio P.149Ds.

Specifications (Fantrainer 400 data)

Accommodation: Student pilot and instructor in tandem stepped cockpits.
Wingspan: 31 ft 10 in (9.70 m).
Length: 31 ft 1¼ in (9.48 m).
Maximum take-off weight: 3968 lb (1800 kg).
Maximum speed: 230 mph (370 km/h).
Range: 1093 miles (1760 km).
Mission performance: Rate of climb at sea level 1550 ft (472 m) per min; ceiling 20,000 ft (6100 m); G limits +6 aerobatic, −3 aerobatic, +4.4 utility, −1.76 utility; endurance 6 h 19 min.
Engine: One 420-shp Allison 250-C20B turboshaft, with 475 liters of fuel standard.

Versions in service

Fantrainer 400: As detailed above.
Fantrainer 600: This model was the first to fly in production form, on 12 August 1984. One 650-shp Allison 250-C30 engine. Maximum take-off weight of 5070 lb (2300 kg), and maximum speed of 259 mph (417 km/h).
Operator: Thailand.

Rockwell B-1B
United States

Intended as a belated replacement for the B-52 in USAF Strategic Air Command, but with vastly wider capabilities, the B-1 program resulted from over 20 years of study. The original B-1 was cancelled in 1977, but in 1981 the B-1B was ordered into full-scale development, with planned production of 100 for SAC. The new B version has upgraded avionic systems, much better stealth qualities, much greater fuel capacity (resulting in gross weight rising from 389,000 lb to 477,000 lb), simple fixed engine inlets and many other changes. Today at last all emphasis is on self-protection by stealth and cunning onboard avionics systems, instead of on supersonic speed. It offers an enemy a radar signature 100 times smaller than that of the B-52 it replaces.

The B-1 pioneered swing-wings for large strategic bombers, the whole main panel of each wing being pivoted. Trailing-edge

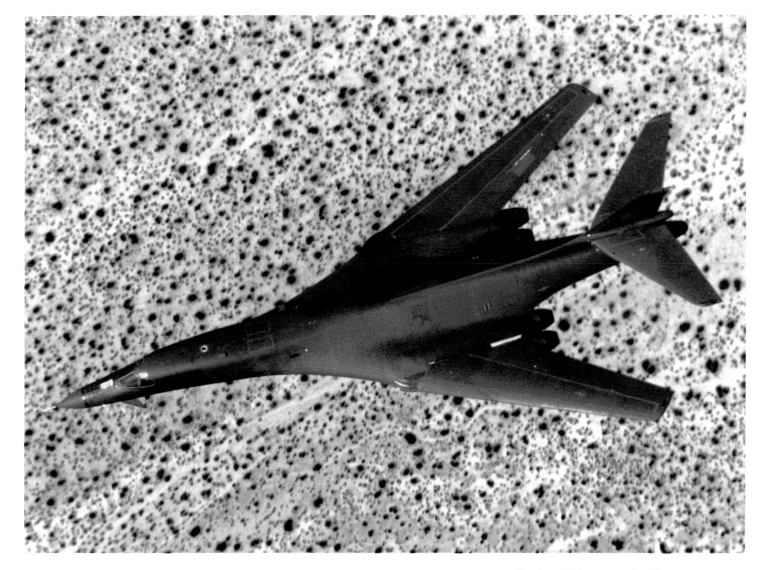

Above: Rockwell International B-1B strategic bomber.

spoilers provide roll control, serving as airbrakes. A challenging design feature was the need to start engines and take off in the shortest possible time, normally within three minutes – in order to get clear of the base before an enemy nuclear missile attack. In any case the structure and the avionics systems are 'hardened' to withstand the blast, overpressure and EMP (electromagnetic pulse) effects of nuclear explosions nearby. Altogether the B-1B is the most complex and probably the most costly bomber in history, approximately half the cost being attributed to the remarkable avionics systems needed for low-level navigation, weapon delivery and self-protection systems.

The first production B-1B flew on 18 October 1984. Initial delivery, to the 96th Bomb Wing at Dyess AFB, took place on 7 July 1985. This base was expected to be operational with 15 aircraft in late 1986, but failed as the result of fuel leaks, a reported overweight problem and many other deficiencies. All are considered rectifiable, and production of all 100 aircraft is proceeding at the planned four per month. It is claimed that the B-1B will penetrate 'present and predicted sophisticated enemy defences well into the 1990s'. Among possible missions are conventional or nuclear bomb delivery, cruise-missile launch, long-range maritime patrol and anti-ship attack, antisubmarine warfare and minelaying.

Specifications
Radar: Westinghouse AN/APQ-164 multimode offensive radar system, with navigation, penetration, weapon delivery and other functions, with a low-observable phased-array antenna. Defensive systems include the Eaton AN/ALQ-161A radio frequency surveillance/ECM system, tail warning function, AN/ASQ-184 management system and an expendable countermeasures system.
Weapons: Three weapons bays and eight underfuselage pylons for up to 22 AGM-86B air-launched cruise missiles, 38 SRAMS, nuclear bombs, or conventional weapons (typically 128 500-lb bombs).
Accommodation: 4 crew.
Wingspan: Spread 136 ft 8½ in (41.67 m), swept 78 ft 2½ in (23.84 m).
Length: 147 ft 0 in (44.81 m).
Maximum take-off weight: 477,000 lb (216,365 kg).
Maximum speed: About Mach 1.25.
Range: About 7455 miles (12,000 km) without in-flight refuelling.
Mission performance: Penetration speed at 200 ft (61 m) altitude over 600 mph (965 km/h).
Engines: Four 30,000-lb (13,610-kg) thrust General Electric F101-GE-102 turbofans.
Version in service
B-1B: First B-1B prototype to fly was the second converted B-1 prototype, on 23 March 1983. 100 production aircraft for delivery up to 1988.
Operator: United States.

Rockwell Commander/Aero Commander series
United States

This series covers a wide range of related twin-engined training, liaison and general-purpose transport aircraft, plus the single-engined Aero Commander/Lark Commander which is thought to be operated by the Indonesian Navy as a trainer. The twin-engined range was originated by Aero (Aero Design and Engineering), formed in 1950 to manufacture the original Aero Commander 520, deliveries to civil users beginning in 1952. Aero merged with North American Rockwell in 1967.

Specifications (Shrike Commander 500S data)
Accommodation: 4 to 7 persons.
Wingspan: 49 ft 0½ in (14.95 m).
Length: 36 ft 9¾ in (11.22 m).
Maximum take-off weight: 6750 lb (3061 kg).
Cruising speed: 203 mph (327 km/h).
Range: 798 miles (1284 km).
Mission performance: Rate of climb at sea level 1340 ft (410 m) per min; ceiling 19,400 ft (5910 m)
Engines: Two 290-shp Avco Lycoming IO-540-E1B5 pistons, with 590 liters of fuel.
Versions in service and Operators
Aero Commander 500B: Two 290-hp IO-540 engines, representing the most powerful version of the early 500/500A/500B range that was manufactured from 1958. Operators are the Bahamas, Benin,

Above: Dominican Republic Aero Commander 560.

Burkina-Faso, Greece (army) and Thailand, the latter using type for survey.

Shrike Commander 500S: Modernized version of the early Aero Commander 500 series for later production (still offered in late 1970s). As detailed above. Operators are Argentina, Iran and Mexico. The latter air force uses its aircraft for photographic reconnaissance as well as transport.

Aero Commander 560: This superseded the 520, the 560E remaining in production until 1980. The 560A was built as a 5/7-seater with 270-hp Avco Lycoming GO-480-B piston engines. The 560A converted to 275-hp GO-480-D1As, the 560E to 295-hp GO-480-C1B6s, and the 560F to 350-hp IGO-540-B1As. It is thought that most 560s in military use are As. Users are Colombia, Dominican Republic, South Korea and the United States (army, as the remaining U-9Cs).

Aero Commander 680: 1955 appearance, with 340-hp Avco Lycoming GSO-480 piston engines and seating for 4 to 6 persons, but upgraded in 1959 to the 680E with greater-span wings. Later models were the 680F and F-P with 380-hp IGSO-540s, the latter representing the pressurized version that was built between 1961 and 1966. Operators

Below: This T-39D, an unusual Rockwell Sabreliner, was modified for testing the Hornet's radar at the Patuxent River test establishment.

are Indonesia (navy and army) and Pakistan.

Turbo Commander 690: Introduced in 1971, the larger 690 offered major improvements to power, weight and performance. The 11-seat 690A has a wingspan of 46 ft 8 in (14.22 m), length of 44 ft 4¼ in (13.52 m) and a cruising speed of 322 mph (518 km/h) on the power of two 700-ehp Garrett TPE331-5-251K turboprop engines. Operators are Argentina (army), Iran and Pakistan (army).

Jetprop Commander 840: Pressurized 11-seat transport, differing from the 690C in having new wings. Two 840-shp Garrett TPE331-5-254K turboprops, bestowing a maximum speed of 333 mph (537 km/h). Certificated in 1979. Operated by the Pakistan Army.

Lark Commander: Four-seat braced high-wing cabin lightplane, powered by a 180-hp Avco Lycoming O-360. Maximum speed 138 mph (222 km/h). Believed to be operated as a trainer by the Indonesian Navy.

Rockwell T-39 Sabreliner
United States

To meet the USAF's UTX combat-readiness trainer and utility transport requirement North American Aviation designed the Sabreliner twin-jet, which first flew on 16 September 1958. Deliveries to the USAF

began in 1962 and production subsequently included versions for the US Navy, all under the military T-39 designation. Today USAF Sabreliners have largely been superseded by C-12Fs and C-21As. Those that remain in USAF and US Navy service are given below, along with those still operated abroad.

Specifications (USAF Sabreliner data)
Accommodation: 2 crew plus 4 to 7 passengers.
Wingspan: 44 ft 5¼ in (13.54 m).
Length: 43 ft 9 in (13.34 m).
Maximum take-off weight: 17,760 lb (8056 kg).
Maximum speed: 595 mph (958 km/h).
Range: 1950 miles (3138 km).
Mission performance: Ceiling 39,000 ft (11,885 m).
Engines: Two 3000-lb (1360-kg) thrust Pratt & Whitney J60-P-3 turbojets, with 3180 liters of fuel standard.

Versions in service
CT-39A and CT-39B: Built as T-39A pilot proficiency and T-39B radar trainers respectively. Now used by Air Force Communications Command and Air Force Systems Command. ATC also has CT-39As for the Instrument Flight Center.
CT-39E and CT-39G: US Navy models, for rapid response airlift of VIP passengers and 10-passenger staff transport roles respectively.
Sabreliner: Used as a VIP transport in Argentina (75A form, with two 4500-lb/ 2041-kg thrust General Electric CF700-2D-2 turbofans), VIP transport in Mexico, and as an ECM trainer in Sweden.
Operators: Argentina (air force and army), Bolivia, Mexico, Sweden and United States (air force and navy).

Rockwell International OV-10 Bronco
United States

Unique in the inventories of the US services, the Bronco was designed by North American Aviation as its bid to satisfy US requirements for a Light Armed Reconnaissance Aeroplane (LARA), producing a pod and twin-boom multimission counterinsurgency aircraft. The initial prototype made its maiden flight on 16 July 1965, and between 1967 and 1969 271 production OV-10As were delivered to the US Marine Corps and USAF. These were

Above: US Marine Corps Rockwell International OV-10D with NOS.

quickly pressed into duty as reconnaissance and forward air control (FAC) aircraft in Vietnam. The Bronco's low speed made it useful also as an armed escort for vulnerable helicopters, while Air Force OV-10As often undertook ground support roles.

In reality, although seven different designations were given to the Broncos delivered to the indigenous forces and export customers, all were basically OV-10As. The only real variations came in the unusual role of the Luftwaffe's aircraft and the NOS (Night Observation Surveillance) conversions that produced the OV-10Ds. However, it has been reported that the OV-10D is likely to become the subject of new production to meet the requirements of South Korea. If this happens, these aircraft will be the only true production-built variants of the OV-10A.

Specifications (OV-10D data)
Equipment: FLIR and laser target designator in nose. Survivability features include radar warning receiver, IR suppressor system for the engines, and chaff and flare dispensers. *Weapons:* One 20-mm General Electric M97 cannon in an underfuselage turret or two anhedral sponsons containing four 7.62-mm M60C machine-guns that also have four pylons for attack weapons. With the underfuselage attachment (only available when the 20-mm cannon is not fitted) the total weapon load can be 3600 lb (1633 kg). *Accommodation:* 2 crew in tandem. *Wingspan:* 40 ft 0 in (12.19 m). *Length:* 44 ft 0 in (13.41 m). *Maximum take-off weight:* 14,444 lb (6552 kg) overload. *Maximum speed:* 288 mph (463 km/h). *Combat radius:* 228 miles (367 km/h) with 3600 lb (1633 kg) of weapons. *Mission performance:* Rate of climb at sea level 3025 ft (920 m) per min; ceiling 30,000 ft (9145 m). *Engines:* Two 1040-ehp Garrett T76-G-420/421 turboprops, with 954 liters of fuel.

Versions in service
OV-10A: Initial version for the USMC and USAF, with two 715-ehp T76-G-416/417 turboprops. Same gross weight and weapon load as the OV-10D.
OV-10B and OV-10B(Z): West German target-towing versions, based on the OV-10A. OV-10B(Z)s differ by each having a pylon-mounted General Electric J85 turbojet to provide auxiliary power.
OV-10C: OV-10A for export to Thailand.
OV-10D: USMC NOS (Night Observation Surveillance) conversion of 17 OV-10As. South Korea reportedly might acquire 24 newly built examples.
OV-10E: OV-10As for Venezuela.
OV-10F: OV-10As for Indonesia.
Operators: West Germany, Indonesia, South Korea(?), Morocco, Thailand, United States (air force and marine corps) and Venezuela.

Rockwell International T-2 Buckeye
United States

The Buckeye was selected for US Navy service as a two-seat general-purpose jet trainer, carrying the necessary equipment for operation from aircraft carriers. The first T2J-1, as the T-2A was originally designated, made its maiden flight on 31 January 1958. The US Navy received three versions, the T-2A, B and C, comprising the majority of the 609 Buckeyes built. The T-2A (two 3400-lb; 1542-kg thrust Westinghouse J34s) was, however, withdrawn by 1973, followed later by the T-2B. To make up for a shortage of T-2Cs, 15 T-2Bs were taken out of store in 1982 and refurbished for service. T-2Ds and Es, similar to T-2Cs, went to Venezuela and Greece.

Specifications (T-2C data)
Weapons: Optional layouts provide for guns, practice bombs, practice bomb clusters or containers, rocket launchers/containers, or target-towing equipment on two underwing attachments, with a total weight of 640 lb (290 kg). Alternatively, up to 3500 lb (1587 kg) of weapons on 6 underwing attachments using an attack kit. *Accommodation:* Student pilot and instructor in tandem. *Wingspan:* 38 ft 1½ in (11.62 m). *Length:* 38 ft 3½ in (11.67 m). *Maximum take-off weight:* 13,191 lb (5983 kg). *Maximum speed:* 530 mph (852 km/h). *Range:* 1070 miles (1722 km).

Above: Hellenic Air Force Rockwell International T-2E Buckeye.

Mission performance: Rate of climb at sea level 5900 ft (1800 m) per min; ceiling 45,500 ft (13,870 m).
Engines: Two 2950-lb (1338-kg) thrust General Electric J85-GE-4 turbojets, with 2616 liters of fuel when including the wingtip tanks.
Versions in service
T-2B: Two 3000-lb (1361-kg) thrust Pratt & Whitney J60-P-6 turbojets. Originally delivered between 1965 and 1969. Up to 15 may remain in active use.
T-2C: Current US Navy version, as detailed above. 231 were built, the bulk of which remain active.
T-2D: Similar to the T-2C but with arrester gear deleted and avionics changes. 24 delivered, half with attack kits. 20 remain in use for training, including all attack models.
T-2E: Similar to T-2C but for the avionics. 40 delivered to Greece with attack kits for training. 36 or 37 remain active.
Operators: Greece (T-2E), United States (navy, T-2B and C) and Venezuela (T-2D).

Below: RTAF-5 forward air control and training aircraft.

RTAF-5
Thailand

The Science and Weapon Systems Development Centre of the Royal Thai Air Force has designed and built prototypes of a tandem two-seat advanced trainer and forward air control (FAC) aircraft as the RTAF-5, the first of which flew initially on 5 October 1984. Resembling in some respects a smaller and very much lighter Rockwell Bronco, which is in Thai service, it is nevertheless an entirely indigenous aircraft and will be expected to enter military service in the coming years. Of conventional pod and twin-boom configuration, its most unusual feature is the choice of mounting the single engine in the rear of the fuselage pod, thereby demanding a pusher propeller.

Specifications (RTAF-5 data)
Weapons: Four underwing pylons for 500 lb (227 kg) of attack weapons.
Accommodation: Student pilot and instructor or pilot and copilot in tandem.
Wingspan: 32 ft 4¼ in (9.86 m).
Length: 32 ft 8 in (9.96 m).
Maximum take-off weight: 4750 lb (2154 kg).
Cruising speed: 132 mph (213 km/h).

Mission performance: Rate of climb at sea level 300 ft (91 m) per min; minimum flying speed 98 mph (158 km/h).
Engine: One 420-shp Allison 250-B17C turboprop, with 220 liters of fuel.
Version in service
RTAF-5: Prototypes only.
Operator: Thailand (eventually?).

Saab J 32 Lansen
Sweden

First flown as a prototype multipurpose combat aircraft on 3 November 1952, the Lansen became a standard Swedish attack aircraft and fighter during the late 1950s. Today the only remaining examples in operational use belong to Flying Unit 32 of squadron F13M based at Malmslatt. This unit flies electronic warfare training missions in support of the SwAF and provides a target-towing service to this air force and others. For the electronic role the unit has 14 J 32Es, converted J 32B all-weather fighters and carrying sophisticated equipment for radar and radio jamming and countermeasures training. As aggressors, these can simulate enemy aircraft to test the effectiveness of air defense systems. A further six J 32Ds operate as target tugs, while three dual-control J 32Bs are used for training and radioactive sampling.

Specifications (J 32E data unless otherwise stated for J 32D)
Accommodation: 2 crew. Target can be streamed to 1.5 km.
Wingspan: 42 ft 7¾ in (13.00 m).
Length: 48 ft 1 in (14.65 m).
Maximum take-off weight: Approx 28,660 lb (13,000 kg).
Maximum speed: Restricted to 340 mph (550 km/h) for J 32D target towing.
Mission performance: G limit 5 for J 32B to prolong the structural life.
Engine: One 14,330-lb (6500-kg) thrust with afterburning Svenska Flygmotor RM6B (Rolls-Royce Avon) turbojet.
Versions in service
J 32B, J 32D and *J 32E:* As detailed above.
Operator: Sweden.

Above: Saab J 32E Lansen ECM-aggressor of Swedish Air Force Squadron F13M.

Saab 35 Draken
Sweden

When it was designed in 1952-54 this 'double delta' was aerodynamically the most advanced fighter in the world, a novel feature being that most items were arranged in the thickened wingroots one-behind-the-other (the wingroot covering most of the length of the aircraft). The huge wing area suited the aircraft to short take-offs and landings, if necessary from straight stretches of country road to escape from vulnerable airfields. The brilliance of this aircraft is seen by the fact that not only did it support 10 years of production totalling 606 aircraft in six major versions, for fighting, reconnaissance, ground attack and dual training, but it outperformed the mission capability of the British Lightning on just one engine of the same type.

The first of three Draken prototypes flew initially on 25 October 1955, followed eventually by the first production J 35A on 15 February 1958. The final J 35F and the versions exported to Finland and Denmark are all still in service, and deservedly popular. They have all-weather interception capability, and some carry heavy ground-attack loads. The last 64 in Swedish service are being upgraded to J 35J standard for continued use to at least 1995. Even some much older Drakens have many years ahead of them after being sold secondhand to Austria.

Specifications (35XD data)
Radar: Nose radar.
Weapons: Provision for two 30-mm cannon in the wings. Up to 9000 lb (4080 kg) of weapons carried under the wings and fuselage, including 4 Sidewinder air-to-air missiles, bombs, rockets, etc.
Accommodation: The pilot.
Wingspan: 30 ft 10 in (9.40 m).
Length: 50 ft 4 in (15.35 m).

Right: Saab J 35F Draken, armed with four Falcon missiles.

Maximum take-off weight: 33,069 lb (15,000 kg).
Maximum speed: Mach 2.
Combat radius: 395 miles (636 km).
Mission performance: Rate of climb at sea level 34,450 ft (10,500 m) per min.
Engine: One 17,650-lb (8000-kg) thrust with afterburning Volvo Flygmotor RM6C, a license-built Rolls-Royce Avon 300 type.
Versions in service
J 35D: Developed from the earlier J 35B fighter, with the more powerful RM6C engine and increased fuel tankage. Deliveries started to the SwAF in 1962. Now out of SwAF active use but 24 sold to Austria.
J 35F: SwAF single-seat all-weather fighter, with a 30-mm Aden cannon and 2 or 4 Saab-built RB27/RB28 Falcon air-to-air missiles. Improved Saab S7 collision-course fire-control system and radar over earlier J 35D. Serving with F10 Wing at Angelholm. See J 35J.
J 35J: Designation of 64 Drakens of F10 Wing, SwAF, being modified to extend their useful life into the 1990s until superseded by Gripens. 6 underwing pylons instead of 4, for 4 missiles and 2 auxiliary fuel tanks or 2 missiles and 4 tanks, modified radar, updated IR target seeker, and other avionics changes.
SK 35C: 2-seat training version of the J 35A, with tandem seating. First flown in 1959.
Saab-35XD: Export version for Denmark, delivered in F-35 attack-fighter, RF-35 reconnaissance and TF-35 training forms.
Saab-35S: Export version received by Finland in J 35BS and J 35XS Valmet-assembled attack-fighter forms. XD and S models have overload take-off weight of 35,274 lb (16,000 kg), allowing nine 1000-lb (454-kg) bombs to be carried.
Operators: Austria, Denmark, Finland and Sweden.

Saab 37 Viggen
Sweden

The generation after the Draken, the Viggen was likewise developed as a family of closely related aircraft: the AJ 37 for attack, the SH 37 for maritime reconnaissance (whose many sensors include radar), the SF 37 for overland reconnaissance (without radar), the SK 37 dual trainer and the extremely advanced JA 37 all-weather fighter. Like all Swedish aircraft, the Viggens are designed for sustained operations from dirt strips and roadways, so they have rapid short take-off and very slow landing, using the giant delta wings and

Above: Saab JA 37 Viggen in the latest color finish.

flapped canard foreplanes, strong tandem-wheel landing gears for 'no flare' landings, and engine thrust reverser.

The first of seven prototypes flew on 8 February 1967, and the AJ version entered service in June 1971. Production of the AJ, SF, SH and SK amounted to 180. The chronologically later JA has a modified engine, new flight controls and totally different avionics for interception of all kinds of aerial targets, with secondary attack capability. A large proportion of the airframe is bonded metal honeycomb construction, and at least the last 20 of the 149 aircraft ordered will have fins of composite carbonfiber material to gain experience for the JAS 39 Gripen. Most unusually, Saab-Scania make their own zero-height zero-speed ejection seats, and nearly all equipment is of Swedish origin. The final JA 37 delivery is due in 1988, when 17 Sw AF squadrons will be Viggen-equipped. Incredibly there have been no export sales.

Specifications (JA 37 data)
Radar: Ericsson PS-46/A multimode pulse Doppler radar, with air-to-air and air-to-ground functions. SATT radar warning system.
Weapons: One 30-mm Oerlikon KCA long-range cannon, with 150 rounds of ammunition, plus four underwing and 3

underfuselage pylons for 2 Sky Flash and six Sidewinder air-to-air missiles or four pods each containing six 135-mm rockets as a ground attack option.
Accommodation: The pilot.
Wingspan: 34 ft 9¼ in (10.60 m).
Foreplane span: 17 ft 10½ in (5.45 m).
Length: 53 ft 9¾ in (16.40 m).
Maximum take-off weight: 37,478 lb (17,000 kg).
Maximum speed: Over Mach 2.
Combat radius: Up to 620 miles (1000 km).
Mission performance: Time to 10,000 m under 1 min 40 sec; take-off distance about 1312 ft (400 m).
Engine: One 28,109 lb (12,750 kg) thrust with afterburning Volvo Flygmotor RM8B turbofan.

Versions in service
AJ 37: First production version, as an all-weather attack aircraft to supersede Lansens. Delivery to F7 at Såtenäs, the first operating Wing, began in 1971. Uses PS-37/A multimode monopulse X-band radar, with search, acquisition, ranging, collision warning, beacon homing and mapping functions. 26,015-lb (11,800-kg) thrust RM8A turbofan.
JA 37: All-weather interceptor with attack capability, as detailed above. Final production version.
SF 37: All-weather photographic reconnaissance aircraft, superseding the S 35E Draken. Delivered from 1977. Engine

as for AJ 37. 2 Sidewinders for self-protection. 4 low-level and 2 high-altitude cameras, a VKA 702 IR camera, IR sensor, and ECM registration equipment.
SH 37: All-weather maritime reconnaissance version, delivered from 1975. Same engine and armament as the SF 37 but with surveillance radar, ECM registration equipment, ECM pods, night reconnaissance pod plus a long-range camera or second night recce pod.
SK 37: 2-seat trainer, with tandem seats, able to carry AJ 37 armament if required. Delivered from 1972. Engine as for AJ 37.
Operator: Sweden.

Saab 39 Gripen
Sweden

The Swedish policy of total self-sufficiency in defense materiel is being continued with this totally new multirole aircraft, whose first prototype is due to fly in late 1987, with entry to service scheduled for 1992. The first prototype was rolled out on 26 April 1987. Naturally, everything possible is being done to minimize risk, and the engine (though made wholly in Sweden) is an advanced version of the well-proven General Electric F404. Moreover, although it follows the currently fashionable canard delta layout, with a basically unstable shape made flyable by fast-acting fly-by-wire control computers, the Gripen is the smallest and lightest of all the new fighters, with a clean gross take-off weight of only 8.4 tons. This is expected to result in low cost, a fixed-price contract of 30 billion Kroner covering the price of all development and the first 30 aircraft. A further 100 are expected to follow.

The full designation is JAS 39, JAS being Swedish initials for 'fighter, attack, reconnaissance,' while the name means Griffon. All JAS 39 pilots will be trained to fly all three missions, and it will be possible to switch from one role to another in minutes. The initial 1992 deliveries will replace AJ 37 Viggens. From 1994 Gripens will begin to replace the J 35J Drakens and SF/SH 37 Viggens, and from 2003 JA 37 Viggens. Every part of the aircraft is as compact as possible. Although the Gripen radar is more capable than that in the JA 37, it weighs only 344 lb (156 kg) compared with 602 lb (273 kg). The airframe has about 30 percent composite materials to reduce weight, with British Aerospace helping with the design and construction of the carbon-fiber wings. Operations will be possible from any 800 m stretch of roadway 9 m wide!

Specifications (JAS 39 data)
Radar: Ericsson/Ferranti PS-05/A multimode pulse-Doppler system, with a radar and FLIR pod, for search and tracking of multitargets, ground and sea attack, and reconnaissance.
Weapons: One 27-mm Mauser BK27 cannon in the fuselage, wingtip-carried Sky Flash, Sidewinder or other air-to-air missiles, and attack weapons or stores on 4 underwing pylons.
Accommodation: The pilot.
Wingspan: About 26 ft 3 in (8.00 m).
Length: About 45 ft 11 in (14.00 m).
Maximum take-off weight: About 18,700 lb (8480 kg).
Maximum speed: Supersonic.

Above: Saab JAS 39 Gripen multimission combat aircraft.

Engine: One approximately 18,000-lb (8165-kg) thrust Volvo Flygmotor RM12 turbofan (General Electric F404J type).
Version in service
JAS 39 Gripen: Under development. For service from 1992.
Operator: Eventually Sweden.

Saab 91 Safir
Sweden

Dating back to the end of World War II, the Safir was designed as a three-seat cabin monoplane. With the Saab 90 Scandia Airliner, it represented the company's introduction to full civil manufacturing activities after passenger conversions of Boeing B-17 Flying Fortress bombers from 1944. The prototype Safir made its maiden flight on the power of a 130-hp de Havilland Gipsy Major IC engine on 20 November 1945, and more powerful versions entered military service as trainers.

Specifications (91D data)
Accommodation: 4 seats in an enclosed cabin.
Wingspan: 34 ft 9 in (10.60 m).

Below: Swedish Air Force Saab 91 Safir.

Length: 26 ft 4¼ in (8.04 m).
Maximum take-off weight: 2657 lb (1205 kg).
Maximum speed: 165 mph (265 km/h).
Range: 658 miles (1060 km).
Mission performance: Rate of climb at sea level 805 ft (245 m) per min; ceiling 16,400 ft (5000 m).
Engine: One 180-hp Avco Lycoming O-360-A1A piston, with 175 liters of fuel standard

Versions in service

Saab 91B: Swedish Air Force designation Sk 50B. 190-hp Avco Lycoming O-435-A piston engine.
Saab 91C: Swedish designation Sk 50C. First flown in 1953. 4-seat version of the Saab 91B.
Saab 91D: As detailed above. More powerful generator fitted, plus rudder trim and new brakes.

Operators: Austria (91D) and Sweden (91B and C).

Below: Austrian Air Force Saab 105Ös.

Saab 105
Sweden

The Saab 105 was developed as a private-venture twin-jet multipurpose aircraft for military operation, with two seats side by side when used as a trainer and light attack aircraft and four seats in liaison form. The prototype made its maiden flight on 29 June 1963. In Swedish service the type undertakes training, light attack and reconnaissance roles, while Austrian trainers have a secondary air defense role in an emergency.

Specifications (Sk 60A data unless otherwise stated)

Weapons: Sk 60B. Up to 1545 lb (700 kg) of weapons on 6 underwing pylons, including air-to-surface missiles, two 30-mm gun pods and twelve 135-mm rockets.
Accommodation: Crew of 2 side by side as a trainer. Alternatively 4 persons in a liaison role.
Wingspan: 31 ft 2 in (9.50 m).

Length: 34 ft 5 in (10.50 m).
Maximum take-off weight: 9921 lb (4500 kg).
Maximum speed: 478 mph (770 km/h).
Range: 1105 miles (1780 km).
Mission performance: Rate of climb at sea level 3935 ft (1200 m) per min; ceiling 44,290 ft (13,500 m).
Engines: Two 1640-lb (743-kg) thrust Turboméca Aubisque turbofans, with 2050 liters of fuel.

Versions in service

Sk 60A: Swedish Air Force trainer, as detailed above. Deliveries began in 1966 to the Ljungbyhed Air Force station.
Sk 60B: Similar to the Sk 60A but with provision for light attack missions as secondary to training. Some SwAF Bs are assigned to the attack role.
Sk 60C: First flown in 1967, this is similar to the Sk 60B but with a Fairchild KB-18 panoramic reconnaissance camera installed in the modified fuselage nose.
Saab 105Ö: The export version, delivered from 1970 to the Austrian Air Force as a

trainer with attack capability. Powered by two 2850-lb (1293-kg) thrust General Electric J85-GE-17B turbojets, maximum speed is increased to 603 mph (970 km/h) and the weapon load of 4410 lb (2000 kg) can include Sidewinder air-to-air missiles.
Operators: Austria (105Ö) and Sweden (Sk 60A, B and C).

Saab Safari and Supporter/Mushshak
Sweden

The two- or three-seat Safari trainer and utility monoplane was originally known by the designation MFI-15 and flew initially on 11 July 1969. A fully militarized derivative became the MFI-17, later Supporter, though the Safari can carry the same weight of weapons for military training. By the end of production in 1978, 250 examples of these aircraft had been built for civil and military use. Only Norway uses the Safari as a military aircraft.

Specifications (Supporter data)
Weapons: Up to 661 lb (300 kg) of weapons on 6 underwing pylons, including 2 twin-gun pods, 6 antitank missiles, rockets, etc. Equipment for other possible roles including reconnaissance, FAC and target towing.
Accommodation: 2 seats side by side, with room at the rear for a third seat.
Wingspan: 29 ft 0½ in (8.85 m).
Length: 22 ft 11½ in (7.00 m).
Maximum take-off weight: 2646 lb (1200 kg).
Maximum speed: 147 mph (236 km/h).
Mission performance: Rate of climb at sea level 805 ft per min (246 m); ceiling 13,450 ft (4100 m); G limits +4.4 utility, −1.76 utility, +6 aerobatic, −3 aerobatic; endurance 5 h 10 min with fuel reserves.
Engine: One 200-hp Avco Lycoming IO-360-A1B6 piston, with 190 liters of fuel standard.
Versions in service
Safari: Trainer and liaison aircraft. 16 used by Norway since the early 1980s.

Supporter: Almost identical aircraft to the Safari, but with a weapon delivery system. Royal Danish Air Force designation is T-17. The Aircraft Manufacturing Factory of the Pakistan Aeronautical Complex was established in 1981 for the license-building of Supporters for the Pakistan Air Force and Army as Mushshaks (approx 140 are in service).
Operators: Denmark (air force and army, Supporter), Norway (Safari), Pakistan (air force and army, Mushshak) and Zambia (Supporter).

SEPECAT Jaguar
United Kingdom and France

In the early 1960s both Britain and France were in the market for a new advanced trainer. As both nations counted their respective pennies or centimes it became clear that it would be desirable to incorporate some attack capability and, eventually, this role became the more important. In the early 1960s there was a growing accord between the British and French aviation industries, leading to a number of Anglo-French collaborations, and this new supersonic strike/fighter trainer proved to be the first of them when the two nations finalized a co-operative agreement in May 1965. A new company, the Société Européenne de Production de l'Avion d'Ecole de Combat et d'Appui Tactique (SEPECAT) was formed, combining Breguet (later Dassault-Breguet) and British Aircraft Corporation (now BAe), to develop this aircraft which became the Jaguar.

To meet the specifications of the RAF's Air Staff Target 362 and the French ECAT (Ecole de Combat et d'Appui Tactique) features of the Breguet Br.121 and British Aircraft Corporation P.45 were taken for development into the Jaguar, and the first of eight prototypes, a French Jaguar E two-seat trainer, made the type's maiden flight on 8 September 1968. Initial planned versions were the Jaguar A single-seat tactical support aircraft for France;

Above: Danish Saab Supporter.

Jaguar B, a UK two-seat trainer; Jaguar E, French two-seat trainer; Jaguar M, single-seat tactical aircraft for the Aéronavale (abandoned in 1973); and the single-seat tactical support Jaguar S for the United Kingdom. Subsequently, an export version known as the Jaguar International was developed; generally similar to the single-seat Jaguar S, this introduced more power and, of course, differed in equipment to meet the requirement of individual nations. The Jaguar International equips the air arms of Ecuador, India, Nigeria and Oman; for the Indian Air Force, which plans to acquire a total of 116, the majority are being assembled or built under license by Hindustan Aeronautics Ltd (HAL). Manufacture of the original versions for the RAF and Armée de l'Air has been completed and comprised 202 and 200 respectively.

Specifications (Jaguar International data)
Radar: No radar normally installed but Thomson-CSF Agave multipurpose radar optional.
Weapons: Two 30-mm Aden or DEFA 553 cannon. One fuselage centerline and 4 underwing hardpoints for up to 10,500 lb (4763 kg) of stores. These can include free-fall or retarded bombs, cluster bombs, rockets, auxiliary fuel tanks and a reconnaissance pack; missiles can include an air-to-surface Martel, 2 Sidewinders or two Matra Magic air-to-air missiles.
Accommodation: The pilot.
Wingspan: 28 ft 6 in (8.69 m).
Length: 55 ft 2½ in (16.83 m) including the probe.
Maximum take-off weight: 34,610 lb (15,700 kg).
Maximum speed: 1056 mph (1700 km/h).
Combat radius: 530 miles (853 km), internal fuel, hi-lo-hi mission.
Mission performance: G limit +8.6.
Engines: 2 Rolls-Royce/Turboméca Adour Mk 804 afterburning turbofans of

Above: SEPECAT Jaguar GR.Mk 1 of No 20 Squadron, RAF, carrying two laser-guided bombs, a Westinghouse ECM pod and a chaff dispenser.

8040-lb (3647-kg) thrust or 2 Adour Mk 811s of 8400-lb (3810-kg) thrust, with 4200 liters of fuel standard.

Versions in service

Jaguar A: French single-seat version with 7305-lb (3313-kg) thrust Adour Mk 102 turbofans.

Jaguar B: UK 2-seater which the RAF designates Jaguar T.Mk 2, becoming Jaguar T.Mk 2A following installation of Ferranti FIN 1064 INS; initially powered by Adour Mk 102s before replacement by uprated Adour Mk 104s of 8040-lb (3647-kg) thrust.

Jaguar E: French 2-seat version with Adour Mk 102 turbofans.

Jaguar S: UK single-seat version which the RAF designated Jaguar GR.Mk 1, becoming redesignated Jaguar GR.Mk 1A after installation of FIN 1064 INS. Like Jaguar B, initial Adour Mk 102s replaced by Adour Mk 104s. Some aircraft used in a dedicated reconnaissance role have a reconnaissance pod beneath the fuselage and can also carry 2 Sidewinders for self-protection.

Jaguar International: Export version of Jaguar S with Adour Mk 804 and Mk 811 turbofans; variations also in armament and other equipment to match the requirements of operating air arms.

Operators: Ecuador, France, India, Nigeria, Oman and United Kingdom.

Shenyang J-8 I, J-8 II and F-8 II
(NATO name Finback)
China

The first indigenous Chinese fighter and the first Chinese fighter to receive its own NATO code name, the J-8 (or Jianjiji-8) is unusual also for having been designed in two quite different forms. Development began as long ago as the 1960s and by the end of that decade a prototype had been built. Understandably, this had some resemblance to the MiGs in Chinese service and manufacture, typified by a nose air-intake with centerbody. Much larger and heavier than the MiG-21, it was hoped that by using two of the 13,448-lb

(6100-kg) thrust with afterburning Chengdu Wopen-7B turbojets found singly in the MiG adequate power would be provided. This did not prove the case and production of the J-8 I is believed to have been kept to only about 50.

Development began in the 1970s of an improved version of the J-8, leading to the J-8 II, which took to the air initially in May 1984. The general change to fuselage configuration can be put down to two major factors: firstly, the selection of two 14,550-lb (6600-kg) thrust with afterburning Wopen-13A II turbojets (Chinese version of the Soviet Tumansky

Below: Prototype of the Chinese Shenyang J-8 II fighter.

R-13-300) to improve performance but requiring a greater volume of air that only large side intakes could satisfy successfully; and better relations with the West could see China acquiring modern airborne radar and other avionics including head-up displays, the former requiring a nose radome. It has been reported that the United States government has permitted the sale of avionics that fall under foreign military sales regulations and that sufficient will be provided initially for 50 production J-8 IIs. These will come off production lines in the early 1990s. As the US avionics would not be permitted for re-export from China, the intended export F-8 II will require avionics from another nation. A model of the J-8 II was displayed at Farnborough International in 1986.

Specifications (J-8 II data)
Radar: Airborne radar. Other avionics will include IFF, ECM and a radar-warning receiver.
Weapons: One 23-mm Type 23-3 cannon in an underfuselage pack, with 200 rounds of ammunition, plus one underfuselage and 6 underwing pylons for air-to-air and attack weapons. Missiles could include Pili 2 (also known as PL-2 or CAA-1) IR homing AA missiles of Atoll type and/or the more advanced PL-7.
Accommodation: The pilot.
Wingspan: 30 ft 8 in (9.34 m).
Length: 70 ft 10 in (21.59 m).
Maximum take-off weight: 39,240 lb (17,800 kg).
Maximum speed: Mach 2.2 estimated.
Range: 1365 miles (2200 km) estimated.
Mission performance: Rate of climb at sea level 39,375 ft (12,000 m) per min; ceiling 65,600 ft (20,000 m); G limit +4.83 in sustained turn at Mach 0.9.

Engines: As detailed with 5500 liters of fuel standard (estimated).
Versions in service
J-8 I: As detailed above. Perhaps 50 production aircraft.
J-8 II: Redesigned and higher power version, for service in the 1990s.
F-8 II: Intended export version, with avionics differences to the J-8 II.
Operator: China.

Shin Meiwa PS-1 and US-1
Japan

Because of its geographical situation, it is hardly surprising that Japan is one of only three nations to operate large military flying-boats for antisubmarine warfare, the other two being China and the Soviet Union. The prototype Shin Meiwa PS-1 made its maiden flight on 5 October 1967 and the JMSDF (Japan Maritime Self-Defense Force) eventually received 23 full production examples for use by the 31st Air Group. Meanwhile, since 1975 the JMSDF has also been receiving US-1 air/sea rescue amphibians, similar to the PS-1 but with an hydraulically retractable undercarriage instead of just the PS-1's beaching gear, more powerful engines from the seventh machine (redesignated US-1A; to be retrofitted to previous US-1s), and equipment changes to suit its different role. Ten US-1As had been accepted by 1987.

To keep take-off and landing speeds and distances low, both aircraft types have boundary layer control system (with power for 'blowing' from a T58 gas turbine engine), high-lift leading-edge slats and large (blown) trailing-edge flaps, especially useful to the PS-1 as this alights many times to lower its sonar for submarine detection. Other PS-1

systems includes Doppler and search radar (as for the US-1), MAD, sonobuoys and Julie echo-ranging equipment.

Specifications (US-1A data)
Radar: AN/APS-80N search radar. AN/APN-187C Doppler radar.
Accommodation: 9 crew and 12 stretchers or 20 sitting casualties. Equipment includes 2 liferaft containers, rescue platform and motorized lifeboat.
Wingspan: 108 ft 9 in (33.15 m).
Length: 109 ft 9 in (33.46 m).
Maximum take-off weight: 94,800 lb (43,000 kg).
Maximum speed: 325 mph (522 km/h).
Mission performance: Rate of climb at sea level 1600 ft (488 m); ceiling 23,600 ft (7195 m).
Engines: four 3490-ehp Ishikawajima/General Electric T64-IHI-10J turboprops, with 22,500 liters of fuel.
Versions in service
PS-1: ASW flying-boat, with 4 bombs, 4 torpedoes in underwing pods and six 5-in rockets. Powered by four 3060-ehp T64-IHI-10 turboprops.
US-1A: Air/sea rescue amphibian.
Operator: Japan (navy).

Shorts 330-UTT and Sherpa
United Kingdom

Developed as a military utility transport from the Shorts 330 regional airliner, the STOL-capable 330-UTT has the same airframe (with a rectangular section fuselage and strut-braced high wing) and engines but with a

Below: JMSDF Shin Meiwa US-1A SAR amphibian.

Above: Shorts Sherpa in service with the USAF as the C-23A.

strengthened floor for up to 8000 lb (3630 kg) of freight or, alternatively, 33 troops, 30 paratroops, or 15 stretchers and four attendants. Two were acquired by the Royal Thai Army in 1984-85, with two more going to the Thai police.

The Sherpa was developed by Shorts as a freighter version of the 330-200 passenger airliner, featuring an hydraulically-operated rear ramp door for straight-in loading to the main cabin. The prototype first flew on 23 December 1982. Eighteen entered USAF service between 1984 and 1985 as C-23As, these being flown by the 10th Military Airlift Squadron of MAC from the base at Zweibrücken in West Germany. Under the European Distribution System Aircraft (EDSA) role, they are tasked to carry vital spares between European USAF bases.

Specifications (C-23A data)
Accommodation: Flight crew of 3 plus up to 7000 lb (3175 kg) of freight (possibly four LD3 or 7 CO8 containers), two ½-ton vehicles of jeep type typically, or passengers (or mixed passengers and freight).
Wingspan: 74 ft 8 in (22.76 m).
Length: 58 ft 0½ in (17.69 m).
Maximum take-off weight: 22,900 lb (10,387 kg).
Cruising speed: 218 mph (352 km/h) at

21,000-lb (9525-kg) AUW.
Range: 225 miles (362 km) with full load, 770 miles (1239 km) with 5000-lb (2268-kg) load.
Mission performance: Rate of climb at sea level 1180 ft (360 m) per min.
Engines: Two 1198-shp Pratt & Whitney Canada PT6A-45R turboprops, with 2545 liters of fuel.
Versions in service
330-UTT and C-23A Sherpa: As described above.
Operators: Thailand (army, 330-UTT) and United States (C-23A Sherpa).

Shorts SC.7 Skyvan
United Kingdom

The Skyvan has been a remarkably successful STOL light transport, finding favor in both commercial and military forms. The root of its success lies in its completely square-section main cabin, reached via a wide rear door through which vehicles, freight or troops can be rapidly loaded/unloaded. The prototype

Below: Shorts Skyvan Series 3M, used by the Singapore Air Defense Command.

Above: SIAI-Marchetti S.208M in Italian markings.

first flew on 17 January 1963 and by 1986 58 had passed into military and police service, not including those of Mexico that are believed to be dual commercial/military and the two used by the government of Ciskei.

Specifications (Skyvan Series 3M data)
Radar: Weather radar optional. Racal ASR 360 surveillance radar on Oman Skyvans for patrol and SAR roles.
Accommodation: Pilot or pilot and copilot plus up to 6000 lb (2721 kg) of freight, 19 staff passengers, 22 troops, 16 paratroops or 12 stretchers and 2 attendants.

Below: SIAI-Marchetti S.211 jet trainer and light attack aircraft.

Wingspan: 64 ft 11 in (19.79 m).
Length: 41 ft 4 in (12.60 m).
Maximum take-off weight: 14,500 lb (6577 kg).
Cruising speed: 202 mph (324 km/h).
Range: 240 miles (386 km) with 5000-lb (2268-kg) payload.
Mission performance: Rate of climb at sea level 1530 ft (465 m) per min; ceiling 22,000 ft (6700 m).
Engines: Two 715-shp Garrett TPE331-2-201A turboprops, with 1332 liters of fuel standard.
Versions in service
Skyvan: Current production versions are the Series 3M and the heavier (15,000-lb/6804-kg) Series 3M-200. Singapore Skyvans are available for SAR.
Operators: Argentina (navy), Austria, Botswana, Ciskei (government), Ecuador

(army), Ghana, Guyana, Indonesia, Lesotho (police), Malawi (police), Mauritania, Mexico, Nepal (army), Oman, Panama (national guard), Sharjah (Amiri Guard), Singapore, Thailand (police) and North Yemen.

SIAI-Marchetti S.208
Italy

The S.208 is a larger companion of the S.205 lightplane and, indeed, uses many of its components. First flown on 22 May 1967, it was initially ordered for the Italian Air Force (24 S.208Ms) as a liaison and training aircraft with a jettisonable starboard cabin door. Construction is all metal and, unlike the S.205, the undercarriage retracts.

Specifications (S.208M data)
Accommodation: 5 persons in an enclosed cabin. Compartment for baggage to the rear of the seats.
Wingspan: 35 ft 7½ in (10.86 m).
Length: 26 ft 3 in (8.00 m).
Maximum take-off weight: 3307 lb (1500 kg).
Maximum speed: 199 mph (320 km/h).
Range: 746 miles (1200 km).
Mission performance: Ceiling 17,715 m (5400 m).
Engine: One 260-hp Avco Lycoming O-540-E4A5 piston, with 215 liters of fuel standard.
Version in service
S.208: As detailed above. Tunisian S.208As were acquired in 1979.
Operators: Italy (S.208M) and Tunisia (208A).

SIAI-Marchetti S.211
Italy

With the Aermacchi MB-339 basic and advanced jet trainer firmly in Italian Air Force service, SIAI-Marchetti has not been able to break into the indigenous air force with its own jet trainer. However, the S.211 has many attractions and at least 40 have been ordered for export, some specifically for a light-attack role. It is a low-cost trainer of the usual tandem cockpit layout with the rear seat raised, claiming also a light airframe due to very extensive use of composite materials.

Specifications
Weapons: 4 underwing pylons for up to 1455 lb (660 kg) of weapons, which can include bombs of up to 331-lb (150-kg) weight each, 12.7-mm or 7.62-mm machine-gun pods, rocket launchers, etc.

Accommodation: Student pilot and instructor in tandem.
Wingspan: 27 ft 8 in (8.43 m).
Length: 30 ft 6½ in (9.31 m).
Maximum take-off weight: 6834 lb (3100 kg).
Cruising speed: 414 mph (667 km/h).
Range: 1035 miles (1668 km).
Mission performance: Rate of climb at sea level 4200 ft (1280 m) per min; ceiling 40,025 ft (12,200 m); G limits +6, −3, +5 with underwing weapons, −2.5 with underwing weapons, +3.4 sustained; endurance 3 h 50 min with reserve fuel.
Engine: One 2500-lb (1134-kg) thrust Pratt & Whitney Canada JT15D-4C turbofan, with 800 liters of fuel standard.

Version in service
S.211: As described above. A version with a HUD, navigation computer and other improvements is being developed for expanded missions. Singapore is the largest customer to date, with 30 ordered for assembly in that country.
Operators: Haiti, Singapore and Somali.

SIAI-Marchetti SF.260
Italy

Developed from the civil SF.260A three-seat lightplane, the military series began with the SF.260M trainer that first flew on 10 October 1970. Suited to basic and night flying, instrument, formation, navigation, and aerobatic training, the 'M' was followed by an armed version for the added role of tactical support (as the SF.260W Warrior). A surveillance and SAR variant of the Warrior is known as the Sea Warrior, which can also carry two containers if required for supply missions. A higher-performance turboprop-powered version of the military SF.260 is known as the SF.260TP.

Specifications (SF.260W Warrior data)
Weapons: Up to 661 lb (300 kg) of light weapons on 2 or 4 underwing pylons, including gun pods, rocket launchers, and bombs of up to 275-lb (125-kg) weight each.
Accommodation: 3 seats under a canopy. The Warrior/Sea Warrior are flown as single-seaters when armed.
Wingspan: 27 ft 4¾ in (8.35 m).
Length: 23 ft 3½ in (7.10 m).
Maximum take-off weight: 2866 lb (1300 kg).
Maximum speed: 190 mph (305 km/h).

Combat radius: 57-345 miles (92-556 km) depending upon mission and stores carried.
Mission performance: Rate of climb at sea level 1250 ft (381 m) per min; ceiling 14,700 ft (4480 m).
Engine: One 260-hp Avco Lycoming O-540-E4A5 piston, with 243 liters of fuel.
Versions in service
SF.260M: Trainer, with 2 or 3 seats.
SF.260W Warrior: Armed trainer, capable also of light attack, forward air control (FAC), reconnaissance using camera pods, and liaison.
SF.260SW Sea Warrior: Surveillance and SAR version of the Warrior.
SF.260TP: Turboprop development of the military SF.260, with a 350-shp Allison 250-BI7C engine. Maximum speed is 262 mph (422 km/h); range 589 miles (949 km) with reserve fuel.
Operators: Belgium (M), Bolivia (W), Brunei

Above: SIAI-Marchetti SF.260MZs in Zambian military service.

(W), Burma (M and W), Burundi (W and TP), Comoros (W?), Dubai (W and TP), Ethiopia (TP), Ghana (TP), Haiti (TP), Ireland (W), Italy (M), Libya (M), Nicaragua (W), Philippines (M), Singapore (M and W), Somali Republic (W), Sri Lanka (TP), Thailand (M), Tunisia (W), Zaire (M), Zambia (M) and Zimbabwe (W).

SIAI-Marchetti SM.1019EI
Italy

The prototype flew initially on 24 May 1969. Eighty SM.1019Es were delivered to the Aviazione Leggera dell'Esercito (Italian Army

Below: SIAI-Marchetti SM.1019 demonstrator.

Light Aviation) during the 1970s for STOL utility transport, light ground attack and helicopter escort, photographic reconnaissance, and observation duties; about 70 remain.

Specifications
Weapons: 4 underwing stations for up to 706 lb (320 kg) of attack weapons, including 7.62-mm machine-gun pods, rocket launchers, 331-lb (150-kg) bombs, etc. Alternative stores could include 2 photographic-reconnaissance pods.
Accommodation: 2 seats in tandem.
Wingspan: 36 ft 0 in (10.972 m).
Length: 27 ft 11½ in (8.52 m).
Maximum take-off weight: 3196 lb (1450 kg).
Maximum speed: 183 mph (295 km/h).
Range: 581 miles (935 km).
Mission performance: Rate of climb at sea level 1440 ft (439 m) per min; ceiling 25,000 ft (7620 m); endurance 6 h 5 min; G limits +3.8, −1.52.

Right: Artist's impression of the Boeing Vertol XCH-62 heavy-lift helicopter.
Below: The US Army's flying-crane helicopter is the Sikorsky Tarhe, seen here lifting a Lance battlefield missile.

Engine: One 400-shp Allison 250-B17B turboprop (derated to 320 shp), with 320 liters of fuel standard.
Version in service
SM.1019EI: Strut-braced high-wing monoplane, as detailed above.
Operator: Italy (army).

Sikorsky CH-54 Tarhe
United States

While development continues of a new heavy-lift helicopter for possible future US Army deployment, under the Boeing Vertol XCH-62 program, the Sikorsky S-64 Skycrane (military CH-54 Tarhe) remains the Army's only specially-designed heavy-lift flying crane. Unlike other helicopters in Western service, the CH-54 has its engines and six-blade rotor mounted above a pod-and-boom type fuselage, leaving the area clear between the very tall main undercarriage legs for the attachment of interchangeable pods, a freight platform, or for sling loads. A rearward-facing seat with flying controls in the cabin enables a third pilot to fly the helicopter while viewing loading or unloading of sling loads. The first prototype Skycrane flew on 9 May 1962 and delivery of production Tarhes started in 1964. Those operated during the Vietnam War air-lifted nearly 400 crashed aircraft back to safety. More than 70 Tarhes remain.

Specifications (CH-54A data)
Accommodation: Crew of 2 or 3 plus a detachable Universal Military Pod for 45 armed troops, 24 stretchers, freight, or equipped for other roles including as a command and communications post. Alternative loads can be carried on an open platform or as a slung cargo, up to a maximum weight of 20,000 lb (9072 kg).
Diameter of rotor: 72 ft 0 in (21.95 m).
Fuselage length: 70 ft 3 in (21.41 m).
Maximum take-off weight: 42,000 lb (19,050 kg).
Maximum speed: 126 mph (203 km/h).

Range: 230 miles (370 km) with reserves.
Mission performance: Rate of climb at sea level 1330 ft (405 m) per min; hovering ceiling in ground effect 10,600 ft (3230 m); hovering ceiling out of ground effect 6900 ft (2105 m).
Engines: Two 4500-shp Pratt & Whitney T73-P-1 turboshafts, with 3331 liters of fuel standard.
Versions in service
CH-54A: As detailed above.
CH-54B: Two 4800-shp T73-P-700 turboshafts, high-lift rotor, and increased payload. Gross weight of 47,000 lb (21,319 kg).
Operator: United States (army).

Sikorsky H-60 Black Hawk, Night Hawk and Seahawk
United States

Under the company designation S-70, Sikorsky developed a combat assault helicopter to supersede the Bell UH-1 Iroquois with the US Army, which first flew as a prototype on 17 October 1974 and went on to win the Army's UTTAS (Utility Tactical Transport Aircraft System) competition. Designed to carry an 11-troop squad and its equipment, and to be sufficiently compact in design to make airlift by USAF transports easy for rapid deployment, delivery of well over 600 UH-60A Black Hawks to the US Army had taken place by early 1986 from the total of 930 ordered to date. To enhance the helicopter's capabilities further, a detachable external stores support system (ESSS) was developed. This centers upon stub wings with four pylons that can be attached to the fuselage when required to carry auxiliary fuel, various weapon loads for anti-armor and suppression, or other stores

Below: US Navy Sikorsky SH-60B Seahawk LAMPS Mk III helicopter.

up to an incredible total of over 10,000 lb (4536 kg), equivalent to 2000 lb (907 kg) more than the helicopter's external sling cargo hook can manage. ESSS systems have been delivered to the Army since 1986, when 395 were on order. The Army has also received eight medevac kits for retrofit to Black Hawks, to support military and civil medical evacuation missions.

Of the other missions undertaken by H-60 type helicopters a special mention should be made of the US Navy's SH-60 Seahawks. First flown as a prototype on 12 December 1979, the SH-60B is an advanced LAMPS (Light Airborne Multi-Purpose System)

Above: US Army Sikorsky UH-60A fitted with ESSS.

Mk III helicopter, complementing the existing Seasprite LAMPS Mk Is but far more capable and with longer mission endurances. Their principal tasks are to operate from destroyers and frigates in antisubmarine and antiship surveillance and targeting roles, carrying the necessary systems for detection, classification and interdiction, while the myriad of other roles include SAR, fleet support and communications relay, and vertical replenishment (vertrep). The SH-60F Seahawk will enter US Navy service from 1988 as

a dedicated carrier-borne antisubmarine helicopter, to supersede the SH-3H Sea King in the defense of the inner zone of a CBG (carrier battle group).

Specifications (UH-60A data)
Equipment: Avionics include Singer Kearfott AN/ASN-128 Doppler navigation system, a radar warning receiver, and Saunders AN/ALQ-144 IR countermeasures set to offer protection against heat-seeking missiles.
Weapons: Optional machine-guns fired from the cabin, plus Hellfire anti-armor missiles, gun pods, rocket launchers or mine-dispensing pods carried on the ESSS.
Accommodation: 3 crew plus 11 to 14 troops or freight.
Diameter of rotor: 53 ft 8 in (16.36 m).
Fuselage length: 50 ft 0¾ in (15.26 m).
Maximum take-off weight: 20,250 lb (9185 kg).
Maximum speed: 184 mph (296 km/h).
Range: 373 miles (600 km).
Mission performance: Ceiling 19,000 ft (5790 m); hovering ceiling in ground effect 9500 ft (2895 m) at 35 degrees C; hovering ceiling out of ground effect 10,400 ft (3170 m); endurance 2 h 18 min.
Engines: Two 1560-shp General Electric T700-GE-700 turboshafts, with nearly 1363 liters of fuel standard.

Versions in service
UH-60A: Assault helicopter, with armaments option. As detailed above. 10 also delivered to USAF with rescue hoists.
EH-60A: US Army communications-jamming helicopter. 80 are required by the US Army; the first EH-60A flew in 1985.
HH-60A Night Hawk: USAF rescue helicopter, equipped to make unescorted sorties at very low level by day or night into unfriendly areas to rescue crews. 1690-shp T700-GE-401 engines. 90 are required but none so far ordered.
VH-60A: US Marine Corps VIP version, for the Executive Flight Detachment of Helicopter Squadron One. Nine required, but none yet in service.
SH-60B Seahawk: LAMPS Mk III helicopter,

Below: RAF Westland Wessex HC.Mk 2.

with 1690-shp T700-GE-401 engines and provision for two Mk 46 torpedoes. Avionics include Texas Instruments AN/APS-124 search radar, ESM, Teledyne Ryan AN/APN-217 Doppler navigation system, sonobuoys and associated equipment, MAD, etc. 62 delivered to the US Navy between 1983 and 1986, of a stated requirement for 204. SH-60Js will be built by Mitsubishi of Japan for the JMSDF, while the Royal Australian Navy will receive S-70B-2 RAWs for use from guided-missile frigates (assembled by Hawker de Havilland in Australia). S-70B-2 RAWs will have MEL Super Searcher radar. Before Japanese or Australian helicopters come off assembly lines, the Spanish Navy will have received its 6 Sikorsky-built S-70Bs (from 1988).
SH-60F: ASW helicopter to supersede the SH-3H Sea King.
S-70A: Export version of the Black Hawk for utility roles.
S-70B: Export version of the Seahawk. See SH-60B above.
S-70C: Commercial model of the Black Hawk, acquired for military use by China (24) and Taiwan (14). Two 1625-shp General Electric CT7-2C or 1723-shp CT7-2D engines.
WS-70: Westland-built S-70A, first flown in April 1987. Contender for UK Ministry of Defence requirement.
Operators: Australia (later, air force S-70A-9 and navy S-70B-2 RAW), China (S-70C), Japan (later, navy SH-60J), Philippines (S-70A-5), Spain (navy, S-70B), Taiwan (S-70C) and United States (later, air force HH-60A; navy SH-60B and SH-60F; later, marine corps VH-60A; army, UH-60A and EH-60A).

Sikorsky S-58, California Helicopters S-58T and Westland Wessex
United States and United Kingdom

Capitalizing on the success of its S-55, Sikorsky used a generally similar configuration for a slightly larger and more powerful develop-

ment, the S-58. The easiest point of recognition was the new helicopter's reshaped rear fuselage, doing away with the S-55's boom. The prototype flew initially on 8 March 1954 and examples joined the US Navy as SH-34 Seabat antisubmarine helicopters and utility UH-34s, the US Marine Corps in UH-34 and VH-34 Seahorse forms, the US Army as CH-34 Choctaw general-purpose and assault transports, and the US Coast Guard as HH-34 SAR helicopters. The S-58 was also exported and manufactured under license in France, Japan and the United Kingdom. The British Westland Wessex was a turboshaft-engined variant, first flown on 17 May 1957 with a 1100-shp Gazelle NGa 11 engine. More powerful Gazelle engines were fitted to various production models of the Wessex until the Commando assault HU.Mk 5 appeared in 1963, when two coupled Rolls-Royce Gnomes took over. Sikorsky also produced a turboshaft version of its S-58, by modification, as the S-58T of 1970 first flight, the rights to which are currently held by California Helicopters. Although once the number of S-58/Wessex operators was larger, today only a few remain in service.

Specifications (Westland Wessex HU.Mk 5 data)
Accommodation: 3 crew plus 16 troops, 4000 lb (1814 kg) of freight or seven stretchers. Can carry armament, such as air-to-surface missiles, rocket launchers and machine-guns.
Diameter of rotor: 56 ft 0 in (17.07 m).
Fuselage length: 48 ft 4½ in (14.74 m).
Maximum take-off weight: 13,500 lb (6123 kg).
Maximum speed: 132 mph (212 km/h).
Range: 478 miles (769 km).
Engines: 2 Rolls-Royce Gnome turboshafts (112 and 113), coupled to give a combined rating of 1550 shp.

Versions in service
Sikorsky H-34: Remaining versions of the H-34 are CH-34 Choctaws with Taiwan, SH-34J Seabat ASW helicopters with Uruguay, and perhaps a very small number of French-built S-58s with Belgium. One 1525-hp Wright R-1820-84B piston engine.

Accommodation for 18 troops or ASW equipment, according to the version.

S-58T: Modified S-58, with the piston engine replaced with an 1875-shp Pratt & Whitney Canada PT6T-6 Twin-Pac turboshaft. A PT6T-3 can also be installed. Maximum weight is 13,000 lb (5896 kg), maximum speed 138 mph (222 km/h), and range 278 miles (447 km) with reserves on 1071 liters of fuel. The Indonesian Air Force received 12, the Royal Thai Air Force 18 and the Argentine Air Force 2.

Wessex: British Gazelle/Gnome turboshaft-powered version. As detailed above. The Mk 31B has a 1540-shp Gazelle engine, the Mk 52 the Gnomes.

Operators: Argentina (S-58T), Australia (navy, Wessex HAS.31B), Belgium (S-58?), Indonesia (S-58T), Iraq (Wessex Mk 52?), Taiwan (army, CH-34), Thailand (S-58T), United Kingdom (air force, Wessex HC.Mk 2 and HU.Mk 5; navy, Wessex HU.Mk 5) and Uruguay (navy, SH-34J).

Sikorsky S-61/H-3 Sea King series and Westland Sea King/Commando
United States and United Kingdom

The remarkable series of S-61-derivative civil and military helicopters began with a contract from the US Navy of September 1957 for an amphibious ASW helicopter that would be large enough to combine the roles of hunter and killer. Sikorsky was therefore faced with having to develop a single design that did the work of two HSS-1s (original SH-34 service designation), carry dipping sonar, other equipment and weapons, and besides have a single-step watertight hull. The resulting prototype S-61 flew for the first time on 11 March 1959 and production examples began entering service in HSS-2 Sea King form in September 1961 with Squadrons VHS-10 and VHS-3, just months before the helicopter received its new Navy designation of SH-3A. Many other H-3 helicopters followed for the indigenous forces and export, for ASW, VIP and troop transport, missile support and drone recovery, SAR and more, with license production or assembly also taking place in Japan, Canada, Italy and United Kingdom.

Italian production of the SH-3H, the final ASW version, continues by Agusta as one of its range of Agusta-Sikorsky types. Meanwhile, back in 1959 Westland Helicopters of the UK received a license for the S-61 which allowed a modified version to be developed and put into production. With Rolls-Royce Gnome H.1400 turboshaft engines fitted and British equipment/avionics, this became the Westland Sea King, which flew for the first time as a production HAS.Mk 1 ASW helicopter for the Royal Navy on 7 May 1969. The Sea King became operational initially with No 824 Squadron. Uprated versions have since followed for the British forces and export, while a nonamphibious tactical military version was first flown on 12 September 1973 as the Commando.

Sikorsky too produced both amphibious and nonamphibious models of its S-61, but retained the amphibious capability when making the design changes necessary to produce the S-61R. Although based on the SH-3A, this was a troop transport and assault helicopter with an hydraulically actuated ramp in the rear of the fuselage to permit direct loading of troops, freight (using a cargo-handling winch) or vehicles, and many changes to the rotor system were introduced to ease maintenance. This entered USAF service under CH-3 designations, along with the HH-3E Jolly Green Giant Aerospace Rescue and Recovery Service helicopter that was intended to work if necessary under enemy fire and thereby incorporated armament, armor and self-sealing fuel tanks. Two Jolly Green Giants entered the record books during 31 May-1 June 1967, by making the first-ever nonstop helicopter crossings of the Atlantic, each using its retractable refuelling probe nine times to take on fuel from tankers. A version without the combat mission equipment became the HH-3F Pelican search and rescue helicopter for the US Coast Guard. While Sikorsky production of the S-61R has ended, Agusta continues to build it in HH-3F SAR form for the indigenous Air Force.

Below: Westland Sea King HAR.Mk 3s flown by No 202 Squadron, RAF, for SAR.

Above: Agusta-Sikorsky HH-3F amphibious SAR helicopter.

Specifications (Agusta-Sikorsky ASH-3H data)

Radar: SMA/APS-707 radar in a chin radome. Optional search radar for a search and rescue role. Other equipment includes sonar, Doppler radar and optional magnetic anomaly detector (MAD).
Weapons: Can be either two or four torpedoes, antiship missiles of Exocet, Harpoon, AS.12 or Marte Mk 2 types, or depth charges.
Accommodation: 4 crew in antisubmarine role. In a transport role up to 31 troops, 15 stretchers and an attendant, or 6000 lb (2720 kg) of internal or 8000 lb (3630 kg) of slung freight. For search and rescue, 25 persons can be accommodated.
Diameter of rotor: 62 ft 0 in (18.90 m).
Fuselage length: 54 ft 9 in (16.69 m).
Maximum take-off weight: 21,000 lb (9525 kg).
Cruising speed: 138 mph (222 km/h).
Range: 725 miles (1166 km) with full standard fuel.
Mission performance: Rate of climb at sea level 2200 ft (670 m) per min; ceiling 12,200 ft (3720 m); hovering ceiling in ground effect 8200 ft (2500 m); hovering ceiling out of ground effect 3700 ft (1130 m).
Engines: Two 1500-shp General Electric T58-GE-100 turboshafts, with 3180 liters of fuel standard.

Versions in service

Sikorsky CH-3E: USAF amphibious transport with roles including evacuation and relief. Two 1500-shp T58-GE-5 engines. Maximum speed 162 mph (261 km/h). Two 7.62-mm General Electric guns.
Sikorsky CH-124: Canadian Armed Forces designation of its SH-3 Sea King antisubmarine and maritime reconnaissance helicopters. Litton AN/APS-503 radar.
Sikorsky HH-3A: SAR helicopter operated by the US Navy and Reserve. Modified from SH-3As and powered by 1250-shp T58-GE-8B engines. Can be armed.
Sikorsky HH-3E Jolly Green Giant: USAF Aerospace Rescue and Recovery Service helicopter, with self-protection features as given above. Now operated also by Air Force Reserve and Air National Guard units.
Sikorsky HH-3F Pelican: Unarmed SAR

helicopter for the US Coast Guard, of similar general type to the HH-3E.
Sikorsky SH-3D: ASW helicopter, flown by the US Navy and others. Two 1400-shp T58-GE-10 engines. Up to 840 lb (381 kg) of weapons. Bendix AN/AQS-13 sonar, Teledyne AN/APN-130 Doppler radar, etc. Maximum speed 166 mph (267 km/h). Range 625 miles (1006 km).
Sikorsky SH-3G: US Navy utility helicopter by stripping SH-3As of ASW equipment.
Sikorsky SH-3H: US Navy multipurpose helicopter, with improved sonar, active/ passive sonobuoys and MAD for ASW, and ESM for ship protection.
Sikorsky S-61A: Basic amphibious multipurpose helicopter, as supplied to Denmark. Can accommodate 26 troops, 12 VIP passengers, 15 stretchers or cargo. Danish aircraft are used for SAR.
Sikorsky S-61A-4 Nuri: Transport and rescue helicopters acquired by Malaysia, with 31 seats, rescue hoists, and long-range fuel.
Agusta-Sikorsky AS-61, ASH-3D and ASH-3H: Similar to US-built models but for some avionics and weapon choices.
Agusta-Sikorsky SH-3D/TS: VIP transport, serving with the Italian Air Force and others.
Agusta-Sikorsky HH-3F: Italian-built version of the S-61R, currently available with two 1500-shp T58-GE-5 engines. 15 stretchers or 5000 lb (2268 kg) of cargo. 35 used by the indigenous air force. Maximum speed 162 mph (261 km/h).
Westland Sea King: British-built version of the S-61/SH-3 type. The Royal Navy operates HAS.Mk 2 and 5 in ASW and SAR roles, the latter carrying MEL Sea Searcher radar, Doppler, electronic support measures, sonobuoys and associated processing equipment, and dipping sonar. Weapons options include up to four torpedoes or depth charges. The RN also has the HC.Mk 4 in service, this being a utility Commando. Sea Kings have been exported. See also Sea King Mk 2 AEW below. The RAF uses the Sea King HAR.Mk 3 for SAR, carrying MEL radar. These accommodate 19 passengers, 6 stretchers or 2 stretchers and 11 sitting casualties. Latest versions use two 1660-shp Rolls-Royce Gnome H.1400-1T turboshafts.
Westland Sea King Mk 2 AEW: As a result of the Falklands war, Thorn EMI Searchwater

radar has been fitted to ten HAS.Mk 2 helicopters to provide Invincible-class aircraft carriers with AEW. The radar is carried in a swivelling container on the fuselage side.
Westland Commando: Tactical version of the Sea King, first flown on 12 September 1973. The Mk 2 version accommodates 28 troops and has a gross weight of 21,500 lb (9752 kg). Egyptian Mk 2Es are equipped for electronic warfare.
Operators: Argentina (air force, S-61R; navy, SH-3D/H and S-61D-4), Australia (navy, Westland SK Mk.50), Belgium (Westland SK Mk 48), Brazil (navy, Sik SH-3D and ASH-3H), Canada (Sik CH-124), Denmark (Sik S-61A), Egypt (air force, Westland Commando Mk 1, 2B and 2E; navy, Westland SK Mk 47), West Germany (navy, Westland SK Mk 41), India (navy, Westland SK Mk 42, 42B and 42C), Iran (navy, ASH-3D), Iraq (air force, SH-3D/ TS?), Italy (air force, AS HH-3 and SH-3D/TS; navy ASH-3D), Libya (AS-61A-4), Japan (navy, Sik SH-3), Malaysia (Sik S-61A-4), Norway (Westland SK Mk 43), Pakistan (navy, Westland SK Mk 45), Peru (navy, ASH-3D), Qatar (Westland Commando Mk 2A, 2C and 3), Saudi Arabia (AS-61A-4 and Commando Mk 2), Spain (navy, SH-3D/G), United Kingdom (air force, Westland S, HAR.Mk 3; navy, Westland SK HAS.Mk 2, 2 AEW and 5 and HC.Mk 4) and United States (air force, Sik CH-3E and HH-3E; navy, Sik HH-3A and SH-3D/G/H; coast guard, HH-3F).

Sikorsky S-62/HH-52A
United States

First flown on 14 May 1958, this helicopter flew before the company's S-61/SH-3 and therefore can lay claim to having been Sikorsky's first amphibious helicopter and with a fuselage shape that was adopted in larger form for the ASW type. It was built in both civil and military versions, the latter as HH-52As for SAR missions with the US Coast Guard (now being superseded by the Aéro-spatiale HH-65A Dolphins as they are delivered) and also delivered to a small number of military forces from US and Japanese (Mitsubishi) production lines.

Specifications (HH-52A data)
Accommodation: 2 crew plus 12 survivors. Rescue hoist, towing gear, rescue platform and sea anchor. Can carry freight, including a sling load which can increase gross weight to 8300 lb (3764 kg).
Diameter of rotor: 53 ft 0 in (16.16 m).
Fuselage length: 44 ft 6½ in (13.58 m).
Maximum take-off weight: 8100 lb (3674 kg).
Maximum speed: 109 mph (175 km/h).
Range: 474 miles (763 km).
Mission performance: Rate of climb at sea level 1080 ft (329 m) per min; ceiling 11,200 ft (3415 m); hovering ceiling in ground effect 12,200 ft (3715 m); hovering ceiling out of ground effect 1700 ft (518 m).
Engine: One 1250-shp General Electric T58-GE-8 turboshaft, with 1560 liters of fuel.
Versions in service:
HH-52A: USCG search and rescue helicopter. As detailed above.
S-62A: General Electric CT58-110 turboshaft,

Above: US Coast Guard Sikorsky HH-52A.

derated to 730 shp. Usual gross take-off weight 7900 lb (3583 kg). 12 troops or 10 VIP passengers. Japanese S-62As are used for SAR.

Operators: Japan (navy, S-62A), Philippines (S-62A), Thailand (S-62A) and United States (coast guard, HH-52A).

Sikorsky S-65A/H-53 Sea Stallion/ Super Stallion and MH-53E Sea Dragon
United States

On 14 October 1964 Sikorsky flew its new S-65A all-weather heavy assault transport helicopter for the US Marine Corps, intended to air-lift 37 armed troops or heavy equipment, or retrieve damaged aircraft. Like the company's S-61R, a loading ramp was placed at the rear of the watertight fuselage/hull to enable vehicles or weapon systems to be carried, such as anti-aircraft missile batteries or two Jeeps. The initial production CH-53A Sea Stallion was followed by several other versions, the D for the USMC but the rest for the US Navy, USAF and export, including a mine-countermeasures (MCM) version for the Navy as the RH-53D. Before actual RH-53Ds arrived, the role of MCM had been initiated by the Navy using fifteen CH-53As loaned by the USMC, and with these it established its first-ever helicopter MCM squadron, HM-12. Purpose-equipped RH-53Ds were received from 1973.

From the CH-53D Sikorsky developed the even larger, heavier and more capable three-engined CH-53E Super Stallion, with the ability to lift a 36,000 lb (16,329 kg) load, about twice that of the Sea Stallion. To date, the Super Stallion is the West's most capable heavy-duty helicopter. The prototype first flew on 1 March 1974 and by 1986 the USMC and US Navy had received a total of 94 for amphibious assault and VOD (vertical on-board delivery) respectively. Also in 1986 the US Navy began receiving MH-53E Sea Dragons, MCM examples of the Super Stallion.

Specifications (CH-53E Super Stallion data)
Accommodation: 3 crew plus 55 troops or up to 36,000 lb (16,329 kg) of freight or vehicles.
Diameter of rotor: 79 ft 0 in (24.08 m).

Fuselage length: 73 ft 4 in (22.35 m).
Maximum take-off weight: 73,500 lb (33,340 kg).
Maximum speed: 196 mph (315 km/h).
Ferry range: 1290 miles (2076 km) without flight refuelling.
Mission performance: Rate of climb at sea level 2500 ft (760 m) per min; ceiling 18,500 ft (5640 m); hovering ceiling in ground effect 11,550 ft (3520 m); hovering ceiling out of ground effect 9500 ft (2900 m).
Engines: Three 4380-shp General Electric T64-GE-416 turboshafts, with 3850 liters of fuel standard.

Versions in service
CH-53A: Initial USMC version, with two 2850-shp General Electric T64-GE-6 turboshafts. Usual gross weight 35,000 lb (15,875 kg). In addition to the payload options given above, it can carry 24 stretchers and four medical attendants.
CH-53C: USAF version, with engines as for

the CH-53G. Just 8 to support the mobile Tactical Air Control System.
CH-53D: USMC version with two 3925-shp T64-GE-413 engines. Accommodation for up to 55 troops. Gross weight 42,000 lb (19,050 kg).
CH-53G: Version for the West German Army, with 3925-shp T64-GE-7 engines built under license by MTU.
HH-53B: USAF version for the Aerospace Rescue and Recovery Service. Same engines as the CH-53G. Gross weight 42,000 lb (19,050 kg).
HH-53C: Same engines as CH-53G but with 1703-liter drop tanks fitted and a flight refuelling probe. Improved performance, and able to accommodate 38 passengers or 18,500 lb (8390 kg) of internal freight/20,000-lb (9070-kg) sling load.
HH-53H: 9 USAF HH-53Cs with Pave Low III equipment for night and adverse weather operations with the Special Operations Forces. Systems include FLIR and radar. 12 HH-53Bs will also be brought up to this standard.
RH-53D: US NavyMCM version as detailed above. Also delivered to Iran.
S-65Oe: 2 rescue helicopters, originally delivered to Austria for duties in the Alps but sold to Israel in 1981.
CH-53E Super Stallion: Heavy lift helicopter, for assault transport and aircraft retrieval with the USMC and VOD with the US Navy. As detailed above.
MH-53E Sea Dragon: MCM version of the Super Stallion. 57 required.
Operators: West Germany (army, CH-53G), Iran (navy, RH-53D), Israel (S-65Oe), Japan (MH-53E) and United States (air force, CH-53C, HH-53B/C/H; navy, CH-53E, RH-53D and MH-53E; marine corps, CH-53A/D, CH-53E).

Below: The West's most powerful helicopter is the US Navy's Sikorsky CH-53E Super Stallion.

Above: Sikorsky H-76 Eagle military derivative of the S-76.

Sikorsky S-76
United States

On 13 March 1977 a new 12-passenger commercial helicopter flew for the first time as the Sikorsky S-76. Of very streamlined appearance, with a retractable undercarriage and twin turboshaft engines, it demonstrated excellent performance and several production versions followed. Like the similar Bell 222, of which one was ordered for the Uruguayan Air Force, the S-76 attracted some military interest, from Jordan (in general-purpose Mark II form), Honduras and the Philippines (17 S-76 Utilities). More specialized military variants are also available.

Specifications (S-76 Mk II data)
Radar: Optional weather radar.
Accommodation: 2 crew plus 8 to 12 passengers/troops, up to 4700 lb (2132 kg) of freight, stretchers, or rescue equipment.
Diameter of rotor: 44 ft 0 in (13.41 m).
Fuselage length: 43 ft 4½ in (13.22 m).
Maximum take-off weight: 10,300 lb (4672 kg).
Cruising speed: 178 mph (286 km/h).
Range: 465 miles (748 km) with 12 passengers.
Mission performance: Rate of climb at sea level 1350 ft (411 m) per min; ceiling 15,000 ft (4575 m); hovering ceiling in ground effect 6200 ft (1890 m).
Engines: Two 650-shp Allison 250-C30S turboshafts, with 1064 liters of fuel standard.
Versions in service
S-76 Mark II: Entered production in 1982 to supersede the original S-76 model. As detailed above.
S-76 Utility: Less well-equipped version of the Mark II for utility tasks. Many possible interior layouts and options. Philippine examples include 12 as H-76s for COIN, transport and stretcher carrying, 2 for SAR, 2 with VIP 8-passenger interiors, and one with a 12-passenger layout.

S-76B: Version of the Mark II with 960-shp Pratt & Whitney Canada PT6B-36 engines. Probably none in military service.
H-76 Eagle: Armed military variant of the S-76B for gunship, assault, SAR, observation and many other possible roles. Equipment can include a mast- or roof-mounted sight. None as yet in service. First flown in 1985.
H-76N: Naval version of the H-76 type with Allison or Pratt & Whitney Canada engines. Many options, including search radar and weapons. First flown in 1986.
Operators: Honduras, Jordan and the Philippines.

Socata Rallye and R 235 Guerrier
France

A design of Morane-Saulnier, the Rallye first took to the air in MS 880A Rallye-Club form in June 1959, powered by a 90-hp piston engine. Many production versions followed for the civil market and examples also found their way into military service as three- or four-seat liaison aircraft and trainers.

In 1966 Socata was formed and took over production and development of new versions, including the purpose-designed Rallye 235G military model with four underwing pylons for weapons, surveillance or other military equipment loads. This STOL version became known as the Guerrier.

Specifications (Guerrier data)
Equipment and Weapons: Up to four Matra F2 launchers carrying six 68-mm rockets each, two AA52 pods each with two 7.62-mm machine-guns (500 rounds of ammunition per gun), or 110-lb (50-kg) bombs, or a mixture of these, on 4 pylons. Alternatively a surveillance pod with scanning TV camera, flares, practice bombs, or other loads.
Accommodation: 4 persons, the front seats with dual controls for training purposes. Can carry a stretcher for casualty evacuation.
Wingspan: 31 ft 11 in (9.74 m).
Length: 23 ft 9½ in (7.25 m).
Maximum take-off weight: 2976 lb (1350 kg).
Maximum speed: Approx 171 mph (275 km/h).
Range: 640 miles (1030 km) with two gun pods and reconnaissance equipment, at cruising speed; or 50 miles (80 km) with two gun pods and two rocket launchers at higher cruising speed with ten minutes over target area.
Mission performance: (Based on Rallye 235GT/Gabier.) Rate of climb at sea level approx 985 ft (300 m) per min; ceiling approx 14,760 ft (4500 m).
Engine: One 235-hp Avco Lycoming O-540-B4B5 piston, with 282 liters of fuel.
Versions in service
MS 885: Early version of Rallye series with 145-hp Continental O-300-C engine and known as Super Rallye.
MS 893: Several 'heavy' sub-variants built as Rallye Commodores, with 180-hp Avco Lycoming O-360-A2A engines. Maximum

Below: Sikorsky S-76 SHADOW, an interesting modification which has placed a new pilot-only cockpit on the nose of an S-76 to evaluate the automated cockpit concepts of the US Army's ARTI (Advanced Rotorcraft Technology Integration) project.

Above: The weapons and other stores available to the Socata Guerrier.

speed 152 mph (245 km/h). Used for liaison missions.

Rallye 100S: 1973 version fitted as 2-seater. Can be spun. Delivered to French Navy training school at Lanvéoc-Poulmic.

Rallye 100ST: Can be spun when flown as a two-seater or carry up to four persons.

Rallye 235A: Early version of 235 series high-performance Rallye.

Rallye 235E: High-performance Rallye with a 235-hp O-540-B4B5 engine, first flown in 1975. Seats four.

Rallye 235G: Similar to 235E but with underwing pylons for military weapons and

equipment. Original designation of Guerrier model.

Rallye 235GT: High performance 'heavy' model with 2645-lb (1200-kg) maximum take-off weight and 235-hp O-540-B4B5 engine. Seats four. STOL performance. Later known as Gabier. Used for liaison missions.

R 235 Guerrier: Armed military version of Rallye 235 series, previously known as Rallye 235G.

Operators: Djibouti (235GT), Dominican Republic (MS 893), France (navy, 100S and 100ST), Libya (Rallye trainers), Morocco (MS 885 and MS 893), Rwanda (Guerrier), Senegal (Guerrier and Rallye, incl 235A) and Seychelles (Guerrier).

SOKO G2-A Galeb
Yugoslavia

The Galeb, since superseded on the production line by the Super Galeb (next entry) is a jet-powered basic trainer which was popular with the air forces of Yugoslavia, Libya and Zambia. The first prototype flew initially in May 1961 and production started two years later for the home air force. Manufacture of the updated export version, the G2-A-E, began in 1975 to fulfill a substantial order from Libya for 50, though Zambia had already received Galebs in 1971 which must

Below: SOKO G2-A Galeb trainers in Yugoslav Air Force markings.

have been of the G2-A type. In all respects the Galeb is a conventional aircraft, with straight wings and tandem cockpits for the student pilot and instructor under separate but adjoining canopies. All Galebs are armed, making them suitable for light strike missions, but their main tasks are flying, aerobatic, navigation and weapons training.

Specifications

Weapons: Two 0.50-in machine-guns with 80 rounds of ammunition each are carried in the fuselage nose. Underwing pylons can carry up to 661 lb (300 kg) of attack weapons, including cluster, 110-lb (50-kg) and 220-lb (100-kg) bombs, bomblet containers or rockets.
Accommodation: 2 crew in tandem.
Wingspan: 34 ft 4½ in (10.47 m) without tiptanks.
Length: 33 ft 11 in (10.34 m).
Maximum take-off weight: 9480 lb (4300 kg).
Maximum speed: 505 mph (812 km/h).
Range: 770 miles (1240 km) with tiptanks fitted.
Mission performance: Rate of climb at sea level 4495 ft (1370 m) per min; ceiling 39,370 ft (12,000 m); endurance 2 h 30 min; G limits +8, −4.
Engine: One 2500-lb (1134-kg) thrust Rolls-Royce Viper 11 Mk 22-6 turbojet.

Versions in service

G2-A: Initial production version, mainly for the home air force. Approximately 150 are in service, some assigned to light attack. Zambia has two in use.
G-2A-E: Updated version for export, Libya becoming the only customer. 2 training squadrons operate about 61 of 70 aircraft delivered in 2 batches, the second in 1983.
Operators: Libya, Yugoslavia and Zambia.

SOKO G-4 Super Galeb
Yugoslavia

Typical of the many new-generation jet trainers that also combine a light strike capability is the SOKO G-4 Super Galeb, designed and produced to supersede the G2-A Galebs and Lockheed T-33As then flown by the Yugoslav Air Force. The first prototype took to the air

on 17 July 1978 and large numbers have since entered service.

Although of much more advanced design than the Galeb, with a considerably longer fuselage carrying stepped cockpits and shorter-span wings that are swept at 22 degrees at quarter-chord, it still relies on the British Rolls-Royce Viper turbojet for power. However, the Viper used for the Super Galeb is a Mk 632, with 60 percent more thrust than the Galeb's Viper 11 Mk 22-6. An interesting feature of the armament is the adoption of a removable pod that fits under the fuselage between the wings, containing a 23-mm GSh-23L twin-barrel cannon.

Specifications

Weapons: One 23-mm GSh-23L twin-barrel cannon in a removable pod, plus 2976 lb (1350 kg) of other stores carried on 4 underwing pylons. The latter can include bombs of various types (including cluster, fragmentation and containers for antiarmor antipersonnel bomblets), napalm and rockets (including 128-mm).
Accommodation: Pilot and instructor.
Wingspan: 32 ft 5 in (9.88 m).
Length: 38 ft 11 in (11.86 m).
Maximum take-off weight for strike mission: 13,955 lb (6330 kg).
Maximum speed: 565 mph (910 km/h).

Above: SOKO G-4 Super Galeb jet trainer and light attack aircraft.

Combat radius: Armed, 186 miles (300 km) at 11,442-lb (5190-kg) AUW.
Mission performance: Rate of climb at sea level 5900 ft (1800 m) per min; ceiling 49,210 ft (15,000 m); G limits +8, −4.2.
Engine: One 4000-lb (1814-kg) Rolls-Royce Viper Mk 632 turbojet, with 1720 liters of fuel standard.

Version in service

G-4 Super Galeb: Basic jet trainer and strike aircraft. Can use detachable rocket packs to boost power during take off. Pilots now train on the UTVA Lasta before progressing to the Super Galeb.
Operator: Yugoslavia.

SOKO J-1 and RJ-1 Jastreb, and TJ-1 Jastreb Trainer
Yugoslavia

The Jastreb flew for the first time in 1967 as a single-seat attack development of the Galeb, with the rear cockpit faired over to merge into the upper fuselage. In addition, the

Below: SOKO J-1 Jastreb light attack aircraft.

communications and navigation avionics were improved, a more powerful engine fitted, and the airframe strengthened to allow for a heavier warload. Also offered was a reconnaissance version, with three cameras in fuselage and tiptank nose positions for daytime photographic missions or a single fuselage camera for night reconnaissance when flash bombs would be carried underwing. Weapons can also be carried by the reconnaissance Jastrebs, though without the rocket options and comprising a lighter load. Conversely, the wing tiptank cameras can be installed on the attack Jastreb if required. Export versions of the J-1 attack and RJ-1 reconnaissance aircraft became the J-1-E and RJ-1-E respectively, each with updated equipment.

One final variant of the Jastreb is the TJ-1 Jastreb Trainer, still capable of attack missions but intended for conversion and proficiency training. A tandem two-seater, the TJ-1 began to enter service in 1975.

Specifications (J-1 and J-1-E data)
Weapons: Three 0.50-in Colt-Browning machine-guns in the nose of the fuselage, each with 135 rounds of ammunition. 8 underwing pylons, the inboard pair able to carry four 551-lb (250-kg) bombs, clusters of lighter bombs, 4 napalm tanks, or rocket pods, while the outer pylons are suited to a 127-mm rocket each. The 4 pylons on reconnaissance Jastrebs can be armed with two 551-lb (250-kg) and two 331-lb (150-kg) bombs.
Accommodation: The pilot, except for TJ-1 Jastreb Trainer which has a crew of 2.
Wingspan: 38 ft 4 in (11.68 m) over tiptanks.
Length: 35 ft 8½ in (10.88 m).
Maximum take-off weight: 11,243 lb (5100 kg).
Maximum speed: 510 mph (820 km/h).
Range: 945 miles (1520 km) with tiptanks fitted.
Mission performance: Rate of climb at sea level 4130 ft (1260 m) per min; ceiling 39,370 ft (12,000 m).
Engine: One 3000-lb (1361-kg) thrust Rolls-Royce Viper 531 turbojet. JATO rockets can be fitted to temporarily boost power.

Below: SOKO Orao with an underfuselage centerline reconnaissance pod.

Versions in service
J-1: Basic attack version, delivered to the home air force.
RJ-1: Tactical 3-camera photographic reconnaissance derivative of the J-1, also for the home air force. Can be armed or used as a target tug.
TJ-1 Jastreb Trainer: 2-seat training model, first flown in 1974.
J-1-E: Export model of the J-1, delivered to Zambia in small numbers. It has been reported that Libya operates one squadron with a large number of Jastrebs.
RJ-1-E: Export photographic reconnaissance model.
Operators: Libya (J-1-E?), Yugoslavia (J-1, RJ-1 and TJ-1) and Zambia (J-1-E and RJ-1-E).

SOKO/CNIAR Orao/IAR-93
Yugoslavia and Rumania

In 1970 in a surprising collaboration, engineers in Rumania and Yugoslavia began to design a close support/ground attack aircraft to meet a joint requirement of their national air forces. Finalized as a neat shoulder-wing monoplane powered by two turbojet engines and built in single- and two-seat versions, manufacture is the responsibility of SOKO in Yugoslavia where the aircraft is designated SOKO J-22 Orao (Eagle), and of CNIAR (Centrul National al Industriei Aeronautice Romãne) in Rumania under the designation IAR-93.

Early progress followed the same pattern in both countries, with a single-seat prototype from each manufacturer being flown simultaneously on 31 October 1974, and the two-seat prototype following on 29 January 1977. Since that date progress has not continued on a parallel basis, but both companies flew their first pre-production aircraft during 1978. Series production began in Rumania during 1979 but in Yugoslavia this phase came about a year later. It has not, so far, been possible to confirm with any degree of accuracy the numbers ordered by each nation and the progress of deliveries. The Rumanian versions are designated IAR-93A with non-afterburning turbojet engines, irrespective of

whether they have single- or two-seat accommodation (the latter with a forward fuselage lengthened by 1 ft 4½ in/0.41 m), and IAR-93B with afterburning turbojets. The Yugoslav equivalents are designated Orao 1 and Orao 2 respectively.

Specifications (CNIAR IAR-93B data)
Radar and weapons: So far as is known none of the variants is equipped with radar. 2 GSh-23L 23-mm cannon, with 200 rounds of ammunition each and external pylons with a combined maximum weapon load of 3307 lb (1500 kg) and suitable for bombs, rocket launchers, drop tanks, or pods containing a GSh-23L cannon, a camera, IR reconnaissance sensors, or night illumination equipment.
Accommodation: One or 2 persons.
Wingspan: 31 ft 6¾ in (9.62 m).
Length: 48 ft 10½ in (14.90 m) (single-seater).
Maximum take-off weight: 24,692 lb (11,200 kg).
Maximum speed: 721 mph (1160 km/h) at sea level.
Combat radius: 329 miles (530 km) for high-altitude mission with maximum external load.
Mission performance: Rate of climb at sea level 13,780 ft (4200 m) per min; ceiling 44,290 ft (13,500 m); G limits +8, −4.2.
Engines: Two 5000-lb (2268-kg) thrust Turboméca/ORAO license-built Rolls-Royce Viper Mk 633-41 afterburning turbojets, with 2950 liters fuel standard.

Versions in service
IAR-93A: Rumanian version of which the first production example was flown in 1981, powered by 4000-lb (1818-kg) thrust license-built Rolls-Royce Viper Mk 632-41R nonafterburning turbojets and available in both single- and 2-seat versions. Initial order for Rumanian air force numbered 20 but it is not known how many have been delivered.
IAR-93B: Rumanian version, generally similar to IAR-93A but powered by the Rolls-Royce Viper Mk 663-41 afterburning turbojet, of which the first production example was flown in 1985. A total of 165, comprising both single- and 2-seat versions, reported to have been ordered for the Rumanian air force.
Orao 1: Yugoslav version of the IAR-93A of which both single-seat tactical reconnaissance and 2-seat operational conversion trainer versions are believed to be in production.
Orao 2: Yugoslav single-seat version of the IAR-93B in production as an attack aircraft, the first having flown on 20 October 1983. It differs from other versions by having a maximum weapon load of 6173 lb (2800 kg) and can deploy a wider range of weapons that includes AM-500 sea mines and Hughes AGM-65B Maverick air-to-surface missiles.
Operators: Rumania and Yugoslavia.

Sukhoi Su-7B
(NATO name Fitter-A and Moujik)
Soviet Union

First flown as a prototype on 8 September 1955, the later production Su-7B attack-fighter became a standard Soviet combat aircraft and was subsequently acquired by other

Above: Polish Air Force Sukhoi Su-7Bs, the nearest having its braking parachutes handled.

Sukhoi Su-17, Su-20 and Su-22
(NATO name Fitter)
Soviet Union

Although the Sukhoi Su-7B was the subject of massive production, its limitations in range and weapon payload somewhat restricted its usefulness, especially when assigned non-nuclear attack weapons. On 2 August 1966 a research aircraft flew as the S-7IG, differing mainly from the standard Su-7B by having variable-geometry outer wing panels, the juncture marked by a large fence. Small though this and other modifications were, the improvement was staggering. In this form the new Su-17 entered production, joining Soviet units in the early 1970s. The initial aircraft were powered by the same Lyulka engine as their predecessors, but a switch to the AL-21F-3 provided the Su-17 with the ability to achieve an enormous leap in performance. Compared to the Su-7B, Fitter-C and later models take off in about half the distance and carry twice the warload. An increase in fuel capacity provided a very significant improvement in range. Today the Soviet Air Force deploys more than 1000 with tactical units, while Naval Aviation has a much smaller but significant number for air support of amphibious landings and anti-shipping in the Pacific and Baltic regions. The Su-20 and Su-22 are export models with reduced standards of avionics and, in the latter case, a Tumansky engine.

nations. However, its long career with the Soviet Air Force has all but ended; it has been superseded by the IAR-93 in Rumanian squadrons, and other nations have either replaced it or will probably do so over the next few years. Nevertheless substantial numbers remained with 11 air forces in 1986.

The Su-7B and the contemporary Su-9 all-weather fighter had remarkably similar airframes, except for the wings, the Su-11 improved fighter in turn being closely related to the Su-9. Neither fighter remains in use. Improvements to the Su-7B have introduced updated versions, though each is covered by the single NATO name of Fitter-A. A feature of all Su-7B types is the light weapon carrying capability, undoubtedly reflecting the intention of arming Soviet-operated aircraft principally with nuclear bombs.

for JATO rocket units to assist take-off.
Versions in service
Su-7B: Original production version, suited also to reconnaissance using available fuselage cameras. Four weapons pylons.
Su-7BM: Changes include uprated engine and avionics, tail warning radar and six weapons pylons.
Su-7BKL: AL-7F-1-200 engine, low-pressure nosewheel tyre, and other changes.
Su-7BMK: Strengthened to carry the heaviest weapon load of any version.
Su-7U: 2-seat trainer. NATO name Moujik.
Operators: Afghanistan, Algeria, Czechoslovakia, Egypt, India, Iraq, North Korea, Poland, Soviet Union (?), Syria, Vietnam and South Yemen.

Specifications (Fitter-C data)
Radar: SRD-5M I-band ranging radar carried in the air-intake cone, known to NATO as 'High Fix'. Radar-warning receiver.
Weapons: Two 30-mm NR-30 cannon in the fixed wingroots, with 70 rounds of ammunition each, plus 4 underfuselage

Below: Sukhoi Su-20 in Polish markings.

Specifications (Su-7BMK data)
Radar: Ranging radar carried in the centrebody of nose air-intake. Tail warning radar.
Weapons: Two 30-mm NR-30 cannon in the wingroots, with 70 rounds of ammunition each, plus 6 underfuselage and underwing pylons for conventional and nuclear bombs, rockets and other weapons. Maximum weapon load is greatly reduced to just 2200 lb (1000 kg) when two 1200-liter drop tanks are fitted under the fuselage. A typical armament is two 1653-lb (750-kg) and two 1102-lb (500-kg) bombs.
Accommodation: The pilot. Moujik seats 2 in tandem.
Wingspan: 28 ft 9¼ in (8.77 m).
Length: 55 ft 1½ in (16.80 m).
Maximum take-off weight: 29,630 lb (13,440 kg).
Maximum speed: Mach 1.6 without weapons.
Combat radius: 215 miles (345 km).
Mission performance: Rate of climb at sea level 29,530 ft (9000 m) per min; ceiling 59,000 ft (18,000 m).
Engine: One 21,165-lb (9600-kg) thrust with afterburning Lyulka AL-7F-1-100 turbojet, with 2940 liters of fuel standard. Provision

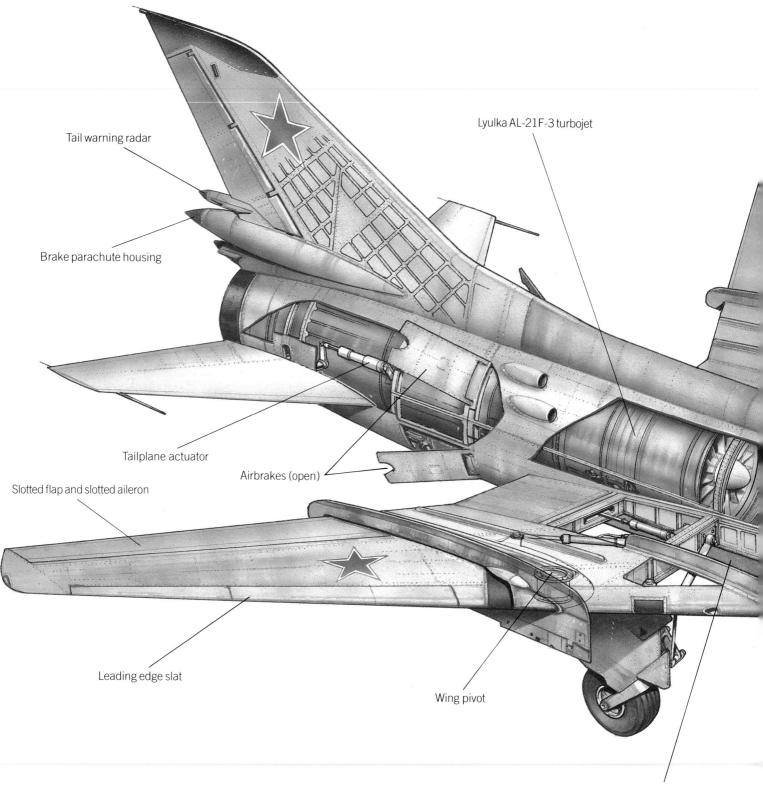

Tail warning radar

Brake parachute housing

Lyulka AL-21F-3 turbojet

Tailplane actuator

Airbrakes (open)

Slotted flap and slotted aileron

Leading edge slat

Wing pivot

Main undercarriage bay

Above: Cutaway drawing of a Sukhoi Su-17
Fitter-D.

pylons for at least 7000 lb (3175 kg) of nuclear or conventional attack weapons.

Accommodation: The pilot.

Wingspan: Spread 45 ft 3 in (13.80 m), swept 32 ft 10 in (10.00 m).

Length: 61 ft 6 in (18.75 m).

Maximum take-off weight: 39,022 lb (17,700 kg).

Maximum speed: Mach 2.09.

Combat radius: 425 miles (680 km) with a 4409-lb (2000-kg) load.

Mission performance: Rate of climb at sea level 45,275 ft (13,800 m) per min; ceiling 59,000 ft (18,000 m).

Engine: One 24,690-lb (11,200-kg) thrust with afterburning Lyulka AL-21F-3 turbojet, with 4550 liters of fuel standard.

Versions in service

Fitter-C: Su-17 variant for the Soviet Air Force and Navy. The first AL-21F-3-powered and earliest model in use.

Fitter-D: Su-17 M. Slightly lengthened fuselage, Doppler navigation radar and a laser rangefinder.

Fitter-E: Su-17 UM. Trainer version, with tandem seats for the two crew under a sectioned canopy. Nose is more conical and the fuselage shape aft of the canopy is revised because of the seating arrangement.

Fitter-G: Su-17G. Trainer version of Fitter-H, with a laser target seeker.

Fitter-H: Improved Su-17 single-seater. Used also for reconnaissance.

Fitter-K: Current production Su-17 single-seater.

Su-20: Fitter-C for export, with lower standard of equipment.

Su-22: Fitter-F is the export version of Fitter-D. As with all Su-22s, it is fitted with a 25,353-lb (11,500-kg) thrust with afterburning Tumansky R-29B turbojet. Can carry Atoll (NATO name) air-to-air missiles for an air defense role. Fitter-G is the Su-22 export model of the Su-17 Fitter-G, while Fitter-J is the Su-22 export model of Fitter-H, but with a greater fuel capacity and Atolls.

Operators: Afghanistan (Su-22), Algeria (Su-20), Angola (Su-22), Czechoslovakia (Su-20), Egypt (Su-20?), West Germany (Su-20*), Iraq (Su-20), Libya (Su-22), Peru (Su-22), Poland (Su-20), Soviet Union (air force and navy, Su-17), Syria (Su-22), Vietnam (Su-22), North Yemen (Su-22) and South Yemen (Su-22).

* Ex-Egyptian aircraft, for evaluation only.

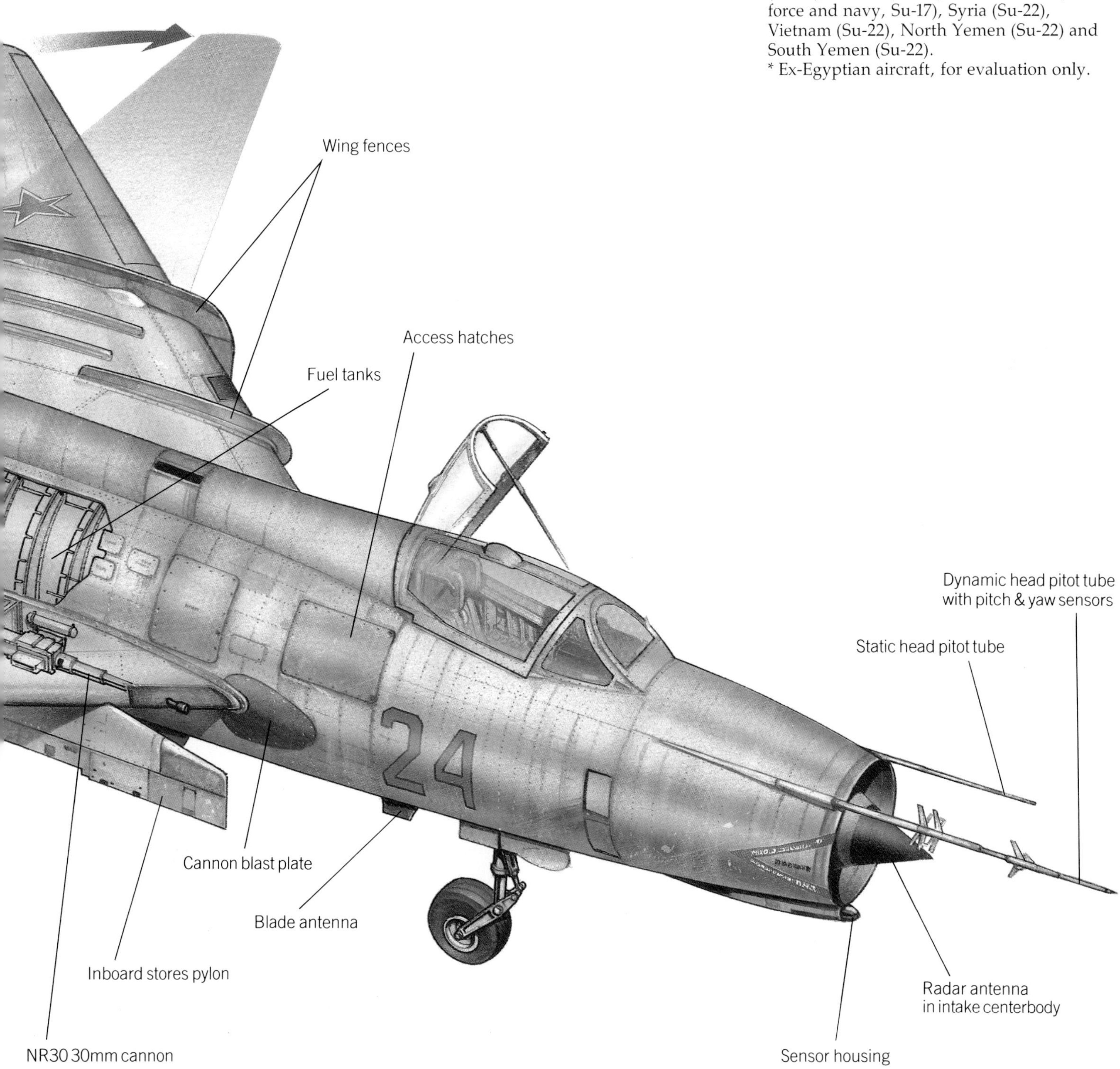

Wing fences

Access hatches

Fuel tanks

Dynamic head pitot tube with pitch & yaw sensors

Static head pitot tube

Cannon blast plate

Blade antenna

Inboard stores pylon

Radar antenna in intake centerbody

NR30 30mm cannon

Sensor housing

Above: Sukhoi Su-21 Flagon-F all-weather interceptor, with Anab AAMs under its wings.

Sukhoi Su-21 (NATO name Flagon)
Soviet Union

This designation may not be familiar to aviation enthusiasts, who might equally wonder at not finding an entry for the Su-15 all-weather interceptor. They are, in fact, more or less the same aircraft. The interceptors first seen publicly at Domodedovo in 1967 were Su-15s, and Flagon-As, Cs and Ds in Soviet service were of this type. However, with more modern aircraft replacing Flagons, only E, F and G versions are thought to remain operational, all of which are much improved and fall under the 'revised' designation of Su-21. Today, some 225 serve with the Voyska PVO as home defense interceptors and more than 300 are with tactical units.

Specifications (Flagon-F data, estimated)
Radar: 'Twin Scan' (NATO name) X-band radar.
Weapons: 2 underfuselage pylons for 23-mm GSh-23L gun pods or other weapons. 4 underwing pylons for Anab and Aphid air-to-air missiles.
Accommodation: The pilot. Flagon-G has a crew of 2 in tandem.
Wingspan: 34 ft 6 in (10.53 m).
Length: 68 ft 0 in (20.50 m).
Maximum take-off weight: 35,270 lb (16,000 kg).
Maximum speed: Mach 2.1.
Combat radius: 450-621 miles (725-1000 km).
Mission performance: Ceiling 65,600 ft (20,000 m); time to 36,100 ft (11,000 m) 2 min 30 sec.
Engines: Two 15,873-lb (7200-kg) thrust with afterburning Tumansky R-13F2-300 turbojets.
Versions in service
Flagon-E: This became the most important version of Flagon, powered by two 14,550-lb (6600-kg) thrust with afterburning R-13F-300 engines. Compared to the earlier versions, the radar detailed above replaced the 1960s-type Skip Spin X-band which had an output of about 100 kW and a scanning limit of perhaps 25 nm, and the wings were

redesigned. Greater range than earlier versions, but subsonic performance with drop tanks fitted.
Flagon-F: As detailed above.
Flagon-G: Unusual for a trainer for carrying a NATO 'F' for fighter reporting name rather than an 'M' name, Flagon-G accommodates 2 persons in tandem and probably has operational capability.
Operator: Soviet Union.

Sukhoi Su-24 (NATO name Fencer)
Soviet Union

By superseding the 1950s'-designed Yakovlev Yak-28 Brewer (NATO name), the Su-24 not only gave the Soviet Air Force a tactical fighter-bomber in the class of the US F-111 but provided a two-seater that could also be added to the strategic inventory, much as the US FB-111A. It is said to be able to hit a target in all weather conditions within an accuracy of 55 meters, fly at Mach 1.2 at 'tree-top' level and, especially for a Soviet aircraft, carry an extremely heavy conventional or nuclear weapon load. Unlike the F-111, Fencer does not have a fuselage bay and only two of its

pylons are on the 'swinging' section of the wings and thereby only these require to be of the more complicated pivoting type. First deployed in 1974, it is believed that some 700 are now in front-line service, two-thirds for strategic use. Fencer variants also include reconnaissance and ECM models.

Specifications (Fencer-C data, estimated)
Radar: Navigation and attack radar, plus terrain avoidance radar. Laser rangefinder and marked target seeker.
Weapons: One 30-mm 6-barrel cannon in the fuselage plus up to 24,250 lb (11,000 kg) of attack weapons. Air-to-surface missiles can include the tactical high-explosive AS-7 Kerry (NATO name), laser-guided AS-10 Karen (NATO name), and the little known AS-14 Kedge (NATO name).
Accommodation: 2 crew side by side.
Wingspan: Spread 57 ft 5 in (17.50 m), swept 34 ft 5 in (10.50 m).
Length: 69 ft 10 in (21.29 m).
Maximum take-off weight: 90,400 lb (41,000 kg).

Below: Soviet Sukhoi Su-24 Fencer-C photographed by a Swedish Air Force pilot.

Maximum speed: Mach 2.18.
Combat radius: 590 miles (950 km) with 2500 kg of weapons and standard fuel.
Mission performance: Ceiling 54,150 ft (16,500 m).
Engines: 2 afterburning engines of unidentified type, although thought to be similar to Su-17 turbojet.

Versions in service

Fencer-A: Initial version, entering service at the end of 1974.
Fencer-B: Minor fuselage differences indicating some equipment changes.
Fencer-C: 1981 version, with extensive equipment updates indicated by various fairings and nose probes.
Fencer-D: Lengthened and latest armed version, from 1983. Flight refuelling system added to enhance its tactical and strategic capabilities. Much new equipment probably including an electro-optical sensor. Reportedly also built in reconnaissance form.
Fencer-E: Likely designation of the ECM tactical jamming variant, to supersede Brewer-E.
Operator: Soviet Union.

Sukhoi Su-25 (NATO name Frogfoot)
Soviet Union

The development of this single-seat close support combat aircraft can be said to have stemmed from two major factors. The first was the deployment by the USAF of the Fairchild Republic A-10A Thunderbolt II for this role and secondly, the subsequent need of the Soviet forces fighting in Afghanistan for an aircraft to perform much the same missions as the Hind gunship helicopters but at higher speed and carrying a much heavier warload. Indeed, so great was its urgency for Afghanistan service that it began initial operations in support of the Soviet army almost two years before becoming fully operational in 1984.

By 1986 it was estimated that some 75 Su-25s were deployed by Soviet units, with Czechoslovakia and Iraq the first export users. Although designed for a similar task, the Su-25 is unlike the US A-10A in configuration, the most obvious differences being its more traditional single fin-and-rudder tail unit, and engines mounted in wingroot nacelles. The pilot occupies a cockpit that is faired into the rear fuselage, having a mirror

Below: Czech Air Force Sukhoi Su-25s.

for glancing rearward but not affording the excellent all-round view that the Thunderbolt II pilot has from his raised bubble canopy. Other features of the Su-25 are armor around the cockpit sides and wingtip pod airbrakes.

Specifications
Equipment: Laser rangefinder and marked target seeker, nose camera, radar warning receiver, and chaff/flare dispenser.
Weapons: One 30-mm twin-barrel cannon, plus up to about 9921 lb (4500 kg) of attack weapons on 8 of the 10 underwing pylons; the outer pylons can carry two Atoll or Aphid missiles for self-protection.
Accommodation: The pilot.
Wingspan: 46 ft 11 in (14.30 m).
Length: 50 ft 7 in (15.40 m).
Maximum take-off weight: 42,329 lb (19,200 kg).
Maximum speed: 609 mph (980 km/h).
Combat radius: 345 miles (556 km) with maximum internal and auxiliary fuel and 4409 lb (2000 kg) of attack weapons.
Mission performance: Rate of climb, ceiling, sustained turn rate and G limits are unknown.
Engines: Two 9337-lb (4235-kg) thrust nonafterburning Tumansky R-13-300 turbojets.
Version in service
Su-25: Initial version, first observed by a US satellite while under test at the Ramenskoye center in 1977.
Operators: Czechoslovakia, Iraq and Soviet Union.

Above: Sukhoi Su-27 Flankers.

Sukhoi Su-27 (NATO name Flanker)
Soviet Union

It has been a belief in the West that the far greater number of combat aircraft available to the Warsaw Pact, and especially the Soviet Union, could be offset if required by the superior technology and sophistication of Western aircraft. Sophistication has, though, been a mixed blessing and at least in the past has greatly contributed to the number of unserviceable aircraft at any one time. The Soviet Union has now not only closed the gap but probably overtaken the West in many vital areas, not least in air-to-air missile armament. In company with the MiG-29 Fulcrum and MiG-31 Foxhound, the Su-27 is every bit as good as its Western counterpart, the US F-15 Eagle. Indeed, a probably specially prepared example has wrested some of the world time-to-height records set over a decade ago by the specially prepared F-15 Streak Eagle, including a climb to 9843 ft (3000 meters) in just over 23 seconds, four seconds less than the Streak Eagle. Its large pulse Doppler radar makes it a very capable antagonist for aircraft and low-flying cruise missiles, while a secondary attack capability is certain. Replacing MiG-21s and Su-21s plus a large number of the MiG-23s, MiG-27s and MiG-25s within air defense and tactical units since 1986, the Su-27 may also be adapted in navalized form for the new Soviet nuclear aircraft carriers.

Specifications (Su-27 data, estimated)
Radar: Advanced lookdown/shootdown track-while-scan radar, with a suggested search range and tracking range of 130 nm and 100 nm respectively.
Weapons: Known armament is six new and very advanced AA-10 medium-range and/or close-range AA-11s. Possibly up to 13,228 lb (6000 kg) of attack weapons.
Accommodation: The pilot.
Wingspan: 47 ft 7 in (14.50 m).
Length: 68 ft 11 in (21.00 m).
Maximum take-off weight: Perhaps up to 60,000 lb (27,215 kg).
Maximum speed: Mach 2.
Combat radius: 932 miles (1500 km).
Engines: 2 turbofans of unknown type, each

perhaps 29,980-lb (13,600-kg) thrust with afterburning.

Version in service

Su-27: First 'seen' by reconnaissance satellite in the late 1970s. Mostly metal-constructed, with a high-mounted cockpit above a drooping nose. Large twin underwing air-intake ducts.

Operator: Soviet Union.

Transall C-160 series
France and West Germany

To undertake the development and production of a military transport aircraft which had been designed to meet the requirements of the governments of Federal Germany and France, the Transall (Transporter Allianz) group was formed in January 1959. It then comprised Messerschmitt-Bölkow-Blohm (MBB), Nord Aviation (later Aérospatiale) and VFW-Fokker GmbH, with the production of assemblies and components being shared also by other manufacturers in France and Germany.

Intended for the military transportation of freight, supplies, troops and vehicles, this aircraft was identified as the Transall C-160, the first prototype making its maiden flight on 25 February 1963. Features of its design include a high-mounted wing to optimize the volume of its pressurized cabin, an upswept rear fuselage incorporating a door/ramp for loading and unloading of vehicles, a freight

Below: Luftwaffe Transall C-160D transports.

door forward and paratroop deployment doors on each side, and wing and landing gear design to permit operation from semi-prepared surfaces. Accommodation is for 93 troops, or 81 equipped paratroops, or 62 stretchers and four attendants, or 35,274 lb (16,000 kg) of freight which can include vehicles. This original program ended in 1972 after deliveries had been completed for France (50), Germany (90), South Africa (9) and Turkey (20).

In 1977 the manufacture of a second series was authorized with production of 25 for France (later increased to 29) to be shared between Aérospatiale and MBB. Basically similar to the original C-160, the second series aircraft benefit by having a reinforced wing that can optionally have a range-increasing fuel tank mounted in the wing center-section and by the introduction of updated avionics. From the initial production order for 25, inflight refuelling equipment of the hose-and-drogue type was installed in the first 10, with provisions for such equipment being incorporated in five more; all have a refuelling probe mounted above and to the rear of the flight deck. The four additional aircraft ordered by the French Air Force are intended to operate from 1987 as communications relay aircraft for the French nuclear deterrent force. Designated Astarté (Avion-station-relais de transmissions exceptionelles), they have a Thomson-CSF VLF communications system similar to that which equips the US Navy's Tacamo EC-130s and will also be equipped to serve as flight refuelling tankers/receivers. Modular kits have been developed

for the C-160 to allow conversion for roles that include electronic surveillance (C-160SE), maritime surveillance (C-160S) and AEW (C-160AAA).

Specifications (C-160 Second series data)

Radar: ESD RDN-72 Doppler navigation radar and Omera ORB-37 weather radar.

Accommodation: As detailed above.

Wingspan: 131 ft 3 in (40.00 m).

Length: 106 ft 3½ in (32.40 m).

Maximum take-off weight: 112,435 lb (51,000 kg).

Maximum speed: 319 mph (513 km/h).

Range with maximum payload: 1151 miles (1853 km).

Mission performance: Rate of climb at sea level 1300 ft (396 m) per min; ceiling at 99,210 lb (45,000 kg) weight 27,000 ft (8230 m).

Engines: Two 6100-ehp Rolls-Royce Tyne RTy.20 Mk 22 turboprop engines, with 19,050 liters of fuel standard.

Versions in service

C-160D: Major production version built for service with the Luftwaffe.

C-160F: French Air Force version.

C-160T: 20 aircraft from the original order of 110 for the Luftwaffe were supplied for use by the Turkish Air Force.

C-160Z: 9 aircraft, basically similar to the C-160D/F, supplied to the South African Air Force for service with its No 28 Squadron.

C-160P: Designation applied to 4 C-160Fs following their conversion for use by Air France in night mail operations.

C-160 (Second Series): Updated version,

generally similar to the C-160F, built for service with the French Air Force. In addition to those built for France, 6 aircraft of this version have been supplied to the Indonesian government for use in the country's transmigration program.

C-160 Astarté: 4 aircraft from the Second Series equipped for a strategic communications relay role, all with a secondary flight refuelling tanker/receiver capability.

Operators: France, West Germany, South Africa and Turkey.

Tupolev strategic bomber
(NATO name Blackjack)
Soviet Union

The development of Soviet strategic bombers over the past half century has been both logical and sustained, achievements the West can no longer claim. Up to the 1960s developments in the Soviet Union and United States can be said to have run in parallel, the postwar US B-52 being matched by the Soviet Tu-95 and Myarishchev M-4, and the supersonic B-58 Hustler having the Tupolev Tu-22 as its Eastern rival. While it had been planned that the USAF would deploy the North American B-70 Valkyrie as a supersonic replacement for the B-52, this idea was dropped in 1963 and the prototypes became test vehicles. The subsonic B-52 remains (in 1987) the main US and NATO strategic bomber, though in 1986 the USAF declared initial operational capability with the B-1B, the single operational aircraft then not having received its cruise missile armament.

The decision to abandon the Mach 3 B-70 was the first blow in the USAF's efforts to keep pace with, or ahead of, Soviet developments, the latter nation subsequently deploying its supersonic Tupolev Tu-26 Backfire swing-wing strategic and theater bomber that has no Western rival. Again, and entirely logically, having gained the initiative with Backfire, while still also keeping the Tu-95 in limited production to make good attrition, Tupolev set about developing an even more formidable supersonic strategic bomber to complement Backfire and carry new-generation nuclear cruise missiles over twice the range. The result is known to NATO as Blackjack.

It was in November 1981 that a US satellite first photographed a Blackjack prototype at the Ramenskoye test center, and in 1986 a total of five were being used in the final stages of the flight test program. According to US official statements, Blackjack was expected to achieve initial operational capability by 1988. While Backfire has no Western counterpart, Blackjack can be seen as equal to the US B-1B, though it is substantially larger and heavier, and very much faster in supersonic dash. At least as many Blackjacks will be built as B-1Bs despite the hundreds of Backfires already in service.

In general configuration, Blackjack is closer to the B-1B than to Backfire, with two pairs of engines mounted below the fixed center sections of the wings and the tailplane carried midway up the fin. Specially developed for this bomber has been the AS-15 (NATO Kent) nuclear cruise missile with a 1860-mile (3000-km) range and the supersonic BL-10 cruise missile with even greater range. The

former has already achieved operational status on newly built Tu-95 Bear-H bombers, prior to Blackjack deployment.

Specifications (Blackjack data, estimated)
Weapons: AS-15 Kent and BL-10 nuclear cruise missiles, other missiles or bombs up to about 36,000 lb (16,300 kg).
Wingspan: Swept 110 ft 0 in (33.75 m), spread 172 ft 0 in (52.0 m).
Length: 166 ft 0 in (50.6 m).
Maximum take-off weight: 551,000 lb (250,000 kg).
Maximum speed: Mach 2.
Combat radius: 4535 miles (7300 km) unrefuelled.
Engines: 4 unidentified engines, possibly related to the Koliesov variable-geometry variable bypass afterburning type as fitted to the Tu-144 supersonic airliner.

Version in service
Blackjack: Prototypes and pre-production aircraft only by 1986.
Operator: Soviet Union (from 1988?)

Above: US Department of Defense impression of the new Tupolev Blackjack strategic bomber launching an AS-15 Kent cruise missile.

Tupolev Tu-16 and Xian H-6
(NATO name Badger)
Soviet Union and China

Although the Tu-4 (Tupolev's copy of the US B-29 Superfortress) only entered service in the Soviet Union after the end of World War II, it was quickly appreciated that future strategic requirements could only be fulfilled by a more advanced bomber. Tupolev responded with prototypes Tu-80 and Tu-85, but as both retained piston engines Stalin gave them the 'thumbs down'. However, although there would be some delay, Tupolev was already working on its Tu-88 and the prototype took to the air in the winter of 1952. This was just what was needed and it entered large-scale

Soviet Tupolev Tu-16 Badger-G, armed with 'Kingfish.'

production as the Tu-16 intermediate-range bomber in 1953.

Equivalent, perhaps, to the USAF's B-47 Stratojet, it was a more modern design in many respects, with the crew occupying a conventional flight deck. The engines were installed neatly at the roots of the swept wings, semirecessed into the fuselage, while seven cannon were provided in the nose, tail, and dorsal and ventral barbettes. Total Soviet Tu-16 production by the 1960s is estimated at around 2000, of which more than 800 currently remain in Soviet Air Force and Navy service in strategic bomber, naval attack, reconnaissance, flight refuelling tanker and ECM forms, the importance of electronic roles indicated by approximately one-quarter of the total force being so equipped. The Tu-16 also entered development and production at Xian in China in about 1962, after the ideological split with the Soviet Union had put an end to China receiving any new Soviet-built examples. Xian H-6s began entering home squadrons in 1968 and production continues. Like Soviet aircraft, some H-6s have a nuclear capability. The latest version that appeared in about 1986 is the H-6D, primarily for antishipping duties with the Aviation of the People's Navy and carrying a modernized radar in an undernose cylindrical radome and two C-601 (CAS-N-1) radar-homing missiles. The Chinese forces are believed to have about 120 H-6s in service, mostly equivalent to Badger-A. It is also known that China has been looking at the H-6 with regard to providing a flight refuelling tanker for its Q-5 force.

Specifications (Badger-G data)
Radar: Radar in a 'chin' radome.
Weapons: Seven 23-mm cannon for defense, plus 19,840 lb (9000 kg) of bombs carried in a weapons bay or 2 'Kelt' or 'Kingfish' (NATO names) air-to-surface missiles.
Accommodation: 6 crew.
Wingspan: 108 ft 0 in (32.93 m).
Length: 118 ft 11 in (36.25 m).
Maximum take-off weight: 165,345 lb (75,000 kg).
Maximum speed: 616 mph (992 km/h).
Combat radius: 1950 miles (3150 km) without flight refuelling.
Engines: Two 20,944-lb (9500-kg) thrust Mikulin RD-3M turbojets, with about 45,500 liters of fuel.
Versions in service
Badger-A: Original bomber version with radar, carrying conventional or nuclear bombs. A number operate as tanker aircraft, transferring fuel by drogue or by a wingtip system that is unique to the Soviet forces.
Badger-B: The air-to-surface missiles formerly carried by this version have now given way to free-fall bombs.
Badger-C: Naval Aviation antiship version, carrying Puff Ball (NATO name) I-band surveillance radar in a large radome on the fuselage nose to detect ship targets over a wide area and perhaps assist in the guidance of the aircraft's Kipper or Kingfish missiles.
Badger-D: Electronic warfare version of the C.
Badger-E: Photographic reconnaissance and elint version, related to the A.
Badger-F: Elint version with a different avionics suite.

Badger-G: Air Force and Navy missile carrier, as detailed above, also able to carry bombs if required. Those armed with Kingfish missiles have different radar midway along the fuselage.
Badger-H: ECM version, with the maximum payload taken up by chaff (radar reflective material cut to a size that will confuse enemy radars).
Badger-J: Electronic jamming and elint aircraft.
Badger-K: Electronic reconnaissance aircraft.
Xian H-6: Chinese version, mostly equivalent to Badger-A and powered by locally-built Wopen-8 engines. The H-6D is the latest version, primarily for antiship missions.
Operators: China (air force and navy), Egypt (D and G), Iraq (G) and Soviet Union (air force and navy).

Tupolev Tu-22 (NATO name Blinder)
Soviet Union

The Blinder medium strategic bomber was the Soviet equivalent of the US Convair B-58 Hustler (which ended its service life prematurely). Both were 1950s' designs and both were their respective country's first supersonic bombers. Blinder was first shown publicly flying over Moscow during the 1961 Aviation Day display, when it became clear that among its weapon options was a huge supersonic nuclear standoff missile known to NATO as Kitchen.

Both the US Hustler and the Soviet Tu-22 had unusual design features. The latter had huge swept wings with trailing-edge pods into

which the main undercarriage units retract and the turbojets are carried either side of the tailfin. It is believed that 250 Tu-22s were built in bomber, reconnaissance and training forms, of which nearly 200 remain in service with Air Force and Naval units. In addition, Libya and Iraq received examples around 1973, of which an estimated seven or so are active with each, though this probably does not take into account Blinder-D trainers in Libyan service. Iraqi aircraft have Kitchen missile options but with high-explosive warheads.

Specifications (Blinder-A data, estimated)
Radar: Reportedly Short Horn (NATO name) J-band navigation and attack radar, also used in Blinder-C.
Weapons: Bomb-bay for conventional or nuclear bombs. One radar-directed 23-mm cannon in the tail.
Accommodation: 3 crew in tandem positions.
Wingspan: 78 ft 0 in (23.75 m).
Length: 132 ft 11 in (40.53 m).
Maximum take-off weight: 184,970 lb (83,900 kg).
Maximum speed: Mach 1.4.
Combat radius: 1800 miles (2900 km) without flight refuelling.
Mission performance: Ceiling 60,000 ft (18,300 m).
Engines: Two 30,865-lb (14,000-kg) thrust with afterburning Koliesov VD-7 turbojets.
Versions in service
Blinder-A: Initial version for bombing and reconnaissance, armed with free-fall

Below: The first Soviet supersonic bomber was the Tupolev Tu-22 Blinder.

Above: Tupolev Tu-26 Backfire-B, photographed by the pilot of a Swedish Air Force fighter.

weapons carried in a bomb-bay.
Blinder-B: Much improved version, with a semi-recessed Kitchen missile as the main armament and associated larger radar. Flight refuelling capability.
Blinder-C: Camera-carrying maritime reconnaissance version, with specialized electronic equipment. Flight refuelling capability. About 35 remain in use.
Blinder-D: Tandem cockpit training version.
Operators: Iraq, Libya and Soviet Union (air force and navy).

Tupolev Tu-26 (NATO name Backfire)
Soviet Union

The Soviet Union has been the only nation to maintain a continuous program of strategic bomber development and production, and in so doing has put or maintained aircraft in service which have no comparisons in the West. According to the US Department of Defense, while NATO only built two new bombers in 1985 (B-1Bs), 50 were completed in the Soviet Union. Examples of maintaining aircraft can be found in the Tu-95/142 Bear and Tu-22 Blinder; the former equivalent of the USAF's B-52 was still being built in new form in 1986, while the Blinder remained active even though its US equivalent (the B-58 Hustler) has long been withdrawn. But more important than these is the Tu-26 Backfire, designed to supersede Blinder as a supersonic medium strategic bomber and tactical attack/maritime reconnaissance aircraft, and a generation of bomber the West forfeited.

Backfire was first seen in prototype form in July 1970 and was the world's first 'swing-wing' bomber of any size; the outer wing panels can be swept up to about 65 degrees. It is thought that a principal aim was to achieve a range of 4775 to 5200 nautical miles without the use of a flight refuelling tanker, though a removable probe to receive fuel is provided. This has been achieved, more or less, with Backfire-B and C, though the first version (Backfire-A) was not so successful and was built in very limited numbers as a result. It is

estimated that the Soviet Air Force has more than 150 Backfires in service and the Navy a further 100 or so for antishipping duties, with production from the Kazan airframe plant adding 30 a year. Indeed, the total force could well be nearly 300 by 1987. Though Backfires could be directed against the contiguous United States, their main areas of operation are over Europe, the Atlantic and the Sea of Japan.

Specifications (Backfire-B data, estimated)
Radar and weapons: Down Beat (NATO name) bombing and navigation radar. Bee Hind radar to control the two 23-mm defensive tail guns. One Kitchen (NATO name) nuclear or high-explosive supersonic standoff missile semisubmerged under the fuselage or 2 under the fixed center-sections of the wings, or up to 26,455 lb (12,000 kg) of conventional bombs. Backfires have been seen with stations for bombs under the air-intakes. Defensive guns as above.
Accommodation: 4 crew.
Wingspan: Spread 113 ft 0 in (34.45 m),

swept 78 ft 9 in (24.00 m).
Length: 140 ft 0 in (42.50 m).
Maximum take-off weight: 286,600 lb (130,000 kg).
Maximum speed: Mach 2.
Combat radius: 2485 miles (4000 km).
Engines: Two 44,092-lb (20,000-kg) thrust turbofans, probably similar to the Kuznetsov NK-144.
Versions in service
Backfire-B: First major production version.
Backfire-C: Latest version, with wedge air-intakes. Little else is known.
Operator: Soviet Union (air force and navy).

Tupolev Tu-28P (NATO name Fiddler)
Soviet Union

First seen in prototype form during the 1961 Tushino flypast, Fiddler is a huge all-weather air defense fighter that has remained active largely because of its ability to intercept at long range. It is, indeed, the largest aircraft designed for this role to go into standard service. The production version became the Tu-28P, first seen by observers in 1967. The Voyska PVO home defense force is believed to include 90 Fiddler-Bs (Tu-28Ps), while a further 25 may serve with tactical units.

Specifications (estimated)
Radar: Big Nose (NATO name) radar.
Weapons: Air-to-air weapons are four Ash missiles, 2 with I R homing heads and 2 radar homing.
Accommodation: 2 crew in tandem.
Wingspan: 59 ft 4 in (18.10 m).
Length: 89 ft 3 in (27.30 m).
Maximum take-off weight: 99,200 lb (45,000 kg).
Maximum speed: Mach 1.65.
Combat radius: 932 miles (1500 km).
Mission performance: Ceiling 65,600 ft (20,000 m).
Engines: 2 unidentified turbojets, possibly in the 27,000-lb (12,250-kg) thrust class with afterburning.

Below: The largest interceptor in use is the Soviet Tupolev Tu-28P Fiddler.

Version in service:
Tu-28P: Referred to by the US DoD as the Tu-128. Does not carry drop tanks to extend range still further.
Operator: Soviet Union.

Tupolev Tu-95 and Tu-142
(NATO name Bear)
Soviet Union

In an age when the air forces of major powers are equipped with new-generation combat aircraft of spectacular performance and awesome capability, interested but uninitiated observers might assume that the Soviet Union's turboprop-powered Tu-95 and Tu-142 are something of an anachronism. In fact nothing could be further from the truth, and it is most interesting to discover that this 33-year-old aircraft, which combines swept wings, highly efficient turbine engines and advanced technology propellers, was still in production in new form in 1986 and is now regarded by some as a pointer to the long-range transport aircraft of the future. One might also make the observation that the reporting name of 'Bear' for this giant is perhaps the most appropriate ever bestowed by NATO.

Contemporary with the USAF's Boeing B-52 Stratofortress, Tupolev's Tu-95 was designed with the same objective, namely to provide the nation's air arm with a strategic

Below: A Tupolev Bear-D maritime reconnaissance bomber flying over the North Atlantic is escorted by two USAF Phantom fighters that took off from Keflavik, Iceland, having been directed onto the bomber by an AWACS aircraft.

bomber of intercontinental range. Flown in prototype form during the summer of 1954, the initial version, to which NATO allocated the reporting name 'Bear' (later amended to 'Bear-A'), was first seen by Western observers during the Soviet Aviation Day flypast at Tushino in July 1955. The type is believed to have entered operational service with the Soviet Air Force shortly after this date, but within two or three years the growing capability of Western defenses hastened the introduction of a cruise-missile-carrying version so that this weapon could be launched well clear of an enemy's defensive perimeter. Since that time the remarkable long-range

Above: The large noser radome and undernose antennae identify this as a cruise missile-carrying Tupolev Bear-H.

performance of these aircraft has seen their adoption for reconnaissance purposes, especially by the Soviet Naval Aviation for maritime surveillance over most of the world's oceans. During 1970 this latter air arm introduced a new ASW version which differed sufficiently from its predecessors to warrant redesignation, as the Tupolev Tu-142, and the latest Bear version (which is in current production) is based on the Tu-142 airframe but configured as a long-range cruise-missile

carrier. In early 1987 it was estimated that rather more than 200 Bears remain in service with the Soviet air arms. The Indian Navy received three Tu-142 Bears in 1984 for land-based antisubmarine, antisurface vessel and patrol missions.

Specifications (Tu-95 Bear-D data)

Radar: Big Bulge (NATO name) reconnaissance and search radar in blister fairing beneath the center fuselage, plus Short Horn weapons delivering and navigation radar, and tail warning radar.
Weapons: Weapon load typically 24,251 lb (11,000 kg) in Bear-A, differs according to variant, and can include a wide range of nuclear or conventional weapons and air-to-surface missiles.
Wingspan: 167 ft 8 in (51.10 m).
Length: 162 ft 5 in (49.50 m).
Maximum take-off weight: 414,469 lb (188,000 kg) estimated.
Maximum speed: 575 mph (925 km/h).
Combat radius: 5148 miles (8285 km) without inflight refuelling.
Mission performance: Ceiling 41,010 ft (12,500 m).
Engines: Four 14,795-ehp Kuznetsov NK-12MV turboprops, with 95,000 liters of fuel standard.

Versions in service

Bear-A: Basic strategic bomber with bomb-bay for nuclear or conventional weapons and defensive armament of 3 pairs of 23-mm cannon in manned tail turret and 2 remotely-controlled dorsal and ventral barbettes.
Bear-B: Similar to Bear-A but equipped to carry the AS-3 Kangaroo (NATO name) supersonic air-to-surface missile of 400-mile (650-km) range and Crown Drum radar.
Bear-C: Similar to Bear B in configuration and role, but with a refuelling probe as standard and an electronic intelligence fairing on each side of the rear fuselage.
Bear-D: Maritime reconnaissance version, with equipment as described above.
Bear-E: Reconnaissance version of Bear-C with 6 camera windows below the normal bomb-bay and one beneath the starboard rear fuselage.
Bear-F: ASW version for Soviet Naval Aviation with Short Horn radar, 2 weapons bays for torpedoes, nuclear depth

charges and sonobuoys, and retaining only the manned tail turret with defensive guns. Some are equipped with MAD.
Bear-G: Based on Bear-B and C, but equipped to carry instead two AS-4 Kitchen supersonic stand-off missiles with a range of 186 miles (300 km).
Bear-H: Current production version, based on Bear-F but with a fuselage of reduced length. Equipped to carry the AS-15 Kent air-launched cruise missile which has a range of 1864 miles (3000 km).
Operators: India (navy) and Soviet Union (air force and navy).

Tupolev Tu-126 (NATO name Moss)
Soviet Union

Based upon the airframe of the Tu-114 airliner, the Tu-126 was developed as a first-generation airborne early warning and control aircraft. Its main task is to serve with the Voyska PVO home defense force, detecting low-flying enemy aircraft and directing Soviet interceptors to them. Operating with tactical air forces it can perform a similar air surveillance task and also assist Soviet fighter and strike aircraft in their bid to evade enemy fighters in the European and Asian theaters. However, it is believed that the radar carried in the above-fuselage rotating radome has proved disappointing in its detection capabilities over land but is useful over water. Such deficiencies are particularly serious now that low-flying cruise missiles are an important part of the military scene. This is undoubtedly the reason why only about nine Tu-126s are flown by the defense forces to be superseded by the Il-76 Mainstay.

Above: The Soviet equivalent of the US Boeing Sentry AWACS aircraft is the Tupolev Tu-126 Moss.

Specifications

Radar and equipment: Surveillance radar of about 11 meters diameter is carried in an above-fuselage rotating radome. Much other electronic equipment is carried by the aircraft, indicated by blisters, dielectric panels and antennae.
Accommodation: Unknown number of crew in air-conditioned cabins.
Wingspan: 168 ft 0 in (51.20 m).
Length: 181 ft 1 in (55.20 m).
Maximum take-off weight: 374,785 lb (170,000 kg).
Maximum speed: 528 mph (850 km/h).
Maximum range: 7800 miles (12,550 km) unrefuelled.
Engines: Four 14,795-ehp Kuznetsov KN-12MV turboprops.
Version in service
Moss: NATO name for this first generation AWACS aircraft.
Operator: Soviet Union.

UTVA-66
Yugoslavia

First flown in prototype form in 1967 or thereabouts, the UTVA-66 is a strut-braced high-wing utility and ambulance light aircraft that has provision for carrying two machine-gun pods under its wings. Those in Yugoslav Air Force service are believed to be assigned mainly to liaison work. To assist the loading

Below: Yugoslavian UTVA-66.

of stretchers or other long items, the rear window hinges upward.

Specifications

Weapons: 2 machine-gun pods optionally.
Accommodation: 4 seats or a pilot and two stretchers and a medical attendant. The UTVA-66-AM can air-drop supplies by parachute from under the fuselage.
Wingspan: 37 ft 5 in (11.40 m).
Length: 27 ft 6 in (8.38 m).
Maximum take-off weight: 4000 lb (1814 kg).
Maximum speed: 155 mph (250 km/h).
Range: 466 miles (750 km).
Mission performance: Rate of climb at sea level 886 ft (270 m) per min; ceiling 21,980 ft (6700 m).
Engine: One 270-hp Avco Lycoming GSO-480-B1J6 piston, with 250 liters of fuel standard.

Versions in service

UTVA-66: Utility and liaison aircraft.
UTVA-66-AM: Ambulance model.
Operator: Yugoslavia.

UTVA-75 and UTVA-75A
Yugoslavia

The UTVA-75 is a two-seat light aircraft, used by the Yugoslav Air Force for training. The first prototype flew initially on 19 May 1976 and production started in 1977. It has two underwing stations, suited to the carriage of 100-liter drop tanks or light armament.

The UTVA-75A is a four-seat derivative of the UTVA-75, using the same airframe and engine but with a maximum take-off weight of 2564 lb (1163 kg). It also has a higher level of avionics fitted as standard but no armament. Production deliveries were scheduled to begin in 1977 and it is possible that it could find use as a military liaison and utility aircraft, though, to date, no such indication has been given.

Specifications (UTVA-75 data)

Weapons: Two 220-lb (100-kg) bombs, machine-gun pods or 2 round rocket launchers, or 2 light cargo containers.
Accommodation: Instructor and student on

Below: UTVA-75.

side-by-side seats.
Wingspan: 31 ft 11 in (9.73 m).
Length: 23 ft 4 in (7.11 m).
Maximum take-off weight: 2116 lb (960 kg).
Maximum speed: 133 mph (215 km/h).
Range: 497 miles (800 km).
Mission performance: Rate of climb at sea level 885 ft (270 m) per min; ceiling 13,120 ft (4000 m); G limits +6, −3.
Engine: One 180-hp Avco Lycoming IO-360-B1F piston, with 160 liters of fuel standard.

Versions in service

UTVA-75: 2-seat trainer, also suited to utility and glider-towing duties. Established also with civil flying clubs.

Above: UTVA Lasta tandem-seat trainer.

UTVA-75A: 4-seat derivative of the UTVA-75, first flown in 1986. Slightly lower maximum speed.
Operator: Yugoslavia (UTVA-75).

UTVA Lasta
Yugoslavia

The Lasta, or Swallow, is a tandem two-seat primary trainer of the general configuration and dimensions of the Chilian Pillán and French Epsilon. It can undertake a variety of training missions, including basic, night, combat maneuver and aerobatic flying, navigation, instrument and weaponry. Once qualified on the Lasta, a student pilot would progress to the Super Galeb. The aircraft also retains a light strike capability. The first prototype made its maiden flight in 1985 and production has started.

Specifications

Weapons: Up to 882 lb (400 kg) of stores on 2 underwing pylons, including bombs, rocket launchers or machine-gun pods.
Accommodation: 2 seats in stepped tandem cockpits.
Wingspan: 27 ft 4½ in (8.34 m).
Length: 26 ft 4½ in (8.04 m).
Maximum take-off weight: 3594 lb (1630 kg).
Maximum speed: 214 mph (245 km/h).
Mission performance: Rate of climb at sea level 1772 ft (540 m) per min.
Engine: One 300-hp Avco Lycoming AEIO-540-L1B5D piston.

Version in service

Lasta: 2-seat trainer.
Operator: Yugoslavia.

Valmet L-70 Miltrainer
Finland

The L-70 is known to the Finnish Air Force as the Vinka, with which 30 are operated as trainers. Originally named Leko-70 and flown for the first time on 1 July 1975, it can be used for primary, aerobatic, instrument and night flying training. The design also allows for two extra seats for liaison and observation roles, while a stretcher and medical attendant or 617 lb (280 kg) of light freight can be accommodated with one pilot only. Four underwing stations for weapons or equipment permit weapon training, photographic reconnaissance, TV monitoring and transmitting, SAR with airdroppable life rafts or rescue packs, target towing and other secondary missions.

Specifications (L-70 data)
Weapons: Up to 661 lb (300 kg) of light armaments on 4 underwing stations, including antitank missiles, 110-lb (50-kg) or 220-lb (100-kg) bombs, rocket pods and/or twin-gun pods. A typical weapon load might be four 110-lb (50-kg) bombs, or 4 pods each with 18 37-mm rockets, or 2 pods each containing two 7.62-mm guns with 1000 rounds of ammunition.
Accommodation: Student pilot and instructor side by side, or 4 persons.
Wingspan: 31 ft 7¼ in (9.63 m).
Length: 24 ft 7¼ in (7.50 m).
Maximum take-off weight: 2756 lb (1250 kg).
Maximum speed: 146 mph (235 km/h).

Below: Valmet L-70 Vinka trainer.

Range: 590 miles (950 km).
Mission performance: Rate of climb at sea level 1122 ft (342 m) per min; ceiling 16,405 ft (5000 m); endurance 6 h 12 min maximum; G limits +3.3 normal, −1.8 normal, +6 aerobatic, −3 aerobatic, +4.4 utility, −2.02 utility.
Engine: One 200-hp Avco Lycoming AEIO-360-A1B6 piston, with 170 liters of fuel.
Version in service
L-70 Vinka: Primary trainer, with many other possible roles.
Operator: Finland.

Vought A-7 Corsair II
United States

The Corsair II was developed initially as a subsonic carrier-borne attack aircraft, capable of carrying a heavier conventional warload than the Skyhawk and fulfilling the US Navy's condition of being based on an existing aircraft, in this case the Crusader fighter. The lower power required for the Corsair II meant that a more fuel-conscious nonafterburning engine could be installed in the shortened Crusader-type fuselage, and that the fighter's variable-incidence wing could be dispensed with. The first prototype A-7 Corsair II made its maiden flight on 27 September 1965 and VA-147 became the first operational squadron with production A-7As in February 1967. Deployment for operations over Vietnam began late the same year.

Other versions of the A-7 followed, and on 5 April 1968 the first flight took place of a close

air support and interdiction version for the USAF as the A-7D, several hundred of which were built up to the mid-1970s. Another land version, this time for the Hellenic Air Force, became the A-7H, and Portugal received refurbished A-7As as A-7Ps.

Vought is currently working on a number of A-7 modification programs to enhance the aircraft's performance and give it a new lease of life. These include fitting Texas Instruments AN/APQ-126 terrain-following radar, FLIR and much else, and a 26,900-lb (12,200-kg) thrust with afterburning General Electric F110-GE-100 engine, to A-7Bs to form the new International Corsair III (an International Corsair II would also be A-7B-based but with an overhauled engine), suited to all-weather day and night attack missions. Other proposals envisage Air National Guard A-7D and Ks modified into Strike-fighters, with supersonic performance bestowed by airframe changes and the installation of a new afterburning engine. None of these are as yet in 'production'.

Specifications (A-7E data)
Radar: Texas Instruments AN/APQ-126(V) terrain-following radar, also used in the A-7D, A-7P and TA-7P.
Weapons: One 20-mm General Electric M61A-1 Vulcan multibarrel cannon in the fuselage, with 1000 rounds of ammunition. Over 15,000 lb (6800 kg) of attack weapons on 8 underfuselage and underwing pylons, 2 of which can alternatively carry Sidewinder air-to-air missiles.
Accommodation: The pilot.
Wingspan: 38 ft 9 in (11.80 m).

Above: Hellenic Air Force Vought TA-7H Corsair II.

Length: 46 ft 1½ in (14.06 m).
Maximum take-off weight: 42,000 lb
(19,050 kg).
Maximum speed: 691 mph (1112 km/h).
Ferry range: 2861 miles (4605 km) with
auxiliary fuel.
Engine: One 15,000-lb (6800-kg) Allison
TF41-A-2 turbofan, with 5678 liters of fuel
standard.

Versions in service
A-7D: USAF close air support and
interdiction version, with a 14,500-lb
(6577-kg) Allison TF41-A-1 engine.
Maximum speed 698 mph (1123 km/h).
Equipment includes Pave Penny laser target
designation pods and some carry FLIR. All
now serve with Air National Guard
squadrons.

A-7E: US Navy version, as detailed above.
A-7H: Hellenic version of the A-7E, for
operation from land. 60 acquired.
A-7K: USAF 2-seat derivative of the A-7D,
powered by a TF41-A-1 engine. Fuselage
length increased by 2 ft 10 in (86 cm). Used
by ANG as operational trainers.
A-7P: A-7As modernized for the Portuguese
Air Force, carrying also ECM pods.
EA-7L: Six TA-7Cs fitted with FLIR and
ECM equipment, in US Navy use.
TA-7C, TA-7H and TA-7P: 2-seat trainers,
based upon the single-seaters of the same
suffix (except for the TA-4C, which
represents both A-7Bs and Cs converted to
2-seat trainers).
Operators: Greece (A-7H and TA-7H),
Portugal (A-7P and TA-7P) and United
States (air force, A-7D and K; navy, A-7E,
EA-7L and TA-7C).

Vought F-8 Crusader
United States

Two aircraft developed in the 1950s changed
the course of naval aviation dramatically,
bringing the performance of carrier-based
fighter and strike-capable aircraft to a level at
least equal to and probably beyond that of
land-based aircraft. One was the McDonnell
Douglas F-4 Phantom II and the other,
earlier, aircraft was the F-8 Crusader.

The difficulty faced by Vought when
designing the new carrier-based fighter was
to achieve the desired high performance and
yet make the aircraft suitable for taking off
and more particularly landing onboard the
relatively short 'strip' of a carrier deck. To

Below: Vought F-8H Crusader land-based fighter
flown by the Philippine Air Force.

overcome these problems Vought designed the Crusader with a two-position variable-incidence wing, providing a high angle of attack for take-off and landing and enabling the fuselage to remain more or less level during the landing approach to assist the pilot's vision. Using an hydraulic self-locking actuator to alter the wing incidence, the ailerons, flaps and dog-tooth leading-edges all drooped automatically. Subsequent French Navy F-8E (FN)s, having to operate from the smaller French aircraft carriers, reduced landing speed still further by using a boundary layer control system to 'blow' the flaps and ailerons and the adoption of two-stage leading-edge flaps.

The prototype Crusader made its maiden flight on 25 March 1955 and US Navy squadrons received initial production F-8A day fighters two years later. The F-8D of 1960 introduced limited all-weather capability. Thirteen versions of the F-8 were built or produced by modernization, production ending in early 1965 with the last F-8E (FN) for France.

Specifications (F-8E (FN) data)
Weapons: Four 20-mm cannon in the nose, plus Matra R.550 Magic and/or Sidewinder air-to-air missiles.
Accommodation: The pilot.
Wingspan: 35 ft 8 in (10.87 m).
Length: 54 ft 6 in (16.61 m).
Maximum take-off weight: 34,000 lb (15,420 kg).
Maximum speed: 1322 mph (2127 km/h).
Combat radius: 600 miles (965 km).
Mission performance: Ceiling 58,000 ft (17,680 m).
Engine: One 18,000-lb (8165-kg) thrust with afterburning Pratt & Whitney J57-P-20A turbojet, with about 5300 liters of fuel.
Versions in service
F-8E (FN): French Navy version, flown initially in 1964. Original missiles carried

Below: Westland TT300 general-purpose helicopter.

were Matra R.530s or Sidewinders.
F-8H: Remanufactured F-8D, with attack capability. First flown in 1967.
RF-8G: Modernized RF-8A photographic reconnaissance model, of which a very small number remain with the US Navy Reserve.
Operators: France (navy, F-8E (FN)), Philippines (F-8H) and United States (navy, RF-8G).

Westland 30 (TT30 and TT300)
United Kingdom

Known successively as the WG 30 and Westland 30, this helicopter is a twin-engined and larger development of the Lynx. The first prototype flew initially on 10 April 1979. The only military order has come from India, requiring VIP transport and others for its air force. To date four versions have been established under the TT30 and TT300 subseries.

Above: Royal Navy Westland Lynx lands on board the Leander-class frigate HMS *Danae*.

Specifications
Accommodation: VIP interior allows for 6 to 11 seats. Utility layout for 14 to 20 troops, or freight, or 6 stretchers plus attendants or sitting casualties.
Diameter of rotor: 43 ft 8 in (13.31 m).
Length including rotors: 52 ft 2½ in (15.91 m)
Maximum take-off weight: 12,800 lb (5806 kg).
Cruising speed: 138 mph (222 km/h).
Range: 293 miles (472 km) (Series 100-60) with 4000-lb (1814-kg) load.
Mission performance: Hovering ceiling in ground effect (Series 100-60) 2600 ft (792 m); hovering ceiling out of ground effect (Series 100-60) 2900 ft (884 m).
Engines: 2 Rolls-Royce Gem turboshafts, of 1260-shp Gem 60-3 type in the TT30 Series 100-60. The TT30 Series 200 and TT300 Series 300 have more powerful General Electric CT7s.
Version in service
TT30/TT300: The initial production version was the TT30 Series 100 with 1135-shp Gem 41-1 engines. The TT30 Series 100-60 followed, with Gem 60-3 engines. First flown in 1984, this is probably the Indian version. TT30 Series 200 uses 1712-shp General Electric CT7-2B turboshafts, has a maximum take-off weight of 12,800 lb (5806 kg) and first flew in 1983. The TT300 Series 300 first flew on 5 February 1986 and has higher performance. Maximum take-off weight is 16,000 lb (7257 kg). This model uses the revolutionary BERP advanced-technology composite rotor blades.
Operator: India.

Westland Lynx and Lynx 3
United Kingdom

The Westland Lynx was one of the three helicopters included in the Anglo-French collaboration program, finalized in April 1968, which united Westland Helicopters in the United Kingdom and Sud-Aviation (later Aérospatiale) in France. The Lynx program was by far the most important for Westland, which had design leadership, and this UK company initiated development of its own

WG.13 design to meet the specific Anglo-French requirements. The original intention was that the helicopter should be suitable for both naval and civil use, but it was soon realized that there was likely to be a worthwhile army requirement for a fast and maneuverable helicopter able to carry as many as 10 armed troops or paratroops. Consequently, in order to minimize the period until production could begin, no fewer than 13 aircraft were involved in the development. The type's maiden flight was on 21 March 1971.

Important aspects of the Lynx design included an innovative four-blade semi-rigid main rotor with a titanium rotor head, the design of the rotor allowing for a negative-pitch setting of 6 degrees that in the naval version could be used to hold the aircraft down on a pitching deck until the best moment for lift-off and to assist in securing the helicopter after landing. Onboard handling capability for the naval version was optimized in a program that involved a rolling platform phase and extensive ship trials. It resulted in the introduction of nonretractable tricycle undercarriage incorporating sprag units to positively lock each main wheel; when combined with optional flotation gear and a harpoon deck-lock system the naval Lynx gains remarkable capability for shipboard operations in most conditions. Army versions have a tubular skid-type undercarriage, to which ground-handling wheels can be attached when required. The company's demonstrator, appropriately registered G-LYNX, was used initially to explore the weapons capability of the type; it was this aircraft which, when equipped with new technology BERP III rotor blades, established on 11 August 1986 a new World Speed Record for helicopters of 249.09 mph (400.89 km/h).

Westland has also developed a dedicated antitank helicopter which it designates Lynx 3; this differs from the standard Lynx by being revised for enhanced battlefield survivability, is equipped to deploy a wide range of antitank missiles, and can operate at a higher weight. The company has also proposed a naval version of the Lynx-3, but so far neither version has gained an order.

Specifications (Lynx HAS.Mk 2 data)

Radar: Ferranti Seaspray search and tracking radar.
Weapons: For primary ASW role can carry 2 depth charges or 2 standard or Sting Ray homing torpedoes and 6 marine markers. Antiship weapons can include 4 Sea Skua or 4 AS.12 missiles.
Accommodation: 2 crew normally.
Diameter of rotor: 42 ft 0 in (12.80 m).
Fuselage length: 39 ft 1¼ in (11.92 m).
Maximum take-off weight: 10,500 lb (4763 kg).
Cruising speed: 144 mph (232 km/h).
Range: 368 miles (592 km).
Mission performance: Rate of climb at sea level 2170 ft (661 m) per min; hovering ceiling out of ground effect 8450 ft (2576 m).
Engines: Two 900-shp Rolls-Royce Gem 2 turboshafts.

Versions in service

Lynx AH.Mk 1: Version for service with the British Army; has Gem 2 turboshafts and can accommodate a pilot and a maximum 10 troops.
Lynx HAS.Mk 2: Royal Navy version for ASW and other duties; has Gem 2 turboshafts and Seaspray radar.
Lynx Mk 2 (FN): French Navy version, similar to HAS Mk. 2 but with wheel brakes, French radar and AS.12 missiles.
Lynx HAS.Mk 3: Royal Navy version with

uprated Gem 41-1 engines developing 1120 shp.
Lynx Mk.4: Second version for French Navy, introducing the Gem 41-1 turboshafts and uprated transmission.
Lynx AH.Mk 5: Version for British Army similar to HAS Mk. 3.
Lynx AH.Mk 7: Improved version for British Army; has composite tail rotor turning in opposite direction for noise reduction and can be operated at a higher gross weight.
Lynx Mk 21: Brazilian Navy version.
Lynx Mk 23: Naval version for Argentina; generally similar to HAS.Mk 2.
Lynx Mk 25: SAR version for Royal Netherlands Navy which designates it UH-14A; generally similar to HAS.Mk 2.
Lynx Mk 27: ASW version for Royal Netherlands Navy which designates it SH-14B; similar to above but with uprated Gem engines.
Lynx Mk 28: Version for State of Qatar Police; similar to AH.Mk 1 but with sand-filters for air-intakes, flotation equipment and a searchlight.
Lynx Mk 80: Version similar to HAS.Mk 2 for Royal Danish Navy.
Lynx Mk 81: ASW version for Royal Netherlands Navy which designates it SH-14C; uprated Gem turboshafts and MAD equipment.
Lynx Mk 86: Naval version, similar to HAS.Mk 2 but with Gem 41-2 turboshafts to equip Royal Norwegian Air Force Coastguard.
Lynx Mk 87: Version similar to Lynx Mk 23 for Argentine Navy but with Gem 41-2 engines.
Lynx Mk 88: ASW version for Federal

Below: Westland Wasp light helicopter.

German Navy; similar to HAS.Mk 2 but with Gem 41-2 engines.

Lynx Mk 89: Naval version, generally similar to HAS.Mk 2, for service with Nigerian Navy.

Super Lynx: New naval version of the Lynx under development with 1120-shp Gem 42 engines, high-efficiency tail rotor, MEL Super Searcher 360-degree radar and capability to deploy Sting Ray torpedoes and Penguin or Sea Skua missiles; new technology main rotor optional.

Lynx 3: Antitank helicopter, not yet in service. See above.

Operators: Argentina (navy), Brazil (navy), Denmark (navy), France (navy), West Germany (navy), Netherlands (navy), Norway, Nigeria (navy), Qatar (police) and United Kingdom (navy and army).

Westland Wasp and Scout
United Kingdom

Developed from an original design by Saunders-Roe (the P.531) that had first flown on 20 July 1958, the antisubmarine Wasp and general-purpose/liaison Scout entered Royal Navy service from 1963 and British Army service from 1961 respectively, though today they have been largely superseded by Lynx. The most obvious difference between the two models is the undercarriage, comprising a tall castoring four-wheel arrangement on the Wasp and a shorter skid-type on the Scout.

Specifications (Wasp data)
Weapons: Two Mk 44 homing torpedoes or other weapons. No detection equipment.
Accommodation: Two crew plus 3 passengers or a stretcher.
Diameter of rotor: 32 ft 3 in (9.83 m).
Fuselage length: 30 ft 4 in (9.24 m).
Maximum take-off weight: 5500 lb (2495 kg).
Maximum speed: 120 mph (193 km/h).
Range: 270 miles (435 km).
Mission performance: Rate of climb at sea level 1440 ft (440 m) per min.
Engine: One 710-shp Rolls-Royce Bristol Nimbus 503 turboshaft.
Versions in service
Scout: British Army AH.Mk 1 five-seater, finally used for liaison. 685-shp Nimbus 101 or 102 engine.
Wasp: Naval helicopter, originally for shipboard operation from frigates and destroyers. Royal Navy designation HAS.Mk 1.
Operators: Brazil (navy, Wasp), Indonesia (navy, Wasp), New Zealand (air force, Wasp), South Africa (air force, Wasp) and United Kingdom (navy, Wasp; army, Scout).

Yakovlev Yak-18 and Nanchang CJ-5 and CJ-6 (NATO name Max)
Soviet Union and China

A varied range of all-metal aircraft have appeared under the Yak-18 designation, mostly for basic training with accommodation for two in tandem under a long canopy but also in cabin form to take in such roles as ambulance, liaison and freight carrying. The original Yak-18 trainer first appeared in 1946 and went to air forces and civil flying schools.

Under the terms of a Sino-Soviet agreement of 1952, China began construction of the Yak-18, the first flying in 1954. Like the Soviet counterpart, its engine was a 160-hp M-11FR. Chinese production then went on to the Yak-18A with a 260-hp Ivchenko AI-14R radial, under the Chinese designation CT-5, to be superseded by the CJ-6 from 1961.

Specifications (Nanchang CJ-6 data)
Accommodation: Student pilot and instructor in tandem.
Wingspan: 33 ft 4¾ in (10.18 m).
Length: 27 ft 9 in (8.46 m).
Maximum take-off weight: 3128 lb (1419 kg).
Maximum speed: 178 mph (286 km/h).
Mission performance: Rate of climb at sea level 1250 ft (380 m) per min; ceiling 16,660 ft (5080 m); endurance 3 h 36 min.
Engine: One 285-hp Zhuzhou Huosai-6A radial piston, with 100 liters of fuel.
Versions in service
Yak-18: First version of 1946 appearance, with a tailwheel type undercarriage. Also built in China following an agreement of 1952.
Yak-18U: Basically a Yak-18 with a tricycle undercarriage.
Yak-18A: Refined Yak-18U, later given a 300-hp AI-14RF engine.
Yak-18P: Single-seat Yak-18A for aerobatics and advanced training.
Yak-18PM: Improved Yak-18P.
Yak-18T: Cabin version of the Yak-18A, with

Above: Nanchang CJ-6 basic trainer.

accommodation for the pilot and three passengers, freight, or a stretcher. First flown as a prototype in 1967 with an AI-14RF engine, but series built with a 360-hp Vedeneyev M-14P. Maximum speed 183 mph (295 km/h).
Nanchang CT-5: Chinese Yak-18A.
Nanchang CT-6: Chinese derivative of the CJ-5, with a 285-hp Zhuzhou Huosai-6A radial piston engine. Maximum speed 178 mph (286 km/h).
Operators: All Yak versions unless otherwise stated. Afghanistan, Albania (Yak and CT-5), Bangladesh (CT-6), Bulgaria, China (CT-5 and CT-6), East Germany, Guinea, Hungary, North Korea (Yak and CT-6), Mali, Mongolia, Soviet Union, Vietnam (Yak and CT-6) and Zambia (CT-6).

Yakovlev Yak-28 (NATO name Brewer, Firebar and Maestro)
Soviet Union

Although looking rather outdated in modern skies, the Yak-28 remains a vital component of the Soviet Air Force, flying such important

Below: Yakovlev Yak-28P Firebar.

missions as all-weather interception, ECM and reconnaissance. It is no afterthought that several roles are undertaken, the Yak having been described by a Soviet commentator as long ago as 1961 as a multipurpose supersonic aircraft. Yet the 'P' suffix for Firebar indicates that the airframe was 'adapted' to suit this role, and ECM Brewer-Es did not become operational until 1970. In fact versions previously in service included three models of Brewer attack bomber with internal bomb-bays, but only those variants of the Yak-28 currently operational are given below. It has also been reported that the Indian Air Force has requested Brewer-E types.

Specifications (Yak-28P Firebar data unless otherwise stated)

Radar: Firebar's dielectric nosecone is larger than Brewer's, housing Skip Spin X-band interception radar. Firebar may have tail warning radar.
Weapons: Firebar armament comprises just 2 air-to-air missiles.
Accommodation: 2 crew in tandem.
Wingspan: 42 ft 6 in (12.95 m).
Length: 75 ft 5½ in (23.00 m).
Maximum take-off weight: 44,090 lb (20,000 kg) estimated.
Maximum speed: Mach 1.88 estimated.
Combat radius: 575 miles (925 km) estimated.
Mission performance: Ceiling 55,000 ft (16,750 m).
Engines: Two 13,117-lb (5950-kg) thrust with afterburning Tumansky R-11 type turbojets.
Versions in service
Brewer-D: An estimated 220 are in Soviet use for reconnaissance, carrying cameras, SLAR and other sensors. (Brewers may have Short Horn weapon delivery and navigation radar. Some are said to carry Look Two I-band radar. SLAR radar is standard to Brewer-D.)
Brewer-E: An estimated 100 or so are in Soviet use as ECM aircraft, tasked to escort strike aircraft. Underwing pylons for antiradiation missiles, rocket pods or chaff dispenser.
Firebar: Some 105 Firebar all-weather interceptors remain with the Voyska PVO home defense force.
Maestro: Trainer for Firebar crew, with 2 individual cockpit canopies.
Operators: India (Brewer-E?) and Soviet Union.

Yakovlev Yak-38 (NATO name Forger)
Soviet Union

The Yak-38 is the world's only rival to the Harrier series as a V/STOL combat aircraft but differs fundamentally in its approach to vertical take-off. Unlike the Harrier, Forger has a large turbojet that exhausts through two vectoring nozzles on the rear fuselage, and two much lower powered 'liftjets' in the fuselage aft of the cockpit to exhaust downward and thereby contribute to the lift thrust and pitch and trim. While Soviet Navy pilots have been capable of making very precise vertical take-offs and landings on board deck, short take-offs (STO) have been a fairly recent maneuver and this indicates continuing development of the aircraft and its modes of operation. An automatic control system is used to find the optimum settings for the liftjets and rotate the vectoring nozzles during STO. But Forger

should not be underestimated. Until recently Western observers doubted its weapon-carrying ability, but now it is known that a heavy armament load is available to it and that Forger has important offensive and defensive missions when operating from the four Kiev-class aircraft carriers. Production is thought to have totalled some 70 aircraft by 1986.

Specifications (Forger-A data, estimated)
Radar: Ranging radar.
Weapons: Up to about 7936 lb (3600 kg) of weapons carried on 4 underwing pylons, including 23-mm GSh-23 cannon pods, AS-7 Kerry (NATO name) tactical air-to-surface missiles, antiship missiles, Aphid air-to-air missiles, 1102-lb (500-kg) bombs, rocket launchers, etc.
Accommodation: The pilot.
Wingspan: 24 ft 0 in (7.32 m).
Length: 50 ft 10 in (15.50 m).
Maximum take-off weight: 25,794 lb (11,700 kg).
Maximum speed: 627 mph (1009 km/h).

Above: Yakovlev Yak-38 Forger-As on board a *Kiev* Class carrier.

Combat radius: Up to 230 miles (370 km) with full weapon load.
Mission performance: Rate of climb at sea level 14,765 ft (4500 m) per min; ceiling 39,370 ft (12,000 m).
Engines: One 17,990-lb (8160-kg) thrust Lyulka AL-21 vectored thrust turbojet, plus two 7870-lb (3570-kg) thrust Koliesov liftjets.
Versions in service
Forger-A: Single-seat ship-borne combat aircraft, the prototype of which appeared in 1971. Some 12 are deployed on board each Kiev-class vessel, with one or more Forger-Bs and 19 Hormone or Helix helicopters.
Forger-B: Unarmed tandem 2-seat training version, without radar.
Operator: Soviet Union (navy).

Below: Yugoslavian government Yakovlev-yak-40.

Yakovlev Yak-40
(NATO name Codling)
Soviet Union

In order to develop a modern short-haul replacement for the piston-engined Lisunov Li-2, to fly from grass strips when required, Yakovlev went completely modern and produced the Yak-40 three-turbofan airliner. The prototype made its maiden flight on 21 October 1966 and began commercial operations with Aeroflot in 1968. A comparatively small number of the 800 or so built were taken into military service.

Specifications
Radar: Grosa-40 weather radar.
Accommodation: Crew of 2 or 3, plus 12 to 32 passengers, according to layout. Maximum payload is 5996 lb (2720 kg). A freighter version was also produced.
Wingspan: 82 ft 0¼ in (25.00 m).
Length: 66 ft 9½ in (20.36 m).
Maximum take-off weight: 33,950 lb (15,400 kg).
Maximum speed: 373 mph (600 km/h) IAS.
Range: 1240 miles (2000 km).
Mission performance: Rate of climb at sea level 1575 ft (480 m) per min.
Engines: Three 3307-lb (1500-kg) thrust Ivchenko AI-25 turbofans; 3910 liters of fuel.
Version in service
Yak-40: As described above. No longer in production. The Soviet Air Force uses its Yak-40s for liaison.
Operators: Bangladesh, Bulgaria, Equatorial Guinea, Ethiopia, Guinea-Bissau, Laos, Poland, Soviet Union, Syria, Yugoslavia and Zambia.

Yakovlev Yak-50 and Yak-53, and Yakovlev/IAv Bacau Yak-52
Soviet Union and Rumania

The Yak-52 was designed to supersede the Yak-18 as a primary trainer, offering tandem two-seat accommodation under a long level canopy but with a more powerful radial engine than the Yak-18 and a tricycle undercarriage as standard. The mainwheels of the undercarriage do not fully retract so that, as with the Yak-18, the airframe is protected in

Below: IAv Bacau Yak-52 trainer.

an emergency 'wheels-up' landing.
The Yak-52, which entered production in Rumania (although a Soviet design) in 1979 and well over 500 have been built, is basically a tandem-seat derivative of the earlier Yak-50 single-seat aerobatic trainer which first flew in 1975. A single-seat aerobatic derivative of the Yak-52 is the Yak-53 which has an airframe stressed for a longer fatigue life.

Specifications (Yak-52 data)
Accommodation: Student pilot and instructor in tandem in level cockpits.
Wingspan: 30 ft 6 in (9.30 m).
Length: 25 ft 5 in (7.74 m).
Maximum take-off weight: 2844 lb (1290 kg).
Maximum speed: 186 mph (300 km/h).
Range: 341 miles (550 km).
Mission performance: Rate of climb at sea level 1380 ft (420 m) per min; ceiling 19,685 ft (6000 m); G limits +7, −5; endurance 2 h 50 min.
Engine: One 360-hp Vedeneyev M-14P radial piston, with 122 liters of fuel.
Versions in service
Yak-50: Single-seat aerobatic trainer with an M-14P engine and a tailwheel undercarriage. Designed to replace the Yak-18PM. Operated in the Soviet Union by DOSAAF, the civil pilot training organization that provides initial training for pilots destined to serve with the Soviet forces.
Yak-52: Soviet-designed two-seat trainer, built in Rumania by IAv Bacau. As described above.
Yak-53: Single-seat aerobatic aircraft, with an M-14P engine, 31 ft 2 in (9.50 m) wingspan, 25 ft 2 in (7.68 m) length, 2337-lb (1060-kg) maximum take-off weight, and 186 mph (300 km/h) maximum speed. Currently manufactured in the Soviet Union, but IAv Bacau may become the future supplier.
Operators: Rumania (Yak-52) and the Soviet Union (DOSAAF, Yak-50, Yak-52 and Yak-53).

Zlin Z-226 Trener, Z-326 and Z-526 Trener-Master, 42M and 43
Czechoslovakia

Two distinct groupings of Zlin aircraft comprise the types covered here; the Trener and Trener-Masters are tandem two-seat basic

Above: Zlin Z-526 Trener-Master.

trainers and the Zlin 42M and 43 are side-by-side seating light aircraft suited to liaison and training but used currently in military service for the former role.

Specifications (Zlin 43 data)
Accommodation: 2 or 4 persons.
Wingspan: 32 ft 0¼ in (9.76 m).
Length: 25 ft 5 in (7.75 m).
Maximum take-off weight: 2976 lb (1350kg).
Maximum speed: 146 mph (235 km/h).
Range: 375 miles (610 km) with standard fuel.
Mission performance: Rate of climb at sea level 670 ft (210 m) per min; ceiling 12,475 ft (3800 m); G limits +4.4 utility, −1.76 utility, +3.8 normal, −1.52 normal.
Engine: One 210-hp Avia M 337A piston, with 130 liters of standard fuel and 55 liters in each wingtip.
Versions in service
Z-226 Trener: Followed on from the Z-26 and Z-126 Treners that were in production from 1948 until 1955. One 160-hp Walter Minor 6-III engine. 137 mph (220 km/h) maximum speed.
Z-326 Trener-Master: First flown in 1957. Developed from the Z-226, with a retractable undercarriage and provision for wingtip tanks.
Z-526 Trener-Master: Similar to the Z-326 but with the instructor seated in the rear cockpit.
Zlin 42M: Side-by-side 2-seat cabin lightplane, first flown in 1972. One 180-hp Avia M 137 AZ engine. Maximum speed 140 mph (226 km/h). Superseded by the Zlin 142 with a 210-hp Avia engine.
Zlin 43: As detailed above.
Operators: Cuba (Z-326), Czechoslovakia (Z-526 and 43), Egypt (Z-526), East Germany (Z-226, 42M and 43) and Mozambique (Z-326).

Index

Note: As entries in the text of this encyclopedia are listed alphabetically by aircraft manufacturer, this index lists their products alphabetically. Thus, for example, the McDonnell Douglas F-15 Eagle is indexed both under Eagle and F-15. *Italics* refer to NATO reporting names for aircraft of Soviet origin, and page numbers set **bold** indicate illustrations.

Acknowledgments

We would like to thank David Eldred who designed this book; Wendy Sacks, the editor; David Mondey, the indexer; Tony Bryan and Peter Sarson who produced the cutaway illustrations; and the following individuals and organizations for the use of their pictures on the pages listed. (B=bottom, C=center, T=top).

Aeritalia 16, 17T; Aero 20B; Aeronautica Macchi: page 19; Aérospatiale 21B, 22T, 24B, 27 (both), 28, 29T; Agusta 30 (both), 50, 51, 52, 19T, 197; Air Photo Supply 43T, 110 (both), 160B, 165B, 166B, 172B; Air Portraits 33B, 172T, 177B; Aircraft Technology 33T, 172T; AMD-BA 62B, 69B, 70, 71, 72, 73, 74 (inset), 76, 77 (both), 78 (both); Atlas Aircraft Corporation 35B, 36T; Luc Aubin/APL 161B; Beechcraft 46T, 47, 48, 49; Bell Helicopter Textron 53 (both); Bison Picture Library 118T, 120B; Boeing 56, 57, 58 (both), 59 (both), 60B, 132T; Boeing Vertol 62T, 193T; British Aerospace 6-7, 8-9, 36B, 38, 39 (both), 40, 41 (both), 42, 43B, 91T, 113T, 132 (both), 147T, 169 (both), 188T, 217T; Austin J Brown 87T, 108T, 119, 121B, 128T, 198T, 220B; Antonio Camarasa 81, 165C; Canadair 63 (both), 64T; CASA 64B, 65B; CATIC 188B; Cessna 65T, 66, 67; De Havilland Aircraft, Canada 80 (both), 81B, 82B; Dornier 83B, 84; Embraer 17B, 88T, 89 (both); ENAER 90B; Equipe de Voltigé 162T; Etablissement Cinématographique et Photographique des Armées 133T; Eurocopter 91B; Euromissile 134; Fairchild 12-13, 125; Federal Directorate of Supply and Procurement 214T; Fleet Air Arm 79T, 111C; Fokker 96, 97T; Gates Learjet 98B; General Dynamics 99 (both); GIFAS 23; Grumman 13 (inset), 102 (both), 103, 107, 108B; K Hinata 123 T&C; Hughes 113B, 180T; IAR 117T; Indian Armed Forces 109T; Israeli Aircraft Industries 22B, 85, 114 (both), 115, 116B; John Jackson 37T; JMSDF 130T; Kawasaki 123T; Letectvi & Kosmonautika/Václar Jukl 207B; Lockheed 9, 126 (both), 128B, 130B, 131; LTV Corporation 83T, 216 (both); MBB 1, 135B; McDonnell Douglas 87B, 136, 137, 138, 142-3 (both), 145 (inset); 147B; Microjet 148T; MOD 4-5, 26, 37B, 61, 79B, 111T, 112, 127; Kenneth Munson 2-3, 117C; Neira 164; Northrop 166T, 167; D Ostrowski 180T; Stephen Piercey/APL 86B; Pilatus 173 (both); Pilatus Britten-Norman 86B; Polish Air Force 203 (both); Rhein-Flugzeugbau 178; Rockwell International 179, 181; Rolls-Royce 18T; Royal Norwegian Air Force 210; Saab Scania 184, 185 (both), 186, 187 (both); Short Brothers 90T, 190 (both); SIAI Machetti 191B, 192T; Sikorsky 8 (inset), 14-15, 194 (both), 198B, 199T; Erik Simonsen 129T; Sperry Flight Systems 10-11; Summit Aviation 68T; Swedish Air Force 55B, 155T, 183T, 209B, 211T; Swiss Federal Aircraft Factory, F & W 168; Tass 219B; Transall 208; US Air Force 212B; US Department of Defense 55T, 122T, 133B, 159 (inset), 160T, 207T, 209T, 220T; US Navy 107; UTVA 213B, 214B; VALMET 215; Vought 193B; Mark Wagner/APL 34B, 148B; Mick West 94B; Westland Helicopters 195, 196, 217B, 218; Gordon S Williams 32B; WSK-PZL Warszawa-Okecie 176B; Zlin 221T.